THE MEANING OF CITIZENSHIP

SERIES IN
CITIZENSHIP STUDIES

· · · · · · · · · · ·

SERIES EDITORS

Marc W. Kruman
Richard Marback

THE MEANING
OF CITIZENSHIP

· · · · · · · · ·

EDITED BY
RICHARD MARBACK AND MARC W. KRUMAN

Wayne State University Press
Detroit

19 18 17 16 15   5 4 3 2 1

Library of Congress Cataloging Number: 2015937850

ISBN 978-0-8143-4130-8 (paperback);
ISBN 978-0-8143-4131-5 (ebook)

Designed and typeset by Bryce Schimanski
Composed in Adobe Caslon Pro

CONTENTS

INTRODUCTION

· · · · · · · · · ·

MARC W. KRUMAN AND RICHARD MARBACK

The essays assembled in this volume are drawn from the tenth anniversary conference of the Center for the Study of Citizenship. The theme of that conference, "The Meaning of Citizenship," provided an appropriate opportunity to reflect on a decade of research in the study of citizenship. Formally chartered in 2002, with a director and advisors drawn from across the Wayne State University campus, the Center for the Study of Citizenship began as an effort to promote campus-wide interdisciplinary research and conversation about citizenship in its many permutations. Initial participants in the center's efforts came together from across disciplines to bring their specific knowledge to bear on charting a single emerging field—the field of citizenship studies. This is not to say that the study of citizenship had previously gone unnoticed within academic disciplines. Far from it. The center's focus on citizenship developed out of recognition that citizenship, as a concept central to modern civilizations, is a key concept across humanistic disciplines.

The idea of citizenship, an idea invoked so broadly across so many disciplines, is a necessarily dynamic idea. Unfortunately, such dynamic ideas often fail to pass disciplinary scrutiny, a failure that threatens to rob those vibrant ideas of some of their incisiveness. The idea of citizenship is no exception. A basic definition of citizenship useable across the widest possible array of disciplines describes citizenship in political terms, as a legitimate personal claim to certain rights, liberties, and immunities. According to this view, the study of citizenship would involve an exploration of such concepts as inclusion and exclusion, possession and dispossession, freedom and slavery, as well as identification with or alienation from a collectivity. In the modern era, the default collectivity associated with citizenship has been the nation-state or its political equivalent, a body with which individuals are legally identified, a body within which they enjoy relations of mutual obligation and privilege.

To articulate the idea of citizenship in terms of its political dimensions is to account for a great deal. At the same time though descriptions of political citizenship only begin to hint at the richer nuances of membership in a political community. There is a broader society beyond government, as Woodrow Wilson pointed out in his book *The State: Elements of Historical and Practical Politics* (1897), "Society, it must always be remembered, is vastly bigger and more important than its instrument, Government. Government should by no means rule or dominate it" (636). Constituent members of society claim to be citizens within a particular polity not because they are legal subjects but because they find the relationships to a society and to fellow citizens to be useful, gratifying, or simply inevitable. As Wilson made clear, in modern democracies, the state "exists for the sake of Society, not Society for the sake of the State." The relationship of citizens to a state, then, does not provide a comprehensive definition of citizenship because the potential associations citizens have with each other exceed relationships to the state. Again in Wilson's words, one of the central limits of the state is that it cannot encompass "necessary cooperation on the part of Society as a whole" (636). Which is to say that citizenship is not exclusively political in nature, it is very much civic in nature as well. Citizens are people who have an opportunity and so a willingness to volunteer themselves to a broader enterprise, to sacrifice a certain amount of their individual autonomy in order to claim the benefits of membership in their communities. Richard Bellamy has recently identified these civic and political dimensions—as well as the tensions between the political and the civic—as fundamental to a definition central to the study of citizenship: "So membership, rights and participation go together. It is through being a member of a political community and participating on equal terms in the framing of its collective life that we enjoy rights to pursue our individual lives on fair terms with others" (Bellamy 2010, xix).

The political membership that is fundamental to any understanding of citizenship establishes conditions for citizens to make associations outside the political community. Recognizing that citizenship broadly understood requires people to give up some measure of their individual autonomy in exchange for the benefits of community membership weaves the study of citizenship into humanistic inquiry—specifically inquiry into the cultural, social, and political fabrics within which human beings live public and private lives. Understood in this way, the study of citizenship raises questions about the proper relationship between individual freedom and civic obligation, about ongoing exchanges between systems of public and private moralization, and about the shifting nature of "self" as it interacts dynamically with collective or alien forces. Across disciplines, scholars generally agree that human beings create structures, frameworks, and languages that bring order and meaning to their lives. As historian Kenneth Karst observed about the American polity in 1989, "To speak of self-definition, of the sense of community, and of the community-defining functions of law [or politics] is not to identify different parts of a machine but to view a complex social process from several different angles" (Karst 1989, 12–13). Language, literature, art—the media through which people express who they are—these are the means by which communities define themselves, placing humanistic inquiry at the very center of the study of citizenship.

Nor do scholars doubt that, since at least 1945, a relatively stable, state-centered system of global organization has been destabilized. As anthropologist Clifford Geertz reminds us, "The function of ideology is to make an autonomous politics possible by providing the authoritative concepts that render it meaningful, the suasive images by means of which it can be sensibly grasped" (Geertz 1973, 218). In the absence of such authoritative symbols, or with the introduction of new, multifaceted, or interlocking symbols—as when a person identifies simultaneously with profession, gender, family, and religion, as well as the state—society threatens to fragment. Alternative systems of identification appear, all of which compose topics long associated with humanistic research: the resurgence of religious doctrines and institutions; new political and social languages; the widespread acceptance of capitalism as both a political and economic ethos; and the transmutation of private systems of identification into primary, public categories.

As W. H. Auden put it, "There is no such thing as the State / And no one exists alone / Hunger allows no choice / To the citizen or the police / We must love one another or die" (Auden 1939). But still the character of human organization and self-identification scarcely resembles its post–World War II antecedent. These changes provide ample justification and fertile ground for sustained humanistic inquiry. In the end, the "pursuit of happiness," a people's ability to work collectively toward the Good, and individuals' willingness to sacrifice degrees of freedom in combination, all seem to require close investigation not only of public structures (governments, laws, institutions) but also of shifting inner landscapes and the ways those changes remap the way that individuals connect themselves to others. As Hannah Arendt cautions, "Democratic freedoms may be based on the equality of all citizens before the law; yet they acquire their meaning and function organically only where the citizens belong to and are represented by groups or form a social and political hierarchy" (Arendt 1973, 312).

Such reflections on the affordances that attend defining citizenship in terms of state-sanctioned rights and responsibilities as well as civic dispositions and valuations figured centrally in the establishment of the Center for the Study of Citizenship. At the same time, it was the terrorist attacks of 9/11 that gave compelling immediacy to those reflections on citizenship and community membership. The year of the first conference of the Center for the Study of Citizenship, 2003, brought together more than three hundred students, faculty, and members of the public to a two-day event titled "The Many Faces of Patriotism." The conference planners aimed to encourage serious contemplation of patriotism and its complex relationship to nationalism, multiculturalism, dissent, and the events surrounding 9/11. Keynote speaker Dennis W. Archer, then president of the American Bar Association and former mayor of Detroit, joined panels of citizenship scholars from around the nation and from South Africa to deliberate these issues. A volume of essays drawn from the presentations, *The Many Faces of Patriotism*, was published by Rowman and Littlefield in January 2007.

In the ten years since 2003 that scholars have been gathering at Wayne State University to discuss the nature and meaning of citizenship, the conference has grown beyond the boundaries of the university to include scholars from across the nation and around the world. As the chapters included in this volume attest, scholars attend the conference from Europe, Asia, and the Middle East, bringing to the event concerns and insights specific to their regions. With scholars from across the globe engaging one another in the study of citizenship, an interdisciplinary field of inquiry has evolved. As an identifiable field of scholarly inquiry, citizenship studies has experienced significant growth in the first decade of the millennium. Not only have issues of citizenship become more pressing over the last ten years, encouraging broader study by greater numbers of scholars, the study of citizenship has also enlarged its concerns and matured into an interdisciplinary field to which multiple academic disciplines make contributions. In an edited collection oriented more toward understanding citizenship in terms of membership in political communities, *Citizenship*, Richard Bellamy and Antonio Palumbo have included chapters covering the major themes of inclusion, rights, outsiders, and sovereignty. They have also included chapters on gender, diversity, and the environment, chapters without which the collection would seem incomplete. Outside the field of citizenship studies itself, across the range of academic disciplines, scholars are assessing the impact of citizenship on their particular fields of study. As documented in *Citizenship in the Humanities and Social Sciences: A Selective Bibliography, 2000–2009*, traditional academic disciplines from anthropology, art, and business, to education, health, psychology, and sociology all share a robust concern for the study of citizenship. The over one thousand journal articles, chapters, and books listed in the bibliography are only representative of a decade of scholarship; as such, it is suggestive of the breadth and the depth of current research on citizenship issues.

As a forum for discussing these issues in all their disciplinary diversity, the Center for the Study of Citizenship constructs conversations that extend beyond the humanistic disciplines to include a broad spectrum of students, public officials, professionals of all kinds, entrepreneurs, and others, at home and abroad. Broad academic interest in citizenship reflects the immediacy of citizenship issues to a larger public. For this reason the mission statement of the Center for the Study of Citizenship commits the center to sustained exploration of actual, possible, or shifting relationships between citizens (that is, members of political, social, economic, religious, intellectual, or ethno-cultural communities) and the broader societies within which these identifications have meaning. Such explorations carry the concerns associated with humanism well beyond traditional boundaries.

A standard criticism of the kind of interdisciplinary research agenda we just defined is that such disciplinary diffuseness gathers under the umbrella of a concept like "citizenship" what is more precisely a series of distinct issues best addressed separately. According to this criticism those distinct issues, despite their relevance, do not, when taken together, add up to a coherent description of just what citizenship is. Certainly the connections are not always clear. For example, David Chaney's "Cosmopolitan Art and Cultural Citizenship" (2002) does appear quite removed from Kibeom Lee and

Natalie Allen's "Organizational Citizenship Behavior and Workplace Deviance" (2002), which is itself removed from the issues Geraldine Boyle (2008) addresses in "The Mental Capacity Act 2005: Promoting the Citizenship of People with Dementia?"

These three references alone—to art, organizational behavior, and dementia—suggest the wide range of issues taken up within the interdisciplinary field of citizenship studies. Whatever else may be gained from such research, there are those who will argue that our attention is better focused on such traditional citizenship issues as, say, civic engagement, human rights, and representation in government. As central as these issues will always be to the proper study of citizenship, we believe their importance does not preclude sacrificing interdisciplinary inquiry. Quite the opposite. If we study issues of civic engagement and representation in government in isolation or even in relation to each other alone, we fail to fully grasp the human dimension that cultural, ethnographic, or gerontological studies provide, and we constrain those citizenship issues to a technocratic realm where their resolution becomes nothing more than a matter of better management. By enlarging our study of civic engagement or representation in government to the interdisciplinary inquiry of citizenship studies, we emphasize the central place of the person in our understanding as well as our resolution of those issues. Interdisciplinary inquiry helps us frame traditional citizenship problems as human problems that involve, among other things, artistic production, organizational behavior, and mental capacity, problems the resolution of which requires the attention, energy, and resolve of people invested in the well-being of their community.

The challenge to citizenship studies today is to continue to articulate as convincingly as possible that a wide range of concerns—from issues associated with art, with aging, with the environment, as well as with progress in technology—are issues of the nature of human belonging in political communities. These issues are the issues at the core of the meaning of citizenship. As a contribution to the conversation on the meaning of citizenship, this volume contains essays that elaborate four themes identified by Rogers Smith in his keynote address to the Tenth Annual Conference of the Center for the Study of Citizenship. Smith has been a major voice in the study of citizenship for over twenty years. His major contribution to the study of citizenship, *Civic Ideals: Conflicting Visions of Citizenship in U.S. History*, documents the history—for better and for worse—of the all-too-human struggle to shape the legal framework for citizenship in the United States. It is a chronicle of narrow-mindedness and unrealized ambitions. From this history Smith nonetheless concludes with the hope that Americans can realize the ambition of their civic ideals, and he presents to them a set of three tasks for doing so. He first recommends to scholars and teachers that they provide a more nuanced account of American history that precludes any mythologizing, so as to "assist reflection from all points of view on the realities of American life, its potentials, and its limitations" (Smith 1997, 505). He next tasks politicians to similarly forego mythologizing and to make the tough political compromises, challenging them to know "when not to push too hard for reforms; but they must also recognize that hard choices in favor of liberal purposes must sometimes be made if they are not to give grimmer meaning to American national life" (505). To American citizens he assigns the task of skeptical attachment and deliberate judgment: "They must recognize that their ties are both to all the real people that inhabit their country, to whom their obligations are deep, and to the ideals which their nation should advance, to which their obligations are also deep even when those ideals point beyond, and against, their country's narrower interests" (505–6). Smith's recommendations at the end of *Civic Ideals* remain prescient for a population of Americans increasingly divided by race and class whose government is stymied by polarizing partisan politics.

In his keynote address to the Tenth Annual Conference of the Center for the Study of Citizenship, published here in this volume, Smith reflects on the ongoing imperative for hard choices, skepticism, deliberateness, and open-mindedness in the form of four questions most critical to our current thinking about the conditions of citizenship:

1. How in theory and practice do we appropriately differentiate citizenship?
2. What are/ought to be the proper horizons of political citizenship (nation-state or other)?
3. What is/ought to be the character of politically sustainable and normatively appropriate civic bonds (including the means used to foster those bonds)?
4. How do we define and resolve conflicting civic and personal obligations?

The essays that follow respond to and elaborate on Smith's four questions. The authors of these essays bring a breadth and depth of interdisciplinary background to their work, including ethnography, literary study, rhetorical analysis, and travel narrative. They also demonstrate the global resonance of Smith's primary questions, focusing on experiences in Brazil, the Caribbean, Germany, Israel, and Pakistan. To highlight the relationship of the individual essays to each other, they are organized into four sections, one each for the four questions Smith raises.

In response to the question of how we ought to differentiate citizenship in both theory and practice, Lawrence Hatter, Nora Gottlieb, and Dani Kranz respond by considering the benefits as well as the drawbacks that attend our practices of differentiating ourselves and others as citizens. Dani Kranz in "Expressing Belonging through Citizenship" uses ethnographic interviews to reveal the dilemmas of national identification faced by third-generation Israeli citizens who are of German descent. On the one hand, these people feel like "Yekkes," or Germans in Israel, even though they are, on the other hand, far more Israeli than German. Focusing on the strategic use of ambiguous national identity, Lawrence Hatter, in "To Acquire the Equivocal Attributes of American Citizen and British Subject," looks back to the early years of the American republic, when the lines drawn between American citizenship and British subjecthood remained usefully malleable. Drawing attention to structural issues inherent in differentiating citizen from noncitizen, Gottlieb, in her essay "State, Citizenship, and Health in an Age of Global Mobility," focuses on the current global expansion of migrant labor to show how policies excluding migrant workers from the health care entitlements of a host country's citizens do not so much protect the rights of those citizens as reveal a more systemic erosion of the rights of all, citizens and noncitizens alike.

Authors who reflect on the theme of the proper horizons of political citizenship—the second of Smith's four concerns—bring their distinct disciplinary perspectives to bear on the problems of identifying citizenship with nation-states. Karen Thomas-Brown, in "Immigrant Teachers and Global Citizenship," describes the practice of training teachers in Jamaica for careers abroad, teaching in the highest-need urban schools in the United States, Canada, and Great Britain. As Thomas-Brown makes clear, the specific geopolitical history of Jamaica has promoted a transnational identity that informs the pedagogical export of Jamaican teachers. Alternatively, in "Exclusion, Island-Style," Kristy Belton examines the denial of rights to stateless persons living in The Bahamas and Dominican Republic, particularly persons of Haitian descent. As Belton argues, the denial of rights to Haitians living in The Bahamas and Dominican Republic demonstrates an ongoing need to preserve the formal recognition of state membership, if for no other reason than that nation-states retain the legal mechanisms for rights provisions. In his contribution to this volume, "Justice for Border-Crossing Peoples," David Watkins encourages us to consider the question of political membership less in terms of categories of inclusion in and exclusion from nation-states and more in terms of people whose lives daily bring them back and forth across established national borders. "'Free' Men and African Colonization" by Eugene Van Sickle returns to the early years of the American republic to describe how the organized movement to repatriate freed Africans reflects the ambiguity of American citizenship.

Smith's third question regarding the sustainability and appropriateness of civic bonds is taken up by several authors who document the intricacies of institutional organization and individual participation. Candice Bredbenner, in "Searching for the Civic Soul of the University" documents the impact of World War I on the evolution of American colleges and universities into partners with the federal government in training students for military preparedness. Bredbenner finds in this history of higher education an institutional imposition of civic responsibilities. Jay Leighter asks, in his contribution, "What Is an 'Average Citizen?'" drawing on a case study of public meetings in Seattle, Washington, to document what people mean when they use the word "citizen." Focusing on participatory budgeting in Porto Alegre, Brazil, Teresa Melgar, in "Voices from the Periphery," weighs the organization and commitment needed to sustain an expanded role for citizens in the management of their government. Howard Lupovitch argues in his essay, "Citizenship and the Ambiguities of Jewish Self-Confidence," that the legal emancipation of Hungarian Jews in 1868 creates a legal demarcation that belies a far more complex and protracted history of a struggle for equal citizenship.

Finally, the essays that engage Smith's fourth question asking how we define and resolve conflicting civic and personal obligations span time, space, and method. Gregory Garvey, in his essay, "Democratic Hopes and Majoritarian Fears," argues for a revision of our understanding of Emerson in light of his responses to the presidential election of 1834. From his reading of Emerson's journals, Garvey proposes a more nuanced view of Emerson, a person at one and the same time hopeful about participatory equality and skeptical of public sincerity. In her essay "French Citizens and Muslim Law,"

Larissa Kopytoff analyzes the consequences that followed from passage in the French National Assembly in 1916 of a law extending French citizenship to colonial subjects in Senegal. As Kopytoff makes clear in her history, the silence in the law regarding, among other things, the status of Muslim law, created opportunities for contesting both colonialism and citizenship status. Finally, Jonah Steinberg, in his essay "Writing Transnationality" takes an autobiographical look at the experience of transnationality, recounting his travels among a global minority Muslim sect, travels he writes about in his book *Isma'ili Modern*, a book that, as he puts it, "moves across a terrain of relationships, intimacies, times, and spaces, the spinning and imagining of multiple overlapping maps and domains of mood and mind."

The four primary concerns identified by Smith and taken up by the contributors to this volume are as timely as they are timeless. Appropriately differentiating citizenship identities and their proper political horizons, clarifying the character of politically sustainable and normatively appropriate civic bonds, and establishing means for defining and resolving conflicting civic and personal obligations will remain primary concerns as long as people continue to live together in communities. The contributors to this volume demonstrate through their engagement with these concerns that the challenges to citizenship in our world today derive from a range of prior practices and require of us that we imagine interdisciplinary solutions. The contributors to this volume in this way advance an ongoing conversation about the full meaning of citizenship.

WORKS CITED

Abbott, Philip. 2007. *The Many Faces of Patriotism.* Lanham, MD: Rowman and Littlefield.

Arendt, Hannah. 1973. *The Origins of Totalitarianism.* San Diego: Harcourt, Brace.

Auden, W. H. 1939. "September 1, 1939." First published in *The New Republic,* October 18, 1939. Available at www.poets.org/poetsorg/poem/september -1-1939.

Bellamy, Richard. 2010. "Introduction." In *Citizenship,* edited by Richard Bellamy and Antonio Palumbo. Burlington, VT: Ashgate.

Boyle, Geraldine. 2008. "The Mental Capacity Act 2005: Promoting the Citizenship of People with Dementia?" *Health and Social Care in the Community* 16 (5): 529–37.

Chaney, David. 2002. "Cosmopolitan Art and Cultural Citizenship." *Theory Culture and Society* 19 (1–2): 157+.

Geertz, Clifford. 1973. *Interpretation of Cultures.* New York: Basic Books.

Karst, Kenneth. 1989. *Belonging to America: Equal Citizenship and the Constitution.* New Haven, CT: Yale University Press.

Lee, Kibeom, and Natalie A. Allen. 2002. "Organizational Citizenship Behavior and Workplace Deviance: The Role of Affect and Cognition." *Journal of Applied Psychology* 87 (1): 131–42.

Smith, Rogers. 1997. *Civic Ideals: Conflicting Visions of Citizenship in U.S. History.* New Haven, CT: Yale University Press.

Van Loon, James E., and Hermina G. B. Anghelescu, eds. 2010. *Citizenship in the Humanities and Social Sciences: A Selective Bibliography, 2000–2009.* School of Library and Information Science Faculty Research Publications. Paper 1. http://digitalcommons.wayne.edu/slisfrp/1.

Wilson, Woodrow. 1897. *The State: Elements of Historical and Practical Politics.* Boston: Heath.

THE QUESTIONS FACING CITIZENSHIP IN THE TWENTY-FIRST CENTURY

· · · · · · · · · ·

ROGERS M. SMITH

As the plethora of outstanding scholarship at the extraordinary Tenth Anniversary Conference of the Wayne State Center for the Study of Citizenship confirmed, serious and sustained academic attention to a wide range of citizenship topics has expanded dramatically in many disciplines since I first began studying American citizenship more than three decades ago. Although I have tried to attend to the growth of that scholarship and the real-world events that have spurred it over time, neither I nor, I venture to say, any other single person can authoritatively delineate the full scope and significance of citizenship developments occurring now and in the years ahead. Yet in an age in which there are many pressures to hyperspecialize, it is valuable from time to time to try to map out the "big picture" onto which our more particular scholarly endeavors fit. In that spirit, this chapter offers an account of the main questions facing both scholars and practitioners of citizenship in the twenty-first century.

As preliminaries, let me note that there are many definitions of citizenship, including legal membership that entitles one to hold a passport from a nation-state; persons who are entitled to rule as well as be ruled within some sort of democratic or republican regime; persons who as a sociological matter are members of communities of "shared fate," whatever their legal statuses in those communities; persons who engage in active service in virtually any type of human association, whether political, civil, private, or even divine, as in St. Augustine's *City of God*; and persons who simply are members of such associations.[1] In common parlance, all these identities and statuses and more are sometimes called "citizens." Although we may rightly identify different conceptions as our specific concerns in particular analyses, I suggest we cannot avoid the fact that any and all uses of the terms *citizen* and *citizenship* will often tacitly invoke a whole range of other meanings. So the broad endeavor of studying citizenship cannot rule any of these meanings wholly out of consideration. To try to do so probably means that we will fail to grasp important dimensions of the phenomena of citizenship we profess to be focusing on in our inquiries.

As a second preliminary, like the great bulk of recent scholarship, I presume that all the different forms of membership, activity, and identity that we may call *citizenship* are products of social and political processes of construction, and indeed, all are also always part of processes of continuing and changing social and political construction and demolition. Scholars are, to be sure, far from agreed on just how to theorize those processes, and we face a daunting array of empirical questions in describing and explaining them, as well as a perhaps still more daunting array of normative questions when we seek to evaluate those processes and the forms of citizenship they have generated and are generating. But virtually all scholars of citizenship, certainly including me, believe they are engaged in a shared endeavor of trying to understand and/or evaluate the social and political processes through which the many things called "citizenship" are created and changed. Most believe this endeavor holds the promise of helping us and others to think how we might best live the forms of citizenship that are available to us or that we can hope to create.

This chapter briefly identifies four large questions of citizenship that I regard as the main ones facing those of us who are engaged in these endeavors of inquiry and of life choice today, in the still-new twenty-first century. These questions have empirical and normative dimensions that are closely linked, and they are all linked to each other, though they are distinct enough to merit separate mention. The four are (1) the question facing both democratic theory and democratic governance of *appropriately differentiated citizenship*; (2) the question of the proper *horizon or horizons* of political citizenship;

(3) the question of the character of *politically sustainable and normatively appropriate civic bonds*; and (4) the question of defining and resolving *conflicting civic and personal obligations*.

The first question, of appropriately differentiated citizenship, has been made central to me through studies of the arc of American civic development in the twentieth century (Smith 2012). But I see it as a central question around the world, in every regime that professes to be some kind of modern democracy or republic, as today most regimes do. The question has become more visible in the United States in the course of its modern history. At the dawn of the twentieth century, due to the clash of the egalitarian post–Civil War amendments with resurgent doctrines and practices of racial as well as ethnic, gender, religious and class inequality, American laws were structured in ways that created putatively equal but visibly first- and second-class forms of citizenship: the second-class forms were enacted in Jim Crow segregation laws; the related voting tests and poll taxes that disfranchised many of the poor and illiterate of all races; "domestic spheres" or "republican motherhood" gendered citizenship laws; the systems of imperial governance of Spanish American war territories and Native American reservations; the segregation by race, gender, class, and religion in systems of public education in much of the nation and at all levels, and much more.

These forms of putatively equal, effectively second-class citizenship led American citizenship struggles in the twentieth century to focus most on achieving legally equal citizenship, understood as *unitary* or *uniform* citizenship—citizenship in which all citizens would legally possess exactly the same bundle of rights and duties, especially voting rights, property rights, and due process rights. Separate could not be equal citizenship, for the races, for the genders, for any subgroup of citizens.

Or it seemed to many, as the battles to enfranchise women, overthrow segregation laws, and establish national antidiscrimination laws were fought during the first two-thirds of America's twentieth century. But even then, many—perhaps even most—who worked on behalf of those causes were not really attracted to, much less committed to, a political society that would be fully color-blind, gender-blind, religion- and culture-blind, one in which all citizens were seen as individuals with identical rights and duties, regardless of other, differing features of their identities. The views of figures like Philip Randolph, W.E.B. Du Bois, and Pauli Murray could not adequately be so described. But they thought the prevailing forms of racial and gender civic differentiation, especially, were clearly unjust, and they joined together under the banner of equal citizenship, widely understood as unitary citizenship, in order to achieve coalitions potent enough to attack those forms of second-class citizenship with considerable success.

But in the last third of the twentieth century, an array of empirical realities and normative considerations became more and more clear. The empirical reality is that neither the United States nor any other democratic society ever has had or ever will have full unitary, uniform legal citizenship. The considerations that contribute to this empirical reality are that in many respects, it does not seem defensible or desirable to define meaningfully equal citizenship as unitary, uniform citizenship. These are facts that the very triumphs of civil rights struggles on behalf of "equal citizenship" can lead us to ignore or deny, in ways that ill equip us to deal with many of the central challenges that democratic civic governance as well as democratic theories and citizenship theories face today.

The empirical reality that the laws of democratic societies never establish fully uniform unitary citizenship is easily shown. Any democracy large enough to have cities, states or provinces, and a national government has at least three levels of citizenship, and the rights and obligations of citizens are sure to vary somewhat between different cities and states and between those levels and national citizenship. Sometimes quasi-colonial forms of territorial citizenship also exist. Some citizens are native-born, almost always some are not, and the latter usually face some legal vulnerabilities the former do not. Some people are able to claim two or more legally recognized national citizenships, some are not. The very young and the severely mentally disabled usually do not possess all the rights of other citizens. For certain very limited but far from trivial legal purposes, corporations are often legally recognized as kinds of citizens and sometimes can claim multiple citizenships, but they are obviously not citizens like any others. A particular society's laws also cannot help but accommodate some religious and cultural practices, sexual orientations, and physical and mental abilities more than others, and this reality among others often leads to successful demands for explicit, counterbalancing legal accommodations for various sorts of minority groups. The reality of legal construction of citizenship in all societies, then, is and will always be differentiated citizenship, not fully uniform, unitary citizenship.

And the truth is, for many differing and often conflicting reasons, that is the way most people believe things ought to be. Many see advantages to having different levels of governance and permitting diversity in the laws of different cities and states or provinces even within the same nation-state. Few in any modern democracy agree that it is just or beneficial to confine citizenship exclusively to the native-born, even though that is how John Rawls theorized about it. Few agree that the very young or severely mentally disabled should possess exactly the same rights as able adults. Most want legal rules that allow corporations to sue and be sued in turn and so find it practical to assign them some kinds of legal citizenship.

More controversially, some still believe, on the one hand, that some traditional laws privileging certain religious, gender, and even racial and ethnic identities over others remain appropriate. And many believe, on the other, that the greatly varying histories, unequal current conditions, and the differing aspirations of particular racial, religious, cultural, and economic groups and persons of different sexes and sexual orientations make it appropriate for laws to treat them differently in important respects. Many think that groups historically subjected to unjust imperial subjugation and/or racial, religious, and gender discrimination, producing economic hardship and social marginalization, merit some forms of affirmative aid and accommodation. Many believe that equality requires restructuring institutions to serve persons with a variety of disabilities as fully as those with more conventional capacities. And some think that special accommodations are warranted even for groups that have not experienced past injustices or other forms of special hardship.

The philosopher Robert Audi, for example, defends a "protection of identity principle," holding that the "deeper a set of commitments is in a person, and the closer it comes to determining that person's sense of identity, the stronger the case for protecting the expression of those commitments tends to be," even if this requires exemption from laws applying to all other citizens (Audi 2011, 42). Audi is thinking of exemptions for religious conscience but stresses the principle applies more broadly, to any deeply valued identities. One might argue that he therefore is defending a kind of "unitary" citizenship, because all are entitled to accommodations for their deeply valued identities. But in practice, this approach means that citizens will possess bundles of rights and duties that are significantly different in their specific content.

Despite this range of normative beliefs and empirical practices, in modern American political rhetoric and in modern political theories more broadly, the bitter historical experiences with legal forms of putatively equal, effectively subordinating second-class citizenship have fostered great and in many ways salutary resistance to recognizing the legitimacy of "differentiated citizenship." But understandable as it is, I submit that the time for such resistance is over. We need to recognize that in reality, governments create and sustain forms of differentiated citizenship all the time. There is always a danger that doing so creates or sustains forms of unjust subordination and domination. There is also always a danger that failing to do so sustains structures of citizenship that are formally equal, but that are in reality, for many important purposes, highly unequal civic statuses. Theories of democracy and citizenship must take the question of what kinds of differentiated citizenship are appropriate in particular, ever-changing contexts as one of their most central questions, as most have not done until now. And we need to recognize that one of the central tasks of democratic governance is to determine on a continuing basis what kinds of differentiated citizenship are and are not appropriate, recognizing that the answers are likely to shift over time and must always be seen as legitimately contestable. So, this first question, the question of appropriately differentiated citizenship, is a very big one indeed.

So is the closely related second question—the issue of the proper horizon or horizons for citizenship. By this I mean above all the question of how far and in what ways we should think about citizenship in the twenty-first century not primarily and paradigmatically as membership in a sovereign nation-state, and should instead think of citizenship far more extensively as involving membership in other sorts of political communities or, indeed, multiple political communities, all of which claim some authority but none of which presents itself as fully sovereign. In this regard, the scholarly literature on citizenship has gone through a cycle that many have noted. In the late 1980s and 1990s, various works by scholars including Yasemin Soysal, David Held, and others began to proclaim that the era of the nation-state was over, that we were seeing simultaneous moves toward new transnational forms of political community like the European Union and new forms of devolution, such as the establishment of greater autonomy for Scotland and Wales in the United Kingdom and Catalonia in Spain (Soysal 1994; Held 1995). Some like Held celebrated these developments as steps toward a cosmopolitan world federation governed by the old Catholic principle of subsidiarity—problems would be dealt with by the most local level of democratic government capable of resolving them (e.g., Held 2003, 471). Others like Saskia Sassen quickly pointed out that we were seeing transnational arrangements that profited cosmopolitan elites who resided in multiple global cities and benefited from the transnational labor of poor migrants, but these arrangements did not obviously promote either economic or political equality (Sassen 1998). And soon, a wave of scholarship argued that it was premature to proclaim anything approach the death of nation-states. They still decisively shape transnational and subnational political associations and remain hegemonic in structuring citizenship and much else, even if they are far from uncontested.

I agree that the era of the predominance of nation-states is not ended, but I am also conscious that it is in fact a relatively recent development in world history—the age of religious and secular multinational empires is not long or even entirely past—that nation-states have not been even in the last century the only form of political community, and that they are indeed undergoing a range of challenges and transformations. The book that received the Wayne State Center for the Study of Citizenship's first book award, Jonah Steinberg's *Isma'ili Modern* (2011), is, for example, a fascinating account of how, with the initial aid of the British empire, the Isma'ili Muslim sect led by the Agha Khan has formed a globe-spanning, relatively wealthy, transnational community with its own constitution, laws, educational, cultural, political, and economic institutions. Its more than two million members are supposed to abide by the laws of the nation-states in which they reside, but often they are more effectively governed through their distinctive institutions, and many feel themselves Isma'ili first, Tajik or Pakistani or Kenyan or English decidedly second.

And though it is true that the project of the European Union that excited many scholars in the 1980s and 1990s has now stumbled over the nationalistic opposition of many of its members, many North Atlantic scholars have so far missed the fact that at its sixth summit in November 2012, the Union of South American Nations, representing Argentina, Bolivia, Brazil, Colombia, Chile, Ecuador, Guyana, Peru, Suriname, Uruguay, and Venezuela, approved a process to advance "in a flexible and gradual manner toward the consolidating of the South American identity . . . with the aim of attaining a true South American citizenship as the backbone of an integrated South American space" (Ishmael 2012). Some leaders hope to establish formal South American citizenship within the next ten years. Whether this will happen is, of course, an open question. But the point is that there is indeed a range of developments that raise pressing empirical questions as to whether and why the nation-state as the horizon of the most important forms of citizenship may be giving way to new forms of political association, and what those new forms will be. They are accompanied by perhaps even more pressing questions about whether the organization of the world primarily as a Westphalian system of nation-states is as desirable from the standpoint of promoting egalitarian democratic citizenship and material well-being as other arrangements. I have argued in favor of seeking to transform our memberships into more fluid and overlapping semisovereign democratic communities of various sorts, but I have many doubts about how empirically feasible and normatively desirable this trajectory really is (Smith 2003). So my point now is simply that the question of the appropriate horizon or horizons for citizenship, in both its manifold empirical and normative dimensions, has to be central to our agendas today.

The third major question is the question of what sorts of bonds can and should serve to hold together political communities, especially in the transformed and transforming world of the twenty-first century. It seems beyond empirical or normative dispute that we need to structure the world in terms of some sorts of political societies with some sorts of governing institutions if we are to create conditions in which human beings can flourish, and whatever sorts of societies we have will need the willing allegiance and cooperation of most of their members if they are to prove sustainable. But we have lots of empirical evidence that many of the ways political leaders and governments seek to foster allegiance either can fail to work to inspire sufficient cooperation to make the society function well, or alternatively can stir up extreme forms of loyalty so chauvinistic that they are accompanied by harsh, unjust policies toward nonmembers. Many have hoped that modern forms of democratic or republican citizenship might prove to be bonded only by "civic" conceptions of "constitutional patriotism," loyalty to principles of equality and freedom that are not accompanied by such chauvinistic nationalism (e.g., Habermas 1996, 491–515). But experience has not given much base for confidence that such purely "civic" bonds of political community are really empirically possible or at least sufficient to sustain regimes. Sociologist John Lie has argued that in fact the most prevalent forms of "modern peoplehood" fostered by modern nation-states are inclusionary but "involuntary" group identities based on ascriptive categories, especially race, ethnicity, or native-born nationality (Lie 2004). He believes the very complexities of modern life make such simplified, involuntary conceptions of peoplehood politically powerful, but they are obviously susceptible to becoming inflamed into virulent racism and xenophobia.

I think that Lie understates the range of forms of peoplehood that are empirically present in the modern world, and to some degree he unduly contrasts them with previous forms, but that only makes me feel more strongly that a central question for modern citizenship is whether it is empirically possible to define bonds of civic membership that work to achieve the good things political societies can do, without being easily distorted into unjust chauvinism of one sort or another. I have explored this issue by examining different sorts of "stories of peoplehood" told by political leaders, and it can be illustrated by citing the contrasting stories told, in explicitly that language, by the last two presidents of the United States.

The first quotation comes from George W. Bush's inaugural address in 2001: "After the Declaration of Independence was signed, Virginia statesman John Page wrote to Thomas Jefferson: 'We know the race is not to the swift nor the battle to the strong. Do you not think an angel rides in the whirlwind and directs this storm?' Much time has passed since Jefferson arrived for his inauguration. The years and changes accumulate. But the themes of this day he would know: our nation's grand story of courage and its simple dream of dignity. We are not this story's author, who fills time and eternity with his purpose. Yet his purpose is achieved in our duty, and our duty is fulfilled in service to one another. Never tiring, never yielding, never finishing, we renew that purpose today, to make our country more just and generous, to affirm the dignity of our lives and every life. This work continues. This story goes on. And an angel still rides in the whirlwind and directs this storm."

Contrast that account with Barack Obama's 2013 State of the Union address: "We may do different jobs, and wear different uniforms, and hold different views than the person beside us. But as Americans, we all share the same proud title: We are citizens. It's a word that doesn't just describe our nationality or legal status. It describes the way we're made. It describes what we believe. It captures the enduring idea that this country only works when we accept certain obligations to one another and to future generations; that our rights are wrapped up in the rights of others; and that well into our third century as a nation, it remains the task of us all, as citizens of these United States, to be the authors of the next great chapter in our American story."

The contrast will be clear. Bush tells Americans that we are not the ultimate authors of the American story; a divine providence is. Obama tells us that we as citizens are the authors. Obama's position is more consistent with democratic or republican or "civic" or "constitutional patriotism" conceptions of civic bonds, while Bush's may seem dangerously providentialist—I have argued that it is (Smith 2008). But notice two things: even Obama does not define American citizenship as fundamentally a matter of legal nationality. Instead, he at least comes close to essentializing it, saying to Americans that their citizenship "describes the way we are made." There is a hint here, to be sure, of the kind of republicanism that says we achieve our human potential in self-governance, as well as Christian social gospel doctrines holding that we do so through service to each other. But there is also at least a faint whiff of doctrines suggesting that Americans are uniquely suited for such republican citizenship.

Even Obama's speech, then, is evidence for the claim that political leaders regard it as empirically necessary to tell their fellow citizens what I have called a "constitutive" story, an account that makes membership in their particular society seem integral to their personal identity in ways they find valuable. And all constitutive stories have at least some xenophobic or chauvinistic potential. How can we find bonds of citizenship that can work empirically to tie political communities together, without falling prey to such bleak potential? That, again, is the third big question of modern citizenship, and it looms all the larger because the primacy of nation-states is being challenged, and many more forms of political community are arising and claiming at least some of our allegiances.

This brings us to the fourth, final, briefest and also oldest, most perennial, question of citizenship. It arises from the certainty that however the first three questions are answered—however we seek to foster appropriately differentiated forms of citizenship, however we define the appropriate bounds or horizons of our civic community or communities, however we define the bonds of those communities, seeking healthy loyalty but not dangerous chauvinism—our answers will be imperfect. They will be unsatisfying even to many who support them, as well as the many who will inevitably oppose them. The social and political processes of citizenship construction, contestation, and transformation will continue.

And so we as individuals will be faced, to some degree every day and some days very acutely, with an ethical dilemma that goes back beyond St. Augustine at least to Socrates. Given that our current forms of civic community are imperfect, how far and in what ways do we give them, their values, principles, policies, and institutions, the obedience and service they demand and undoubtedly often need if they are to do whatever good they are capable of doing—and how far instead do we decide that we have other, higher obligations? What do we do when our duties as good citizens conflict with our duties as good human beings? Probably even more than other persons, scholars of citizenship, who probably recognize more than most others how constructed, fragile, imperfect, but often valuable our forms of civic community are, must carefully explore the very wide range of empirical and normative questions involved in deciding what forms of citizenship can and should be sustained or resisted.

And if we scholars of citizenship wish not only to be good scholars but also good people, we, like our students and readers, must address these issues as questions we seek to answer as well as we can, not just for the audiences of our work, but for ourselves in our own personal lives. For me, at least, it is part of the great promise and appeal of studies of citizenship in the twenty-first century—studies superbly represented in the chapters of this volume—that they may help us approach better answers to all of the four large questions I have sketched. But it is perhaps especially this question that matters most: the quest to shed insight into what each of us and all of us should strive to do, as human beings pulled in many directions, yet always inescapably engaged in conceiving, constructing, and inhabiting much needed but always imperfect forms of citizenship.

NOTES

1. For taxonomies of different conceptions of citizenship, see e.g., Bosniak 2006, 17–36, and the papers collected in Isin and Turner 2002.

WORKS CITED

Audi, Robert. 2011. *Democratic Authority and the Separation of Church and State.* New York: Oxford University Press.

Bosniak, Linda. 2006. *The Citizen and the Alien: Dilemmas of Contemporary Membership.* Princeton, NJ: Princeton University Press.

Bush, George W. 2001. "First Inaugural Address," January 20, 2001. www .presidency.ucsb.edu.

Habermas, Jürgen. 1996. *Between Facts and Norms: Contributions to a Discourse Theory of Law and Democracy* .Translated by William Rehg. Cambridge, MA: MIT Press.

Held, David. 1995. *Democracy and the Global Order: From the Modern State to Cosmopolitan Governance.* Stanford, CA: Stanford University Press.

———. 2003. "Cosmopolitanism: Globalization Tame?" *Review of International Studies* 29: 465–80.

Ishmael, Odeen. 2012. "UNASUR Proposes Single South American Citizenship." www.guyanachronicleonline.com/site/index.php?option=com_content &view=article&id=52638:unasur-proposes-single-south-american-citizen ship&catid=2:news&Itemid=3.

Isin, Engin F., and Bryan S. Turner, eds. 2002. Handbook of Citizenship Studies. London: Sage.

Lie, John. 2004. *Modern Peoplehood.* Cambridge, MA: Harvard University Press.

Obama, Barack. 2013. "State of the Union Address," February 12, 2013. www. nytimes.com/2013/02/13/us/politics/obamas-2013-state-of-the-union-address.html?pagewanted=all.

Sassen, Saskia. 1998. *Globalization and Its Discontents.* New York: New Press.

Smith, Rogers M. 2003. *Stories of Peoplehood: The Politics and Morals of Political Membership.* Cambridge: Cambridge University Press.

———. 2008. "Religious Rhetoric and the Ethics of Public Discourse: The Case of George W. Bush." *Political Theory* 36: 272–300.

———. 2012. "Equality and Differentiated Citizenship: A Modern Democratic Dilemma in Tocquevillian Perspective." In *The Anxieties of Democracy: Tocquevillian Reflections on India and the United States,* edited by Ira Katznelson and Partha Chatterjee, 85–118. New Delhi: Oxford University Press.

Soysal, Yasemin N. 1994. *Limits of Citizenship: Migrants and Postnational Membership in Europe.* Chicago: University of Chicago Press.

Steinberg, Jonah. 2011. *Isma'ili Modern: Globalization and Identity in a Muslim Community.* Chapel Hill: University of North Carolina Press.

I

. . . .

Appropriately Differentiating Citizenship
in Theory and Practice

2

TO ACQUIRE THE EQUIVOCAL ATTRIBUTES OF AMERICAN CITIZEN AND BRITISH SUBJECT

· · · · · · · · · ·

Nationality and Nationhood in the Early American West, 1796–1819

LAWRENCE B. A. HATTER

James Wilkinson, governor of the Louisiana Territory, issued a proclamation in August 1805 banning anyone "the Citizen or Subject of a foreign Power" from entering the Missouri River at Saint Louis for the purpose of trading with Indians.[1] Wilkinson considered the exclusion of foreigners from the Missouri River an essential measure to secure US sovereignty over the native peoples inhabiting the vast trans-Mississippi territory, only recently acquired from Napoleonic France.

Wilkinson soon discovered that it was impossible to enforce his proclamation because traders had learned to exploit the ambiguity of nationality in the early American West to move between American citizenship and British subjecthood. The governor complained to secretary of war Henry Dearborn that traders from Canada had "availed themselves of an extraordinary clause in the [Jay] treaty . . . to acquire the equivocal attributes of American Citizen and British Subject, which they acknowledge or deny as may best suit their interests."[2] Traders exploited the difficulty of differentiating between American citizens and British subjects to maintain their transnational trade between Montreal and the hunting grounds of the upper Missouri River Valley.

The difficulties that Wilkinson encountered in Saint Louis reveal the protean nature of American citizenship in the early republic and the practical problems that federal officials faced in differentiating between their own nationals and those of the British Empire. Such difficulties are easy to understand during the first few years of independence. The United States secured its independence through a bitter civil war within the British Atlantic world, in which the loyalties of Anglo-Americans were constantly shifting (see Jasanoff 2011, 21–53). But the frustrations Wilkinson faced took place almost thirty years after independence in a city that had never been part of the British Empire.

Why, then, did American citizenship and British subjecthood remain intertwined in the early American West? The answer lies in understanding the inchoate nature of the border between the United States and the British Empire before the War of 1812. British subjects were "semicitizens" of the United States. As Elizabeth F. Cohen has explained, citizenship is best understood as a continuum of different combinations of rights enjoyed by different groups, rather than as a normative category (Cohen 2009, 15). Euro-Americans in the early American West could appeal to overlapping rights of citizenship in both the American republic and British Empire to negotiate state authority, particularly with regard to nationality. British subjects enjoyed core rights of nationality—free movement and residence—within the United States, which made it difficult for federal officials to distinguish between them and full citizens or American nationals.

This essay explores the problem of differentiating American citizenship from British subjecthood. Rogers Smith identifies the theme of appropriately differentiated citizenship as one of the key questions facing scholars, theorists, and policy makers in the twenty-first century. It is a question whose historical roots extend back to the founding of the United States. Indeed, the challenge of codifying categories of citizenship was integral to the creation of American nationhood in the early nineteenth century. While Great Britain recognized the formal political independence of the United States by the Treaty of Paris in 1783, the allegiance of Americans remained up for grabs, particularly in the region west of the Appalachians, where separatist movements threatened the survival of the American union (see Onuf

1987; 1995, 50–80; Lewis 1998, 12–40; Kastor 2004, 36–42; Hammond 2007). The clear ideological divide British and American policy makers envisioned between the democratic republican United States and the monarchical liberal constitutionalism of British North America did not reflect the reality of the northern borderlands. Scholars of citizenship in the early American republic have tended to focus on the ideological dimensions of republican citizenship, contrasting the new responsibilities and rights American citizens enjoyed in the postrevolutionary era with the nature of subjecthood in the colonial period (Kerber 1998; Kettner 1978; Pocock 1995, 29–52; Wood 1991).[3] The distinction between citizenship and subjecthood meant little to borderlands peoples for whom the face-to-face interactions of kinship and trade provided a more compelling framework for their sense of identity and belonging.

Overlapping British and American rights of nationality in the trans-Appalachian West posed a significant challenge to the federal government's efforts to exercise sovereignty over the northern borderlands. First, the difficulty of differentiating American citizens from British subjects retarded the development of civil society in the West. In an ideological sense, the presence of crypto-monarchists within the body politic was troubling to a founding generation who believed that the survival of the republic depended on the virtue and vigilance of active republican citizens (see Wood 1969, 65–70; McCoy 1980, 48–75). In more concrete terms, British subjects exploited their status as semicitizens to enjoy rights of residence and free movement while evading important civic responsibilities, including militia service and jury duty. Second, westerners used the ambiguity of categories of citizenship to evade federal regulation of the Indian trade, which was a critical part of the US government's policy to undermine the sovereignty of native peoples. The process of forcing political subjection on native peoples as domestic dependents of the federal government was tied up with resolving the problem of differentiating between British subjects and American citizens.

Geopolitics is critical to understanding the process of differentiating between British subject and American citizens in the early American West. The porous conditions in the northern borderlands meant that categorizing citizenship did not just involve negotiations between the federal state and different groups and individuals, but it also included Anglo-American diplomacy. Prior to 1796, British soldiers continued to garrison the military posts in the West at places such as Niagara, Detroit, and Michilimackinac. After the evacuation of the British garrisons in 1796, the United States agreed by the Jay Treaty of 1794 to maintain a porous border in the Great Lakes. British diplomats advocated on behalf of their nationals who were resident in the United States, interceding between them and the federal government. The free movement of peoples between the British Empire and the American republic denied the federal government the ability to use nationality as a tool to control western peoples by undermining their efforts to define American citizens and British subjects as mutually exclusive national groups (Cohen 2009, 144, 150).

The War of 1812 finally freed the United States to categorize citizenship. The conflict and its diplomatic resolution made possible an exclusivist border regime that helped to define the American people as a sovereign community within the family of nations. The Laurentine Indian trade offers unique insight into the making of American nationhood. Its protagonists, merchants and traders engaged in the Indian trade of the extended Saint Lawrence River valley, formed a transnational community of kinship and commerce. The expanding Indian trade was truly continental in scope, connecting the Atlantic entrepôt of Montreal in British Canada to a riverine commercial network that extended to the Columbia River and the Pacific Northwest by the outbreak of the War of 1812. Border crossings defined the lives of Laurentine merchants and traders; their livelihoods depended on traversing cultural and geopolitical boundaries. Most importantly, these individuals occupied an undefined position on the continuum of differentiated citizenship. The War of 1812 created the geopolitical conditions necessary for the US government to categorize American citizenship through a regular system of naturalization and stricter border controls. After 1815, Laurentine merchants and traders lost the ability to move between British subjecthood and American citizenship.

––––––

The British troops garrisoning Fort Lernoult crossed the Detroit River, which formed the international border between the United States and British North America, into the province of Upper Canada in July 1796. But a sizeable community of British subjects remained in the town of Detroit, which boasted a population of around two thousand souls, making it the most populous settlement in the federal Northwest Territory. In June 1797, the Detroit merchant George Sharp registered a petition with federal officials to record the election of 113 male heads of household to remain British subjects, residing on American soil. One-third of the adult male population of Detroit claimed critical rights of American nationality—the right to reside in the United States and the right of free movement—while declaring themselves British nationals.[4]

The British subjects at Detroit filed their petition under the second clause of the Jay Treaty of 1794. The Treaty of Amity, Commerce, and Navigation (Jay Treaty) negotiated by US chief justice John Jay and British foreign secretary Lord Grenville successfully averted an Anglo-American war by resolving long-standing tensions in the trans-Appalachian West and the Atlantic world. As part of this process, the British government agreed to remove their garrisons from Detroit, and the other western posts south of the Great Lakes, in return for a controversial agreement that protected a porous border between the United States and British North America. As such, the Jay Treaty granted important rights of nationality to British subjects on American soil by guaranteeing their residence and free movement in the United States.[5] At the same time, these British subjects avowed themselves foreign nationals, uninterested in taking up the treaty's offer of American naturalization. They possessed elements of American nationality, but were British nationals.

The residency of a large number of influential British subjects in Detroit undermined American nationhood. By granting British subjects some rights of nationality, the Jay Treaty limited the ability of the United States to make an American people "legible" by defining the boundaries of the political community (Cohen 2009, 150). To put it simply, the presence of British subjects on American soil blurred the borders of nationhood; residence did not denote full citizenship. The alien population posed a series of problems for establishing federal authority and a healthy body politic at Detroit in the late 1790s. Firstly, the British subjects at Detroit refused the civic duties the federal government demanded of its citizens. Chabert Joncaire, the lieutenant colonel of the Wayne County militia, declared the military force unreliable in the winter of 1796. Only twenty-nine of 111 men on the town's roster of two companies mustered arms. Moreover, the delinquent militiamen had refused to pay their fines for failing to appear because "they considered themselves as British Subjects" or informed Chabert's sergeants that "they had business of their own to attend to." Chabert blamed "a few Carreactors of the Town in the Mercantile line" for influencing the *Canadien* residents of Detroit from fulfilling their civic duty. Whatever the cause, the lieutenant colonel declared that he would not muster the militia until "some forceable measure is adopted to compel the Citizens of the Town to do their duty."[6] The citizen militia, the bulwark of liberty, could not be relied upon to defend the republic.

The federal garrison was no more reliable. Security concerns led General James Wilkinson to proclaim martial law in Detroit on July 12, 1797, barely a year after federal troops had taken possession of the settlement. "To guard the National Interests against the Machinations of its enemies, secret or ouvert, Foreign or Domestic," Wilkinson resolved to treat "all persons resorting to or residing within the limits" of Detroit as "followers of the army."[7] Wilkinson blamed a recent spate of desertions from the federal garrison at Detroit on the town's merchants and traders plying his soldiers with liquor.[8] The general grew increasingly suspicious that the British merchants were aiding the "dismemberment of the military force & the dispersion of a desperate band of Villains among these settlements, ripe for revolution, & ready to ride on any tempest which may be excited." As magistrates across the straits in Upper Canada, these individuals willingly administered oaths of allegiance to the British Crown to American deserters.[9]

The federal magistrates and sheriff of Wayne County shared Wilkinson's sense of alarm in the summer of 1797. They sent a memorial supporting the general's declaration of martial law to Winthrop Sargent, the acting governor of the Northwest Territory. The memorialists believed that "internal and increasing factions" threatened the operation of civil government in Detroit. "Twelve months ago, we Knew of no more than Ten of its Inhabitants that were avowed British Subjects," the magistrates wrote, but this handful of malcontents had since succeeded "by direct insinuations and circulating-papers to corrupt the minds of the Inhabitants and alienated their affections from the Government of the States." They reported that the consequent loss of civic manpower at Detroit was such "that it was with difficulty that the Sherrif could procure a Jury of real Citizens to attend the last Sessions, or Ballifs to do their duty."[10] Patrick McNiff, a justice of the peace for Wayne County, considered civil government in Detroit to be "unequal to counteract the Machinations of the present prevailing factions." Such was the sense of alarm, that McNiff urged Sargent to abandon civil government in Wayne County in favor of limited military rule.[11] The body politic was simply not healthy enough to support republican government.

Faction infected all aspects of life in Detroit society. Merchant communities from Montreal to Detroit traditionally formed dining clubs and other associations to entertain themselves during the long winter months when frozen rivers cut off communication from the upper country and the Atlantic world. In the winter of 1797/98, Detroit merchants forged an unlikely alliance with US army officers from the garrison at Fort Lernoult "to form with them a Separate and distinct Society for this Winter's amusements to which no Citizens of any respectability has been or is to be admitted." Peter Audrain, the prothonotary of Wayne County, spied a deliberate plot by the "British faction" to excite animosity between the civil and military authorities at Detroit. Audrain explained to Sargent that the merchants had made "an Easy conquest of certain Officers of the army who through fol[l]y or want of prudence, have involved themselves in debts, and have felt the Severe and impartial Justice of our Court." "Those officers," the prothonotary wrote, "have joined heart and hands with a party whose objective is to depress the dignity and destroy the respect due to our Magistrates."[12]

Political faction was anathema to a republican system of government designed to achieve political consensus through the organization of a homogeneous body politic. Faction seemed to infect all aspects of private and public life in the early years of American rule in Detroit, even religious observance. Audrain also wrote Sargent that he believed that the "the british faction have carried their intrigue as far as the roman Catholic Church" by "effecting a misunderstanding between the respectable & rev'd Monsr. Levadoux, pastor of this parish, and the wardens of the Church." In preaching a sermon celebrating George Washington's birthday and extolling the virtue of the US constitution as "the best in the World," Father Levadoux questioned whether British subjects could serve as parish wardens. In particular, Levadoux queried whether Philip Belangé could serve a third term in this capacity. The *cure* referred the question to the magistrates of Wayne County, who decided that Belangé "could not serve in any office of Trust." The decision sparked a violent demonstration among Belangé's supporters, who only dispersed after "the riot act was read in English & french." Audrain reported that "Phillip Bellengié makes no secret that he was advised & supported by John Askin Senr George Meldrum & others."[13] The presence of British subjects in Detroit divided confessional and social life in ways that undermined the civil authority of the federal government.

British subjects at Detroit may have rejected full US citizenship, but they still made use of important rights of American nationality. To be sure, British subjects sometimes impugned the dignity of some federal officers. But they also made frequent use of federal civil courts. British subjects made up one-fourth of the plaintiffs who filed suit in the Wayne County Court of Common Pleas between 1796 and 1804. Indeed, the individuals who Audrain identified as exercising the most caustic effects on federal authority, Laurentine merchants, used the court more than anyone else in Detroit; fifteen British merchants filed 241 separate causes in court, accounting for one-fifth of the business before the Court of Common Pleas between 1796 and 1804.[14] The severity of the problem British subjects posed to federal authority in Detroit was less their resistance to American rule than it was the unsettling influence of the ways in which they negotiated federal governance. By rejecting allegiance and the duties of citizenship, while enjoying the benefits of civil society, British subjects in Detroit destabilized categories of nationality.

The Jay Treaty's western provisions obscured the boundaries of nationality by granting some rights of American citizenship to British subjects and, importantly, failing to put in place a formal naturalization process that would allow federal officials to distinguish between people who enjoyed rights of nationality and individuals who were American nationals. Audrain warned Sargent that the British subjects in Detroit promised to have "every person now in Commission turned out of office" because they planned to "fill the vacancy by remaining on our side [of the straits] and taking the oath of allegiance to the United States."[15] The ability of individuals to claim American citizenship by the simple utterance of an oath meant that it was difficult for federal officials to determine who was and who was not a full member of the body politic. Indeed, several signers of Sharp's declaration held commissions in the US military. Jonathan Schieffelin, who replaced Colonel Meigs as the garrison engineer for Fort Lernoult; Hugh Heward, who served as a commissary; and Jonathan Nelson, the commander of the sloop USS *Detroit*, had all made a written declaration of their decision to remain British subjects.[16]

While General James Wilkinson promised to remove from office any British subjects in the federal service, this proved more difficult than he anticipated. Six candidates ran for election in the second contest held in the Northwest Territory after it entered the second stage of territorial government in 1798. George McDougal, Chabert Joncaire, and Jonathan Schieffelin defeated Benjamin Huntington, Joseph Cissne, and James May to claim the county's three seats in the territorial House of Representatives (Burton et al. 1922, 1: 268). Huntington contested the election on the grounds that Schief- felin was ineligible to run for election because he had signed Sharp's declara- tion in 1797. The defeated candidate protested that his rival was "not a citizen of the United States, but a subject of his Britanic Majesty." It was inconceiv- able to Huntington that Schieffelin would claim "the right of remaining here a citizen of the United States and of filling a seat in our Legislature under (what you call) the taut implications of our Treaty with the British Government." Allowing an avowed British subject to sit and vote in the legislature represented a dangerous intrusion "on the domestic affairs of this Government . . . [in] an illegal attempt to influence its deliberations."[17] The Court of Quarter Sessions heard Huntington's petition on October 19 in "rather noisy" proceedings that lasted "from ten o'clock in the forenoon until five o'clock in the afternoon."[18] While legal proceedings over the contested election continued until December 1802, Schieffelin traveled to Chillicothe to take his seat in the House of Representative for the opening of the second General Assembly on November 23, 1801 (Burton 1922, 2: 269).[19]

Schieffelin's election to the territorial House of Representatives helps to reveal the ways in which American nationhood remained ambiguous at the turn of the nineteenth century. He had signed Sharp's declaration as a Brit- ish subject in 1797, served in the employ of the federal government in 1798, and was a voting member of the territorial legislature in 1801 without having become a naturalized citizen of the United States. Despite this, members of the House of Representatives of the Northwest Territory were satisfied that he was an American citizen because the Jay Treaty had exempted him from the formal naturalization procedures Congress established in the 1790s. All that Schieffelin had to do to become an American citizen was to swear an oath.

The ambiguous bounds of the American body politic increasingly blurred the distinction between domestic and international politics. Patrick McNiff wrote Albert Gallatin, the new treasury secretary in Thomas Jeffer- son's cabinet, of the rise of "aristocratic" Federalist faction in Detroit in the fall of 1801. Addressing Gallatin because of his support for Jefferson in the disputed presidential election of 1800 against a "Nefarious and daring faction of Aristocrats Introduced by foreign (I mean British) Influences," McNiff explained to the Pennsylvanian that Democratic Republicans encountered an equally dangerous movement in local politics. The Detroiter described an alliance between "Bandittis" from Pittsburgh and "a number of British

Subjects still remaining among us [who] have formed one faction giving themselves the appellation of Aristocrats." McNiff accused the faction, led by Mathew Ernest, of using "every artful means in their power to bring over undiscerning Ignorant people to their principles," and decried their occupation of civil offices at Detroit.[20] While McNiff's letter to Gallatin was unquestionably part of his strategy to secure the lucrative position as federal collector for the port of Detroit, his argument is demonstrative of the way in which volatile loyalties and the ambiguity of nationality intersected with partisan politics to exacerbate divisions within the body politic.

British subjects retained rights of American nationality even after they moved across the straits of the Detroit River into the new townships of Sandwich and Amherstburg in the province of Upper Canada. The movement of these merchants from the United States to British Canada helped to create a transnational community that bridged the Detroit River because they still retained the right of open entry to the United States. Certainly, the migration of these merchants did little to quell the fears of federal officials in Detroit. Writing in December 1802, Peter Audrain, again, complained of the continued presence of British subjects at Detroit, who were "not acquainted with the worth of our present executive." Reflecting on the state of civil society in the settlement after six years of American rule, Audrain did not consider Detroit suited for incorporation into the federal union. He wrote John Cleves Symmes that he thought it best if the settlement and its environs remain a "Colony of the United States," as he thought the local population, including the "illiterate" *Canadiens*, "not fit for a Self Government."[21]

In the summer of 1805, a brigade of traders from Montreal made their way through the Great Lakes bound for the Missouri River. They entered their goods and paid duties with the federal collector of customs at Michilimackinac and continued down the Illinois River to its confluence with the Mississippi. "To their utter astonishment," the traders found their passage across the Mississippi River to Saint Louis barred by a proclamation issued by their old advisory, James Wilkinson. The governor of the Upper Louisiana territory had forbade the entry of foreign nationals from the Missouri River. Moreover, the traders complained, Wilkinson had imposed "the most extraordinary test that was offered to any, but more especially to British Subjects; nothing less than abjuring their Allegiance and Faith to their lawful

Prince & Sovereign, or to be excluded from that Trade."[22] Wilkinson was determined to differentiate between American citizens and British subjects to protect federal authority in a vast territory inhabited by native and Euro-American populations who were largely strangers to the laws and customs of the United States.

Federal control over the Indian trade was essential to establishing US hegemony over the Indian nations of the Missouri River Valley. The close connection between politics and trade in Indian diplomatic culture meant that federal officials looked upon British traders as agents of the British government, spreading dangerous foreign influence on American soil. Regulation of the Indian trade, then, was an important part of US Indian policy to limit the autonomy of native peoples by confining them within national borders. Moreover, it was also a way of forcing a form of differentiated citizenship on native peoples. While Indians were denied formal American citizenship until the twentieth century, the US government sought to undermine the sovereignty of native peoples by denying Indian nations the right to conduct diplomacy with rival European empires (see Jennings 1976, 118). As such, the problem of differentiating American citizens from British subjects was intertwined with the complementary process of forcing a semicitizenship status on native peoples as domestic dependents of the federal government.

The trade between the Saint Lawrence and Missouri River valleys was of long standing by 1805. Arthur St. Clair, the governor of the Northwest Territory, described the Mississippi trade in 1791 as being "almost entirely in the hands of the british—even much the greatest part of the merchandize for the trade of the Missouri River is brought from Michilimackinac by that of the Illinois, partly by spanish Subjects themselves, and partly by british Traders."[23] Laurentine merchants and traders hoped to put the trade, which had formerly relied on the illicit cooperation of Spanish officials, on a more regular footing now that Louisiana was under American rule. The merchants believed that the nationality rights they enjoyed under the Jay Treaty would extend to the newly acquired territories of the Louisiana Purchase. Wilkinson's proclamation excluding foreign nationals from the Missouri River threatened to destroy their trade by saddling the merchants with the additional expense of hiring boatmen and traders in Saint Louis. Indeed, Wilkinson issued his proclamation to coincide with the arrival of the Laurentine traders at Kaskaskia, opposite Saint Louis, to inflict grievous financial losses on their patrons by ensuring that merchants had already invested in goods that would realize no returns from the Missouri hunting grounds.

Far from creating a clear distinction between American citizens and British subjects, Wilkinson's proclamation only revealed the extent to which these ill-defined categories collapsed into each other. The Laurentine trade depended on access to both Montreal and the hunting grounds of the American West. Montreal supplied manufactured goods, such as textiles and metalwork, and received furs to sell on the London market; the native peoples who stalked the hunting grounds of the American West supplied furs in return for manufactured goods. The Jay Treaty had allowed merchants and traders to maintain their cross-border trade in Ohio and Illinois as British subjects, but Wilkinson and the Jefferson administration argued that the treaty's commercial rights did not extend across the Mississippi River because the territory of the Louisiana Purchase was acquired after the Anglo-American agreement. In short, traders needed to be British subjects in Montreal and American citizens in Saint Louis to access the trans-Mississippi trade.

This is precisely what Laurentine traders did. Exploiting the ambiguity of the Jay Treaty's western provisions, they claimed American citizenship on arriving in Saint Louis based on their residence at one of the western posts, including Niagara, Detroit, and Michilimackinac, in 1796. "A Mr Aird a Scotchman has just arrived with a considerable quantity of goods from Michilimackinac, and A Mr. Dickson his Countryman, is daily expected with a large Cargo from the same Place," Wilkinson wrote secretary of war Henry Dearborn in September 1805. On arriving in Saint Louis, Aird, an employee of Robert Dickson & Co., had "claimed the right of Citizen-ship, under the last clause of the British Treaty," and Wilkinson expected that "Mr. Dickson will no doubt follow his example." The western provisions of the Jay Treaty did not create dual nationality, or permit individuals to move between subjecthood and citizenship. Rather, the treaty failed to provide a regular system for recording and verifying individual claims to nationality. Wilkinson complained that he had no effective means of querying Aird and Dickson's claims to citizenship. He recognized that "I can barely require proof of residence, which I have no doubt they will find, coming as they do prepared for this occasion." Consequently, he called for "some extraordinary provisions . . . to detect or repel the impositions daily practiced by persons calling themselves American Citizens, but who are in fact Zealous British Partizans." Wilkinson questioned the ease with which Aird and Dickson claimed American citizenship. He asked Dearborn whether it was "proper to admit such Characters to take the oath of Allegiance and abjuration? Or is this Oath sufficient, to entitle them to all the Privileges of American Citizenship?"[24] The fluid boundaries of American citizenship allowed Aird and Dickson to maintain their transnational trade between British Canada and the United States.

Federal officials did not find a way to differentiate between American citizens and British subjects in the American West before the War of 1812. Figures such as Dickson and Aird exploited their liminal status to cement their position as power brokers in the Indian trade of the trans-Mississippi West. Jean Baptiste Lucas, a territorial judge in Saint Louis, complained in 1807 of the ability of Laurentine traders to access the Missouri River trade. Lucas wrote Henry Dearborn that traders from Michilimackinac "declared on oath that they were citizens of, or residents in the united states," though the judge was "credibly informed that several of these traders are well known to be residents in montreal or Near that place in Canada." Echoing Wilkinson's sentiments from two years earlier, Lucas informed the secretary of war that "som[e] better evidence than an oath ought in my opinion ought to be required of an Indian Trader."[25] Two years later, Governor William Clark warned of "the British interference with our Indian affairs in this country," pointing to their activities at Prairie du Chien on the upper Mississippi River, which "is the inroad of the British Canadian Traders to all the upper country; and the Grand Mart for several nations & Tribes of Indians."[26] The inability of federal officials to differentiate between American citizens and British subjects meant that the territorial borders of the United States remained porous. Merchants and traders exercised their right to freely move between the British Empire and the American republic, maintaining a transnational trade that worked against federal efforts to confine native peoples within the borders of a nation-state.

———

In the summer of 1818, Jacques Porlier, a trader at Green Bay, decided to claim American citizenship.[27] The *Canadien* Porlier was a British subject, having resided at Detroit and Michilimackinac since at least 1791, and a seasoned veteran of the Laurentine trade. The exclusive Beaver Club of Montreal had elected him a member in 1801, reflecting his growing influence in the trade.[28] Porlier made his claim to American citizenship by appealing to the rights he enjoyed under the Jay Treaty as a resident of the western posts at the time of the British evacuation in 1796. Unlike the countless merchants and traders who had made the same claim before him, Porlier found no easy path to citizenship in 1818.

The War of 1812 was a critical moment in the making of American nationhood because it made it possible for federal officials to differentiate between American citizens and British subjects. The US Congress, at the behest of the Madison administration, declared war on Great Britain in June 1812 in large part because of the threat that the porous boundaries of nationality posed to American sovereignty in both the Atlantic world and the trans-Appalachian West (Hatter 2012, 106). The conflict abrogated the Jay Treaty, invalidating the commercial and residential rights of British subjects on American soil. Moreover, the American peace commissioners in Ghent refused to renew the Jay Treaty's provisions in the new peace treaty and commercial convention that followed. The bitterness of the war along the Anglo-American border also created a popular clamor to exclude foreign traders from the Indian trade of the United States.[29] In December 1815, the Philadelphia *Aurora* newspaper campaigned for the exclusion of ruthless British traders from American soil, asking of its readers, "do not the practices of her *Dicksons* and her *Elliotts*, and other agents along our whole frontier, from Detroit to Chickago, and from thence to the Mississippi, demand of the United States government, the protection of our settlers from the instigated massacres of those barbarous agencies?"[30] The US Congress agreed, passing the Indian Intercourse Act in 1816, which ensured that only American citizens could obtain Indian trade licenses.[31]

The enforcement of the Indian Intercourse Act by federal agents in the Great Lakes helped to differentiate between British subjects and American citizens. Jacques Porlier spent a dispiriting winter in Saint Charles, across the Missouri River from Saint Louis, in 1816/17. Unable to obtain an Indian trade license, he wrote Pierre Rocheblave, a trader at Michilimackinac, "the tribunal of a mercantile inquisition has not allowed me to go and winter with the Sacs as I had proposed. I was not clothed with the spotless robes, without which one could not be admitted to the number of the privileged ones." Porlier had few options but to rent a second-floor store in Saint Charles, where he tried, largely in vain, to sell his goods.[32] The plight of traders like Porlier convinced the Montreal merchant houses to sell their interest in the Indian trade of the United States to John Jacob Astor's New York–based American Fur Company in early 1817.[33]

Communities of British subjects remained in the United States, despite the withdrawal of Laurentine commercial operations from American territory. At Green Bay, the local US Indian agent, John Bowyer, reported that "Mr. John Lawe, The Grignons, Mr. Porleur and others have a number of engages in their service who are all british subjects . . . married to Indian Women." Bowyer explained to Lewis Cass, the governor of the Michigan Territory, that "if they are suffered to remain here as British Subjects, the laws prohibiting Foreigners to trade with the Indians living in the United States will have no effect." Bowyer suggested to Cass that federal agents either remove these individuals or force them to become American citizens, favoring the latter course in the case of the "Lower Class of the French."[34] The remaining British traders, however, found it hard going making a living in the Indian trade. John Lawe complained in November 1818 that in the three years since the peace he had grown "Grey and worn" because of the "oppression" of British subjects by the federal authorities.[35] Louis Grignon, also of Green Bay, complained to Robert Dickson the following February that "British Subjects are always black Sheep."[36]

Porlier's attempt to claim American citizenship in the summer of 1818 foreshadowed a growing wave of applications among British subjects for whom the crystallization of categories of citizenship threatened to isolate them as aliens in a foreign land. William Woodbridge, secretary of the Michigan Territory, initially confirmed Porlier's status as an American citizen in September 1818.[37] John Lawe, Louis Grignon and his brothers Pierre, Augustin, and Charles all applied, providing documents to local federal agents to establish their residency in the United States in 1796. Federal officials, however, did not agree on the status of these individuals or the naturalization procedure they ought to follow. Adam Stewart, the US customs collector at Michilimackinac, considered Lawe and Pierre, Augustin, and Charles Grignon to be bona fide American citizens for whom "it is not necessary for them to take the oath of allegiance to the U.S. Government," while the Indian agent Bowyer insisted on administering the oath.[38] Federal agents at both Michilimackinac and Green Bay rejected the claims of Louis Grignon, who appealed to Governor Cass "to be recognized as a Citizen."[39] While the difference between American citizens and British subjects was beginning to come into focus in the years following the War of 1812, the federal government still lacked a clear system for naturalizing westerners.

US attorney general William Wirt established a naturalization procedure for claimants under the Jay Treaty in the opinion he issued on Jacques Porlier's application for citizenship in September 1819. Cass appealed to the Monroe administration for authoritative instructions on how his agents ought to proceed in registering individual claims to citizenship. Secretary of war John C. Calhoun referred Porlier's case to Wirt to determine whether the trader, by not subscribing to Sharp's petition in 1797, had become a citizen of the United States. Wirt decided that he had not. The attorney general considered the wording of the Jay Treaty's second article to imply "not that they [foreign residents of the United States] shall, thereby become citizens, *ipso facto:* but that they shall be considered as having *elected to become* Citizens; the manner and terms of their admission, remained to be prescribed by the U.S." Wirt argued that the Alien Act of January 29, 1795, had prescribed "an uniform rule of naturalization" by which Porlier was qualified to apply for US citizenship in 1797—after two years residence under the jurisdiction of the United States. Wirt noted that "the various laws which have since passed on the subject have always contained a provision keeping open this privilege in behalf of the settlers prior to 1795." Wirt concluded that Porlier was "not yet, in my opinion, a citizen of the United States."[40] The attorney general's opinion ensured that the Jay Treaty no longer offered a shortcut to citizenship. Rather, British subjects resident on American soil in 1796 now fell under regular US naturalization laws.

Wirt's ruling framed the instructions that Cass sent to federal agents at Michilimackinac, Green Bay, Chicago, and Fort Wayne in October 1819. The governor explained that the US attorney general "has given it as his opinion, that persons, whose cases are comprehended in the 2d Article of the treaty of 1794, commonly called Jay's treaty, do not by the mere force of that article become American Citizens, but that they must also be naturalized under the acts of Congress." The Jay Treaty did not confer citizenship on the residents of the western posts in 1796; rather, it offered them the "right to become American Citizens." As such, Cass instructed the agents that "no license will consequently be granted to any person claiming to be an American Citizen under the article before referred to, unless such a person has also been naturalized agreeable to the acts of Congress."[41] The ability of federal officials to differentiate between American citizens and British subjects was an integral part of the making of American nationhood. By 1820, the American people comprised a distinct political community in equal standing with the other nations of the world.

The difficulty of differentiating between American citizens and British subjects reveals the extent to which allegiances were volatile in the early American West. That Laurentine merchants and traders exercised rights of both American and British nationality prior to the War of 1812 suggests that choices about loyalty were most often shaped by pragmatic calculations about personal advantage, rather than an abstract ideological commitment to republicanism or monarchy. Appreciating how the federal government dealt with the practical problems of categorizing citizenship in a contested borderlands region is critical to understanding the making of American nationhood.

The process of codifying citizenship and formalizing naturalization in the early American West also shows the extent to which the process of defining the American people took place in an international space. In other words, categorizing the continuum of American citizenship did not simply involve determining the internal composition of the body politic, but also of distinguishing members of the American nation from the other nations of the world, most notably, the provinces of British North America. Consequently, Anglo-American diplomacy played an important role in both obscuring and fixing the boundaries of nationality in the early American West. The Jay Treaty, by granting British subjects important nationality rights of residence and free movement, created the necessary geopolitical conditions for Laurentine merchants to exploit the ambiguity of American citizenship to maintain their transnational trade. The Treaty of Ghent and Anglo-American commercial convention of 1815 ensured that the territorial border dividing the British Empire from the American Republic also defined separate British and American peoples.

The War of 1812 was the critical moment in the making of American nationhood. For future generations of British-Canadians and Americans, the conflict came to occupy a central place in the collective memory of the two nations. The later nineteenth-century development of American and Canadian nationalism was only possible, however, because the war had helped to differentiate between American citizenship and British subjecthood so that the categories of "American" and "Canadian" proved capable of assuming cultural significance.

NOTES

1. Proclamation by Governor Wilkinson, August 26, 1805, in Carter (1934–62, 13: 203).

2. Governor Wilkinson to Secretary of War, September 8, 1805, in Carter (1934–62, 13: 198).

3. This paper builds on Bradburn (2009) by seeking not only to understand who could be considered members of the American nation, but also to explain how the changing nature of the Anglo-American border helped to transform the amorphous boundaries of American citizenship into a fixed category of nationality.

4. George Sharp to Peter Audrain, May 20, 1797, Ms. Hershel Whitaker, Burton Historical Collection (hereafter BHC), Detroit Public Library. The declaration contained 113 signatures or marks. A further five individuals, whose names are absent from the declaration registered by George Sharp, signed a letter to James Wilkinson as British subjects. "The Petition of Sundry British Magistrates, Merchants and others holding property residing in and resorting to the Town of Detroit," July 24, 1797, RG 59, Notes from Foreign Legations, Great Britain, vol. 2 (hereafter British Legation Notes), National Archives of the United States, Washington, DC. According to the census of 1796, 106 men above the age of sixteen resided in the city of Detroit, of whom thirty-six (34 percent) elected to remain British subjects (Russell 1982, 59, 60–62, 74).

5. Elizabeth Cohen identifies residence and movement as the fundamental rights associated with a "legal/territorial" definition of nationality (Cohen 2009, 144).

6. Chabert Joncaire to Winthrop Sargent, December 6, 1796, Microfilm edition of the Winthrop Sargent Papers, Massachusetts Historical Society, 4: 211. Hereafter Sargent Papers.

7. By James Wilkinson Brigadier General and Commander in Chief of the Troops of the United States, A Proclamation, July 12, 1797, British Legation Notes, vol. 2.

8. James Wilkinson to the British Magistrates, Merchants, and others holding property, residing in and resorting to the Town of Detroit, n.d., British Legation Notes, vol. 2.

9. James Wilkinson to the Justices of the Peace of the Western District of Upper Canada, July 16, 1797, in Quaife (1928–31, 2 [1931]: 116–17).

10. "Machinations against the United States Government," July 12, 1797, in Quaife (1928–31, 2 [1931]: 112–13).

11. Patrick McNiff to Winthrop Sargent, July 12, 1797, Sargent Papers, 4: 333–35.

12. Peter Audrain to Winthrop Sargent, January 20, 1798, Sargent Papers, 4: 522.

13. Peter Audrain to Winthrop Sargent, January 20, 1798, Sargent Papers, 4: 523–24.

14. Wayne County Court of Common Pleas Records, 1796–1804, Michigan Supreme Court Records, 1796–1857, Series I, Boxes 1–6, Bentley Historical Library, University of Michigan, Ann Arbor.

15. Peter Audrain to Winthrop Sargent, January 20, 1798, Sargent Papers, 4: 523.

16. Peter Audrain to Winthrop Sargent, January 26, 1798, Sargent Papers, 4: 527–28.

17. Notice of Contest of Election of Jonathan Schieffelin, October 18, 1800, in *Historical Collections of the Michigan Pioneer and Historical Collections*, 8: 517–18. Hereafter *MPHC*.

18. Peter Audrain to Governor St. Clair, October 20, 1800, in Smith (1882, 2: 500).

19. November 23, 1801: *Journal of the House of Representatives of the Territory of the United States, North West of the Ohio, at the First Session of the Second General Assembly, A.D. 1801* (1801, 11).

20. Patrick McNiff to Albert Gallatin, October 22, 1801, Albert Gallatin Papers, Reel 3: 248, New-York Historical Society.

21. Peter Audrain to John Cleves Symmes, December 15, 1802, Albert Gallatin Papers, Reel 3: 6, New-York Historical Society.

22. Memorial of Montreal Merchants, November 8, 1805, *MPHC*, 25: 219–20.

23. Report of Governor St. Clair to the Secretary of State, February 10, 1791, in Carter (1934–62, 2: 331)

24. Governor Wilkinson to Secretary of War, September 8, 1805, in Carter (1934–62, 13: 196–98).

25. Judge Lucas to Secretary of War, February 9, 1807, in Carter (1934–62, 14: 96).

26. William Clark to the Secretary of War, April 30, 1809, in Carter (1934–62, 14: 271).

27. William H. Puthuff to Lewis Cass, August 24, 1818, William Woodbridge Papers, Box 15, Folder March–September 1818, Burton Historical Collection, Detroit Public Library.

28. "Rules of the Beaver Club," February 1807, Beaver Club Minute book, 1807–27 (P305), Musée McCord, Montreal.

29. With Britons, Americans, and native peoples fighting on both sides of the conflict, Alan Taylor persuasively argues that the War of 1812 is best understood as a civil war (Taylor 2010).

30. *Aurora General Advertiser*, December 15, 1815.

31. An act supplementary to the act passed the thirtieth of March, one thousand eight hundred and two, to regulate trade and intercourse with the Indian tribes, and to preserve peace on the frontiers, April 29, 1816, *U.S. Statutes-at-Large*, III, 332–33.

32. Jacques Porlier to Pierre Rocheblave, c. Winter 1816–1817, in Thwaites (1888–1931, 19: 445–46).

33. American Fur Company's Agents, John Jacob Astor to Ramsey Crooks, March 17, 1817, in Thwaites (1888–1931, 19: 451).

34. John Bowyer to Lewis Cass, May 16, 1818, in Thwaites (1888–1931, 20: 56–57).

35. John Lawe to Thomas Anderson, November 13, 1818, in Thwaites (1888–1931, 20: 90–91).

36. Louis Grignon to Robert Dickson, February 6, 1819, in Thwaites (1888–1931, 20: 102–3).

37. William Woodbridge to John Bowyer, September 8, 1818, Woodbridge Papers, Box 15, Folder March–September 1818.

38. Adam D. Stewart to John Bowyer, September 2, 1819, in Thwaites (1888–1931, 20: 120–21).

39. Louis Grignon to Lewis Cass, August 27, 1819, in Thwaites (1888–1931, 20: 120).

40. William Wirt to J. C. Calhoun, September 3, 1819, in Thwaites (1888–1931, 20: 121).

41. Lewis Cass to Agents at Michilimackinac, Green Bay, Chicago, Fort Wayne, and Piqua, October 11, 1819, in Thwaites (1888–1931, 20: 127).

WORKS CITED

Manuscript Sources

Aurora General Advertiser.

Beaver Club Minute Book, 1807–27.

Bentley Historical Library, University of Michigan, Ann Arbor, Michigan.

British Legation Notes (microfilm edition).

Burton Historical Collection, Detroit Public Library, Detroit, Michigan.

Gallatin, Albert. Papers.

Massachusetts Historical Society, Boston, Massachusetts.

Michigan Supreme Court Records, Series I: Northwest Territory and Indiana Territory, 1796–1805.

Musée McCord, Montreal, Quebec.

National Archives of the United States, Washington, DC.
New-York Historical Society, New York, New York.
Record Group 59: US State Department Records.
Sargent, Winthrop. Papers (microfilm edition).
Whitaker, Hershel. Papers.
Woodbridge, William. Papers.

Edited Manuscript Collections

Carter, Clarence Edwin, ed. 1934–62. *Territorial Papers of the United States.* 26 vols. Washington, DC: US Printing Office.

Historical Collections of the Michigan Pioneer and Historical Society. 1874–1929. 40 vols. Lansing, MI: The Society.

Journal of the House of Representatives of the Territory of the United States, North West of the Ohio, at the First Session of the Second General Assembly, A.D. 1801. 1801. Chillicothe, OH: N. Willis.

Quaife, Milo M., ed. 1928–31. *The John Askin Papers.* 2 vols. Detroit: Detroit Library Commission.

Russell, Donna Valley, ed. 1982. *Michigan Censuses 1710–1830 under the French, British, and Americans.* Detroit: Detroit Society for Genealogical Research.

Smith, William Henry, ed. 1882. *The St. Clair Papers: The Life and Public Services of Arthur St. Clair, Soldier of the Revolutionary War; President of the Continental Congress; and Governor of the North-Western Territory, with His Correspondence and Other Papers.* 2 vols. Cincinnati: Robert Clarke.

Thwaites, Reuben Gold, et al., eds. 1888–1931. *Collections of the State Historical Society of Wisconsin.* 20 vols. Madison: The Society.

United States. 1845–46. *The Public Statutes at Large of the United States of America: from the organization of the government in 1789 to March 3, 1845.* 4 vols. Boston: Charles C. Little and James Brown.

Secondary Sources

Bradburn, Douglas. 2009. *The Citizenship Revolution: Politics and the Creation of the American Union, 1774–1804.* Charlottesville: University of Virginia Press.

Burton, Clarence M., et al., eds. 1922. *The City of Detroit Michigan, 1701–1922.* 5 vols. Detroit: S. J. Clarke.

Cohen, Elizabeth F. 2009. *Semi-Citizenship in Democratic Politics.* New York: Cambridge University Press.

Hammond, John Craig. 2007. *Slavery, Freedom, and Expansion in the Early American West.* Charlottesville: University of Virginia Press.

Hatter, Lawrence B. A. 2012. "Party Like It's 1812: The War at 200." *Tennessee Historical Quarterly* 71: 106.

Jasanoff, Maya. 2011. *Liberty's Exiles: American Loyalists in the Revolutionary World*. New York: Random House.

Jennings, Francis. 1976. *The Invasion of America: Indians, Colonialism, and the Cant of Conquest*. New York: Norton.

Kastor, Peter J. 2004. *The Nation's Crucible: The Louisiana Purchase and the Creation of America*. New Haven, CT: Yale University Press.

Kerber, Linda K. 1998. *No Constitutional Right to Be Ladies: Women and the Obligations of Citizenship*. New York: Hill and Wang.

Kettner, James. 1978. *The Development of American Citizenship, 1608–1870*. Chapel Hill: University of North Carolina Press.

Lewis, James E., Jr. 1998. *The American Union and the Problem of Neighborhood: The United States and the Collapse of the Spanish Empire, 1783–1829*. Chapel Hill: University of North Carolina Press.

McCoy, Drew R. 1980. *The Elusive Republic: Political Economy in Jeffersonian America*. Chapel Hill: University of North Carolina Press.

Onuf, Peter S. 1987. *Statehood and Union: A History of the Northwest Ordinance*. Bloomington: Indiana University Press.

———. 1995. "The Expanding Union." In *Devising Liberty: Preserving and Creating Freedom in the New American Republic*, edited by David Thomas Konig, 50–80. Stanford, CA: Stanford University Press.

Pocock, J. G. A. 1995. "The Ideal of Citizenship since Classical Times." In *Theorizing Citizenship*, edited by Ronald Beiner, 29–52. Albany: State University of New York Press.

Taylor, Alan. 2010. *The Civil War of 1812: American Citizens, British Subjects, Irish Rebels, and Indian Allies*. New York: Knopf.

Wood, Gordon S. 1969. *The Creation of the American Republic, 1776–1787*. Chapel Hill: University of North Carolina Press.

———. 1991. *The Radicalism of the American Revolution*. New York: Vintage.

3

STATE, CITIZENSHIP, AND HEALTH
IN AN AGE OF GLOBAL MOBILITY

··········

A Comparative Study of Labor Migrants' Health Rights
in Germany and Israel

NORA GOTTLIEB

INTRODUCTION

This chapter examines health policies toward documented and undocumented labor migrants in Germany and Israel, focusing in particular on
the rationales underlying governmental decisions to grant or restrict labor
migrants' entitlement and access to publicly funded health care. By today,
approximately one hundred million labor migrants live and work in host
countries worldwide. An estimated thirty million persons do so without
holding the required residence and/or work permit (UNDESA 2013; IOM
2010). Documented and undocumented labor migration is part of the larger
phenomenon of globalization whose effects on countries around the world
cannot be overestimated (Castles and Miller 2003). Liberal welfare states
struggle with the question of labor migrants' entitlement to publicly funded
health care because it brings to the fore tensions between universalistic
concepts of health rights on the one hand and between more exclusionary national frameworks of citizenship and rights on the other (Filc and

Davidovitch 2007; Morris 2003). Illustrating the emergence of divergent forms of "differentiated citizenship" (Smith 2015), the case studies presented in this chapter allow for insights into the reconfigurations of social citizenship in an age of globalization and migration.

Migration, Membership, and Health Rights—The Dilemma of the National Welfare State

People have always been—and presumably will always be—on the move in search of a better life (Castles and Miller 2003). Today, worldwide approximately 232 million persons—3.2 percent of the world population— live outside their country of origin. Approximately half of them have left their home for the purpose of finding employment and better pay abroad ("labor migrants"). Twenty to thirty million people live and work in a host country without holding the required authorization ("undocumented labor migrants") (UNDESA 2013). The presence of large noncitizen populations in nation-states brings to the fore tensions between confined national frameworks and increasingly globalized realities, or, in Rogers Smith's words, "the question of the proper horizon or horizons of . . . citizenship" (2015). Membership and health rights of migrants thus continue to be shaped by "the inverse movements of universality and exclusion" (Balibar 2004, 61). As a result migrants often obtain only partial membership rights or remain barred from national social and health care schemes, sometimes in spite of long-established de facto residence and employment in the host country (Filc and Davidovitch 2007; Groβ 2005; Scott 2004; Morris 2003). The particular scope of migrants' formal health entitlements as well as modes of health care delivery result from the interaction between country-specific citizenship and immigration regimes, social policies, characteristics of the welfare and health system, and institutional practices (Filc and Davidovitch 2007; Morris 2003).

Citizenship has been described as a status that endows the individual with substantial rights vis-à-vis the state, including the right to health. However, the nation-state bases citizenship on territorialized notions of belonging, thus creating "mutually exclusive sets of persons . . . identifying those who cannot be included because they belong somewhere else" (Bauböck 1994, 205). A more dynamic notion of citizenship understands it as active practice and participation in public affairs. From this perspective rights are the results of constant social and political processes of renegotiation of the contents and conditions of citizenship (Balibar 2004; Isin 2009;

Smith 2015). Such a concept of citizenship evidently accommodates—or even necessitates—greater inclusion. The question of migrants' health rights is part of a larger debate on the role and future of the citizenship concept in view of globalization processes that transcend the nation-state framework, such as migration and the internationalization of rights. This debate has yielded two main strands of thought. Some perspectives dismiss traditional notions of the national state and national citizenship as obsolete and suggest new forms of citizenship (Bauböck 1994; Soysal 1996). For example, Yasemin Soysal purports that (postwar Western European) states have developed a "postnational" form of citizenship based on universal personhood and codified in international human rights legislation. She claims that this new form of membership decouples national identity from rights and is "not easily distinguishable from a formal citizenship status in terms of the rights and privileges it confers" (Soysal 1996, 20). However, many other authors have voiced dissent, pointing out that states uphold almost unchanged national sovereignty when it comes to immigration and migrant policies (Balibar 2004; Brettell and Holifield 2008; Joppke 1998; Brubaker 1992). From this perspective migration challenges the nation-state, but ultimately the legal and institutional frameworks of the national state continue to determine the status and rights of migrants.

The national welfare state operates amid above-described tensions between universalistic and exclusionary principles. States introduced welfare systems, inter alia, as a tool to mitigate inequalities generated by industrialization, urbanization, and capitalism; to continuously expand access to social services to marginalized populations; and to thus establish the conditions for broad political participation. The latter is in turn an essential source of legitimacy for the liberal democratic state (Bauböck 1994; Esping-Andersen 1990). The welfare state concept implies state responsibility for ensuring the basic needs of its members in an equitable manner. However, distinguishing between recipients and nonrecipients and granting differential benefits, the welfare state functions also a system of exclusion, stratification, and control (Esping-Andersen 1990; Piven and Cloward 1971). Many states have expanded social benefits also to migrant populations. Nonetheless, citizenship status often continues to play a role in the determination of health entitlements by discriminating between full-fledged, partial, temporary, and nonmembers (Filc 2009; Fix and Laglagaron 2002; Morissens and Sainsbury 2005; Morris 2003).

Within states, exclusionary health policies toward migrants often exist alongside inclusionary health care solutions. This ostensible paradox can be explained by divergent rationales that inform policy and practice in the health sector (Cuadra 2011; Filc and Davidovitch 2007; Karl-Trummer, Novak-Zezula, and Metzler 2010). Migrants' health entitlements are continuously reshaped through the negotiation of these conflicting reasons, forces, and interests on political and practical, national and local levels (Filc and Davidovitch 2007; Morris 2003). In this process, migrants' claim making may be regarded as a "disturbance" from the a priori exclusionary perspective of national citizenship. From the perspective of a political conceptualization of citizenship it is, on the contrary, part of essential reconfiguration processes thereof (Balibar 2004; Isin 2009; McNevin 2009). A more nuanced understanding of the development of migrants' health rights and its meaning for emerging forms of citizenship requires a more profound comprehension of the rationality of context-specific policies. To this end, this research examines and compares two pertinent case studies—Germany and Israel—with regard to their decision-making processes concerning documented and undocumented labor migrants' entitlements and access to health care.

Labor Migration and Labor Migrant Health Policies in Germany and Israel

Germany recruited millions of "guest workers" between 1955 and 1973 to satisfy the needs of its labor market (Geddes 2003; Gutiérrez Rodríguez 2007; Joppke 1998). In 2009 noncitizens made up approximately 8.2 percent of Germany's population and 6.9 percent of its workforce (DESTATIS 2011); the estimated number of undocumented migrants was 330,000 persons (0.4 percent of the population) (Vogel and Gelbrich 2010). Germany has a long-established complex system that interlinks immigration, labor, and social laws for the regulation of migrants' social rights (Mohr 2005; Morris 2003). The German statutory health insurance is employment based; thus, legally employed labor migrants are included equal to German citizens. Undocumented migrants' access to care, on the contrary, is severely restricted. German social law entitles all irregular migrants, including asylum seekers, nondeportable persons, and undocumented migrants, to treatment of acute and painful conditions, of conditions that are life threatening or that can cause irreversible damage, as well as to prevention and treatment of a range of infectious diseases (Classen 2008). However, in practice the provisions of

German residence law hinder the latter group from realizing these entitlements by obliging public servants to report undocumented persons to the immigration authorities.[1] Thus out of fear of disclosure and arrest, undocumented migrants do not take advantage of their health rights (Castañeda 2009; Classen 2008; Groß 2005).

In Israel international labor migration was introduced as late as the early 1990s. Overseas labor migrants were recruited in order to replace Palestinian day laborers who had hitherto provided cheap labor in low-skilled sectors (Raijman and Kemp 2007). Today approximately 200,000 documented and undocumented labor migrants reside in Israel. Estimated at up to 14 percent of the Israeli workforce, some economic sectors such as construction, agriculture, and care work strongly rely on foreign labor (Nathan 2011). Eligibility for Israeli national health insurance is conditioned by permanent residence status. As a result all labor migrants—documented and undocumented—are excluded from national health coverage. Employers are obliged by law to purchase private health coverage for nonresident workers (Fried 2003; Leventhal, Berlovitz, and Chemtob 2003). However, NGO activists as well as academics have voiced serious concerns regarding the translation of labor migrants' health entitlements into practice. They argue that the respective laws link health entitlements to labor migrants' workforce in an unethical manner,[2] and that, furthermore, the commercial character of the current labor migrant health insurance scheme produces significant "informal deficits" (Morris 2003); that is, the factual denial and/or restriction of rights that are formally held through the development of institutional practices that exploit legal loopholes, power differentials, and weak enforcement mechanisms (Filc and Davidovitch 2007; PHR-IL 2008).

Hitherto, variations between and within different countries' health policies toward labor migrants have not been adequately explained (Morris 2003; Spencer and Pobjoy 2011). This paper contributes to filling this void by using Germany and Israel as test cases that can provide valuable insights into the production of migrants' membership and health rights. Both states have in common: (a) an exclusive citizenship concept that bases membership on ethno-cultural belonging;[3] (b) a universal public health care scheme; and (c) an increasingly globalized labor market. However, the German public health care scheme operates independent of legal status parameters, while eligibility for public health insurance in Israel is based on permanent residence status. This combination of similarities and differences constitutes an excellent point of departure for a comparative analysis of decision-making processes regarding labor migrant health policies, which allows for a better comprehension of conceptualizations of health rights and social citizenship in an age of globalization and migration.

The goals of this essay are to illuminate the context-specific interplays of rationales that shape policy decisions concerning labor migrants' entitlement to publicly funded health care in Germany and Israel, and to gain insights into underlying conceptualizations of health rights and citizenship. To this end, this paper (a) examines exclusionary arguments that are brought forward as part of the political debate on labor migrant health care in each context and (b) scrutinizes how context-specific notions of deservingness and membership frame labor migrants' access to care, and what other logics inform policies regarding the granting, denial, or restriction of these populations' health rights.

Study Design and Methodology

The paper focuses on labor migrant populations in Tel Aviv–Yafo, Israel, and Berlin, Germany. The comparative approach allows for the recognition of general patterns in labor migrants' health rights, while being sensitive to context-specific phenomena. It builds on the assumption that political, cultural, and institutional differences help to unveil presumptive social orders, concepts, and norms, thus helping us to develop a better understanding of how social phenomena are systematically related to the similarities and particularities of each setting (Armer and Grimshaw 1973; Øyen 1990). For the purpose of this work, any person whose migration was primarily motivated by the search for employment and by prospective improvements of income and socioeconomic position was considered a labor migrant. Names have been changed to ensure anonymity.

Qualitative and quantitative research methods were applied in a complementary manner in order to help capture the complex nature of decision-making processes concerning labor migrants' health entitlements (Johnson and Onwuegbuzie 2004). Qualitative methods include (a) the analysis of policy documents such as legal texts, administrative guidelines, and protocols of parliamentary discussions, and (b) the analysis of seventy-one semi-structured in-depth interviews with national- and local-level government officials, health care providers, representatives of nongovernmental organizations, insurance companies and sick funds, and documented and undocumented labor migrants. Interviews were conducted in Germany and in Israel between 2009 and 2011; they were digitally recorded and transcribed.

Interviewees received transcripts and/or contextualized quotes for valida-tion (Mays and Pope 2000; Strauss and Corbin 1994). Approved transcripts were subjected to software-aided (ATLAS.ti 6) analysis based on grounded theory, as part of which analytical codes and theoretical categories were gen-erated both deductively and inductively in a circular heuristic process (May-ring 2000; Strauss and Corbin 1994).

Quantitative methods comprise (a) the analysis of sociodemographic and health-care-related data that was retrieved from NGO-run walk-in clinics. The respective datasets include 9,379 patient records and 683 advocacy files for the Israeli setting, and aggregated data based on 16,265 patient records for the German setting. The data were analyzed by means of SPSS.17 software, using single- and multivariate tests, and (b) an economic assessment of the Israeli labor migrant health care scheme, based on published data on labor migrants' health insurances (Chertoff 2009; Ziv and Cohen 2009).

RESULTS

Labor Migrants' Stratified Health Rights

The comparative policy analysis reveals that both countries maintain mul-titiered systems of stratified health rights. Within the respective systems, documented and undocumented labor migrants' access to health care is shaped by partial and limited forms of membership and health entitlements, rather than by clear-cut in-/exclusion. Yet the particular policies and institu-tional structures produce distinct categories and exclusions in each setting—along the lines of legal/illegal residence and employment in the German context and along the lines of migrant/resident status in the Israeli context. The qualitative results of this study furthermore show that labor migrant health policies are shaped by a context-specific interplay of divergent ratio-nales—such as the logic of health rights, of public health, of medical ethics, of humanitarianism, of health economy, of the labor market, of immigration control, of welfare protectionism, and of the social contract—which will be explored in the following sections.

The Israeli Discourse on Labor Migrants' Entitlement to Health Care

In the Israeli context health rights, humanitarian, and public health rationales are cited in support of an expansion of labor migrants' health entitlements that will allow for access to primary care independent from legal/migrant status. For example, a representative of the Israeli Ministry of Health explained that "from a public health perspective it is right to give treatment to every person. . . . This is a basic right that has to be granted independent of [legal] status." Also from the logic of health economics it is argued that labor migrants' greater inclusion would benefit the public health care system. This tenet is bolstered by the study's quantitative results. The analysis of health-care-related data verifies that labor migrants are of a young age as compared to the general population (with an average age of 36.8 ± 10.1 years in our sample and more than 90 percent (8,508) of the sampled persons under the age of fifty years), and that their health care utilization is low especially with regard to secondary health care. In our sample, the mean number of visits to a primary health care clinic per year was 1.9 ± 1.8 and only 17 percent (1,597) of all patients received one or more referrals for further diagnostic procedures or secondary medical services. Many migrant interviewees, too, reported that they hardly used any health services. For example, Frede, a forty-nine-year-old from Latin America, said: "I cannot tell you anything about the health care here—I did not see a doctor in fifteen years." Economic assessments, too, indicate that labor migrants' inclusion would financially strengthen the public health care system with an additional up to US$13.5 million per year. Under the current arrangement, private insurance companies reap these revenues.

In addition, many labor migrant interviewees reported problems in realizing their formal entitlements vis-à-vis the insurance companies. The study's quantitative findings, too, point to the development of institutional practices that significantly restrict labor migrants' de facto access to health services. For instance, our data reflect that significant numbers of labor migrants resort to NGOs for health care in spite of holding private health insurance. As a matter of fact, it shows that the proportion of insured labor migrant patients at the Tel Aviv Open Clinic has risen from 7.6 percent in 2001 to 13.8 percent in 2009. Moreover, large numbers of undocumented as well as documented labor migrants remain without insurance altogether (76 percent and 13 percent respectively). This frequently leads to situations in which un- and underinsured labor migrants ultimately seek emergency health care in public hospitals. The manager of a large medical center in the Tel Aviv area explained that such a situation "causes harm to health care providers and increases their deficits. . . . [All of this] within a system that is already economically very tight. . . . We are talking about expenses of several million

[Israeli New] Shekels per year, which are dealt out [in services] without getting reimbursement."

Many interviewees suggested that labor market considerations played an important, though subliminal, role in the determination of labor migrants' health rights. They held that the current policies allow insurance companies and employers to compromise labor migrants' health care access for the pursuit of pecuniary goals, and that they furthermore help the regulation of the workforce. For example, an NGO worker explained that the current labor migrant health insurance scheme "adds another system of control. It's not only the Ministry of Interior with the visa; it's not only the employer with his conditions—well, it's also the insurance company that keeps the worker on a short leash. It regulates him: you get [health care], you don't get [health care]. If you complain we notify the Ministry [of Interior] that you are sick. . . . It's another mechanism that bends the worker's head." The labor market thus benefits from the contingent character of labor migrants' health care access in that it contributes to the various pressures on labor migrants to sell their workforce at a low price and under any condition.

Exclusionary policies are justified mainly by economic, welfare protectionist, and immigration control arguments. These strands of thought are epitomized in the frequently cited "pull factor argument," that is, the assumption that the granting of health entitlements will act as an incentive for irregular and "bogus" migration: "We don't want to become a center of attraction for migrants. Tomorrow they'll know . . . you arrive to the Holy Land—you get all the services. So why shouldn't all of Ghana's poor start flowing into Tel Aviv?" (Local Health Office representative, Israel). Such framing of migration motives stands in stark contrast to how labor migrants themselves described their expectations; for example, one migrant interviewee vigorously rejected the suggestion that access to health care should be free and unconditional: "It doesn't work like this! You have an obligation to work hard and pay your taxes. And the taxes help the state to give health care." However, this study shows that the pull factor argument nonetheless dominates the Israeli discourse, underlain by fears that are stirred by waning welfare resources and social security. For instance, an employee of the Tel Aviv Health Office explained, "Many [Israeli] taxpayers feel that they . . . pay and pay and only get ripped off. Thus, it's very hard to tell this public 'Let's also take care of the weak.' Not only of migrants, also of weak Jewish Israelis—not to talk about Arab Israelis. . . . [O]f anyone who is not part of the dominant hegemony. . . . [T]he feeling that we don't have money for anything . . . is practically translated into a kind of formula that . . . the one who belongs [comes] first, and the one who doesn't belong after." Most interviewees maintained that the current exclusionary health policies toward labor migrants were also a means to maintain a clear division between citizens and noncitizens. This assumption is verified by the following assertion, which concluded one of the parliamentary debates on the Israeli labor migrant health care model: "It is forbidden . . . to cross this boundary that distinguishes between the citizen . . . and the noncitizen who is here only for a limited time. It is our duty to give him all services, but it will be better to give them in a way that maintains this separation" (MP, Israel). Several interviewees explained that membership in a public health care scheme signified also social membership, whereas the labor migrants' separate, private health insurance "is not perceived as something that makes you think 'I am citizen of this state'" (Ministry of Finance representative, Israel). They concluded that the Israeli government wants "to leave [migrant] workers' [insurance] in the private insurance companies, because this draws a very clear separation between those who are residents and those who are not" (NGO worker, Israel). The current labor migrant health care scheme is thus ultimately entrenched in the political goal to preserve the Jewish identity of the state and its institutions. From this perspective, obviously, the settlement and social integration of non-Jewish migrants should be prevented "so the state won't lose its religious character. . . . [T]he state must preserve some . . . Jewish character. . . . It can well be that, if we lose this identity, we also lose our state" (Professional Association, Israel).

The German Discourse on Labor Migrants' Entitlement to Health Care

In Germany, claims for the improvement of undocumented migrants' access to care are rooted in the logics of health rights, of medical ethics, and of public health. Compared to the Israeli case, the German health rights discourse promotes a predominantly legalistic conceptualization of health rights, which draws heavily on guarantees enshrined in national legislation such as basic and social law. From this perspective, current policies are sharply criticized among others for denying undocumented migrants health benefits, which they are formally entitled to. For example, a church representative challenged the national government, "why do you grant a right . . . and then you make another law whose obvious result is that, de facto, they cannot realize this right?" Furthermore, many German public health professionals expressed a strongly value-driven approach to public health, exemplified in a local government official's emotive exclamation that "public health [policy] is a policy of justice in the health sector!" Their outspokenly political conceptualization of the role of public health professionals stood in stark contrast to their Israeli counterparts' political ambiguity and restraint.

Compared to the Israeli discourse, economic arguments are not readily used by German health rights advocates. This is in spite of the fact that the quantitative results on labor migrants' sociodemographic and health-related characteristics in the German context draw a similar picture as in the Israeli setting: Labor migrant populations are on average of young age, with almost 90 percent being under the age of fifty, and they mostly present with relatively simple health needs (such as antenatal care, treatment of acute infections, or chronic noncommunicable diseases) that clearly fall into the realm of primary and preventive medicine. Thus, in the German context, too, more inclusive health policies that enable universal access to primary health care would be the better choice in terms of public health and health economics.

Ultimately, also the German debate on labor migrants' entitlement to health benefits is framed by welfare austerity and shrinking social citizenship. Several interviewees emphasized that "the gaps in the health care system are getting bigger and bigger and more and more people fall through.... The [NGOs] have more and more people in their clinic[s] who are not at all illegalized but they are German or ... EU citizens. But they don't have health insurance" (NGO worker, Germany). Such a situation raises essential questions concerning the meaning and future of the health rights concept for citizens and noncitizens alike: "Actually the entire society is concerned [by the question] 'Who gets what and who can pay for what?' We're not gonna get around this discussion anyway" (Church representative, Germany). In this context, it is mainly the logics of immigration control and of welfare protectionism that are used to rationalize current policies. Many interviewees denounced the respective arguments—and in particular the above-described pull factor argument—as unfounded and deceptive "bar-room slogans" (Church representative, Germany) and "hand-knitted fairy tales" (Parliament representative, Germany). Veteran politicians asserted that "we were able to prove ... [that] not more [migrants] arrived after [we granted more rights]. You cannot simply say that it's all pull- and push-effects" (Parliament representative, Germany).

Nonetheless, the same arguments continue to play a central role in the public and political discourse on labor migrant health policies.

Ultimately, restrictions on undocumented migrants' access to health benefits are justified with reference to the social contract. For example, an NGO worker reasoned, "The state creates ... a health care system ... and it creates options for people to participate. And now the question is: How does it deal with illegal work, with illegality, with ... immigrants who ... use this system for their own purposes? ... You can say: We don't want to tolerate illegal work, because the tax losses become too big. And if we have only tax losses, then the system cannot function." From this point of view, it is legitimate and even necessary that whoever wants to enjoy the benefits of the social contract will in return comply with its norms and principles such as solidarity, reciprocity, and respect for the rule of law. Interestingly, undocumented migrants themselves stated by the same token that they did not deserve recourse to publicly funded health care. For instance, Ivanka, a migrant from Bulgaria who had been working illegally in Germany for several months, reasoned: "I did not give anything to the state. I did not contribute. So I don't have any expectations." Based on this supposition of undocumented migrants' undeservingness for publicly funded health care, restrictions on undocumented migrants' health care access are justified as a means to reserve health resources for those who are regarded as "righteous" members of the social contract.

DISCUSSION

Discourses of Deservingness

Taken together, the results of this study lead to the conclusion that more inclusive health policies toward labor migrants would be favorable not only from the point of view of various ethical frameworks but also from evidence-based, "practical" perspectives such as the perspective of health economics and public health.[4] However, in spite of the above-described tangible arguments in support of greater inclusion and in spite of many exclusionary arguments' manifest lack of evidential basis,[5] both states uphold restrictions on labor migrant populations' health rights, thus "creat[ing] and sustain[ing] forms of differentiated citizenship" (Smith 2015) in the health realm. This raises a fortiori questions regarding the respective political decision-making processes: What causes policy makers to reject policy options that would help resolve normative tensions and yield economic and public health benefits? For what reasons do they hold on to policies whose negative implications are known? And how can we explain that the respective discussions are centrally shaped by arguments that lack or even contradict scientific evidence? This study suggests that the answer to the above questions lies in context-specific hegemonic discourses of deservingness. These discourses interweave evidence-based and value-based arguments to relate deservingness for health benefits to deeply rooted concepts of membership and rights, thus rationalizing each state's in-/exclusionary choices. They thus explain—in reference to one of Rogers Smith's four big questions of contemporary citizenship (in this volume)—what forms of differentiated citizenship particular societies in a particular historical, political, social, and economical context deem "currently appropriate" (ibid.), that is, in line with the social order and the citizenship they want to create and inhabit at this point in time. Both case studies illustrate that, indeed, differentiated citizenship is apparently "the way most people believe things normatively ought to be" (ibid.) also with regard to social and health rights. Yet at the same time the disparities between the two discourses of deservingness—which, in turn, lead to health rights restrictions for different migrant populations—help unearth fundamentally divergent "stories of peoplehood" (ibid.), membership, and rights.

The German Discourse of Deservingness—The Moral Economy of Migrants' Health Rights

In Germany the dominant discourse of deservingness evolves mainly around the give and take of the social contract. Social and health rights are conceptualized as inherently based on the existence and functioning of the mutually supportive community. Consequently, deservingness for publicly funded health care is linked to the fulfillment of duties toward the community and abidance by its rules. Following Didier Fassin's works on immigration policies in Europe, we can call this framework for granting rights a "moral economy" in the sense of a "traditional view of social norms and obligations, of the proper economic functions of several parties in the community" (Thompson, in Fassin 2005). This moral economy allows for the denizenship, that is, quasi-citizenship status with regard to social rights (Bauböck 1994), of documented and legally employed labor migrants. Contrary to its reputation for upholding an exclusionary ethno-cultural concept of the nation (Brubaker 1992; Fulbrook 1996), Germany thus actually invokes contractual and "republican" themes in its conceptualization of social citizenship. It constructs rights as flowing from a discrete contractual exchange of equivalents—such as workforce, tax payments, public goods, and services—between free and equal persons, and it emphasizes willful choice and identification with social norms and values as a condition for membership (see also Faist, Gerdes, and Rieple 2004). Such conceptualization of citizenship accommodates, with qualifications, a postnational transformation of social citizenship. Yet on the other hand, such contractual understanding of citizenship and rights, which is a central motif of liberal political thought (Fraser and Gordon 1992), could well be interpreted as a sign for the insidious renunciation of communitarian norms and for a neoliberal reconfiguration of the German welfare state. Furthermore, this seemingly postnational health rights expansion comes at the price of the exclusion from health rights of one, though arguably small, population group: undocumented labor migrants. The framing of their lack of legal status as a willful choice and violation of the social contract de-contextualizes the phenomenon by blanking out the state's role in the production of illegality[6] (Balibar 2004; De Genova 2004) and by denying the political economy that enfolds the phenomenon (De Genova 2004; Spencer 2011).

The Israeli Discourse of Deservingness—Who Belongs and Who Deserves?

The Israeli discourse on migrant health care is framed by persistently strong links between ethno-national belonging and deservingness that are deeply entrenched in Israel's national self-concept as a Jewish state. The goals of maintaining the state's Jewish identity and, to this end, containing non-Jewish immigration, tower over any policy decision concerning labor migrants' entitlement and access to health care. The Israeli case study thus exemplifies a context in which many "still believe that . . . laws privileging certain religious, gender, and even racial and ethnic identities over others remain appropriate" (Smith 2015). In particular, the results of this study illustrate the Israeli government's tenacity in reserving health rights for permanent residents and citizens, that is, for persons who are deemed to "belong" to Israeli society. The denial of access to publicly funded health care thus serves to delineate a symbolic boundary that cuts across the Israeli de facto resident population in order to distinguish between members and non-members. In other words, labor migrants, instead of crossing Israel's national border, carry it with them and thus remain in a peculiar status of internal exclusion (Balibar 2004, 109–10). Hence, this study shows that the Israeli discourse of deservingness is entrenched in a conceptualization of access to health care as a national right (Filc and Davidovich 2005). It thus supports Davidovitch and Filc's (2007) previous conclusions that eventually "the ethnonational conception of citizenship still plays the dominant—though not unique—role in the development of health care services for migrant workers [in Israel]" (Filc and Davidovitch 2007). However, the essentialist character of such ethno-national conceptualization of citizenship leaves little room for the constant processes of renegotiation and transformation of rights that has been described as a necessary condition for ensuring the democratic legitimacy of the citizenship concept in an era of migration (Arendt 1958; Balibar 2004; Isin 2009).

Exclusion as Protection, Exclusion as Exception, and Circles of Exclusion

The above discourses of deservingness represent also a form of othering, that is, a mechanism that draws a clear boundary between "Us," the community whose right to health is established and protected by virtue of its members' social citizenship, and "Them," to whom this protection does not apply by virtue of their outsider status. The construction of the other as a threat—to public health, to national identity, or to an overstretched social system—helps to justify exclusionary policies (Grove and Zwi 2006). From this perspective, exclusionary contentions like the pull factor argument and framings of migrants as an economic burden are useful rhetorical tools inasmuch as they evoke fears and fuel a sense of competition for increasingly scarce resources: "They want what we have" (Grove and Zwi 2006, 1936). Notwithstanding their lack of evidential base, such arguments thus serve as powerful mechanisms to reinforce the boundaries between the deserving "us" and the undeserving "others," all the more in a socioeconomic context that is shaped by the welfare state's contraction.

In both countries, labor migrants' exclusion from full membership and health rights is thus conceptualized as exception[7] (inasmuch as it applies only to the other) and as protection (of citizens' right to health). As such, it becomes reconcilable with the concept of citizenship and of a universal and equal right to health. Ironically, it is the partial and limited character of labor migrants' membership and health entitlements that serves their submission to a neoliberal economic order. This is especially the case in Israel, where the current policy framework reifies the notion that "[labor migrants] are entitled to health care services only in their capacity as workers" (Filc and Davidovitch 2007). The concerted conditions of labor migrants' legal vulnerability, social marginalization, and provisional entitlements act to regulate their workforce in accordance with the requirements of the globalized neoliberal labor market.[8]

However, to frame labor migrants' exclusion as exception and as protection is to ignore the fact that also citizen populations' health rights have long been compromised by welfare retrenchments. This has been demonstrated by a multitude of studies (Coburn 2000; Crimmins and Saito 2001; Donkin, Goldblatt, and Lynch 2002; Mackenbach et al. 2003; Marmot 2005; Navarro and Shi 2001; Plavinski, Plavinskaya, and Klimov 2003). In this light, it would be remiss or even delusive to call limited and partial forms of health rights exceptional. Instead, it may well be that they herald the erosion of social citizenship from the margins, that is, "the state of exception becomes the rule" (Fassin 2005, 377) in the sense that no citizenship is fully recognized and realized. Hence, instead of two distinct spheres, one in which social citizenship ensures the enjoyment of equal full health rights, and another one in which health is less or unprotected, the metaphor of concentric "circles of exclusion" (Filc 2009) may be more appropriate to capture a reality in which citizens and noncitizens are similarly affected by diminishing health rights. A political discussion on labor migrants' health rights that fails to account for this larger context obscures the proliferation of multitiered systems of inequities and directs the public and political attention away from the structural core causes of the erosion of social citizenship. This study thus underscores that exclusionary health policies toward labor migrants are at best ineffective as a means to protect social citizenship. At the worst, they bolster the neoliberal restructuring of labor markets and social systems and thus reinforce the disintegration of the welfare state.

NOTES

1. It should be noted that since 2009 the administrative guidelines to residence law prohibit medical personnel as well as third persons to impart personal information that has been disclosed within the framework of a clinical encounter. This has eased undocumented migrants' access to emergency care, but not to primary and elective services (since the latter require a prior administrative procedure).

2. For instance, in the case that a labor migrant falls seriously ill and is found not to be fit for work for a period of ninety days ("loss of work capacity"), the insurance company is authorized to terminate his/her insurance policy. As a result, the person in question will also lose his/her work and residence permit.

3. In the German case, the exclusionary citizenship concept has been softened by subsequent legal amendments since the 1990s. However, several authors have argued that these changes have left the ethno-national core of the German citizenship regime untouched (Joppke 2005; Anil 2005).

4. It would go beyond the scope of this paper to elaborate on the intricacies of making clear-cut distinctions between the practical and the normative, the factual and the value based, the professional and the political. For the purpose of this study, it is important to note that, ultimately, evidence- and value-based frameworks are always interconnected and that, therefore, there can be no value-free generation or perception of what we like to regard as objective knowledge (Bhopal 2012; Daniels, Kennedy, and Kawachi 1999). Nonetheless, one vital distinction can be made between the two kinds of arguments. As Spencer and Pobjoy have pointed out, practical contentions can—and arguably should—be based on empirical evidence (Spencer and Pobjoy 2011), whereas normative arguments cannot be verified or disproved on the basis of data, but only agreed or disagreed with based on a personal choice of certain moral values.

5. Numerous studies have disproved economic and immigration control arguments for migrants' exclusion; for example, by showing that health benefits do not act as a significant incentive for irregular migration, and that migrants do not become a drain on their host countries' social system. On the contrary, some studies have shown that local economies benefit from the presence of documented as well as undocumented migrants (Chauvin, Parizot, and Simonnot 2009; Robinson and Segrott 2002; Romero-Ortuño 2004; Spencer 2011).

6. Several authors have pointed out that states' immigration regimes, in combination with macro-social push and pull factors, play a central role in the production of "illegality." For example, in the German context the reunification and the EU expansion in the 1990s have resulted in restricted options for legal entry for non-EU nationals. At the same time, sociodemographic trends (such as an aging population) as well as neoliberal reforms of the social system and the labor market (such as the privatization of geriatric care) created a high demand for cheap and flexible labor, especially in sectors such

as domestic and care work, agriculture and construction (Castañeda 2009; Alt and Bommes 2006). With regard to the Israeli migrant worker scheme it has been noted that the "binding arrangement," which ties labor migrants' work permits and visas to specific employers, significantly contributes to illegality (Raijman, Schammah-Gesser, and Kemp 2003; Willen 2007). This claim is substantiated by a government-commissioned study that found that the most frequent reason for loss of legal status is that migrant workers leave their employers due to substandard conditions or salary withholding (Bar-Tsuri 2005; Ida 2004).

7. See also Ong (2006) for a detailed discussion of the discursive creation of frameworks of exception for migrants' rights in the Asian context.

8. This is not to suggest the purposeful abuse of health policies as leverage, but rather does the subjugation of labor migrants transpire in the sense of Nikolas Rose's advanced liberal governmentality; that is, "not [as] a matter of the implementation of idealized schema in the real by an act of will, but of the complex assemblage of diverse forces . . . techniques . . . [and] devices . . . that promise to regulate decisions and actions of individuals, groups, [and] organizations" (Rose 1996, 42).

WORKS CITED

Alt, Jörg, and Michael Bommes, eds. 2006. *Illegalität: Grenzen und Möglichkeiten der Migrationspolitik*. Wiesbaden: VS Verlag.

Anil, Merih. 2005. "No More Foreigners? The Remaking of German Naturalization and Citizenship Law, 1990–2000." *Dialectical Anthropology* 29 (3): 453–70.

Arendt, Hannah. 1958. *The Origins of Totalitarianism*. 2nd ed. Cleveland: Meridian Books.

Armer, Michael, and Allen Day Grimshaw, eds. 1973. *Comparative Social Research: Methodological Problems and Strategies*. New York: Wiley.

Balibar, Etienne. 2004. *We, the People of Europe? Reflections on Transnational Citizenship*. Princeton, NJ: Princeton University Press.

Bar-Tsuri, Ran. 2005. *Chinese Workers Employed In Israel without a Permit*. Jerusalem: Ministry of Industry, Trade and Labor.

Bauböck, Rainer, ed. 1994. *From Aliens to Citizens: Redefining the Status of Immigrants in Europe*. Aldershot: Avebury.

Bhopal, Raj S. 2012. "Research Agenda for Tackling Inequalities Related to Migration and Ethnicity in Europe." In *Health Inequalities and Risk Factors among Migrants and Ethnic Minorities*, vol. 1, edited by David Ingleby, Allan

Krasnik, Vincent Lorant, and Oliver Razum, 25–38. Antwerp-Apeldoorn: Garant.

Brettell, Caroline B., and James F. Hollifield, eds. 2008. *Migration Theory: Talking across Disciplines.* London: Routledge.

Brubaker, Rogers. 1992. *Citizenship and Nationhood in France and Germany.* Cambridge, MA: Harvard University Press.

Castañeda, Heide. 2009. "Illegality as Risk Factor: A Survey of Unauthorized Migrant Patients in a Berlin Clinic." *Social Science and Medicine* 68 (8): 1552–60.

Castles, Stephen, and Mark J. Miller. 2003. *The Age of Migration: International Population Movements in the Modern World.* New York: Guilford.

Chauvin, Pierre, Isabelle Parizot, and Nathalie Simonnot. 2009. *Access to Healthcare for Undocumented Migrants in 11 European Countries.* Paris: Médecins du Monde.

Chertoff, Yacov S. 2009. *Transfer of Foreign Workers' Health Insurance from Private Insurance Companies to the Sick Funds—An Economic Analysis.* Jerusalem: Knesset Center for Research and Information.

Classen, Georg. 2008. *Sozialleistungen für MigrantInnen und Flüchtlinge.* Handbuch für die Praxis. Karlsruhe: Loeper Literaturverlag.

Coburn, David. 2000. "Beyond the Income Inequality Hypothesis: Class, Neo-Liberalism, and Health Inequalities." *Social Science and Medicine* 58 (1): 41–56.

Crimmins, Eileen M., and Yasuhiko Saito. 2001. "Trends in Healthy Life Expectancy in the United States, 1970–1990: Gender, Racial, and Educational Differences." *Social Science and Medicine* 52 (11): 1629–41.

Cuadra, Carin Björngren. 2011. "Right of Access to Health Care for Undocumented Migrants in the EU: A Comparative Study of National Policies." *European Journal of Public Health* 22 (2): 267–71.

Daniels, Norman, Bruce P. Kennedy, and Ichiro Kawachi. 1999. "Why Justice Is Good for Our Health: The Social Determinants of Health Inequalities." *Daedalus* 128 (4): 215–51.

De Genova, Nicholas. 2004. "The Legal Production of Mexican/Migrant 'Illegality.'" *Latino Studies* 2: 160–85.

DESTATIS (German Federal Statistical Office). 2011. "Migration and Integration." www.destatis.de/jetspeed/portal/cms/Sites/destatis/Internet/DE/Navigation/Statistiken/Bevoelkerung/MigrationIntegration/MigrationIntegration.psml, accessed December 7, 2011.

Donkin, Angela, Peter Goldblatt, and Kevin Lynch. 2002. Inequalities in Life Expectancy by Social Class, 1972–1999. *Health Statistics Quarterly* 15: 5–15.

Esping-Andersen, Gosta. 1990. *The Three Worlds of Welfare Capitalism*. Princeton, NJ: Princeton University Press.

Faist, Thomas, Jürgen Gerdes, and Beate Rieple. 2004. "Doppelte Staatsbürgerschaft: Determinanten der Deutschen Politik des Staatsangehörigkeitsrechts." Working Paper No. 6. Bremen: COMCAD Center on Migration, Citizenship and Development.

Fassin, Didier. 2005. "Compassion and Repression: The Moral Economy of Immigration Policies in France." *Cultural Anthropology* 20 (3): 362–87.

Filc, Dani. 2009. *Circles of Exclusion: The Politics of Health Care in Israel*. Ithaca, NY: Cornell University Press.

Filc, Dani, and Nadav Davidovich. 2005. "Health Care as a National Right? The Development of Health Care Services for Migrant Workers in Israel." *Social Theory and Health* 3: 1–15.

———. 2007. "Rights, Citizenship, and the National State: Health Policies toward Migrant Workers in Comparative Perspective." In *Transnational Migration to Israel in Global Comparative Context*, edited by Sarah S. Willen, 103–21. Lanham, MD: Lexington Books.

Fix, Michael, and Laureen Laglagaron. 2002. *Social Rights and Citizenship: An International Comparison*. Washington, DC: Urban Institute.

Fraser, Nancy, and Linda Gordon. 1992. "Contract versus Charity. Why Is There No Social Citizenship in the United States?" *Socialist Review* 22: 45–68.

Fried, Mordechai. 2003. "Healthcare for Migrant Workers in Israel." *Harefuah* 142 (6): 429–32.

Fulbrook, Mary. 1996. "Germany for the Germans? Citizenship and Nationality in a Divided Nation." In *Citizenship, Nationality, and Migration in Europe*, edited by David Cesarani and Mary Fulbrook, 88–105. London: Routledge.

Geddes, Andrew. 2003. *The Politics of Migration and Immigration in Europe*. London: Sage.

Grove, Natalie J., and Anthony B. Zwi. 2006. "Our Health and Theirs: Forced Migration, Othering, and Public Health." *Social Science and Medicine* 62 (8): 1931–42.

Groß, Jessica. 2005. *Möglichkeiten und Grenzen der Medizinischen versorgung von Patientinnen und Patienten ohne Legalen Aufenthaltsstatus*. Berlin: Flüchtlingsrat Berlin e.V. / Büro für medizinische Flüchtlingshilfe Berlin / PRO ASYL / IPPNW Deutschlan Internationale Ärzte zur Verhütung des Atomkrieges / Ärzte in sozialer Verantwortung e.V.

Gutiérrez Rodríguez, Encarnación. 2007. "The 'Hidden Side' of the New Economy." *Frontiers: A Journal of Women's Studies* 28 (3): 60–83.

Ida, Yoram. 2004. *The Factors Affecting Foreign Workers' Transition to Illegal Employment.* Jerusalem: Ministry of Industry, Trade, and Labor.

International Organization for Migration (IOM). 2010. "World Migration Report 2010. The Future of Migration: Building Capacities for Change." http://publications.iom.int/bookstore/free/WMR_2010_ENGLISH.pdf, accessed March 4, 2015.

Isin, Engin F. 2009. "Citizenship in Flux: The Figure of the Activist Citizen." *Subjectivity* 29 (1): 367–88.

Johnson, R. Burke, and Anthony J. Onwuegbuzie. 2004. "Mixed Methods Research: A Research Paradigm Whose Time Has Come." *Educational Researcher* 33 (7): 14–26.

Joppke, Christian. 1998. "Why Liberal States Accept Unwanted Immigration." *World Politics* 50: 266–93.

———. 2005. *Selecting by Origin: Ethnic Migration in the Liberal State.* Cambridge, MA: Harvard University Press.

Karl-Trummer, Ursula, Sonja Novak-Zezula, and Birgit Metzler. 2010. "Access to Healthcare for Undocumented Migrants in the EU: A First Landscape of NowHereland." *Eurohealth* 16 (1): 13–16.

Leventhal Alex, Yitzhak Berlovitz, and Daniel Chemtob. 2003. "Migrant Workers—Development in the Israeli Healthcare System's Approach to a New Social Phenomenon." *Harefuah* 142 (9): 632–35.

Mackenbach, Johan P., Vivian Bos, Otto Andersen, Mario Cardano, Giuseppe Costa, Seeromanie Harding, Alison Reid, Örjan Hemström, Tapani Valkonen, and Anton E. Kunst. 2003. "Widening Socioeconomic Inequalities in Mortality in Six Western European Countries." *International Journal of Epidemiology* 32 (5): 830–37.

Marmot, Michael. 2005. "Social Determinants of Health Inequalities." *The Lancet* 365 (9464): 1099–104.

Mayring, Philipp. 2000. "Qualitative Content Analysis." *Forum Qualitative Sozialforschung / Forum: Qualitative Social Research* 1 (2): 1–10.

Mays, Nicholas, and Catherine Pope. 2000. "Assessing Quality in Qualitative Research." *British Medical Journal* 320: 50–52.

McNevin, Anne. 2009. "Doing What Citizens Do: Migrant Struggles at the Edges of Political Belonging." *Local-Global: Identity, Security, Community* 6: 67–77.

Mohr, Katrin. 2005. "Stratifizierte Rechte und soziale Exklusion von Migranten im Wohlfahrtsstaat." *Zeitschrift für Soziologie* 34 (5): 383–98.

Morissens, Ann, and Diane Sainsbury. 2005. "Migrants' Social Rights, Ethnicity, and Welfare Regimes." *Journal of Social Policy* 34 (4): 637–60.

Morris, Lydia. 2003. "Managing Contradiction: Civic Stratification and Migrants' Rights." *International Migration Review* 37 (1): 74–100.

Nathan, Gilad. 2011. *Non-Israelis in Israel: Status Quo, 2010–2011.* Jerusalem: Knesset Center for Research and Information.

Navarro, Vicente, and Leiyu Shi. 2001. "The Political Context of Social Inequalities and Health." *Social Science and Medicine* 52 (3): 481–91.

Ong, Aihwa. 2006. *Neoliberalism as Exception: Mutations in Citizenship and Sovereignty.* Cambridge: Cambridge University Press.

Øyen, Else. 1990. *Comparative Methodology: Theory and Practice in International Social Research.* London: Sage.

Physicians for Human Rights Israel (PHR-IL). 2008. "Problems in the Private Health Insurance Arrangement for Migrant Workers." Submitted to the Knesset Committee on the Foreign Worker Problem. Tel Aviv: Physicians for Human Rights Israel (PHR-IL).

Piven, Frances Fox, and Richard Cloward. 1971. *Regulating the Poor: The Functions of Public Welfare.* New York: Pantheon Books.

Plavinski, Sviatoslav L., Svetlana I. Plavinskaya, and Alexey N. Klimov. 2003. "Social Factors and Increase in Mortality in Russia in the 1990s: Prospective Cohort Study." *British Medical Journal* 326 (7401): 1240–42.

Raijman, Rebeca, and Adriana Kemp. 2007. "Labor Migration, Managing the Ethno-National Conflict, and Client Politics in Israel." In *Transnational Migration to Israel in Global Comparative Context*, edited by Sarah S. Willen, 31–50. Lanham, MD: Lexington Books.

Raijman, Rebeca, Silvina Schammah-Gesser, and Adriana Kemp. 2003. "International Migration, Domestic Work, and Care Work: Undocumented Latina Migrants in Israel." *Gender and Society* 17 (5): 727–49.

Robinson, Vaughan, and Jeremy Segrott. 2002. *Understanding the Decision-Making of Asylum Seekers.* Research Study No. 243. London: Home Office.

Romero-Ortuño, Román. 2004. "Access to Health Care for Illegal Immigrants in the EU: Should We Be Concerned?" *European Journal of Health Law* 11 (3): 245–72.

Rose, Nikolas. 1996. "Governing 'Advanced' Liberal Democracies." In *Foucault and Political Reason: Liberalism, Neo-Liberalism, and Rationalities of Government*, edited by Andrew Barry, Thomas Osborne, and Nikolas S. Rose, 37–62. Chicago: University of Chicago Press.

Scott, Penelope. 2004. "Undocumented Migrants in Germany and Britain: The Human 'Rights' and 'Wrongs' Regarding Access to Health Care." *Electronic*

Journal of Sociology. www.sociology.org/content/2004/tier2/scott.html, accessed September 2, 2008.

Smith, Rogers. 2015. "The Questions Facing Citizenship in the Twenty-First Century." This volume.

Soysal, Yasemin Nuhoğlu. 1996. *Changing Citizenship in Europe.* London: Routledge.

Spencer, Sarah. 2011. *The Migration Debate.* Bristol: Policy Press.

Spencer, Sarah, and Jason Pobjoy. 2011. *The Relationship between Immigration Status and Rights in the UK: Exploring the Rationale.* Working Paper No. 86. Oxford: COMPAS.

Strauss, Anselm, and Juliet Corbin. 1994. *Grounded Theory Methodology: An Overview.* Thousand Oaks, CA: Sage.

United Nations Department of Economic and Social Affairs, Population Division (UNDESA). 2013. "International Migration Report 2013." http://esa.un.org/unmigration/documents/worldmigration/2013/Full_Document_final.pdf, accessed March 4, 2015.

Vogel, Dita, and Stephanie Gelbrich. 2010. *Update Report Germany: Estimate on Irregular Migration for Germany in 2009.* Hamburg: Hamburg Institute of International Economics.

Willen, Sarah. S. 2007. "Introduction." In *Transnational Migration to Israel in Global Comparative Context,* edited by Sarah S. Willen, 1–17. Lanham, MD: Lexington Books.

Ziv, Sani, and Ran Cohen. 2009. *The Economic Profitability of Insuring Foreign Workers within the Public Healthcare System.* Tel Aviv: Physicians for Human Rights Israel (PHR-IL).

4

EXPRESSING BELONGING
THROUGH CITIZENSHIP
· · · · · · · · · ·
Are We Talking Third-Generation Israelis,
Third-Generation Yekkes, or Third-Generation
Diasporic German Citizens?

DANI KRANZ

If they outlaw multiple citizenship in Israel, they can have my Israeli passport back. The German one stays with me.

Ben, born 1977 in Tel Aviv

I have a German passport, but I never use it. Not knowing the language
stops me from doing so.

Gal, born 1974 in Nahariya

I am proud to be a Yekke! A German passport is a strong passport, a good one!

Nati, born 1986 in Nahariya

Ben, Gal, and Nati are three of the Third Generations[1] I interviewed over the
years concerning their ideas of Germanness, Israeliness, and their respective German and Israeli citizenships. Given the specific focus of this chapter
the quotes already indicate the different relationships these three have to
their German citizenship. All three have an emotional investment in the

issue; it is not neutral for them. They raise key questions concerning the meaning of citizenship, and more so appropriately differentiated citizenship (Smith 2013), which is complicated by way of the sociohistoric events, restitution praxes, and the ethnically underpinned citizenship regimes in both Germany[2] and Israel. Indeed, are these three Third-Generation Israeli citizens, or Third-Generation German citizens? While this issue is important it says little about how the likes of Nati, Ben, and Gal construct the meaning of their citizenship, and how they express belonging within the complex, fraught, and historically heavily infused matrix of German/Jewish/Israeli history and relationships. What intersections apply to these citizens, how do they assign meaning and/or belonging to their German citizenship, Germanness, and why do they care about these issues at all? Focusing on these questions is particularly fruitful for the study of citizenship because these three are full German citizens, yet besides Nati—who constitutes an exemption—they lack linguistic capital of German, all three lack native and local knowledge of Germany on all levels, Germany has never tried to involve these citizens in its nation-building project,[3] and they come from families who fled Germany, who were expelled from German citizenship, and who have seen all their rights of revoked and their belonging questioned (Bodemann 2006; Kranz 2013).

In order to contextualize these three (as well as the fifty plus other Third-Generation Israeli citizens of German descent who I interviewed formally or informally since 2003), and unravel their ideas concerning German citizenship, Germanness, and belonging, I will move along the following structure: first, I will outline German citizenship law and German Israeli relations to allow for insights into the dynamics on the legal level and on the level of these particular binational relations. In the second part I will move on to Israeli social structures, because the relationship of Third-Generation Israelis to their German citizenship needs to be contextualized within the specific social structure of Israel, which underpins the wish to renaturalize as a German citizen, as well as their family histories, which need to be appreciated sociohistorically within the wider framework of Israeli history, and which shapes the base of their ideas of Germanness (Kranz 2013). This line of analyzing the meaning of German citizenship for Third Generations leads to appreciating in-depth their perspective on German citizenship, and allows one to understand that the relations to becoming or being a German citizen are both rational and emotional, and effectively expand on the theories concerning differentiated citizenship. In the concluding part I will offer an explanation of the meaning of German citizenship, and the underlying Germanness that emerged through my fieldwork, and contextualize the ethnographic, legal, and sociohistoric data citizenship theories.

THE LEGAL AND THE BINATIONAL RELATIONS FRAMEWORK: THE GERMAN BASIC LAW, CITIZENSHIP LAW, AND GERMAN ISRAELI RELATIONSHIPS

The Basic Law of the Federal Republic of Germany came into force in May 23, 1949. It enshrines the basic rights of German citizens, the basic tenets of German democracy, and it functions as a constitution. Section 116, point 1, lays out who fits the definition of being German; who has the right to renaturalize as a German citizen in post-Nazi Germany is outlined in point 2:[4]

(1) Deutscher im Sinne dieses Grundgesetzes ist vorbehaltlich anderweitiger gesetzlicher Regelung, wer die deutsche Staatsangehörigkeit besitzt oder als Flüchtling oder Vertriebener deutscher Volkszugehörigkeit oder als dessen Ehegatte oder Abkömmling in dem Gebiete des Deutschen Reiches nachdem Stande vom 31. Dezember 1937 Aufnahmegefunden hat.

German in spirit of the basic law and pending other legal stipulations is a German citizen, or a refugee or displaced person of German ethnicity or their spouse or their children who had settled on the territory of the German Reich in its borders of December 31, 1937.

(2) Frühere deutsche Staatsangehörige, denen zwischen dem 30. Januar 1933 und dem 8. Mai 1945 die Staatsangehörigkeit aus politischen, rassischen oder religiösen Gründen entzogenworden ist, und ihre Abkömmlinge sind auf Antrag wieder einzubürgern. Sie gelten als nicht ausgebürgert, sofern sie nachdem 8. Mai 1945 ihren Wohnsitz in Deutschland genommen haben und nicht einen entgegengesetzten Willen zum Ausdruck gebracht haben.

Former German citizens, whose German citizenship was revoked for political, racial, or religious reasons between January 30, 1933, and May 8, 1945, as well as their descendants must be naturalized upon their request. They are defined as not denaturalized, should they have been German residents after May 8, 1945, and should they have not made a statement to the contrary (Deutscher Bundestag).

The German state has no discretion concerning Section 116, if the line of descent or affiliation can be proven, and individuals must be naturalized as German citizens.[5] In regard to German Jews and their descendants in Israel or other countries, that means that if they wish, they will be renaturalized as German citizens immediately if they qualify according to the Basic Law, and German citizenship law. The latter outlines the gritty details of German citizenship, and it has undergone a number of major changes since 1949. Concerning German Jews and their descendants, the most crucial change occurred January 1, 1975.[6] Since that date, either parent can pass on German citizenship. Prior to that date the child of a German mother and a non-German father was only German if the child would have been stateless otherwise, or if the child had been born out of wedlock. Otherwise, such a child was not a German citizen, lest the German mother registered it with the respective German administration by December 31, 1977. According to my interviews with mothers of Third-Generation Israelis/Germans they had not been informed of this deadline, and they perceived it as—understandably—unfair.[7] They outlined time and again that their own parents had not been asked to be displaced from Germany, or to be stripped of their German citizenship. Indeed, conversations like this brought up major resentment against German restitution practices, and regularly the old German passports from the 1930s, at times stamped with a "J" for "Jude" (Jew), were shown as proof not only of citizenship but also to emphasize the racism that had been leveled at Jews during the Nazi reign.

However much upset this legal framework might cause to the single Jew of German descent, from the side of the German state the situation is legally clear. The legal framework of the Federal Republic of Germany stated explicitly that German Jews and their descendants were part of post-Nazi citizenry again, if they fit the categories of citizenship law applied to all and any German citizen.[8] It is of course debatable if it is ethical to apply the same legal framework to a group of people who had been treated completely different from all other Germans citizens under Nazi rule. Bearing in mind the atrocities that had been waged against Jews, and the general attitudes in Israeli society concerning Germany when this law came into force, the amount of German Jews seeking immediate renaturalization was unsurprisingly low, yet they existed:

> It is not that uncommon that I have Third Generations turn up at my office, handing papers over and asking for renaturalization. A couple of weeks later we get a letter back from the BVA (Bundesverwaltungsamt / Federal Office of Administration)[9] that states that so and so is a German citizen already because the grandparents naturalized in 1953. In that case I often have to explain to the applicants that they have been German citizens all along, and that they just never had a passport issued. The issue of passport and nationality is often completely unclear, and the clients are completely startled that they have been German citizens all along. (Interview with Alexandra Margalith, lawyer and notary, Tel Aviv, January 2013)

Margalith went on to explain that the German citizenship of the grandparents had been kept a secret from the children (Second Generation) and grandchildren (Third Generation), which again is little surprising against the backdrop of the Holocaust/Shoah,[10] the lack of diplomatic relationships between Germany and Israel in the immediate post-Shoah period, and the complicated perception of German Jews, also called Yekkes, in Israel. Diplomatic relations came only into place in 1965, yet economical ties had existed since state foundation, and that not alone because of German restitution and hence resulting in business with Israel (Geller 2005). Jews from Germany who had been displaced to Palestine did not necessarily cut all ties with Germany. The keeping of these contacts needs to be appreciated in the light of the way of German Jews came into Palestine/Israel. Only two thousand to three thousand came as Zionists pre-1933 (Worman 1970, 76), the vast majority arrived as refugees (Erel 1983; Rosenstock 1956; Worman 1970), and had been part of German mainstream society prior to their displacement (Rosenthal 2005; Miron 2009; Sela-Sheffy 2006, 2011; also the edited volume by Zimmermann and Hotam 2005). The film *The Flat* (hrydh, 2011) picks up on this issue; when sorting through the flat of the recently deceased grandparents, the filmmaker and his mother find that the grandparents/parents had a vivid, yet secret, life that connected them with non-Jewish Germans throughout their life. The Third-Generation filmmaker is intrigued while the Second-Generation mother seems baffled, and speechless, indicating the shifting identities and perception of Germany by the Second, and Third, Generation. The Second-Generation mother feels that her own, precarious construct as an Israeli is endangered (Kranz 2013), while the Third-Generation son reacts with positive curiosity about these new finds of the family history (Harpaz 2009; Kranz 2013).

ISRAELI SOCIETAL STRUCTURES AND THE IDEA OF ALIYAH

Israel for the most part is a country of Jewish immigrants who arrived at different times and from different countries. It is rare that Israeli Jewish families have roots in the country that reach back more than three generations. The amount of Jews who came to the British mandate of Palestine as part of the Yishuv movement is small compared to the amount of Jewish refugees in the 1930s and 1940s from Europe, after state foundation from Arabic-speaking countries, and since the collapse of the Soviet Union from various Eastern European and Central Asian countries. Israeli discourse refers to Jewish immigrants as Olim, literally ascenders, and the single migration wave of Jews to Israel as Aliyah, literally ascend, regardless of the actual reason for the migration. German Jews arrived primarily as part of the Fifth Aliyah between 1929 and 1939. The issue of the arrival of their families in Palestine, the Israeli discourse concerning immigration and integration, the complicated history of Jews and non-Jews in the Diaspora, as well as societal structures of Israel play into the identity configurations of the Third Generation and their contemporaries in present-day Israel, and they have direct relations to the general trend to obtain a European passport (Harpaz 2009, 2012, 2013; Hirsch and Lazar 2011; Kranz 2013).

The major institutional structures of current Israel were set up by the Jews of the early Yishuv, who were by and far Ashkenazim (European Jews) from Eastern European countries and territories of the Russian empire. While only very few of them were German Jews, these too influenced the elite of the Yishuv and in consequence upon foundation the State of Israel (Sela-Sheffy 2006, 2011). Inequalities between Ashkenazim and other Jewish groups, especially Spharadim/Mizrahim,[11] prevail to date (Khazzoom 2003, 2005, 2012; Yaish 2001), although Ashkenazim have lost some of their power.

During the first decades of the existence of Israel the inequalities were so strong that Ashkenazim and with them Yekkes and their descendants were "transparent" (Harpaz 2009), they were not forced to reflect on their identity, while other Jewish groups were perceived as "ethnic groups" (Khazzoom 2003, 2005, 2012; Kimmerling 2010), or as "religious sects" (Khazzoom 2003, 2005, 2012; Kimmerling 2010). Yet the domestic dynamic of Israeli Jewish identity negotiations underpinned the decline of the Ashkenazi hegemony in the 1970s by way of the Spharadim/Mizrahim challenging it. This dynamic forced Israeli Jews in general to reflect on the matter of Jewish Israeliness. The previous transparency of Ashkenazim had been based on their hegemonic power (Harpaz 2009), which in turn finds it roots in the Yishuv, which bore the structure and ideologies of immigrating Ashkenazim.[12] After state foundation these early structures morphed into the foundation of Israeli administration, and in effect forced Spharadim/Mizrahim into integrating into societal and social structures, which were defined by Ashkenazic culture as both dominant and superior to any other inner-Jewish culture. In some respects this societal structure compares to colonial countries, as Aziza Khazzoom (2003) argued convincingly. Yet despite the all stigma, and remaining inequalities (Sagiv 2014), the non-Ashkenazic Jews had been raised to believe that they were Israeli Jews too, and thus equals. This discourse of being an Israeli Jew first and foremost was part of the social engineering of Israeli Jewish society. It meant to increase the social cohesion between all Israeli Jews and to create what has been referred to as the new Jew (Almog 2000). Be that as it may, the social engineering worked in parts for the Second Generation; that is, for the parents of Ben, Gal, and Nati. Their parents grew up as being ethnically transparent Israeli Ashkenazi Jews, and they were furthermore keen on being Israelis only, while forgetting about their diasporic roots. At this point in time diasporic roots were a source of identity that was stigmatized, clinging on to it was nondesirable, which found its most vivid expression in the embarrassment of the publicly spoken German of the parents (Kranz forthcoming), or one's own refusal to reply in German, let alone pass the language on to one's own Third-Generation children (Kranz 2013). In praxis the countries of origin, and the family histories of the parents and respective grandparents, influenced the identity formations (Harpaz 2009; Kranz 2013). Yet for the Second Generation the strategy to identify first and foremost as Israeli worked for a while, and the Second Generations only had to reflect on their identities from the 1970s onward because the societal dynamic had changed (Kranz 2013; Levy-Sasson 2008). The Third Generation of Israelis did not grow up in an unspoken Ashkenazi hegemony, but with parents who had positioned themselves within the dynamic framework of Israeli society (Kranz 2013). They had to base their identity on something more than being Israeli Jews (ibid). The question was what to base it on. As it turned out, the basis was going to be the diasporic culture, which had been transmitted within families from the First to the Second Generation. For the Third Generation this meant that both their First-Generation grandparents and their Second-Generation parents passed on their diasporic roots as well as their ideas of Israeliness. Yet in the present the situation has gained a new momentum because besides the dynamics of Israeli society, and family history, other features have started to play into this matrix of Israeli identity options. Israel is part of the global system of flows of good, people, and cultures, and Israelis are increasingly mobile. Until 1959 Israelis had to negotiate exit permits to be able to leave Israel (Cohen 2009; Rozin 2010); any Israeli leaving was perceived a threat to the nation-building project (Cohen 2009; Rozin 2010; Silber 2008). This meant in turn that it was hard for First Generations to leave Israel even if their arrival in Palestine, and later Israel, had not been their desired choice of residence. This means for those who did leave, they suffered from incomprehension at the best of times, and those wanting to go to Germany kept their planned emigration secret (Kranz 2009). The derogative term coined for Israeli Jews who left Israel was Yored, meaning somebody who descends (cf. Cohen 2007; Magat 1999; Shokeid 1988, among others). Meanwhile, it has been recognized that not all Israelis want to remain in Israel, and the new policy recommendations lean toward the direction to implement diasporic Israelis (Rebhun and Lev Ari 2010); to entice the highly qualified to come home (Cohen 2007); to see diasporic Israelis as a resource for, and not a threat to, Israel (Cohen and Kranz 2014); and to engage their children abroad in Israeli-style activities (Cohen 2007). Historically, the trend to venture abroad started with the Second Generation who went abroad in higher number than the First Generation, but this trend is dwarfed by the lust to work, live, or to travel by Third Generations.

GAINS FROM GERMAN CITIZENSHIP: RATIONAL AND EMOTIONAL

Ben, Gal, and Nati all have one Second-Generation German parent, who in turn had two German parents. Ben's mother is a German native speaker, so is Nati's father, Gal's father is not, or at least he did not speak any German with me. All grandparents but Ben's learned Hebrew and resumed their lives in Palestine, later Israel. This was not the case with Ben's grandparents who did not reenter their professions in Palestine/Israel and worked in unrelated, lower-skilled professions. His mother remained their translator for life; according to her, and him, they remained in their "Yekke Bubble," meaning their social circle comprised of other German Jewish refugees.

Ben harbors regrets that he did not learn German at home. His mother spoke Hebrew with him and his siblings, and she had forbidden her own parents to speak German with her children. Being a German native speaker did not necessarily have good connotations for Ben's mother; she felt horribly lonely when she started school in 1948, because she did not speak anything but German. She wanted to spare her children this kind of loneliness. Problematically, there is a specific stigma attached to Germanness; anything relating to Germany, or the German language, can be put into a direct connection with the Shoah. To date, jokes about the Nazis or remarks concerning the Shoah remain overabundant in Israel; the Shoah constitutes a cultural trauma (see Kidron 2004). Nati, who is bilingual in German and Hebrew and outspoken on his Germanness, remarked in an interview: "I have been called a Nazi in school."[13] Gal did not mention that this insult had ever been directed at him, while Ben did. Ben also mentioned that "at work, there was that one guy who kept on calling me Yekke. Yekke here, Yekke there." Dani: "Did it piss you off?" Ben: "No, not really. [laughs] He actually made me laugh. [...] and he was Moroccan."[14] Interestingly, for Ben and Nati, being of German descent, or being a Yekke, is a compliment, despite the offense that can come with it. Both interpret their German descent as setting them positively apart from other Israelis; it is a marker of positive distinction (cf. Greif 2000; Sela-Sheffy 2006). Ben's remark concerning the ethnic origin of his coworker underlines this further: being Moroccan connotes being of a lower social class, less educated (even if they were colleagues in this case), not being Ashkenazi, and in many cases not having access to a desirable EU passport (see Harpaz 2009), and especially not a German passport. In other words, Ben found his self-perception confirmed by his coworker and overheard a possible negative slant of the term Yekke.

Ben's as well as Nati's interpretations relate directly to the Yekke myth (Sela-Sheffy 2006, 2011; Kranz 2013). This myth refers to the popular culture depiction of the first generation of German Jewish immigrants/refugees as unable to adjust to the British mandate of Palestine and later Israel, and hanging on to their values, habits, and language (see the edited volume by Zimmermann and Hotam 2005) while being unwilling to learn Hebrew, assimilate, or adapt to the new surroundings. Yekke literally means jacket in Yiddish. The term was used to mock the stiff and climatically ill-fitting attire of German Jews of the First Generation. The term came to be a shortcut of their depiction as unwilling immigrants, as the second meaning of the term emphasizes even more. If the Hebrew letters are taken as an acronym—יקה—they stand for Yehudi Kshe Havanah, a Jew with problems understanding. There might be a kernel of truth to the unwillingness of Yekkes to integrate, and them picking up Hebrew slowly, yet it needs to be taken into consideration that most were refugees, not immigrants, and that they had been highly integrated in pre-Shoah Germany (Kranz 2013). This sets German Jewish arrivals notably apart from other incoming Jews at the time; their displacement overshadowed their accomplishments, as well as integration into Palestine, and later into Israel (Kranz 2013; Sela-Sheffy 2006, 2011). This is not to say that other Jews came to Palestine/Israel based on their free will, just the opposite: immigration waves to Palestine/Israeli were often underpinned by upheaval and persecution, ranging from the Pogroms in the Pale region in the 1880s, to the displacement of Jews from Arab countries poststate foundation, and the vast immigration of Jews from the (former) Soviet Union in the 1990s. The comparison is warranted that unlike German Jews these early waves from Eastern Europe and the Arab countries had not been part of the societal mainstream of their native countries, and unlike Yekkes they were often not part of the middle classes of their countries of origin. In the 1990s this was mirrored by the often highly qualified, assimilated, and highly integrated "Russian" Jews, who, similar to the Yekkes some fifty years earlier, have been mocked as well as criticized for their clustering, their slow uptake of Hebrew, and their hanging on to their Russianness (Elias and Lerner 2012; Rebhun 2010; Remennick 2004). Going back to the Yekkes, but bearing the Russian Jewish comparative in mind, it is not surprising that the settling-in process of German Jews was different, and took longer compared to those Jews who came based on Zionistic motives, or of those who had not been integrated in the mainstream of their previous native countries.[15] At the same time, it does not hold true that German Jews were a marginalized group in Palestine/Israel, and that they did not have access to centers of power, or were indeed part of the elite of the country (Sela-Sheffy 2006, 2011, 2013; Stone 1997). However, these German Jewish immigrants/refugees/Zionists created a particular myth, a myth of all sorts of positive values that they related to being a Yekke: being correct, being on time, working hard and diligently, being reasonable, reliable, and so on (Sela-Sheffy 2006, 2011, 2013). Herman (Haim) Cohen, who was going to be an Israeli Supreme Court judge, went so far as to stress: "My client was a Yecke and it was inconceivable that he would not speak the truth" (Shashar 1989, 201, quoted in Sela-Sheffy 2011, 94).

Amusing as all of this may sound, First-Generation Yekkes created this myth consciously and unconsciously to obtain a viable identity in a new setting and to establish themselves by way of distinction (Sela-Sheffy 2006). Their children, the Second Generation, suffered from it. Thus the Yekke descent was best forgotten for the Second Generation, and only lived out among Yekkes or out of view of "other" Israelis, while the Third Generation reaps the harvest of the myth. Nati went as far as to tell me, in German: "I am perfect." His slightly odd figure of speech referred to the fact that he is a perfectionist. Ben stresses the same about himself. Gal, the one who doesn't use his German passport and who is more ambiguous about his Germanness than Nati or Ben, mentioned that he had no interest in obtaining the other, Eastern European, EU citizenship he could have got via his mother, and reacted in a surprised way when I asked if he wanted to visit this other ancestral homeland. He had no interest, while he had a definite interest in Germany. Yet like Ben and Nati, Gal expresses Germanness by way of specific habits, which he interprets as German virtues, and which draw on the Yekke myth. While he did not refer to himself as a perfectionist, he is meticulous, and proud of it. He harbors the belief that he mixes Israeliness and Germanness, taking the best of both. Yet Gal relates specific habits to his Germanness. He needs to have access to a wristwatch at all times to be on time, a habit he traces back to his German grandfather, because one must know what time it is at any given time (despite having the time on his mobile phone). Drawing on Fuss (1989) and Spivak (1993), Judith Gerson (2001) refers to expressions like Gal's watch habit as "strategic essentialisms," which she defines as highly condensed expressions of identity that can be displayed rather easily and without appreciation of the complexities of the culture they refer to, its disjunctures, and irregularities. I would extend this notion to strategic embodied essentialisms, because the expressions of Nati, Ben, and Gal were not necessarily verbal; indeed, eating nonkosher, German-style or German food is a key element to their identities as Third-Generation Yekkes; the same goes for a specific kind of politeness that they deem German, which they all claim sets them apart from other Israelis, and their take on professionalism.

The German passport serves a similar function. It underpins a specific positioning within Israeli society, vis-à-vis other Israelis, other Germans, and it permits access to a desired in-group, that is, EU Europeans. Israelis have a clear ranking of EU passports; again, the Yekke myth plays into it as much as the perception, or more so ideas, of present-day Germany. The German passport is the highest-ranking of EU passports, which can be obtained via descent. The sheer amount of nearly 100,000 renaturalized German citizens (see Harpaz 2009, 2013) in Israel bears witness to that, as well as the transmission of Germanness within families with German roots (Kranz 2013). Given the integration and assimilation into German mainstream society "before,"[16] it is not surprising that they passed on Germanness to their descendants. This Germanness in turn is positively connected to especially the Third Generation, who is the major group of those who want to renaturalize, and who involve their Second-Generation parents into the process (Harpaz 2009). Harpaz found that on the surface, reasons given for the renaturalization as an EU citizen can be rational, such that one has a safe second passport to leave Israel with in case of war, that one has an EU work permit, that one can travel to countries that are otherwise inaccessible to Israeli citizens, or that one pays lower fees at EU universities. Some of the Third-Generation Yekkes gave similar reasons: Gal sees his German passport as a life insurance; his sister argued to their grandmother that obtaining the passports was a way to "get back at the Germans." Nati and Ben did offer some rational reasons, yet they mentioned no vitriol directed at "the Germans," strikingly, they experience themselves as Germans and not only as German citizens, and they experience their German passport as their right to their heritage on a formal level, and within Israel as a means of distinction (see Sela-Sheffy 2006 for First Generations). However, even for the likes of Gal and his sister the rational reasons hide reasons that are emotional, such as attachment to German culture as a means of distinction, a statement that one is not Israeli only (frequently mentioned by Gal's sister, at times by him too), an expression of a general cosmopolitan identity, the stressing of one's other, diasporic roots, as well as a means of expressing discontent with Israeli society.

THE MEANING OF GERMAN CITIZENSHIP

The meaning of German citizenship to the descendants of German Jews, and in particular of Third Generations in Israel, must be seen within the Israeli context, as part of the family history, as well as part of international developments and global trends. Dual nationality has become increasingly common, and it is furthermore increasingly accepted (Bauböck 2010; Bloemraad 2004, Böcker and Thränhardt 2006). Generally, it has been found that citizenship takes all sorts of meanings, ranging from strategic citizenships (Ong 1999) that can be used à la carte (Fitzgerald 2008) to emotional connectors to an ancestral homeland, or to an expression of a postnationalistic, cosmopolitan identity (Bloemraad 2004; Sejersen 2008).

The case of the Jews of German descent is a highly interesting one, because dual citizenship is neither perceived as desirable by the German nor by the Israeli state. These two countries apply with few exceptions ethnically based citizenship regimes and privilege one specific ethnic group at the expense of other ethnic groups and non-co-ethnic immigrants in the country (see Joppke and Rosenhek 2002). Ironically, these ethnically driven citizenship regimes enable Jews of German descent to renaturalize as German citizens, while maintaining Israeli citizenship. Yet underneath the legal framework lie complex expressions and contradictions of identity on various levels, which beg uneasy questions about the respective citizenship regimes.

In regard to Ben, Gal, and Nati's Israeli citizenship, it is worth noting that while all three are fully functioning as Israelis in Israel, and are active citizens who fulfilled their civic duties with army service, theirs and similar cases show that Israeliness is always flavored with something else that lies well beyond the foundation of the state, and which even with the Third Generation of Israelis feels a strong repercussion. While the main characters agree that they are Israelis by birth and citizenship, all express an attachment to what they see as German and express their personal take on Germanness by way of an array of habits and in the shape of strategic essentialisms, while simultaneously underlining it by way of the official, formal, and legal token of belonging: German citizenship. For the ethnically based citizenship regimes of both countries these Third Generations beg the uneasy question, if they are Third-Generation Israelis, or Third-Generation Yekkes, or Third-Generation diasporic Germans.

Ben, Gal, and Nati reflect examples of the three main groups that emerged from more then fifty interview partners and countless fieldwork conversations conducted since 2003. Generally, cases like Gal—the same goes for his sister, who I only mentioned in passing—are most common among the Third-Generation Yekkes. On the surface Gal is extremely ambiguous about this German citizenship, but underneath his ambiguity hides an array of expressions of identity that he connects positively with his German descent within the Israeli context. It might well be the case that he is more ambiguous then Nati and Ben because his family arrived in Palestine only in the early 1940s, and his German grandmother in particular had witnessed atrocities firsthand. Ben's and Nati's German grandparents came to Palestine in the early 1930s, and only witnessed the Nazi raise to power, but they had left Germany before 1935 when the Nuremberg Laws were passed and the prosecution of Jews in Germany reached new levels.

Ben is not ambiguous about being a German, or a German citizen, but he lacks the ability to speak the language, and hence resorts to strategic essentialisms to express Germanness vis-à-vis other Yekkes, Israelis, and other Germans (non-Jews) he encounters. Nati, who is fully conversant in German, expresses some strategic essentialism, but by way of access to the language resource he has a different access to actual Germany. He is not restricted to some imaginary Yekke Wonderland that serves as a smoke screen for wishes, desires, and the opposite of Israel. Unable to speak any German, the group of individuals like Gal commonly claimed that they naturalized for rational reasons, yet the data show that Gal uses Germanness to stress his Ashkenazi descent vis-à-vis other Israelis and dwells on belonging to the ruling class of Israeli Jews. For Gal, his Germanness and German citizenship has relevance within the Israeli framework, yet it has little or no meaning beyond Israel. Gal, like Ben, is extremely critical of Israel and complains vociferously about its increasing neoliberalization, (alleged) lack of manners among Israelis, the failing political class, and the stagnant peace process.[17] Scratching the thin veneer of his defensiveness concerning his renaturalization, and filtering in all his issues with Israel, a different story emerges, that of an emotional attachment to a culture lost, and which he can only express by way of embodying an imagined Germany. Yet it makes sense to refer to Gal as a Third-Generation Israeli of German descent because Israel is the main anchor of his identity, and it is the focal point in which his Germanness and German citizenship has currency.

However, Ben, too, employs Germanness to express unhappiness with Israeli society, by way of projecting wishes and desires on the other, actual, and yet imaginary belonging. If none of that would matter to individuals like Ben and Gal, they would not bother to renaturalize, because effectively, the rational gains of a German passport are not that great; fees at EU universities are based on residence, and not on EU citizenship; one can travel to about ten more countries with a German passport; plus, various EU countries have policies that allow highly qualified Israelis to obtain work permits easily. However, based on their different knowledge bases and family histories, these three allow insights into the complex of appropriately differentiated citizenship (Smith 2013), but I would argue into appropriately differentiated diaspora citizenships; while Gal is best identified as a Third-Generation Israeli, Ben is best described as a Third-Generation Yekke, and Nati as a Third-Generation diasporic German citizen. Ben has more knowledge about Germany and German language skills than Gal, yet Germany is still more or less an imaginary space. Nati holds language skills, and could function in Germany rather easily, but he acknowledges freely that he is anchored in both countries.

In terms of theories of citizenship, and theories of expressions of identity, these Third-Generation Israelis/Yekkes/Germans allow for some highly valuable insights. As already mentioned they expand the notion of "strategic essentialisms" (Gerson 2001) to "strategic embodied essentialisms" because most of their Germanness lies in the realm of the nonverbal. On the one hand this is based on the lack of language transmission down the generations; on the other hand, it underlines the strength and the resilience of nonverbal aspects of identities that become embodied habits, and thus expressions of (shared) identity across generations.

Smith (2013) argues for an appreciation of what he calls an appropriately differentiated citizenship, a concept I would amend by the appropriately differentiated diasporic citizenship as stated above. Of particular relevance is his argument concerning cultural and social citizenship. Legally, the likes of Nati, Ben, and Gal are German citizens like any other German, yet the meaning they give to this citizenship lies in the realm of the cultural, social, and emotional, but it does not hinge on the territorial.

Bearing Smith's argument in mind, the Yekke descendants question the German concept of *jus sanguinis*, the idea of Germanness, and its relationship to citizenship, and effectively German restitution practices. By and far, article 116, section 2, that allowed for the renaturalization of Ben, Gal, Nati, and their respective family members, did not undo the losses caused to German Jews by the Nazis. While all three hold the same citizenship as any other German citizen, only Nati would function rather easily and independently in Germany. Ben and Gal can only deal with German administration with the help of friends, First- and Second-Generation family members, or lawyers, setting them apart from those German citizens who were born and raised in the country, and making them more similar to immigrants than to native Germans. This means as well that none of them has a native understanding, or native knowledge, of Germany, ranging from not knowing their way around the administration of the country, to struggling with ticket machines for public transportation, and as mentioned before, acting different from Germans. Nati's sister reflected on this critically, underscoring that: "I feel more Israeli than German. But at the same time, it was always quieter in our house [in Israel] than in the homes of [non-Yekke] Israelis, but it was way noisier than in German homes." His sister offers a rare self-reflective insight into the praxes of Yekkes, and she is not shy to outline the Israeli aspects of their home life, issues that Ben, Gal, and Nati blissfully overlooked in their quest for Germanness. Inasmuch, their German citizenship adds another layer to the idea of a differentiated citizenship as put forward by Smith: while they are ethnically defined citizens, they unhinge the idea of an ethnic group that rests on shared descent, and they call for an extension of this theory by what Nir Cohen (2007) described in his case study of Second-Generation diasporic Israelis in the United States. Cohen outlined how the everyday praxes of these Second-Generation Israelis in particular challenged the Greek, territorially based concept of ethnic citizenship regimes, and he argued that their praxes lay more in the area of the Roman, culturally expressed, and de-territorialized concept of citizenship (Cohen 2007). Yet Cohen underlines that diasporic citizenship is always contradictory (Cohen 2007, 137), and this is where he offers a crucial link to the Third Generations of this paper: what does it mean to be a Third-Generation Israeli, Third-Generation Yekke, or Third-Generation diasporic German while belonging to the formally same group of citizens?

Their family history and displacement makes for a layer of differentiated citizenship that calls into question how different the same citizens of the same country are, and in this case in particular what it actually means to be a German citizen, while, problematically, they challenge the ubiquitous claim of Israel to its citizens at the same time. Citizenries of countries that apply descent-based citizenships for one or the other reason contain individuals who cannot and do not function in their "homeland," and these countries thus need a (legal) framework that outlines what happens if these "Germans come home," because the inequalities between the different German citizens are still deeply marked by the aftermath of Nazi terror for the specific group at the focus of this chapter.

Effectively, by way of its legal framework, Germany has not been able to undo the aftermath of Nazi terror, and different classes of ethnic German citizens remain as a result.[18] This structure also reflects in the likes of Ben and Gal, being "inactive diasporic" German citizens; they are formally German citizens, and they might well feel like Yekkes, or Germans in Israel, yet unlike Germans with native knowledge they can only become active German citizens after undergoing another socialization, and acculturization in Germany that resembles those of immigrants. Inasmuch, their citizenship, and their take on Germanness, allows adding a new layer to Smith's differentiation approach (2013) and to extend Cohen's (2007) idea of diasporic citizenship: these German citizens are ethnically, yet inactive diasporic, citizens of Germany, while carriers of a specific, embodied Germanness in Israel. Thus applied differentiated citizenship must filter in the local situatedness and local context of diasporic, ethnic citizens in particular of countries that—preferably—adhere to ethnically based citizenship regimes because these diasporic citizens can range from the nearly fully active, to the fully inactive.

NOTES

I would like to thank the Yekkes across generations for their insights, trust, and time. I would also like to thank A. Margalith for her numerous explanations about the German and Israeli legal frameworks, their dynamics and interrelatedness, countless conversations, and her superior patience to stand the nosiness of an anthropologist who analyzes law, and I would also like to thank M. Schlezinger for research assistance on Israeli law and policy. Finally, my gratitude goes to M. Kruman and H. Callow of the Center for the Study of Citizenship at Wayne State for the invitation to present a first draft of this work in progress, and to A. Rothe for offering me her home during the conference.

1. A Third Generation is the grandchild of one or more Shoah survivors (First Generation). The underlying concept of generation is that of Mannheim (1952), as a cohort that shares similar experiences due to the time in which they were born.

2. While it is beyond the scope of this paper, it is worth noting that Germany did not define itself as an immigration country, and that naturalization as a German citizen has been a long, complex process for nonethnic Germans, and subject of much contention (for example: Böcker and Thränhardt 2006; Canefe 1998; El-Tayeb 1999; Joppke and Rosenhek 2002; Halfmann 1997;

Kurthen 1995; Mandel 2008; Nathans 2004; Preuss 2003; and the volume *Challenging Ethnic Citizenship*, 2002, edited by Levy and Weiss).

3. While Germany did not involve these citizens, Israel had little interest to see them involved abroad either, as the case study of Silber (2008) outlines for Poland.

4. All translations are mine. The laws were translated from German into English. Interviews and fieldwork was conducted in English, German, and Hebrew.

5. Unlike other European countries like the United Kingdom, Germany only knows the category "citizens" to relate to its citizens, which is also exemplified in German identity records. They only bear the mark "deutsch" (German) under the section "citizenship." Furthermore, the German terms of citizenship—Staatsangehörigkeit—literally derives from the terms state (Staat) and Angehöriger, which literally translated into kinsman. Citizenship and nationality (Nationalität) are synonymous in German legal discourse.

6. Other changes concern birth out of wedlock; children born before July 1, 1993, will be naturalized if the paternity of the German father has been proven, if the ordinary residence of the child has been in Germany for the last three years, and the child is under twenty-three. Since July 1, 1993, children of a German father are automatically German citizens. This part of the law reflects the recognition that an increasing amount of children have been born out of wedlock over the last decades. However, this law will be important for Fourth-Generation children in Israel, too, because a growing number of children are born out of wedlock. I did not come across any Third Generations who were born out of wedlock in Israel.

7. It did not come up in interviews that Israeli policy makers are extremely ambiguous about Israeli citizens renaturalizing as citizens of their ancestral home countries (see Harpaz 2009), and that the secrecy about this deadline might be part of the complex of German/Israeli diplomatic relationships.

8. The lawyer and notary Dan Assan, Tel Aviv, acknowledged in an interview that the citizenship praxis did indeed cause upset to those who saw their application declined. He stated that he explains to his clients that "they cannot have it better than anybody [any other German] else." Interview, November 2009.

9. The BVA is the federal ministry responsible for matters of renaturalization and other citizenship-related matters.

10. As all of my research participants were Hebrew native speakers, they used the Hebrew term Shoah when relating to discrimination, racism, and the mass murder of Jews under the Nazis.

11. The term Spharadim refers to Jews who originate in Spain (Spharad in Hebrew), who were displaced during the inquisition and who settled—mainly—in North Africa. Mizrahi literally means "Eastern" and refers to Jews from Arabic-speaking countries, and Asia. However, both terms are problematic, contentious, and self-ascriptions between individuals from these countries, between generations, and more so between individuals of mixed ancestry (see Sagiv 2014).

12. Ashkenazim are not a monolithic block, and differences in ideology, religious practices, language, and culture exist (see Kranz 2013). Yet Ashkenazim tend to be more similar to one another than other Jewish groups if considering these parameters as a benchmark.

13. Nati went to school in the 1990s and 2000s.

14. This situation occurred in late 2012.

15. It is worth noting that the settling-in process in Palestine/Israel deviated between groups, and individuals. Miron (2009) depicted differences between individual women from Germany, while Hertzog's (1999) ethnography depicts in great detail the complicated settling-in process of Ethiopian Jews.

16. The notion "before," meaning before the Shoah, is rather common among Yekke. The breakdown in "before" and "after" bears a direct connection to the trauma they experienced, because traumatic events cannot be integrated into one's autobiography, but split it into "before" and "after" (Fresno 1981; Kranz 2009, forthcoming; Raczymov 1986).

17. Harpaz (2009) found similar results among Israelis who renaturalized as EU citizens in general. The renaturalization was also seen as a critique toward Israeli ethno-nationalism, the unique claim of Israel toward its citizens, and fears about the declining Jewish Israeli population.

18. There are of course many more classes of citizens in Germany, ranging from naturalized foreigner in the country who repeatedly complained about discrimination and not being taken as Germans, to ethnic German Spätaussiedler (resettlers), to children of foreign residents in Germany who must decide if they want to maintain German citizenship at age twenty-three or take their parents' citizenship and so on. The list of differences within German citizenry is long, and comprehensive, and these examples are not comprehensive.

WORKS CITED

Almog, Oz. 2000. *The Sabra: The Creation of the New Jew.* Translated by Haim Watzman. Berkeley: University of California Press.

Bauböck, Rainer. 2010. "Studying Citizenship Constellations." *Journal of Ethnic and Migration Studies* 36 (5): 847–59.

Bloemraad, Irene. 2004. "Who Claims Dual Citizenship? The Limits of Postnationalism, the Possibilities of Transnationalism, and the Persistence of Traditional Citizenship." *IMR* 38 (2): 389–426.

Böcker, Anita, and Dietrich Thränhardt. 2006. "Multiple Citizenship and Naturalization: An Evaluation of German and Dutch Policies." *Revue de l'integrationet de la Migration Internationale / Journal of International Migration and Integration* 7 (1): 71–94.

Bodemann, Y. Michal. 2006. "Between Israel and Germany from the 'Alien Asiatic People' to the new German Jewry." *Jewish History* 20: 91–109.

Canefe, Nergis. 1998. "Citizens versus Permanent Guests: Cultural Memory and Citizenship Laws in a Reunified Germany." *Citizenship Studies* 2 (3): 519–44.

Cohen, Nir. 2007. "State, Migrants, and Negotiation of Second-Generation Citizenship in the Israeli Diaspora." *Diaspora* 16 (1/2): 133–58.

———. 2009. "From Legalism to Symbolism: Anti-Mobility and National Identity in Israel, 1948–1958." *Journal of Historical Geography* 36: 19–28.

Cohen, Nir, and Dani Kranz. 2014. "State-Assisted Highly Skilled Return Programmes, National Identity and the Risk(s) of Homecoming: Israel and Germany Compared." *Journal of Ethnic and Migration Studies.* http://dx.doi.org/10.1080/1369183X.2014.948392.

Deutscher Bundestag. n.d. *Grundgesetz für die Bundesrepublik Deutschland. XI: Übergangs- und Schlussbestimmungen.* www.bundestag.de/bundestag/aufgaben/rechtsgrundlagen/grundgesetz/gg_11.html.

Diner, Dan. 2005. "Jeckes-Ursprung und Wandeleiner Zuschreibung." In *Zweimal Heimat: Die Jeckes Zwischen Mitteleuropa und Nahost,* edited by Moshe Zimmermann and Yotam Hotam, 100–103. Frankfurt am Main: Beerenverlag.

El-Tayeb, Fatima. 1999. "'Blood Is a Very Special Juice': Racialized Bodies and Citizenship in Twentieth-Century Germany." Supplement, *International Review of Social History* 44: 149–69.

Elias, Nelly, and Julia Lerner. 2011. "Narrating the Double Helix: The Immigrant-Professional Biography of a Russian Journalist in Israel." *Forum Qualitative Sozialforschung / Forum: Qualitative Social Research* 13 (1): Art. 15. http://nbn-resolving.de/urn:nbn:de:0114-fqs1201155.

Erel, Shlomo. 1983. *Neue Wurzeln: 50 Jahre Immigration deutsch-sprachiger Juden in Israel.* Göttingen: Bleicher Verlag.

Fitzgerald, David. 2008. "Citizenship a la Carte: Global Migration and Transnational Politics." Working Paper No. 3, George Mason University. http://cgs.gmu.edu/publications/gmtpwp/gmtp_wp_3.pdf.

Fresno, Nadine. 1981. "La diaspora des cendres." *Nouvelle Revue de Psychanalyse* 24: 205–20.

Geller, Jay H. 2005. *Jews in Post-Holocaust Germany, 1945–1953.* Cambridge: Cambridge University Press.

Gerson, Judith M. 2001. "In Between States: National Identity Practices among German-Jewish Immigrants." *Political Psychology* 22 (1): 179–98.

Greif, Gidon, ed. 2000. *Die Jeckes: Deutsche Juden aus Israel erzählen.* Cologne: Böhlau.

Halfmann, Jost. 1997. "Two Discourses of Citizenship in Germany: The Difference between Public Debate and Administrative Practice." *Citizenship Studies* 1 (3): 301–22.

Harpaz, Yossi. 2009. "Israelis and the European Passport: Dual Citizenship in an Apocalyptic Immigrant Society." Unpublished master's thesis, Tel Aviv University.

———. 2012. "The Demand for European Passports in Israel: Dual Citizenship as Intergenerational Transfer and Status Symbol." *Megamot* 3 (4).

———. 2013. "Rooted Cosmopolitans: Israelis with a European Passport—History, Property, Identity." *IMR* 47 (1): 166–206.

Hertzog, Esther. 1999. *Immigrants and Bureaucrats: Ethiopians in an Israeli Absorption Center.* Oxford: Berghahn.

Hirsch, Tal Litvak, and Alon Lazar. 2011. "Belonging Here, Not There: The Case of Attaining European Passports by Grandchildren of Holocaust Survivors." *International Journal of Intercultural Relations* 35: 387–94.

Joppke, Christian, and Zeev Rosenhek. 2002. "Contesting Ethnic Immigration: Germany and Israel Compared." *European Journal of Sociology* 43: 301–35.

Khazzoom, Aziza. 2003. "The Great Chain of Orientalism: Jewish Identity, Stigma Management, and Ethnic Exclusion in Israel." *American Sociological Review* 68: 481–510.

———. 2005. "Did the Israeli State Engineer Segregation? On the Placement of Jewish Immigrants in Development Towns in the 1950s." *Social Forces* 84 (1): 115–34.

———. 2011. "Intra-Jewish Conflict in Israel: White Jews, Black Jews." *Journal of Israeli History* 30 (1): 108–11.

Kidron, Carol A. 2004. "Surviving a Distant Past: A Case Study of the Cultural Construction of Trauma Descendant Identity." *Ethos* 31 (4): 513–44.

Kimmerling, Baruch. 2010. *Clash of Identities: Explorations in Israeli and Palestinian Societies.* New York: Columbia University Press.

Kranz, Dani. 2009. "Shades of Jewishness: A Liberal Jewish Community in Post-Shoah Germany." Unpublished PhD dissertation, University of St. Andrews.

——. 2013. "Being a Yekke Is Big Deal for My Mum!" *Austausch* 2 (1): 43–66.

Kurthen, Hermann. 1995. "Germany at the Crossroads: National Identity and the Challenges of Immigration." *International Migration Review* 29 (4): 914–38.

Levy, Daniel, and Yfaat Weiss, eds. 2002. *Challenging Ethnic Citizenship: German and Israeli Perspectives on Immigration.* New York: Berghahn.

Levy-Sasson, Orna. 2008. "'But I Don't Want an Ethnic Identity': Social Boundaries and Their Erasure in Contemporary Discourses of Ashkenaziut." *Theory and Criticism* 33: 101–25 (Hebrew).

Magat, Ilan N. 1999. "Israeli and Japanese Immigrants to Canada: Home, Belonging, and the Territorialization of Identity." *Ethos* 27 (2): 119–44.

Mandel, Ruth Ellen. 2008. *Cosmopolitan Anxieties: Turkish Challenges to Citizenship and Belonging in Germany.* Durham, NC: Duke University Press.

Mannheim, Karl. 1952. "The Problem of Generations." In *Essays on the Sociology of Knowledge*, edited by Paul Kecskemetied. New York: Routledge and Kegan Paul.

Miron, Guy. 2009. "From Bourgeoise Germany to Palestine: Memoirs of German Jewish Women in Israel." *Nashim* 17: 116–40.

Nathans, Eli. 2004. *The Politics of Citizenship in Germany: Ethnicity, Utility, and Nationalism.* Oxford: Berg.

Ong, Aihwa. 1999. *Flexible Citizenship: The Cultural Logics of Transnationality.* Durham, NC: Duke University Press

Preuss, Ulrich K. 2003. "Citizenship and the German Nation." *Citizenship Studies* 7 (1): 37–55.

Raczymov, Henri. 1986. "La mémoire trouée." *Pardès* 3: 177–82.

Rebhun, Uzi. 2010. "Immigration, Gender, and Earnings in Israel." *European Journal of Population* 26: 73–97.

Rebhun, Uzi, and Lilach Lev Ari. 2010. *American Israelis: Migration, Transnationalism, and Diasporic Identity.* Amsterdam: Brill.

Remennick, Larissa I. 2004. "Providers, Caregivers, and Sluts: Women with a Russian Accent in Israel." *Nashim* 8: 87–114.

Rosenstock, Werner. 1956. "A Survey of Jewish Emigration from Germany." In *Yearbook of the Leo Baeck Institute*, 373–90.

Rosenthal, Rubik. 2005. "Vom intimen zum Geschichtlichen und zurück. Zur Blumenstraße 22." In *Zweimal Heimat: Die Jeckes Zwischen Mitteleuropa und Nahost*, edited by Moshe Zimmermann and Yotam Hotam. Frankfurt am Main: Beerenverlag.

Rozin, Orit. 2010. "Israel and the Right to Travel Abroad, 1948–1961." *Israel Studies* 15 (1): 147–76.

Sagiv, Talia. 2014. *Half/Half: About Israelis of Mixed Ethnicity*. Tel Aviv: Kibbutz Hapoalim.

Sejersen, Tanja Brøndsted. 2008. "'I Vow to Thee My Countries'—The Expansion of Dual Citizenship in the 21st Century." *IMR* 42 (3): 523–49.

Sela-Sheffy, Rakefet. 2006. "Integration through Distinction: German-Jewish Immigrants, the Legal Profession, and Patterns of Bourgeois Culture in British-Ruled Jewish Palestine." *Journal of Historical Sociology* 19 (1): 34–59.

———. 2011. "High-Status Immigration Group and Culture Retention: German Jewish Immigrants in British-Ruled Palestine." In *Culture Contacts and the Making of Culture: Papers in Homage to Itamar Even-Zohar*, edited by Rakefet Sela-Sheffy and Gideon Toury, 79–100. Tel Aviv: Unit of Culture Research, Tel Aviv University and Authors.

———. 2013. "'Europeans in the Levant' Revisited—German Jewish Immigrants in 1930 Palestine and the Question of Cultural Retention." In *Tel Aviver Jahrbuch für deutsche Geschichte*, edited by José Brunner, 40–59. Göttingen: Wallstein Verlag.

Shokeid, Moshe. 1988. *Children of Circumstance: Israeli Immigrants in New York*. Ithaca, NY: Cornell University Press.

Silber, Marcos. 2008. "'Immigrants from Poland Want to Go Back': The Politics of Return Migration and Nation Building in 1950s Israel." *Journal of Israeli History: Politics, Society, Culture* 27 (2): 201–19.

Smith, Rogers. 2013. "The Questions Facing Citizenship in the 21st Century." Keynote lecture at "The Meaning of Citizenship" conference, Wayne State University, Detroit, Michigan, March 21.

Stone, Lilo. 1997. "German Zionists in Palestine before 1933." *Journal of Contemporary History* 32 (2): 171–86.

Worman, Curt. 1970. "German Jews in Israel: Their Cultural Situation since 1933." In *Yearbook of the Leo Baeck Institute*, 73–103.

Yaish, Meir. 2001. "Class Structure in a Deeply Divided Society: Class and Ethnic Inequality in Israel, 1974–1991." *British Journal of Sociology* 52 (3): 409–39.

Zimmermann, Moshe, and Yotam Hotam. 2005. *Zweimal Heimat: Die Jeckes Zwischen Mitteleuropa und Nahost*. Frankfurt am Main: Beerenverlag.

II

....

Proper Horizons of Political Citizenship

5

IMMIGRANT TEACHERS AND GLOBAL CITIZENSHIP

· · · · · · · · · ·

Perspectives from Jamaica

KAREN THOMAS-BROWN

INTRODUCTION

Out-migration from Jamaica is prevalent regardless of economic, social, and education levels because many Jamaicans are socialized to seek social and economic success outside of the island. Despite the reasons and intent of the migrating and migrant Jamaican, notions of citizenship in its legal/political, cultural identity and lived experiences are foremost because citizenship influences the migrants' move to and the actions they are most likely to take once they arrive in their destinations. This is certainly true of many Jamaican teachers, for whom global or transnational citizenship is becoming more common. As a result of the lack of sufficient economic opportunities in Jamaica, the appeal of working in more economically successful countries grows. Because of recruitment drives and advertising for qualified and skilled Jamaican teachers, the outmigration of teachers from the island spiked between 2001 and 2004 and has continued at a steady pace since. Many immigrants, not only teachers, tend to define their citizenship in terms of ties to their homeland (Jamaica). With relatives and friends left behind, the need to return to Jamaica for a range of reasons and the common assertion that regardless of the country of legal citizenship, many feel they "will always be Jamaican." This narrowly focused perception of citizenship suggest that Jamaican migrant teachers do not readily identify themselves as global and transnational citizens, yet their actions and lived experiences suggest otherwise. This is a clear indication of the need to prepare future teachers from Jamaica to be more globally aware.

Jamaica, like most of the islands of the Caribbean, is a highly globalized sphere, having experienced its first incorporation into the global economy through the Columbian voyages of the 1400s. The islands of the Caribbean experienced further global incorporation through colonial imperialism, and later through neoliberalism. While all these phases of global incorporation have focused primarily on the economic and political fortunes of many of the islands, the inherent policies have had significant impacts on the mandates, structure, function, and purpose of education (Thomas-Brown 2013; Thomas 2003). Historically, education on many of the Caribbean islands was instrumental in meeting the needs of the mother country. However, with the post-1950s independence of many islands, including Jamaica, the focus of education shifted to meet the needs of the newly independent country. Since the mid- to late 1970s, islands like Jamaica experienced the rise of the neoliberal age, and with this rise, the need to prepare more global citizens. This was especially so, given the new, more globally competitive economic realities and more capitalistic political/governmental expectations. Hence, the general notion that education mirrors society—and in a rapidly globalizing world it is imperative that education meets the needs of this globalized society—is pertinent to the context of many in these small island states. Given the substantial and foundational role of teachers in this and most societies in shaping future citizens, ground zero for such discussions, debates, and discourses has to be teacher preparation programs.

Since the mid-1990s Jamaica has experienced increased emigration of its qualified teachers. This emigration has raised several important questions pertaining to the curriculum mandates on the island, the preparation levels of the migrating teachers, brain drain, brain circulation, remittances and return flow gains, and the impact of the loss in qualified teachers on the quality of education on the island. Using the dialogues within existing citizenship debates, this research will begin to address some of these questions.

In Jamaica, many players in the teacher education sector have begun to grapple with the question of how to prepare teachers capable of purporting the global citizenship ideals. These are the ideals that allow for productive, informed, global citizens who are able to independently deliberate on existing and emerging global matters. The other challenge they face is figuring out what role, if any, do teacher trainers within the context of global education have on influencing teachers' perceptions of and assertions about their own citizenship/s. Citizenship scholars are actively engaged in debates about what constitutes a global as opposed to a transnational citizen, and although the distinctions are not yet quite clear, the fundamental understanding of this research is, be it global or transnational citizen, teacher educators in the Caribbean are attempting to train future and current teachers to be citizens who are equipped with the skills to function effectively in any country while still contributing to the greater good of their island-state and the globe. As this research attempts to answer some of the more pertinent questions, it also seeks to place the narratives reported on in this study within broader questions of citizenship and democratic theory, horizons of political citizenship and civic bonds, and it also attempts to contextualize conflicting civic and personal obligations (Smith 2013).

TEACHER EDUCATION AND GLOBAL EDUCATION

For the purposes of this research, global/transnational citizenship is an analytical lens through which conversations about teacher preparation programs globally can be constructed. So the arguments supporting the preparation of teachers everywhere for global education may be subsumed within the notion of global or transnational citizenship. As such, the need to be familiar with one's national and global contexts, connectivity(ies), is critical. This paper presents findings from ongoing research on a group of Jamaican immigrants working in the United States. The research methodology is qualitative, and it documents the lived experiences of these immigrants. The participants were selected using a combination of snowball and convenience sampling with a total of twelve immigrants and ten potential immigrants (in the process of migrating) being interviewed. In an attempt to learn more about the current teacher preparation procedures and the national response to teacher emigration, two government officials and five teachers college administrators and lecturers (professors) in Jamaica were also interviewed for this project. The study participants all agreed to an in-depth, face-to-face interview to discuss a range of topics pertaining to migration, citizenship, teachers' immigrant experiences, and the impact of permanent migration on forms of citizenship. The interview instrument has twenty-six questions. All except for the first three are open-ended and topics based. The questions ask the migrants and teachers to recount their immigrant experiences, their experiences working in urban schools, their perceptions of their citizenship/s, and their contact with their home country. All the interviews were tape recorded, transcribed, coded, and cross-coded to ascertain the emerging and dominant themes. The participants' stories were aligned with the dominant themes in the theoretical and contextual domains of global and transnational citizenship. Narrative analysis and critical discourse analysis are used to allow the teachers' culture and thinking to be heard, while preserving their voices. Using their personal histories helps to facilitate an understanding from the inside, hence rendering their lived experiences meaningful. One primary methodological feature and approach in the overall project is the presentation of small stories from the study participants. This narrativization of particular experiences in the overall teacher immigration story/experience acts as supporting data for the theoretical arguments advanced, while allowing for the immigrants' own perspectives on their citizenship identities (Georgakopoulou 2006).

Because this research focuses on educators who are global and transnational in both the lived and theoretical spaces, one is compelled to examine the nuances and debates surrounding global education. One of the fundamental challenges the participants in this study faced was how to reconcile their legal political citizenship with their transnational existences that tied them to their conflicting civic and personal obligations and how this conflict might impact their decisions about their legal political status and their cultural identities within the context of their roles as global educators.

According to Bremer (2007), "international education matters and philanthropic organizations are taking notice by funding projects that support the mission and goals of international educators" (41). Globalization's impact on higher education raises several fundamental questions; chief among these is how to serve the common good within the context of global norms (Segrera 2010). Learning and work can no longer occur within the vacuumed confines of national contexts because today's global marketplace demands workers who are internationally competent and equipped with new and emerging skill sets in order to solve global problems. Gaudelli (2009), quoting May (2008), confirmed this point by noting that capitalist globalization fosters solidarity, while offering workers internationalism as the path to their futures. This, according to Gallavan (2008), is rooted in the essence of global education, the content and processes for which involve cultivating a global perspective. This global perspective contains the attributes for ethical, pluralistic, and interdependent deliberations needed to efficiently navigate the world and be active citizens. Herein lies a complicated set of reciprocal factors and dimensions that have given rise to the Jamaican teacher as a global and/or transnational citizen. Citizenship categorizing of many Jamaican immigrants is dependent upon when, how, and why these individuals left the island, where these individuals migrated to, the category of migration (temporary/visitor, permanent, circular, work-based, or illegal) the individual falls into, the education level of the migrant, and how the migrant perceives the return flows that he/she facilitate to the island.

In Jamaica, as in many other places in the global south, the primary intersections between globalization and education begin with three main measures of globalization. These are trade, private cross-border financial flows including foreign direct investments (FDI), and migration. These measures of globalization influence the competitiveness and adaptability of a place to globalization through years of schooling (elementary/primary and high school/secondary school), and through vocational, college level, and international education (Thomas-Brown 2013). Trade and FDI have a positive effect on education and training. This is both direct, through more training, and indirect, through the available resources. However, according to Velde (2005), the overall effects are more positive in countries that are already relatively well endowed with education to start with. The complexity of international migration results in both positive and negative outcomes. The positive outcomes may be seen in the network effects on trade in goods, services, and remittances, whereas emigration from smaller countries results in apparent capacity losses in specific professions such as teaching. For many developing countries, vocational and college-level education are useful in attracting FDI; however, they need to be appropriate and include engineering and other technical skills (Velde 2005). Similar to Jamaica, there are examples from Thailand and South Korea that demonstrate how a pool of well-educated nationals abroad can act as a source for exports goods and services, and as a source for diaspora investment back into the home country, much of which goes toward daily living expenses and education.

"Global citizenship curriculum lacks natural consistency" (Gaudelli 2009, 77), making the need to examine notions of teaching for globalization that more pertinent within the context of the bigger picture. The big picture in this instance is that the core dimensions of global education include attention to global issues such as justice, equity, and sustainability. There is also a spatial dimension that focuses on global-local flows and perspectives; a temporal dimension that focuses on the interconnected nature of places over time; and a process dimension, which is the one most critical to teacher educators since it focuses on participatory actions, pedagogy, and the actualization of global citizenship (Zong, Wilson, and Quashiga 2008). This research found that the Planning Institute of Jamaica (PIOJ), the arm of the Government of Jamaica (GOJ) that monitors the number of teachers employed, unemployed, and trained each year, is of the view that teacher training institutions and departments on the island need to make three fundamental changes. The first measure they suggest is to train more STEM (science, technology, engineering, and math) teachers. Second, they recommend that there needs to be a reduction in the number of teachers who are trained in social science disciplines such as history, social studies, and music. The third and last measure they suggest is to incorporate more materials that allow trained teachers to be more globally adaptable. In the meantime, in order to improve the global opportunities for Jamaican teachers, the PIOJ in conjunction with the Ministry of Education on the island, have partnered with several recruiting agencies in Japan, China, Canada, and the United States in order to extend as well as provide new overseas employment opportunities for Jamaican teachers. This research finding clearly answers the questions on the purpose of global education and where the primary focus should lie. In the case of Jamaica, emphasis is on trade in human resource/capital, growth, poverty reduction, nation building, and sustainable development. Here is a clear case of education being viewed as a commodity; hence, it is a tradable in services. This is not unique, as examples may be drawn from the Philippines in Asia and several other Caribbean islands where many college-educated individuals are encouraged to migrate with the assumption that they will still contribute to the islands' economies through remittance. Evidence of this may be seen in the organization of annual diaspora conferences in Jamaica,[1] as well as the GOJ monitoring of the monetary value of not only remittances from the island's migrant population but also the monetary values of gifts reported to the diaspora organization. Taking all this into consideration, what then should the role of teacher education on the island be and what do teachers need to know in order to aid students as they navigate the world?

According to Holden and Hicks (2007), long-standing global issues include such things as poverty, the environment, and conflict and social justice. These issues, they argue, impact the world within which students live (see also Hutchinson 1996; Oscarsson 1996; Hicks and Holden 1995). Merryfield (2002) notes that "by examining different points of view, students develop the habit of looking for and considering other perspectives, especially those of people of minority cultures or from other continents" (19). It is important to note that the administrators interviewed for this project made the point that many of these topics and issues are slowly seeping into the materials presented to future teachers on the island.

According to Velde (2005), "the quality of education and training determines whether and how countries can participate in the process of globalization, such as global value chain, fragmentation, increased trade in final products, and migration" and this is fundamental to mapping one's citizenship (6). According to Tye (1999) in Holden and Hicks (2007), "global education involves learning about those problems and issues which cut across national boundaries and about the interconnectedness of systems, cultural, ecological, economic, political, and technological" (14). Thomas-Brown (2013) reports that in the context of Jamaican immigrants, global education is a demonstration of understanding, empathy, and appreciation for those perceived to be "others" and "neighbors." Such categorizing allows for more insightful interactions that penetrate cultural, geographic, economic, and social obstructions.

The participants' also intimated struggles with defining, naming, and categorizing their citizenship status in the United States; this was regardless of their actual legal status in the country. One of the struggles pertains to feeling that their American citizenship is "second class." They held this view because they thought that despite their work and contribution to the American education system, as well as the fact that they were living and working in this country legally, their Jamaican accents and overall socialization prevented them from being accepted as American by many of the American born/socialized individuals they interact with. While this finding immediately ties into the forever foreigner discourse, a more salient point is the fact that for these individuals, citizenship acceptance by others is not a function of the immigrant's level of education, but instead about the ability to assimilate to the extent that his/her immigrant status is not immediately identifiable. Many of the participants have acknowledged that by getting to that level of assimilation, questions such as "where are you from?" in reference to their speech patterns in particular, are avoided. This outcome increases their sense of belonging while simultaneously reducing occasions for them to vocalize an outsider status; see excerpts from two study participants:

> Citizenship is about belonging to somewhere and having something to identify with. Identifying with the norms of the environment in which you find yourself. For me citizenship is not static, it varies based on where you are. So it would be fair to say I am an American right now although I still hold on to some aspects of my Jamaican self. How do you throw away everything that you have known since birth, and growing up? I do not think I will truly be an American, even after I swear in, and because of this I think my American citizenship would be second-class in a sense. (Immigrant teacher in North Carolina—Ruth, forty-six years old, six years teaching in North Carolina)

> For me, my American citizenship is second class because I do not think I will ever be perceived as American. Americans will never look at me as an American ever, regardless of the passport as an artifact to prove my citizenship. I am fine with that. I am fine with being considered a second-class American citizen because deep down I am Jamaican and that is something I will never lose, because of my culture, socialization, and heritage. (Immigrant teacher in New York—Juliette, forty-five years old, seven years teaching in New York)

Alazzi (2011), Gaudelli (2009), and Merryfield (2002) have all noted that significant elements of global education include knowledge and inquiry into global interconnectedness, global issues, and the need to be open-minded, as it facilitates sensitivity to varied perspectives. This in essence allows for the recognition of biases, stereotyping, and exotification and is best practiced within the context of intercultural experiences, understandings, and competencies. As it related to immigrants, however, research has shown that only a small number of teacher preparation courses around the globe attempt to actively promote global education. Although this is the case, the nature of teacher training programs in many developed countries does allow instructors and professors opportunities to infuse global education and global perspectives into their lessons. According to Segrera (2010), when instructors are given the latitude to infuse some global education into their classes, it allows for a broader social mandate that provides more relevant and innovative curricula. Much of the global education aspect of teacher education programs is still somewhat limited though, as the focus themes tend to be reformist education, wealth, and power and rights disparities. This limited infusion of global education in education programs so far means that the open-mindedness and sensitivity that can be facilitated by broader focuses and themes is yet to materialize. This point was evident in the stories of many of the migrant Jamaica teachers, who when interviewed indicated their objection to being perceived or described as exotic. For them, exotification disparages their past and present struggles to achieve success, puts them into the category of "other," and effectively makes them second-class citizens in their adopted country.

Increased diversity in many countries around the world has led to an augmented push for global education. This push is steeped in dialogues around issues of citizenship, race equality, sustainability and climate change, political conflicts, global economic flux, and social and cultural changes. This brings to the fore contestations and problems regarding the impact of these changes on notions of identity and sense of belonging. The other issue highlighted is the logistical issue of where these conversations should be facilitated. According to Gaudelli (2009, 75) there has been a "shift evident in the past 60 years away from national citizenship and towards standing as a person irrespective of national affiliations or the lack thereof."

Since the postindependence period, the islands of the Caribbean, including Jamaica, have strived toward greater self-determination. In the region, as in many other parts of the world, teacher education derives its curriculum agenda from a range of stakeholders, focusing primarily on national and regional standards and themes such as planning, assessment, and classroom behavior management. This has left little or no room for the infusion of global education themes and global citizenship. The postindependence period saw Caribbean islands, led by Jamaica, Barbados, and Trinidad, diligently changing school curriculums, exit requirements, and high school/secondary level standardized examinations to reflect Caribbean and island-specific themes, topics, and issues. This was essentially a postcolonial shift toward a more nationalist focus that was seen by the GOJ as being more relevant to local needs. However, with a chronically slow growing economy, high unemployment, and large foreign debt, the GOJ has acknowledged the significant role played by remittances to the island from its migrant population (January to March 2013 remittances to the island accounted for USD 309.3 million: see PIOJ publication for 2013[2]) in sustaining the fragile economy. One direct impact of this acknowledgment is on teacher training where a gradual move toward encouraging stakeholders to increasingly infuse global topics, themes, issues, and technology into teacher education is being adopted as a strategy to make Jamaican teachers more globally marketable over time.

INCLUDING GLOBAL EDUCATION AND GLOBAL CITIZENSHIP THEMES IN EDUCATION

Holden and Hicks's (2007) study found that most future teachers wish to learn more about global issues because they think this will allow them to better facilitate their own students when such discussions, questions, and topics are raised because there is a fundamental link between active citizenship and global awareness. Similar studies from Banks (2008) and Hanvey (1976) found that many future teachers, while enthusiastic about infusing the global perspective into their future teaching, were hesitant about how and when to do so, particularly as it pertains to sensitive topics that have inherent biases. These concerns expressed by future teachers are a direct outcome of the limited and/or fragmented infusion of the global perspective into their teacher preparation courses. While here in the United States students seems to have the opportunities to be exposed to global perspectives and themes in the courses they take, there are regulatory groups and time constraints that influence how much of this information is made available to these future teachers in usable form for classroom practice. This is important because it calls into questions notions of academic mobility within the context of continued national structure.

What has been evident from this research is that there needs to be some modification of the roles and pedagogy of teachers as well as increased exposure to and training in the use of new and emerging information technologies. These elements, according to all the participants in this study, are essential. In fact, all the immigrants interviewed noted that teacher preparation programs in Jamaica could have done more to prepare them for the pedagogical and technological classroom expectations they encountered once they migrated from the island. While there are obvious shortfalls related to pedagogical and technological preparation in these courses, more than three-quarters of the immigrants interviewed noted that with regard to content-knowledge, teaching experience, and ability to handle difficult situations and students, their Jamaican teacher training provided them with superior skills. The other issue arising from the interviews was related to the certification process and how best to organize this so that national and state interests/needs could be maintained, while infusing the global issues that would allow the teacher to be academically mobile. In this sense, academic mobility allows for credentials earned in one country or state to be transferable to another academic body, country, or state setting without the requirement of complete retraining. The challenges that face many educators are the absence of an agreed-upon definition for global competence and the inability to immediately ascertain whether the teachers and the students they serve meet the basic standards of global preparedness. According to an American Council for Education (ACE) report (1988) in Hunter (2004, 8), in order "to be globally competent, one must have four or more international college courses and have an unspecified ability to speak a foreign language." This is, however, a very limited view of such an important concept because it does not meaningfully provide for the complexity of global education, experience, and competencies aforementioned. Excerpts from several participants in this study indicate that for many immigrant Jamaican teachers, this is a real-life issue.

> Myself along with many other teachers who migrated from the Caribbean are currently facing the challenges of being granted state teaching certification. I applied for New York teaching certification and basically had to go back to school and redo all the teaching courses I had done in Jamaica. I also had to do the same when I lived in Virginia. When I applied for the New York teaching certification under the process of reciprocity, they informed me that I had to redo another set of courses before I could become eligible for the teaching certification, despite the fact that I was reciprocating and had completed a master's of education in the United States. I know of two ladies who came to the United States on permanent residency cards (green card) who are having the same issues.

(Immigrant in Long Island, New York—Ariel, thirty-six years old, four years teaching in New York)

Just to do my master's in early childhood education my university told me that I needed more credits in math and English. Based on what I was told by the academic advisor at the university I applied to, while completing my bachelor's degree in Jamaica, I should have done more prerequisite courses in language, math, and humanities. They refused to accept my teachers' college credits from Jamaica because they say that my teachers' college diploma was not a bachelor's degree. It's like an associate degree so it does not count. (Immigrant in New Jersey—Jody, thirty-eight years old, three years teaching in New Jersey)

Notable is the fact that the study participants indicated that they do possess global competence, which is important to them as cross-border workers. For them, global competence is the possession of cultural capital that allows one to understand, empathize with, and communicate in an array of cultural settings, but their foreign-gained credentials are not as readily accepted despite their demonstrated skill set. It is the knowledge and awareness of global topics, trends, events, issues, and debates that allow one to be able to effectively communicate across geographic, cultural, and linguistic borders. All of the study participants have accepted this as a fact of life, and that makes them competent teachers in US schools. "Global educators help students explore other cultures through literature, history, news, and Web Sites from other parts of the world (Merryfield 2002, 19). This, for Merryfield (2002) and Alazzi (2011), allows these individuals to be open-minded, resistant to stereotyping, and able to communicate across cultures while establishing connections between themselves and other countries, international organizations, and cultures, thus allowing students to participate more meaningfully as global citizens.

Based on my experience, socialization, and culture I think I am able to help my students to see the world in a bigger framework, show them that it is bigger than their city, which is where they know. I also see that the values that they have are far different from how I was raised in Jamaica, so sometimes during my class time I may find a little moment to include a character lesson or moral value to show them that not everyone shares their views on life and the world. (Immigrant in Long Island, New York—Ariel, thirty-six years old, four years teaching in New York)

What I do makes my students better global citizens. I know I impact them based and what I hear in informal conversations with them. Many of the kids have no idea about the world, and their perceptions of other places are limited. When I talk to them and show them pictures of people and places in Jamaica and other places globally they seem to constantly have the a-ha moments. Most of my kids have never been outside of their city, South Bronx, so I can see where I am making a difference with them wanting to know about other people and places and wanting to explore what else is out there apart from just where they live. (Immigrant in the Bronx, New York—Sandra, thirty-five years old, four years teaching in New York)

In the United States, the research literature on schools and citizenship proves otherwise. Knight Abowitz and Harnish (2006), as well as Westheimer and Kahne (2004a), indicate that traditional/personally responsible views of citizenship are dominant discourses in schools. Furthermore, in a Westheimer and Kahne (2004b) study, it was found that citizenship education is hardly discussed in the public schools (in this case, Chicago) and it is feared that the lack of citizenship education is typical in the United States. The immigrants interviewed for this research taught global citizenship education as an appendage to the formal curriculum because they thought that their students' knowledge of global issues was limited. For all the immigrants who did this, their justification are steeped in comparisons between the Jamaican and American education systems as well how children are socialized and exposed to the world around them.

ARE THERE REALLY MULTIPLE FORMS OF CITIZENSHIP?

Before I became a transnational citizen, I would have said that citizenship meant to me where you belong. The particular country or place you are from. But now it is more a mental thing of where I see myself, where I fit in. (Immigrant in Florida—Althea, thirty-three years old, eight years teaching in Florida)

For me it's pretty cut and dry, I'm a Jamaican. Yes, I have a green card, but living somewhere does not make you of that place. I live here, I worked here, and that's just because of circumstances. My citizenship is who I am, so even if I did carry around a passport or papers that say I am an American citizen, am I really? Am I going to feel like I am? (Immigrant in New York—Juliette, forty-five years old, seven years teaching in New York)

I'm Jamaican, I'm American, I'm transnational, and I'm global. I have integrated myself into the American society but that does not make me any less Jamaican. It does not take away from what I've learned in Jamaica. I think what I learned in Jamaica has prepared me for where I am today. I am here and I'm appreciative of what I'm doing in this country. However, I do not want to throw away what I have gotten from my home country. (Immigrant in North Carolina—Valerie, thirty-nine years old, seven years teaching in North Carolina)

This section starts with three excerpts from interviews with migrant Jamaica teachers in New York and North Carolina. There narratives confirm research that indicates that there are different forms of membership, activity, and identity that we may call citizenship, and they are products of social and political processes of construction (Smith 2013). Correspondingly, figure 5.1 shows that notions of citizenship in Jamaica are connected to the global, and as it is constructed and reconstructed, there is a tendency for it to correspond with the changing and declining economic fortunes on the island. In Jamaica, there are strong connections between economic fortunes and levels of education. Education is highly valued, and for many, it is seen as one of the most acceptable routes out of poverty as indicated by nearly all the participants in this study.

The nature of education in Jamaica and its connection to the global may be contextualized by figure 5.1 (adapted from Gaudelli 2009, 70). In this figure, the X axis is the tangible-imaginary and represents the extent to which global citizenship is suffused into national institutions and processes. The Y axis represents competitive-cooperation and indicates the level of competitiveness or cooperativeness of citizenship actions. In Jamaica, the vision of global citizenship intersects to produce competitive-tangible-cooperative individuals, given the nature of K–12 curricula and the outcome. Despite this,

FIGURE 5.1. Jamaica added to Gaudelli's heuristic of global citizenship

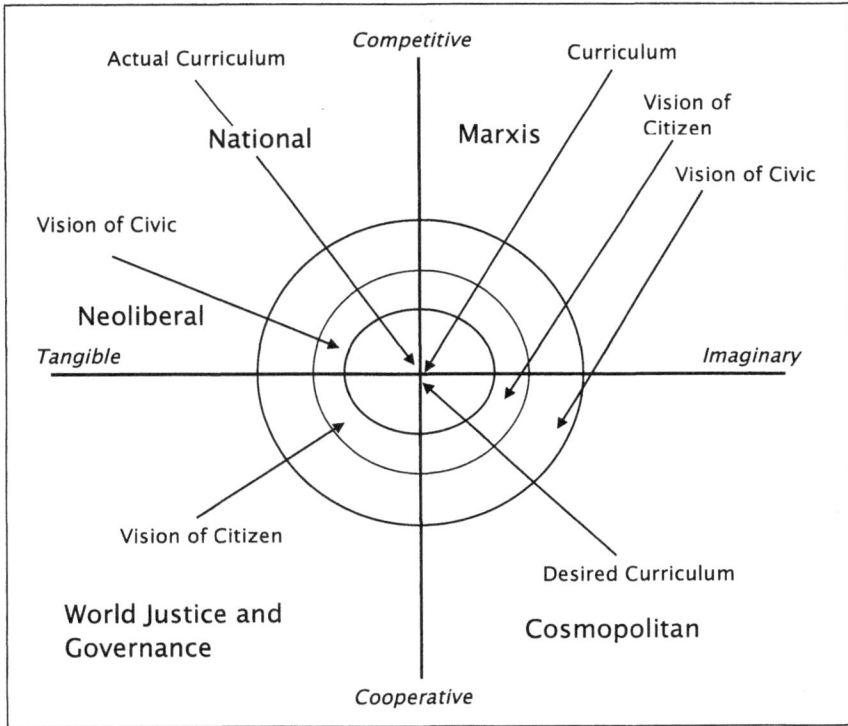

the desired outcome is a global citizen who is more cosmopolitan (Thomas-Brown 2013).

For an island like Jamaica, the concept of the nation-state goes far beyond the political realm. Figure 5.1 shows that nation-state and nationalist ideas still play a significant role in education. This is punctuated by the regional ideals that are also important, though less so when compared to the global perspectives that are needed. It is important to note that since the 1960s, the Caribbean has had several regional agreements that have attempted to make the region more integrated, but they have seen little success. In addition, while some Jamaican immigrants will migrate to other Caribbean islands, the United States, Canada, and the United Kingdom are often seen as more attractive migration destinations. Therefore, while regional knowledge is useful, it does not carry as much importance because many Jamaicans do not perceive that the titles "Caribbean" or "West Indian" denote that they are citizens with rights to and within the region. They really see themselves as citizens of Jamaica, which happens to be located in the region and citizens of the world. This is because becoming a citizen of the United States, Canada, and the United Kingdom carries more overall value than becoming a citizen of another Caribbean island.

Citizenship is a socially, politically, and academically contested construct, with implications for responsibilities to and rights of the state. All these aspects of citizenship intersect and often conflict for the migrant Jamaican teachers interviewed for this project. Almost all the interviewees indicated that while they have no intentions of ever living in Jamaica again, they do retain their Jamaican citizenship, opting to remain green card holders because for them, surrendering their Jamaican citizenship made them feel like they were betraying their home country. A few of the teachers represented the counternarrative because they were able to separate their citizenship into legal/political and cultural, and for those individuals, their legal/political citizenship as Americans, did not diminish their cultural claims to Jamaica. The following excerpts are examples of these narratives.

> I am a dual citizen. I am very American in the way I talk and my lifestyle. I also consider myself a transnational or even global citizen, I am Jamaican all around. (Immigrant in Florida—Althea, thirty-three years old, eight years teaching in Florida)

> Becoming a citizen of this country means I can do so much more, I can vote; I have a say. My accent may be different, many Americans may not see me as equal, but I still have a say in whatever happens. For me, citizenship doesn't really have anything to do with belonging. I don't know if the Americans I have to interact with daily make me feel like I belong or not. I still refer to Jamaica as home, even though this is home to me now. I however, feel like this is where I want to be. So citizenship for me is not so much belonging, it's more of where I feel like I want to be, it's about my having a voice, it's about my being able to vote, it gives me the opportunity to improve my life. (Migrant teacher in North Carolina—Ruth, forty-six years old, six years teaching in North Carolina)

It is important to add that many of the study participants perceive themselves as global or transnational citizens because of their ties to both Jamaica and the country to which they migrated. Also important is the fact that many Jamaicans, premigration, view themselves as global citizens because of their connections to countries that their relatives and friends have migrated to as well as their connections to countries that they hope to migrate to in the future. A related debate is the intrinsic limited value placed on Jamaican citizenship by some, because it is not associated with economic and social successes and global citizenship from the Jamaican perspective.

Incorporating the conversation on nation-state into the value placed on Jamaican citizenship, Rapoport (2009, 23) adds that citizenship is often interpreted as an individual's relationship with a nation-state. Within the context of this study, notions of the nation-state's ties to these discourses and categorizations of citizenship have diminished, due mostly to the impact and pervasiveness of globalization and the ideological nature of the concept of nation-state and its ancillary, nation building. Hence, the concept of the nation-state is a vulnerable one, because of a state's implicit predisposition to change in response to internal and external forces.

The transformative nature of the nation-state and notions of citizenship are precipitated by the rise in global consciousness and global citizenship as seen in the migrant Jamaican teachers interviewed in this study. Shifts from nationalistic focus to transborder changes and their impacts on individual choice, tolerance, vulnerability, and social participation are important within the numerous definitions and conceptions of citizenship and in the lived citizenships of these study participants. Fundamental to this study is the notion of cosmopolitan citizenship. For the immigrants, fostering tolerance, being willing to engage openly with others, and seeking out diverse social and cultural experiences among their students are integral parts of their professional role. For them, these are practices they have had to incorporate into their own lives since migrating from Jamaica. Hence, these statements by the study participants cement them as global citizens because they have been able to maintain a dual existence steeped in patriotism toward Jamaica, despite their physical absence from the island. They are also fiercely loyal to principles of equality and freedom, which can be attributed to their insider-outsider perspective on issues of race, ethnicity, and native-born nationality.

PERSPECTIVES FROM JAMAICA

There has been accelerated out-migration of teachers from several Caribbean islands in response to recruitment drives that originate in the United States,

Canada, and the United Kingdom since the mid-1990s. These recruitment drives have attracted the most qualified, highly skilled, and experienced teachers in exchange for the possibility of improved economic prospects in developed countries. The islands' responses to this teacher emigration ranges from lack of awareness to improved local working conditions, changed national curricula, increased wages and salaries for teachers, and facilitation of the emigration process (Degazon-Johnson 2008, 2007; Ministry of Education of Jamaica 2004). One of the problems teachers in Jamaica face is the disparity between the numbers of teachers graduating each year and the number of teaching positions available in K–12 schools. According to one GOJ official at PIOJ, each year teacher training institutions and teaching departments graduate an average of one thousand new teachers, but during the last five years (2008–13) fewer than five hundred new teaching positions were created in the approximately 1,007 public schools (K–12) on the island. The outcome of this obvious oversupply of teachers is high levels of unemployment. In 2013, the GOJ through the Ministry of Education hosted a teachers' fair to ascertain the number of unemployed teachers on the island as well as to establish a registry. At the end of the fair, over two thousand unemployed teachers had attended the event and signed up to the registry. In response, the GOJ has continued to encourage the migration of teachers from the island, and according to unofficial statistics from PIOJ, approximately three hundred teachers have migrated through these recruitment drives between 2011 and 2013. This figure is unofficial because the GOJ has not been able to efficiently track the out-migration of teachers. This is because when migrating many teachers have not actually reported that their move is precipitated by a job offer or for the purposes of family reunification. It is anticipated that the number of individuals leaving the island for the purpose of teaching overseas will triple within the next two years (2014–16) in response to an articulation agreement that the GOJ is negotiating with Canada and China to employ Jamaican teachers.

Migration from Jamaica is not a new phenomenon. Historically, the island experienced droves of out-migration during the pre- and early independence periods of the late 1950s to mid-1960s and during periods of political crisis (for example, 1979–81). The negative impacts of emigration from this island, such as brain drain, loss of local earning power, negative multiplier effect, import dependency, and human capital loss are well studied. The last decade has seen the islands of the Caribbean as a whole losing as much as 70 percent of their college-trained workforce to developed countries (Degazon-Johnson 2007; Mishra 2006). For example, between 2001 and 2003, Jamaica lost approximately one thousand teachers to the United Kingdom alone. While acknowledging the human capital loss, several studies (Thomas-Brown 2013; Dodman 2009; Timms 2008; Kingsbury 2005) have pointed to the benefits many of the Caribbean islands derive from the skilled migration of some of their educated population; chief among them being return flows (remittances, barrels, other gifts, and returning residents/circular migrants). However, these benefits tend to add to speculations about the migrants' citizenship and legal nationality as well as the transnational nature of the flows they facilitate. This is a point emphasized by all the teachers interviewed for this project. They all noted that they contribute the remittance flows to care for relatives and friends on the island. Additionally, many of them spend an average of USD 1,500 on trips "home," and they contribute to brain circulation via contributions to the schools they attended and/or worked at prior to migrating from the island. Below are two excerpts that demonstrate this point.

I am taking care of my younger siblings who still live in Jamaica. It often comes down to the money! Teaching wherever you are, you are not going to be a millionaire, but I find that working here my money has more value than when I was living and working there [Jamaica]. I go back to Jamaica twice a year, usually during spring break and summer time and trips are normally USD 3,000 at minimum, so that is USD 6,000 yearly just on the trips, and every month I send USD 200 = USD 2,400 each year. (Immigrant in the Bronx, New York—Sandra, thirty-five years old, four years teaching in New York)

I feel obligations to be back to Jamaica. I work in a great classroom that has the latest technology and I am working with an organization to set up a similar classroom in my old school in Jamaica. I also Skype lessons so that kids there can see what's going on here. Whenever I can I go back home and use some of what I've learned here, for example, new methodologies, new materials, and new techniques. I share ideas and lesson plans with teachers back home. If I know of someone who is going to Jamaica to visit, I will send stuff, like charts to give to a teacher down there. (Migrant teacher in North Carolina—Ruth, forty-six years old, six years teaching in North Carolina)

In Jamaica, the general consensus among those who work in teacher training institutions and in the university department devoted to teacher education is one of lack of inclusion in the recruitment and emigration of teachers. The advertisements that attract the best of the island's teachers are placed in local newspapers and on the Internet with no collaboration taking place between the local teaching institutions and the recruiting agencies. There is also the lack of knowledge among those who work in teacher training institutions about the recruitment protocols used, as well as the extent to which the rights of the recruited teachers are considered during the recruiting process. Despite this, it is generally accepted that the migration experience enhances one's proficiencies, and there are benefits for both the recruiting country and the home country of the teachers. Conversations with teachers' college administrators and lecturers in Jamaica indicate some consensus about how the emigration of teachers is perceived. According to one lecturer interviewed, "we do not see globalization as a threat, we see it as a positive, widening scope that always enhances a person's development, and the bicultural experience/exchange whether temporary or permanent, can benefit countries." While such perspectives acknowledge the potential benefits of teacher emigration, there are no published studies to substantiate or refute these claims. Also absent are studies that indicate the possible negative impact of teacher emigration on the quality of the island's K–12 education system. The other concerning factor is that neither the study participants nor teachers planning to migrate from the island in the future seem knowledgeable about the adjustment process for immigrants after they move. This was a critical point for the immigrants interviewed for this project. All the teachers indicated that despite the content knowledge they acquired during their teacher training in Jamaica, they felt unprepared for the social and cultural adjustments they needed to make upon migrating to the United States. An additional point that came out of these conversations was the notion that if the island of Jamaica wanted to continue "exporting" teachers, then more global topics, themes, and information about the education system in countries like the United States needed to be included into their teacher training programs. All the immigrants interviewed noted that recruiting agencies tend to disproportionately place the recruited immigrants into urban schools, even though most of them know little to nothing about urban education in the United States prior to their arrival at their teaching jobs.

The notion of differentiated citizenship is the norm for some immigrants. Some of the immigrants interviewed for this study acknowledged that the differentiated nature of their citizenship due to the legal vulnerabilities were precipitated by the fact that they are naturalized. Many were not saddened by this reality, instead finding comfort and solace in the fact that they "will always be Jamaican" and if necessary, could return "home" at any time. Such sentiments must be contextualized by the fact that the study focused on highly educated (a minimum bachelor's degree) legal immigrants, who would, if they returned to Jamaica, have the potential to live relatively survivable lives on Jamaican incomes. The unanswered question in this study is, how would lesser-educated individuals and those who are not legal immigrants perceive references to their citizenship in the United States as not fully uniform or unitary or semicitizenship. Overall, the immigrants had strong connections to national citizenship, which they ascribed to Jamaica, and they often connected it to their cultural identity, which was generally more important to them than their legal citizenship status in the United States. All the immigrants interviewed recognized their role as transnational citizens but did not view their continued participation in Jamaica as completely obligatory. When asked outright questions about how they saw themselves, they were more inclined to describe themselves as global educators. This is because they saw themselves as exposing their American students to more global contexts. In fact, they are transnational citizens who contribute both economic and social remittances to Jamaica while maintaining citizenship ideals, practices, and status that is not Jamaican.

Spring (2008), while quoting the Global Commission on International Migration (2005), indicated that brain circulation is a process "in which migrants return to their own country on a regular or occasional basis, sharing the benefits of the skills and resources they have acquired while living abroad." Another finding from this research indicates that this contextualizes some of the debates around teacher emigration in Jamaica. Many Jamaicans believe that with teacher emigration, the island loses valuable human capital, while others focus on the return flows to the islands. Few discussions focus on the notion of brain circulation, which the PIOJ incorporates under the broad umbrella of social remittances. Brain circulation is relevant to those teachers who choose to return to the island after their contracts overseas end. Those teachers who choose to return to the island convey an enhanced worldview that has the potential to positively impact the teaching and learning process.

Relevant theories of critical, crisis, and transformational pedagogies (Freire, 2000) suggest that those who work in teacher training institutions encourage their students and graduates to be global citizens. This is not always the case, because the curricula taught are structured and assessed by one governing body (the Joint Board of Teacher Education) and as mentioned earlier in this paper, the primary focus remains on nationalist themes to meet the needs of Caribbean-based standardized testing at the end of primary (elementary) and high (secondary) school. Therefore, it was the general consensus that global citizenship themes were not routinely infused in the curriculum, and when infused, were limited to the teacher's/lecturer's knowledge, perceptions, and experience with globalization. Additionally, those conversations with college lecturers indicate that there is a growing demand for local teachers to be more globally focused, more tolerant of those they perceive as different from themselves, and that they be able to communicate more clearly using a global language.

Some language barriers also exist in the process of preparing the ideal global-citizen-teacher. Many would perceive English as the global language, and in the Jamaican context, English is the language used in schools and it is the island's official language. However, for many Jamaican children, English is not usually the first language learned. Given this fact, an ordinary assumption would be that English in schools would be taught as a second language; however, this is not the case. This approach to the teaching and learning of (British) English on the island does present some communication challenges for many future teachers. There is also consensus that given the extent of transnational migration and the numbers of local teachers who emigrate to developed countries in response to recruitment drives, there should be some standardization of teaching certifications that would allow those who choose to emigrate, the opportunity to transition more smoothly into the new country. An anecdote from one immigrant working in Virginia puts one aspect of this adaptation into perspective.

Language-wise, the standard Jamaican English is pretty much British English. However, I did not have an American accent so I had to work my American accent for the kids to understand what I was saying. I had to reshape the vowels to get the sound that they would understand. Because, when I spoke to them in standard Jamaican English they did not understand me and I could see that there was a language barrier developing. As for spelling, I had to abandon my spelling. I remember once I wrote a letter home to a parent with the word behavior and the spelling had the U in it. The boy came back and said to me, "My mama says you don't know how to spell." (Immigrant in Virginia—Simone, thirty-six years old, three years teaching in Virginia)

Similar to teacher educators in the United States, teacher educators in Jamaica are faced with the need to incorporate global citizenship principles into curricula and pedagogy as they respond to the transformational nature of globalization and increased global interdependence. Zong (2009) notes that in an interconnected world, one's survival is directly tied to one's capacity to understand and effectively interact with changes that originate outside of national settings. Several of the migrant Jamaican teachers view themselves as more Jamaican than American; however, they hold loyalties to both countries. For the most part, American naturalization does not negate their feelings of obligation to their home country. Many noted that they feel compelled to remain involved politically, especially via social media through such campaigns as "speak you mind Jamaica," "on the ground report," and "think Jamaica" on Facebook and Twitter. They say that while they cannot return home to vote in elections, they are still able to contribute to the political process on the island, by voicing their opinions.

> I do feel obligated to contribute money and other assistance to my family who live there. I know a lot of people down there if they get help they would be better off, so I offer that help when I can. Despite this, nothing will cancel out the fact that I am a brain-drainer, if I were in Jamaica teaching in the classroom I would've given more than whatever I sent to Jamaica in remittances or whatever other contributions I make. (Immigrant teacher in New York—Juliette, forty-five years old, seven years teaching in New York)

TEACHER EDUCATION AND JAMAICAN IMMIGRANTS: A WAY FORWARD

The 2012–13 congressional debates on immigration and the passing of the "Dream Act" in 2012 are among a plethora of factors that point to the importance of discussing the citizenship experiences and perceptions of this group of migrant teachers. Also important is the question of how teacher training in the Caribbean, and Jamaica in particular, will adapt to the increasing impetus of many their graduates to emigrate. To address these questions and concerns, several cultural conversations must be rearticulated to encourage potential migrants to be more culturally and socially adaptive and responsive to their potential work environments. Within these conversations, Smith (2013) postulates that empirical realities seem morally desirable to define meaningfully equal citizenship as unitary, uniform citizenship and that civil rights struggles on behalf of "equal citizenship" are not just normative but tangible. These are factors that current and potential immigrants need to become informed about. This brings to the fore the pervasiveness of citizenship education, that is, encouraging students to become "good citizens." The incorporation of these principles into all aspects of teacher training on the islands should facilitate the creation of the "global citizen/teacher," one who possesses the skill sets that make him/her an effective teacher in any country or setting within which he/she chooses to work.

Globalization is reflected in two aspects of teacher education programs in many national systems: in the diversity of the student population that teacher candidates are required to support, and in the rhetoric of the proclaimed goals of these programs. The achievement of the stated goals, however, is influenced by Jamaica's historical and political realities that have determined the economic, social, and cultural climate of the island. These factors have encouraged many to look outward, rather that inward. The tensions between global and local aspects of teacher education are important considerations for the immigrant from Jamaica. As it stands now, the education necessary to prepare college graduates to be globally competent lacks clarity, uniformity, and direction. Therefore, a rethinking/reimagining of the regional (Caribbean) and nationalist focus of the island's education addenda as well as exit standards for teachers will have to be embedded within the curriculum and pedagogy practices for teacher education. Such efforts should be aimed at emboldening practitioners to begin to feel comfortable enough to attempt to infuse global and cosmopolitan citizenship into their lived identities and daily teaching.

Second-class citizenship rhetoric of unequal citizenship due to race, genders, country of origin, speech patterns, cultural practices, and other-ness, are issues highlighted by the Jamaican immigrants in this study. According to these individuals notions of color and a foreign accent are seen as the major indicators by which they perceive their American citizenship second class because they must first acclimate to the racially divided nature of this country and adjust to a country that uses equal opportunity laws and rules to meet diversity requirements within the context of several racially tense contemporary issues. Additionally, these immigrants grapple with gaining acceptance from those they label as "other," and this often includes African Americans, whom they perceive as having some hostility toward them. This point must be underscored by the fact that many of these immigrants have never lived in a society that is divided strictly along racial lines, and for the most part, the discrimination they have experienced in Jamaica is more economic discrimination, or home-address discrimination, which is a subcategory of economic discrimination. Paradoxically, they also perceive their American citizenship as an ideologically and tangibly prized possession because it attaches them to a country they hold in high regard. Having American citizenship removes many of the visa restrictions that are placed on the travels of Jamaicans and offers them the opportunity to gain an array of successes. It also allows them to facilitate a plethora of return-flows to the island. US citizenship is viewed as something desired by many "back home," hence, a form of upward mobility, and for some it is something to boast about.

NOTES

1. Jamaica Diaspora Organization: http://www.jamaicadiaspora.org/#.
2. Review of Economic Performance, January–March 2013, Planning Institute of Jamaica: http://pioj.gov.jm/Portals/o/Economic_Sector/Press%20Confer ence%20v17n4%20website-new.pdf.

WORKS CITED

Alazzi, Khaled. 2011. "Teachers Perceptions and Conceptions of Global Education: A Study of Jordanian Secondary Social Studies Teachers." *Journal of Multiculturalism in Education* 7: 1–19.

Banks, J. A. 2008. *An Introduction to Multicultural Education.* 4th ed. Boston: Allyn and Bacon.

Beetham, David. 1999. *Democracy and Human Rights.* Malden, MA: Blackwell.

Bremer, Darlene. 2007. "Missions Driven." *International Educator* 16 (3): 40–47.

Bromley, Patricia. 2009. "Cosmopolitanism in Civic Education: Exploring Cross-National Trends, 1970–2008." *Current Issues in Comparative Education* 12 (3): 33–44.

Degazon-Johnson, Rolande. 2007. *Migration and Commonwealth Small States— The Case of Teachers and Nurses* (Report). University of The West Indies

Sir Arthur Lewis Institute of Social and Economic Studies (SALISES) and Commonwealth Secretariat Conference. Barbados, May 2007. www .Thecommonwealth.Org/Files/182470/Filesname/Uwisaliseslabourmarket conference_May2007_1.Pdf, accessed November 1, 2011.

————. 2008. "Ethical Recruitment Standards: The Case of the Commonwealth Teachers Recruitment Protocol." Paper presented at the American Federation for Teachers Migration Conference, Chicago. www.Thecommonwealth.Org/Files/182468/Filename/Aftmigrationforumpresentation_July08_.Pdf, accessed November 1, 2011.

Dodman, D. 2009. "Globalization, Tourism, and Local Living Conditions on Jamaica's North Coast." *Singapore Journal of Tropical Geography* 30: 204–19.

Freire, Paulo. 2000. *Pedagogy of the Oppressed 30th Anniversary Edition*. New York: Bloomsbury Academic.

Gallavan, Nancy. 2008. "Examining Teacher Candidates' View on Teaching World Citizenship." *Social Studies* (November/December): 249–54.

Gaudelli, William. 2009. "Heuristics of Global Citizenship Discourses towards Curriculum Enhancement." *Journal of Curriculum Theorizing* 25 (1): 68–85.

Gaudelli, William, and William Fernekes. 2004. "Teaching about Global Human Rights for Global Citizenship." *Social Studies* 95 (1): 16–26.

Georgakopoulou, Alexandra. 2006. "Thinking Big with Small Stories in Narrative and Identity Analysis." *Narrative Inquiry* 16 (1): 122–30.

Hanvey, Robert G. 1976. *An Attainable Global Perspective*. New York: Global Perspectives in Education.

Hicks, David, and Cathie Holden. 1995. *Visions of the Future: Why We Need to Teach for Tomorrow*. Stoke-on-Trent: Trentham Books.

Holden, Cathie, and David Hicks. 2007. "Making Global Connections: The Knowledge, Understanding, and Motivation of Trainee Teachers." *Teaching and Teacher Education* 23: 13–23.

Hunter, William. 2004. "Got Global Competency?" *International Educator* 13 (2): 6–12.

Hutchinson, Francis. 1996. *Educating beyond Violent Futures*. London: Routledge.

Kammen, Michael. 1993. "The Problem of American Exceptionalism: A Reconsideration." *American Quarterly* 45 (1): 1–43.

Kingsbury, P. 2005. "Jamaican Tourism and the Politics of Employment." *Geoforum* 36: 113–32.

Knight Abowitz, Kathleen, and J. Jason Harnish. 2006. "Contemporary Discourses of Citizenship." *Review of Educational Research* 76 (4): 653–90.

Lee, Wing On, and Sai Wing Leung. 2006. "Global Citizenship Education in Hong Kong and Shanghai Secondary Schools: Ideals, Realities, and Expectations." *Citizenship Teaching and Learning* 2 (2): 68–84.

Levy, Daniel, and Natan Sznaider. 2004. "The Institutionalization of Cosmopolitan Morality: The Holocaust and Human Rights." *Journal of Human Rights* 3 (2): 143–57.

Merryfield, Merry. 2002. "The Difference a Global Educator Can Make." *Educational Leadership* 60 (2): 18–21.

Ministry of Education of Jamaica. 2004. *Protocol for the Recruitment of Commonwealth Teachers* (Report). www.Thecommonwealth.Org/Shared_Asp_Files/GFSR.Asp?NoDeid=39311, accessed November 1, 2011.

Mishra, Sangay. 2006. "Citizenship, Political Participation, and Transnationalism: South Asian Immigrants in the U.S." Paper presented at the Annual Meeting of the American Political Science Association, Philadelphia, August 31–September 3.

Oscarsson, V. 1996. "Young People's Views of The Future." In *Teaching for Citizenship in Europe*, edited by Audrey Osler, Hanns-Fred Rathenow, and Hugh Starkey. Stoke-on-Trent: Trentham Books.

Pogge, Thomas. 2008. *World Poverty and Human Rights: Cosmopolitan Responsibilities and Reform.* Malden, MA: Polity Press.

Rapoport, Anatoli. 2008. "We Cannot Teach What We Don't Know: Indiana Teachers Talk about Global Citizenship Education." Paper presented at the National Council for the Social Studies Annual Meeting, Houston, Texas, November 14, 2008.

———. 2009. "Lonely Business or Mutual Concern: The Role of Comparative Education in the Cosmopolitan Citizenship Debates." *Current Issues in Comparative Education* 12 (1): 23–32. www.Tc.Edu/Cice.

Schweisfurth, Michele. 2006. "Education for Global Citizenship: Teacher Agency and Curricular Structure in Ontario Schools." *Educational Review 58* (1): 41–50.

Segrera, Francisco. 2010. *Trends and Innovations in Higher Education Re-Form: Worldwide, Latin America, and in the Caribbean.* Research and Occasional Paper Series: CSHE.12.10 Center Doe Studies in Higher Education, University of California, Berkeley.

Smith, Rogers. 2013. "The Questions Facing Citizenship in the 21st Century." Keynote lecture at "The Meaning of Citizenship" conference, Wayne State University, Detroit, Michigan, March 21, 2013.

Spring, Joel. 2008. "Research on Globalization and Education." *Review of Educational Research* 78 (2): 330–63.

Subedij, Binaya, ed. 2005. *Critical Global Perspectives: Rethinking Knowledge about Global Societies*. A Volume in Research in Social Education. Charlotte, NC: Information Age Publishing.

Thomas, K. 2003. "Postcolonial Transformation of Small and Medium-Sized Urban Settlements in Jamaica." *Caribbean Geography* 13 (2): 114–29.

Thomas-Brown, Karen. 2013. "Preparing Teachers for Global Citizenship: Perspectives from One Caribbean Island." In *Exploring Globalization Opportunities and Challenges in Social Studies: Effective Instructional Approaches*, edited by Lydiah Nganga, John Kambutu, and William Russell III, 51–66. Vol. 26 of Global Studies in Education. New York; Frankfurt: Peter Lang Gmbh, Europaischer Verlag Der Wissenschaften.

Timms, B. F. 2008. "Development Theory and Domestic Agriculture in the Caribbean: Recurring Cries and Missed Opportunities." *Caribbean Geography* 15 (2): 102–17.

Tully, James. 2008. "Two Meanings of Global Citizenship: Modern and Diverse." In *Global Citizenship Education: Philosophy, Theory, and Pedagogy*, edited by Michael A. Peters, Alan Britton, and Harry Blee, 15–41. Rotterdam: Sense Publications.

VanSledright, Bruce. 2008. "Narratives of Nation State, Historical Knowledge, and School History Education." *Review of Research in Education* 32 (1): 10946.

Velde, Dirk Willem te. 2008. *Globalisation and Education: What Do the Trade, Investment, and Migration Literatures Tell Us?* London: Overseas Development Institute. www.Odi.Org.Uk/Resources/Docs/2484.Pdf, accessed June 16, 2012.

Westheimer, Joel, and Joseph Kahne. 2004a. "Educating the "Good" Citizen: Political Choices and Pedagogical Goals." www.apsanet.org, *Psonline*, accessed June 12, 2012.

———. 2004b. "What Kind of Citizen? The Politics and Educating for Democracy." *American Educational Research Journal* 41 (2): 1–30.

Zong, Guichun. 2009. "Developing Preservice Teachers' Global Understanding through Computer-Mediated Communication Technology." *Teaching and Teacher Education* 25 (5): 617–25. doi:10.1016/J.Tate.2008.09.016.

Zong, Guichun, Angene H. Wilson, and A. Yao Quashiga. 2008. "Global Education." In *Handbook of Research in Social Studies Education*, edited by Linda S. Levstik and Cynthia A. Tyson, 197–216. New York: Routledge.

6

EXCLUSION, ISLAND STYLE

· · · · · · · · · ·

Citizenship Deprivation and Denial in the Caribbean

KRISTY A. BELTON

INTRODUCTION

As the tide ebbs and flows, Luzena Dumercy looks out across the sea and explains how many Bahamian-born individuals of Haitian descent feel like they exist in limbo, "The Bahamas don't want to claim you and Haiti don't either. . . . We are on our own because we don't really have anyone looking out for us or looking for our interests to protect us."[1] Some seven hundred miles to the south, Dumercy's story of exclusion is repeated like the constant crash of waves against the shore as hundreds of thousands of Dominican-born persons of Haitian descent are stripped of their Dominican nationality. Denied or deprived of citizenship in the country of their birth, many such persons are at risk of statelessness.

Statelessness is the condition of having no nationality,[2] and it affects more than twelve million people globally (UNHCR 2013b). Statelessness first became an issue of international concern during the World War II era when an atmosphere of instability, "disintegration," and "[h]atred" (Arendt 2004, 342) permeated war-ravaged Europe. During those dark times, people were forcibly pushed across borders, denationalized, compressed into ghettoes, and, in many instances, exterminated because of their ethnicity or political persuasion. This picture seems far removed from the "tourist-friendly" Caribbean, which lures people voluntarily to its shores with its swaying palms, balmy weather, and array of top-notch accommodations and activities for people to enjoy. Despite the two seemingly disparate pictures, however, a common characteristic unites those affected by statelessness in both accounts—minority status. In fact, "[d]eprivation or denial of national-ity based on discriminatory practices, particularly against racial, ethnic or religious minorities . . . is perhaps the most important cause of statelessness worldwide" today (Manly 2007, 256).

This chapter examines how the denial or deprivation of the human right to a nationality (UN 1948, Article 15) affects the lives of a specific minority in the Caribbean—the descendants of Haitian migrants. It illustrates how the Arendtian notion of the "right to have rights" has yet to be surpassed in the contemporary era and demonstrates the continued precariousness of belong-ing, even among democratic states. The first section of the chapter presents the concept of a "right to have rights" and the challenges that have been lev-eled against it in contemporary scholarship. It then pinpoints the gaps in this scholarship and explains how the present work sets about addressing these gaps through an investigation of statelessness in the Caribbean. The second part describes the methodology and the case studies justification, while the third offers an overview of why statelessness is a problem in the region. The final section provides an overview of the ramifications of statelessness and demonstrates why the "right to have rights"—in the form of formal citizen-ship in the state—continues to be significant in accessing rights, protections, and freedoms.

THE FRAMEWORK

To be stateless means that a person "is not considered as a national by any State under the operation of its law" (UN 1954, Article 1). When Hannah Arendt, herself a stateless person for many years, first wrote about stateless-ness in the aftermath of World War II, she described a rightless people who were everywhere outlaws. The community of nations, premised as it was and continues to be, on people belonging formally to some state through citizen-ship, was unable to deal with those who held citizenship from nowhere. In *The Origins of Totalitarianism* ([1948] 2004), Arendt wrote, "it turned out that the moment human beings lacked their own government and had to fall back upon their minimum rights, no authority was left to protect them and no institution was willing to guarantee them (370). . . . The Rights of Man, supposedly inalienable, proved to be unenforceable . . . whenever people appeared who were no longer citizens of any sovereign state" (372). Whereas Arendt strongly believed that one had to be a citizen of an organized polity—or state—in order to enjoy access to human rights, protections, and freedoms, many scholars today challenge this notion. Due to the advent and incorporation of human rights into domestic legislation and policies, as well as the diverse forms of political membership that exist in the contemporary era, some contend that formal citizenship in the state is a "waning," "partially obsolete," or "decomposi[ng]" institution (Benhabib, Shapiro, and Petranovic 2007, 14; Hailbronner 2003, 75; Cohen 1999, 247). Personhood, whether "the right . . . to be a *legal person*, entitled to certain inalienable rights, regardless of the status of their political membership" (Benhabib 2004, 3) or the right to "recognition as a moral equal" (Somers 2008, 25), is now allegedly the basis for accessing rights.

Soysal's *Limits of Citizenship* (1994) is perhaps the best-known and earliest work to describe how citizenship is losing its importance in a globalizing world of increased migratory movements and human rights provisions. Through her study of guest workers in Europe, Soysal observed that citizens and noncitizens were basically treated in the same way when it came to rights provisions. She found that the basis for this similarity in treatment was host-state respect for the human rights regime, which acknowledges the rights of all *persons* regardless of race, or national or social origin. Soysal found that the "[r]ights that used to belong solely to nationals are now extended to foreign populations, thereby undermining the very basis of national citizenship" (137).

Post–*Limits of Citizenship*, various authors have taken up one or more of the postnationalist threads presented in Soysal's work. Some have sought, like Soysal, to illustrate that human rights are now decoupled from citizenship. Benhabib and Jacobson posit, for example, that "one does not have to be part of a territorially defined people to enjoy human rights" (Benhabib 2001, 36; Jacobson 1996, 2; see also Basok, Ilcan, and Noonan 2006), while Bosniak, studying the "citizenship of aliens" in the United States, argues that "[c]itizenship . . . is *not* actually 'the right to have rights,' despite the conventional wisdom. In many situations, only personhood is required" (2006, 117).

Other scholars have centered on Soysal's exploration of "the emergence of membership that is multiple in the sense of spanning local, regional, and global identities, and which accommodates intersecting complexes of rights, duties, and loyalties" (Soysal 1994, 166). These authors examine the myriad citizenship types or ways of belonging that exist in the contemporary era. From cultural (Kymlicka 1995), transnational (Bauböck 2007), deterritorialized (Teune 2009), denationalized (Sassen 2006), flexible (Ong 1999; Nyamnjoh 2007), anational (Kostakopoulou 2008), postnational (Soysal 1994; Benhabib and Resnik 2009), post-sovereign (Murphy and Harty 2003), global (Cabrera 2010), quasi (Gilbertson 2006), and the "citizenship of aliens" (Bosniak 2006), these scholars illustrate that formal legal citizenship is no longer so important to act in and belong to a polity.

Since "the distinction between 'citizen' and 'alien' has eroded" (Jacobson 1996, 8–9 and 39; see also Bosniak [2006, 34 and 94] and Soysal [1994, 137]), and the legitimate space for rights claims is now external to the state (Cohen 1999; Jacobson 1996; Sassen 2006), it appears that the Arendtian portrayal of the stateless as a "rightless people" (Arendt [1948] 2004, 373) no longer holds. "Rights and status [have become] relatively autonomous" (Bosniak 2006, 89) and, as a result, questions arise as to whether "the idea of territorial state citizenship—as distinct from personhood—remain[s] important? Are human rights replacing citizenship as the most important rights-bearing ideas and legal norms?" (Jackson 2009, 443). Several limitations present themselves within much of the aforementioned scholarship on the relationship between human rights and citizenship and the weakening of citizenship as status, however. Many of the studies examining noncitizens, their rights, participation and treatment, have focused on developed-world, democratic states. Very few have examined the relationship between citizenship status and access to rights and protections in the developing world.

This is somewhat surprising given that Soysal clearly stated that her postnationalist arguments "are not exclusive to Europe. As the transnational norms and discourse of human rights permeate the boundaries of nation-states, the postnational model is activated and approximated world-wide" (1994, 156). More recently, Bosniak asserts that "the status of aliens in liberal democratic societies is, in many respects, hardly distinguishable from that of citizens" (2006, 34) as "a great many of the rights commonly associated with equal citizenship and economic citizenship are not confined to status citizens at all but are available to territorially present persons" in "most other liberal democratic states" (117).

Additionally, the majority of these studies focus on noncitizens who are actually citizens of some state when they make claims about the decoupling of human rights from citizenship or the weakening of citizenship as a formal institution. The groups studied generally include refugees, guest workers, and immigrants of various kinds who are recognized as citizens of some state according to its law. They are not stateless. The present work therefore challenges the aforementioned arguments about citizenship and human rights by evaluating how well they "travel" to developing-world, democratic states and by applying these claims to those who hold no citizenship from any state.

CASE STUDIES JUSTIFICATION AND METHODOLOGY

The Caribbean region stands as a valid testing ground for evaluating claims about the decoupling of human rights from citizenship because "no other region" in the developing world "has had, for so long, so many liberal democratic polities" (Domínguez 1993, 2). Freedom House, which scores countries according to their behavior in the areas of civil liberties and political rights, classifies all the countries in the Caribbean—with the exception of Cuba and Haiti—as "free" (2013). Caribbean states thus score well in the categories of political participation, freedom of speech and of the press, social and economic freedoms, and the rule of law, among other criteria. Specifically, The Bahamas and the Dominican Republic, which are the two case studies for this work, score well on these criteria. The Bahamas earns the highest freedom scores possible (1 out of 7) in both civil liberties and political rights, while the Dominican Republic scores slightly lower, earning a score of 2 (out of 7) in each category, respectively.

Beside the comparative "liberal" nature of the region, statelessness is "an issue of . . . concern in the Caribbean" (UNHCR 2012b). In fact, the problem is of such significance that the United Nations High Commissioner for Refugees' (UNHCR) office for the Americas stated that one of its four strategic priorities for 2012 was to: "[p]revent statelessness in the Caribbean by advocating for accession to international instruments, mapping the population concerned or at risk, providing technical and legal support and helping them with their registration and documentation" (UNHCR 2012a). For 2013, this theme is continued as "there will be a strong focus on the prevention and reduction of statelessness and other nationality issues, mainly through birth registration and documentation" (UNHCR 2013a). Moreover, the organization is expressly focused on "ensur[ing] access to a national-ity for undocumented people of Haitian descent" (UNHCR 2012a). This is important because in both The Bahamas and the Dominican Republic, indi-viduals of Haitian descent struggle to obtain, or retain, their citizenship. They are left in political and legal limbo because state bureaucrats, often arbitrarily, determine whether or not they can "formally belong" to the only country they have ever known.

In order to examine critically the claims made about the decoupling of human rights from citizenship and the weakening of citizenship as an institution I analyzed the nationality laws and constitutions of The Bahamas, the Dominican Republic, and Haiti; the status of their treaty ratifications dealing with statelessness or the right to a nationality; and the reports of various nongovernmental organizations (NGOs) and the United Nations (UN) on the subject. Additionally, I engaged in fieldwork on statelessness in The Bahamas and the Dominican Republic between 2009 and 2013. In 2009 I conducted sixteen semistructured, elite-level interviews. Fourteen of those interviews took place in Nassau, Bahamas, while the remaining two were conducted via telephone. Participants included former and current government officials, academics, community leaders, lawyers, a civil servant, a journalist, an amateur film documentarian, and a graduate student who had worked in the local Haitian communities. None of those interviewed was stateless or at risk of statelessness, but two of them were Haitian and held prominent positions in the Haitian community. The people who par-ticipated in the 2009 study were chosen via purposive sampling because of their leadership positions in either the government or the nascent human rights community or because of their expertise on Bahamian migration or nationality law.

I returned to The Bahamas in the fall of 2012 where I conducted thirteen interviews in the capital, Nassau, and seven on the island of Abaco. Partici-pants included lawyers, activists, elected and appointed officials, educators, businesspersons, health care professionals, a police and a defense force officer, and the Haitian ambassador and some Bahamian-born students of Haitian descent from the College of The Bahamas. An official from the Ministry of Foreign Affairs provided the ministry's perspective via e-mail.

Of the twenty-one persons interviewed in 2012, eight had either faced the risk of statelessness or were stateless at some point. As in the 2009 study, I performed purposeful sampling, but limited such sampling to government officials and lawyers. I obtained interviews with the other participants via snowball sampling or because I came into contact with them at a public forum on statelessness[3] at the College of The Bahamas (COB) and requested interviews from them. Those who participated in the 2012 portion of the study reflected a broad set of opinions, from those affected by statelessness and those affected by the presence of Bahamian-born individuals of Haitian descent in their communities, to those who held leadership positions in diverse professions that come into contact with individuals of Haitian descent (such as the armed forces, the police, the Ministry of Foreign Affairs, health professionals, lawyers, and teachers).

In addition to the thirty-seven interviews from The Bahamas, I traveled to the Dominican Republic in the summer of 2012 and the spring of 2013. I interviewed ten individuals in the capital, Santo Domingo, and five in the *batey*[4] of El Caño in the province of Monte Plata. Four of the five participants from the *batey* were stateless, while one had previously been in that situation but now had her documents to prove Dominican citizenship. The interviewees from Santo Domingo consisted of two United Nations (UN) officials, nongovernmental organization (NGO) activists, lawyers, a diplomat from the Haitian embassy, academics, and the local representative of the Open Society Justice Initiative (OSJI).

Participants for this part of the fieldwork once again reflect diverse viewpoints on the effects, and existence, of statelessness in the country. As in the Bahamian 2009 portion of the study, I selected the majority of the interviewees from Santo Domingo via purposeful sampling, although a few individuals were contacted via the snowball technique. I did not purposefully select the participants from El Caño, however. I was part of a group that went to listen to a town hall meeting on nationality deprivation in that *batey* and I consequently ended up informally interviewing five of the attendees (all women). Two additional interviews were conducted in New York City with two other members of OSJI earlier in 2012 on the subject of statelessness in the Caribbean.[5]

THE PRESENCE OF STATELESSNESS

The Bahamas and the Dominican Republic are both primary destination sites for Haitian migrants. It is estimated that between 30,000 and 60,000 Haitian migrants reside in The Bahamas (International Organization for Migration 2005, 98), and around 380,000 live in the Dominican Republic

(Wooding and Moseley-Williams 2004). The number of stateless persons making up this population in both countries is unknown, although several factors facilitate the risk of statelessness in both countries. First, neither country allows for the automatic acquisition of citizenship via *jus soli* (birth on the territory).[6] The Bahamas allows for children born on its soil to non-citizen parents to apply for citizenship within a one-year time frame when they reach the age of eighteen (Government of The Bahamas 1973, Article 7), while the Dominican Republic does not grant it to "children born to foreigners who are part of diplomatic and consular delegations, and foreigners who are in transit or who live illegally in the Dominican Republic" (Dominican Republic 2010, Article 18.3).[7]

Second, the governments of both states deny that statelessness is an issue in their respective countries (Castro 2011; El Nuevo Diario 2012; Rolle 2012; Turnquest 2011), despite the fact that neither country has statelessness status determination procedures in place to support this claim. Both states rely on Article 11 of the Haitian Constitution to make their case that children born in their countries of Haitian ancestry cannot be stateless. This particular article states that "[a]ny person born of a Haitian father or Haitian mother who are themselves native-born Haitians and have never renounced their nationality possesses Haitian nationality at the time of birth" (Republic of Haiti 1987).[8] The Bahamian and Dominican governments thus contend that the children born on their soil of Haitian descent are Haitian citizens through their parents. It therefore does not matter whether or not they have Bahamian or Dominican citizenship.

A third reason why children born to parents of Haitian descent are at a heightened risk of statelessness is lack of parental documentation. Neither the Haitian embassy in The Bahamas nor the one in the Dominican Republic provides citizenship to those who cannot either provide proof of their parents' Haitian nationality or who cannot produce two witnesses to attest to this fact. As the former Attorney General of The Bahamas, Alfred Sears, notes, "When someone has no evidence of another nationality, has never applied for a Haitian passport, has never had a Haitian passport . . . because they've never had any documentation to evidence a Haitian nationality . . . this is where the issue of statelessness comes in."[9] Moreover, as Gonçalves Margerin and Teff (2008) point out, children born to undocumented parents or parents seeking asylum do not acquire Haitian citizenship at birth, and Wooding asserts that "[t]he reality is that under the Haitian

Constitution and Haiti's 1984 law on nationality, there are several groups of people of Haitian origin born outside Haiti who do not have automatic access to Haitian nationality" (2009, 24).

A fourth reason for the heightened risk of statelessness in both countries is their failure to ratify the two statelessness conventions and incorporate preventive measures against statelessness into national legislation. The *Convention relating to the Status of Stateless Persons* (UN 1954) delineates the rights and duties that a stateless person has, while the *Convention on the Reduction of Statelessness* (UN 1961) provides means of preventing and reducing statelessness globally. As of 2014 neither the Bahamian nor the Dominican government had ratified the conventions.[10]

Despite these similarities, a primary distinction between the Dominican and Bahamian cases concerning statelessness is that people born in the Dominican Republic of Haitian descent appear to be the target of "a concentrated State policy to deny and deprive" them of citizenship in the Dominican case.[11] This purported "state policy" of citizenship denial and deprivation takes several forms in the Dominican Republic. A well-known example of the first instance is the *Case of the Girls Yean and Bosico v. Dominican Republic* (IACHR 2005), wherein Dominican authorities refused to give Dilcia Yean and Violeta Bosico their Dominican birth certificates, thereby making it difficult for them to prove they were Dominican citizens. The case made its way to the Inter-American Court of Human Rights (IACHR) in 2005 where the court determined that the Dominican Republic had violated the girls' rights to a nationality, a juridical personality, a name, and equal protection before the law.

Even before the IACHR gave its opinion in the *Yean and Bosico* case, the Dominican Republic instituted Ley 285-04. This law established the distinction between resident and nonresident noncitizens in the country (Dominican Republic 2004) to the alleged detriment of children born of Haitian noncitizen parents. Resident noncitizens may be "permanent" or "temporary." The former enter the Dominican Republic with permission from the relevant authority and with the intention of permanently residing within it. The latter only reside for a limited amount of time (Articles 29 through 31). Nonresident noncitizens, however, are "in transit" (Article 10) and allegedly have no intention of making the Dominican Republic their home (Article 32). Previously, "in transit" was understood to mean a person who spent no more than ten days in the country. Since the passage of Ley 285-04, however, "the category of 'non-resident' [has become] conflated with the concept of 'in transit' status, thus all non-resident migrants and undocumented migrants are considered to be 'in transit' and their children born on Dominican soil are denied citizenship" (UN Human Rights Council 2008, 18).

Allegations exist that Ley 285-04 is being retroactively applied to those who were recognized as Dominican citizens prior to the passage of the 2004 law. Since the issuance of Circular No. 17 and Resolución No. 12/2007, which demand that civil registries investigate the issuance of birth certificates to children born of parents who are in "irregular" status, registry officials have purportedly begun to "equat[e] being of Haitian descent with fraud" and denationalized many such persons (Gonçalves Margerin and Teff 2008, 2). Others of Haitian descent have allegedly had their names removed from the Dominican birth registry and put into the foreigners' birth registry, even though they were previously holders of citizen birth certificates or are entitled to such birth certificates because they were born to legal, permanent residents (US Department of State 2010b, 19).

Additionally, two of the individuals I interviewed in the *batey* of El Caño found out when they went to obtain certified copies of their birth certificates that they had been "suplantada." That is, the local Dominican civil registry officers had already issued their birth certificate to other people. Without the regular resident birth certificates, they were unable to acquire a government-issued *cédula*. This *cédula*, or national ID, is needed to access "formal sector jobs, public education past the eighth grade, marriage and birth registration, formal economy services such as banks and loans, access to courts and judicial procedures, and ownership of land or property" (US Department of State 2010b, 18).

In addition to Ley 285-04, Circular No. 17, and Resolución No. 12/2007, the Dominican government amended its constitution in 2010 in the area of nationality.[12] Whereas the constitutions issued from 1939 to 2002 allowed for *jus soli* citizenship acquisition, with the exception of those born to diplomats or persons "in transit" under the ten-day definition, the 2010 constitution adds those who "reside illegally on Dominican territory" as another exception to the *jus soli* rule and incorporates the post-2004 understanding of "in transit" (Article 18). Those of Haitian descent are the primary group affected by this change.[13]

While The Bahamas has not modified or created any laws for allegedly discriminatory purposes, the US Department of State found that the

Bahamian government "has not effectively implemented laws and policies to provide certain habitual residents the opportunity to gain nationality in a timely manner and on a nondiscriminatory basis" (2010a, 11). Every one of the eight Bahamian-born interviewees who were stateless or at risk of statelessness at some point in their lives[14] described the difficulties they had in completing the Bahamian citizenship application process: information on what documents were needed was unclear; it was often difficult to obtain original documents, like birth certificates, from Haiti; identity documents were sometimes "lost" by immigration officers during the process; and immigration officers sometimes failed to update applicants on the status of their applications, or never provided them with the correct date of their swearing-in ceremony, thus prolonging the acquisition of Bahamian citizenship. Several interviewees noted that the only way they could actually get their citizenship was by surreptitiously involving an elected official in the process who could put pressure on the appropriate Department of Immigration officer.

Whereas the Dominican Republic has been known to deny birth certificates to children born on their territory prior to the 2010 constitutional amendment,[15] The Bahamas provides the same birth certificate to all children born on its territory. As noted by an official at the Office of the Registrar, it is "very rare" for a child born in The Bahamas not to receive a birth certificate. However, the same interviewee noted that the parent must have a "valid government issued picture identification" in order to register their child and obtain a birth certificate.[16] Without such a valid ID, the ability of the child to acquire a Bahamian birth certificate—and consequently Bahamian citizenship at eighteen—is placed in jeopardy. Gwendolyn Brice-Adderley, the chief lawyer at the Nationality Support Unit[17] in Nassau, offers an account where a child was unable to obtain a Bahamian birth certificate precisely on these grounds:

We have a case where that was brought to my attention. The father was born in The Bahamas. He's from Haitian parentage. He is thirty-two years old. I think he may have submitted his documents for citizenship, but they haven't come through as yet, for whatever reason. The mother was an illegal immigrant, but she came here somehow and stayed for two years, met him, had a child. But two months ago she was detained and repatriated. But before, in between being detained and being repatriated, they called me in to see if I could assist her because she had a young baby. The young baby was not documented . . . so the mother was the one who would have taken the child to be registered, but because she was illegal for whatever reason, she did not have any ID. So she couldn't do anything for the child. . . . She couldn't get the notice of birth from the hospital because she didn't have an ID.

Whether this is an instance of an exceptional case or one that represents a more systemic problem of undocumented mothers being unable to obtain birth certificates for their Bahamian-born children must be left unanswered at present. What appears to be apparent, however, is that the acquisition of Bahamian citizenship is no simple process for those born to noncitizens in the country, and that lack of citizenship affects their lives in many different ways.

PRECARIOUS BELONGING

Individuals born of Haitian descent in The Bahamas and the Dominican Republic are the primary ethnic group affected by citizenship denial and deprivation. Despite the distinct causes for their respective statelessness, Bahamian-born and Dominican-born persons of Haitian descent face similar problems in their countries of birth. Both are susceptible to limited educational and career opportunities, indirect and direct forms of discrimination, as well as poverty and myriad human rights violations due to their stateless status. Many also confront societal rejection and feelings of insecurity or confusion regarding their nationality status.

In the Dominican Republic, children struggle to continue their education past the eighth grade if they do not have a certified copy of their birth certificate, and nearly all are unable to pursue a tertiary education. Francía Calis García encountered both of these problems.[18] A twenty-one-year-old born in the Dominican Republic to Haitian or "foreign" parents, she had difficulties finishing her high school degree because the civil registry office would not give her a certified copy of her birth certificate, despite being born in the country. After overcoming many obstacles, she finished high school, but has been unable to attend university or secure a job because the authorities will not grant her a *cédula*. As noted earlier, in the Dominican Republic, a *cédula* is needed to engage in all sorts of activities. Without a *cédula*, reports an anonymous program official of the United Nations Development

Program in the Dominican Republic, "They cannot cash a check. They cannot get a credit card. They can't enter into a contract. They are not subjects of the law. They don't exist as citizens."[19] Without a *cédula*, Calis García and the many others who she knows in this situation face limits on their ability to advance professionally and socioeconomically. "I think that my rights as a Dominican are being violated," she says.

Several of the participants from El Caño confirmed that they were unable to pursue their university studies after completing high school. One also noted that although she received good grades in high school and was the recipient of a scholarship for her work, the scholarship was never given to her because she was "from a *batey*."[20] She feels like she was discriminated against because of her Haitian heritage and adds that the denial of scholarship opportunities to Dominican-born students of Haitian descent "happens a lot." Interviewees in Civolani Hischnjakow's work (2011)[21] similarly note how the lack of certified documentation from the civil registry stopped them from taking the national exam, continuing their postsecondary studies, or taking part in overseas athletic opportunities. "It prevents me from doing many things," says Eduardo Dierdito Exilien (29), while Nico Paredes and Rogelio Exil de La Rosa explain how their athletic careers were cut short (30).

Unable to pursue tertiary education and other career opportunities that come their way, many of these Dominican-born students are confined to low-paying or menial jobs. Calis García explains how although she has taken courses in accounting, computing, and Basic English, without a *cédula*, she cannot find employment as a teacher. Once, when she found employment as a teacher's aide, she was paid very little money and was told that she could not continue because she did not have a *cédula*. She has faced many such career limitations, and it has left her despondent. "Many times I don't feel like going on." Dierdito Exilien likewise expresses dejection: "They killed me morally because when you are in a society and you cannot have a career, you cannot be in a job unless you are doing things that a person who has no worth does," it is like being "an immigrant, an unknown, an undocumented person" (Civolani Hischnjakow 2011, 35). He adds that he has had to take on jobs that he would not have voluntarily pursued if he had been given his *cédula* and been able to pursue the opportunities that had been presented to him (42). Other interviewees agree and lament their inability to advance economically as a result.

Dim educational and economic prospects are not the only problems these individuals face, however. Sometimes others question their Dominican identity, and Dominicans of Haitian descent themselves become "confused about what their nationality is and where they belong" (Civolani Hischnjakow 2011, 24). The participants in Civolani Hischnjakow's study readily admitted that it affects them to the point where "your personality changes. If you're not from here or there, where are you from?" (ibid.). Ramona Petion declares, "We don't know where we belong. It's like when you have an animal and you let it loose without its brand. . . . We're not even in that position; we're not even branded animals because, without those documents, nobody recognizes us" (ibid., 25). Exil de La Rosa adds that without any Dominican documentation it is as if "I were a stranger, but in my own country or in my own nation . . . it's like I am physically here, but when it comes to the laws it's as if I don't exist" (ibid., 26). As a result, these Dominican-born individuals of Haitian descent feel "anguish, anxiety and insecurity" (ibid., 36), humiliation, confusion, and frustration (ibid., 34 and 27).

The effects of citizenship deprivation are not only individual, however. Three of the five participants from El Caño were mothers and related how they were unable to register their Dominican-born children because of their own lack of a birth certificate or a *cédula*. "I feel terrible," confesses one.[22] Beside the multigenerational and individual effects of denationalization, the social ramifications may be significant as well. Francisco Henry Leonardo, a lawyer and spokesperson for the Centro Bonó, sees an increase in the unemployment rate and believes that "the lack of opportunities, unemployment, lack of education and extreme poverty" are creating a volatile situation. "It's a time bomb. You're dealing with a population that is conscious that they are being crushed and there's going to be a reaction."[23] He believes that segments of this population "are going to enter into crisis. They are going to enter into crisis and look for their own identity because even though they are Dominicans, they are rejected. . . . They are going to start a process of differentiation."

Although a "state policy" of citizenship denial and deprivation against persons of Haitian descent does not appear to exist in The Bahamas, the effects of a lack of citizenship are the same. The interviews from the "Haitian-Bahamians"[24] were replete with stories exemplifying the ways in which they had been reminded that they did not "belong" in the country where they were born. Education, jobs, and discrimination were the three key areas in which their exclusion was made evident. Several explained how they had to pass up educational opportunities overseas because they could not study in the United States on the Bahamian government-issued "travel document," or certificate of identity. Others noted how they had to pay the non-Bahamian school tuition or "foreigner's fee" at their tertiary institutions, while most expressed their frustration at being unable to apply for scholarships. Akin to some of the participants in the Civolani Hischnjakow study, interviewees recounted how they were unable to take advantage of athletic opportunities that came their way. Gillard Louis, a student at the College of The Bahamas, describes how "growing up there are many opportunities that came my way but because I didn't have a passport, it kind of like hindered me. I could just give you one [example]. In high school, I was in athletics, into sports pretty good. I had an opportunity to be a part of the Bahamian national soccer team, but that chance was crushed because, you know, they said that I don't have a Bahamian passport. . . . I was hurt."²⁵ Natacha Jn-Simon, a student at the College of The Bahamas who has yet to acquire her Bahamian citizenship, relates how her friend had been offered a basketball scholarship in the United States to study. He held a Bahamian passport, but when he went to renew it at the age of sixteen, an employee at the passport office revoked it because his parents were "Haitian." He was told that he should never have had a Bahamian passport. His athletic opportunity consequently never came to fruition, and he ended up not graduating from high school. He is currently unemployed with two children. Jn-Simon relates how another friend "who got the highest [Bahamas Government Certificate in Secondary Education exam results] in the government schools in her year . . . didn't even have an opportunity to go to school because . . . she wouldn't be able to get a scholarship."²⁶ Jn-Simon says that after working so hard in high school, her friend now "has to work and settle for mediocrity. Like certain jobs that she would never see herself doing, she has to settle for them in order to get where she wants to get in life."

Moreover, after-school programs, such as the police and nursing cadets, were also off limits for the interviewees. One participant, who chose to remain anonymous, explains how in grade twelve she "wanted to join the cadet corps and I remember the police officer—she was a lady—telling me you can't join the cadet corps because you don't have a Bahamian passport. Yes, I remember that. And then it hinders you from moving forward."²⁷ Jn-Simon similarly adds how the police cadets, which is "a very, very good program . . . once you go to school under them, they pay for your school tuition," is unavailable to

Bahamian-born students of Haitian descent. "If you don't have a passport, you can't join the police cadets. Then there is the nursing cadet program where they have this nursing program in high school and then when you get out of high school, they pay for your tuition to go to nursing school. However, if you don't have a passport, you don't get the nursing grant."

Due to limitations on their ability to pursue tertiary education and also facing a limited job market due to their lack of a Bahamian passport, many Bahamian-born children of Haitian descent also end up working in menial jobs with little opportunity for career advancement. Government jobs are out of the question without a Bahamian passport, as are many jobs in the private sector. Mark Desmangles, one of the founders of Sakpase Bahamas, notes how many young Haitian Bahamians "take menial positions and then some of them they get stuck in them."[28] Dumercy adds that "[t]he stigma of the last name" haunts those who get an education and who try to advance in a career. She says that "local employers here, they look at your name and not at your qualifications." One anonymous interviewee, who previously worked in the health care industry, explains how, "when I applied for jobs . . . they see the qualifications there" but that "just by looking at my name . . . you won't get hired."

Although a Haitian identity is firmly attributed to many Haitian Bahamians by their non–Haitian Bahamian counterparts, several of the interviewees explained how they felt as if they were rejected by both Haiti and The Bahamas. Harry Dolce, a Bahamian policeman of Haitian descent, observes how, "You have one group of people saying, 'You are this' and the other person saying that you are not. It's like you are stuck in between. . . . You're saying I am Haitian, but if I go to Haiti they say that I am not Haitian, I am Bahamian."[29] Desmangles relates the story of how he went to Haiti when he was fifteen and people there told him, "'Oh, no, no. You're not Haitian, you know.' They look at me . . . I say, 'Ah my parents are Haitian. I understand that once you're Haitian, you're Haitian.' 'No, no, no! That's not the case. You have to be born here.' . . . And the thing is, with Haiti, they don't really want individuals who were born in the Bahamas to be Haitians. That's not something that they want to practice." Dumercy similarly narrates,

[Haitians say], "You wasn't born here, you're a Bahamian." But then . . . it's the same thing where the Bahamians say, "Well you're born of Haitian parents, you're Haitian." So that's why a lot of us

[are] saying we're stateless or we're in limbo because the Haitians don't look at us as part of them. . . . Haiti don't look at you as part of their country and, well, literally you could say the Bahamas don't want you to be part of their country until you're eighteen, until you're an adult. That means as a child, I mean nothing to you. . . . Literally, that's what they're saying by their law. You are worthless to me.

Dumercy adds that "[t]hey don't make us feel like we belong here. So it's a sense of belonging. . . . You shouldn't be stateless in the place you were born and where you feel like you're not included or not wanted." One of the anonymous Bahamian-born participants of Haitian descent, discussing the personal and societal rejection that many of them feel from both The Bahamas and Haiti, remarks that "to be stateless means you have no identity. You have no say in what's going on. . . . It feels like you're nonexistent. . . . You feel like you're trapped; you're held a prisoner. . . . Yeah, you feel like you're trapped and there's no way out for you. You have no identity."[30] Louis had a similar definition of statelessness and identity: "to be stateless is to not have a nationality that is publicly known or I can say that falls under a country's group of identity."

These limitations not only serve to remind the Bahamian-born interviewees as they grow up that they do not belong and that they are not "Bahamian," but they also present problems for the "community" that is denying their equal treatment. Brenda Claridge, a business owner in Marsh Harbour, Abaco, explains how "people make them [Haitian Bahamians] a problem" by setting limitations on them in the form of bank loan denials, delays in granting Bahamian citizenship, and lack of educational opportunities. She wonders "how likely is it that they are going to educate their own children" when they "try hard" in school, but are "crushed" in return?[31] Louis similarly remarks how the country should be "trying to create positive assets for the future," but by denying these Bahamian-born children of Haitian descent opportunities, "you're pushing them away. . . . You say that the crime rate is high. You say that our young men are into drugs, into gang violence, but then you're not giving them opportunities and programs to better themselves."

As these interviewees' accounts illustrate, the denial of citizenship—and the effects thereof—to persons who are born and raised in The Bahamas results in various forms of exclusion. A lack of national identity documents from Haiti and the possession of a certificate of identity from the Bahamian government, which, in the words of Desmangles, only leads you to be "treated as though you are a foreigner," highlights the sense of nonbelonging that many of them felt—or continue to feel—growing up. As Dolce points out, "The Bahamas is losing a lot of its citizens. I call them citizens because they were born here. They are losing them . . . because when they remain here they don't have that sense of belonging."

In conclusion, the ramifications of citizenship denial and deprivation move far beyond the strictly legal realm. As this chapter illustrates, although statelessness is arrived at through the application, or not, of certain constitutional or nationality laws, statelessness is not simply a legal problem. Statelessness affects individuals in many ways, including emotionally, socially, and economically. It leaves them in an insecure position in the countries where they were born and has potential negative repercussions for society in terms of development, democracy building, and stability. The chapter demonstrates that even in democratic states, where human rights provisions are supposed to be strongest, those who are noncitizens everywhere continue to face challenges in accessing rights, freedoms, and protections. In our allegedly postnational world, then, where rights are allegedly decoupling from citizenship as status, formal recognition of membership in a state continues to be significant. Thus even though an ocean and more than a half century of distance separates the stateless of Arendt's war-torn Europe from those who are stateless in the Caribbean, the Arendtian notion of a "right to have rights" remains as relevant as ever to those who are stateless in the Caribbean today.

NOTES

1. Personal interview, Marsh Harbour, Abaco, The Bahamas, November 12, 2012. All the quotations that I attribute to Dumercy throughout the rest of the chapter took place in Marsh Harbour on the aforementioned date.
2. Nationality and citizenship are used interchangeably in this chapter, as is common in statelessness scholarship.
3. The conference, "21st Century Slavery in The Bahamas: A Discussion on Statelessness," took place on October 24, 2012, in the Harry C. Moore library at COB.
4. A *batey* is the traditional name for a settlement where sugarcane workers resided during the heyday of the sugarcane industry in the Dominican Republic, from the 1930s to the 1980s. Today, these settlements are primarily

shantytowns where many Dominicans of Haitian descent, many of whom continue to work in the sugarcane industry, live.

5. In addition to the primary and secondary source analysis and the fifty-five semistructured interviews, I engaged in participant observation in a number of settings in the Caribbean and the United States as a means of assessing how individuals engage with each other on questions surrounding stateless-ness, migration, and human rights.

6. Besides the Dominican Republic and The Bahamas, the majority of states in the Caribbean have constitutional clauses that state that a child born on their territory does not gain citizenship automatically if neither of his or her parents is a citizen.

7. Author's translation.

8. The 2011 amended constitution does not change this (Republic of Haiti 2012).

9. Personal interview, Nassau, The Bahamas, November 8, 2012.

10. The Dominican Republic signed the 1961 Convention, but never ratified it.

11. Personal interview with Indira Goris, New York, New York, February 22, 2012. Goris was formerly a program officer on equality and citizenship for OSJI in New York. She is now the director of administration for OSJI. Cristóbal Rodríguez and Noemi Méndez, both Dominican attorneys who have worked closely on the issue of citizenship deprivation in the Dominican Republic, agree with Goris's position. They asserted at the "Simposio sobre Derecho a la Nacionalidad y Estado de Derecho en República Dominicana: Retos y Perspectivas," that denationalization is "una política de estado."

12. This is but one of the areas in which the constitution was amended.

13. Since I first wrote this chapter, the Dominican Constitutional Court passed Sentence TC/0168/13 (Government of the Dominican Republic 2013b), which ruled that civil registry officers were not acting unconstitutionally when they refused to issue citizenship and identity documents to persons whose parents' residency status was unclear or illegal when they were born in the country. This has resulted in tens, and possibly hundreds of thousands, of Dominicans of Haitian descent being stripped of their citizenship (Archibold 2013; Edmonds 2013; Rojas 2013).

14. Seven of the interviewees were of Haitian descent, while one was of British parentage.

15. Prior to the 2010 constitutional amendment the Dominican constitution allowed for citizenship to be acquired through birth on the territory unless a child was born to a parent who was a diplomat or "in transit" (ten days or less) through the country.

16. Personal interview, Nassau, The Bahamas, November 9, 2012.

17. The NSU is a legal clinic housed at the Etienne Dupuch Law School in Nassau, The Bahamas. It partners with UNHCR to assist children born of Haitian descent in the country to acquire their Bahamian citizenship.

18. I translated all quotes from Calis García, which are from the online video "Statelessness in the Dominican Republic" (MOSCTHA 2012).

19. Personal interview, Santo Domingo, Dominican Republic, July 13, 2012. Author's translation.

20. Personal interview, El Caño, Monte Plata, Dominican Republic, February 6, 2013.

21. All interviewee quotes from the Civolani Hischnjakow source are my own translations.

22. Personal interview, El Caño, Monte Plata, Dominican Republic, February 6, 2013.

23. Personal interview, Santo Domingo, Dominican Republic, July 13, 2012.

24. "Haitian-Bahamian" and "Haitian Bahamian" are terms used to identify those who are born in The Bahamas of Haitian descent.

25. Personal interview, Nassau, The Bahamas, November 5, 2012. All the quotations that I attribute to Louis throughout the rest of the chapter took place in Nassau on the aforementioned date.

26. Personal interview, Nassau, The Bahamas, November 1, 2012. All the quotations that I attribute to Jn. Simon throughout the rest of the chapter took place in Nassau on the aforementioned date.

27. Personal interview, Nassau, The Bahamas, November 1, 2012.

28. Personal interview, Nassau, The Bahamas, October 30, 2012. All the quotations that I attribute to Desmangles throughout the rest of the chapter took place in Nassau on the aforementioned date. Sakpase is an organization founded by Haitian Bahamians to raise awareness about the activities of individuals of Haitian descent in the Caribbean.

29. Personal interview, Nassau, The Bahamas, October 29, 2012. All the quotations that I attribute to Dolce throughout the rest of the chapter took place in Nassau on the aforementioned date.

30. Personal interview, Nassau, The Bahamas, November 1, 2012.

31. Personal interview, Abaco, The Bahamas, November 14, 2012.

WORKS CITED

Archibold, Randal C. 2013. "Dominicans of Haitian Descent Cast into Legal Limbo by Court." *New York Times.* www.nytimes.com/2013/10/24/world/

americas/dominicans-of-haitian-descent-cast-into-legal-limbo-by-court.
html?emc=edit_tnt_20131024&nlid=55818265&tntemailo=y&_r=0, accessed
March 4, 2015.

Arendt, Hannah. [1948] 2004. *The Origins of Totalitarianism*. New York:
Schocken Books.

Basok, Tanya, Suzan Ilcan, and Jeff Noonan. 2006. "Citizenship, Human
Rights, and Social Justice." *Citizenship Studies* 10 (3): 267–73.

Bauböck, Rainer. 2007. "Political Boundaries in a Multilevel Democracy." In
Identities, Affiliations, and Allegiances, edited by Seyla Benhabib, Ian Shapiro,
and Danilo Petranovic, 85–109. Cambridge: Cambridge University Press.

Benhabib, Seyla. 2001. *Transformations of Citizenship: Dilemmas of the Nation
State in the Era of Globalization*. Assen: Koninklijke Van Gorcum, University
of Amsterdam.

———. 2004. *The Rights of Others: Aliens, Residents and Citizens*. Cambridge:
Cambridge University Press.

Benhabib, Seyla, and Judith Resnik. 2009. *Migrations and Mobilities: Citizenship, Borders, and Gender*. New York: Ney York University Press.

Benhabib, Seyla, Ian Shapiro, and Danilo Petranovic. 2007. "Editors' Introduction."
In *Identities, Affiliations, and Allegiances*, edited by Seyla Benhabib, Ian Shapiro,
and Danilo Petranovic, 1–14. Cambridge: Cambridge University Press.

Bosniak, Linda. 2006. *The Citizen and the Alien: Dilemmas of Contemporary
Membership*. Princeton, NJ: Princeton University Press.

Cabrera, Luis. 2010. *The Practice of Global Citizenship*. New York: Cambridge
University Press.

Castro, Aníbal de. 2011. "A Response from the Embassy of the Dominican
Republic in the United States." www.economist.com/blogs/newsbook/
2011/12/our-blog-post-haitian-dominicans, accessed March 4, 2015.

Civolani Hischnjakow, Katerina. 2011. *Vidas suspendidas: Efectos de la Resolución
012–07 en la población dominicana de ascendencia haitiana*. Santo Domingo,
Dominican Republic: Centro Bonó.

Cohen, Jean L. 1999. "Changing Paradigms of Citizenship and the Exclusive-
ness of the Demos." *International Sociology* 14: 245–68.

Domínguez, Jorge I. "The Caribbean Question: Why Has Liberal Democracy
(Surprisingly) Flourished?" In *Democracy in the Caribbean: Political, Economic,
and Social Perspectives*, edited by Jorge I. Domínguez, Robert A. Pastor, and
R. DeLisle Worrell, 1–25. Baltimore: Johns Hopkins University Press.

Dominican Republic. 2004. "Ley 285: Sobre Migración." www.acnur.org/
biblioteca/pdf/4414.pdf?view=1, accessed March 4, 2015.

————. 2010. "Constitución de 2010." http://pdba.georgetown.edu/
Constitutions/DomRep/vigente.html, accessed March 4, 2015.

Edmonds, Kevin. 2013. "Dominican Republic 'Denationalization' Program
Seeks to Strip Citizenship from Haitian Descendants." North American
Congress on Latin America. https://nacla.org/blog/2013/10/3/dominican-
republic-"denationalization"-program-seeks-strip-citizenship-haitian-
descen, accessed March 4, 2015.

El Nuevo Diario. 2012. "Canciller de RD refuta afirmaciones contra el país
publicara periódico canadiense." January 3. www.elnuevodiario.com.do/app/
article.aspx?id=270058, accessed March 4, 2015.

Freedom House. 2012. "Americas." www.freedomhouse.org/regions/americas,
accessed March 10, 2015.

————. 2013. "Freedom in the World 2013: Democratic Breakthroughs in the
Balance." www.freedomhouse.org/sites/default/files/FIW%202013%20
Booklet%20-%20for%20Web_1.pdf, accessed March 4, 2015.

Gilbertson, Greta. 2006. "Citizenship in a Globalized World." Migration Policy
Institute. www.migrationinformation.org/Feature/display.cfm?ID=369,
accessed March 4, 2015.

Gonçalves Margerin, Marselha, and Melanie Teff. 2008. "Dominican Republic:
Time to Move Forward to Resolve Statelessness." Refugees International.
www.refugeesinternational.org/policy/field-report/dominican-republic-
time-move-forward-resolve-statelessness, accessed March 4, 2015.

Government of The Bahamas. 1973. The Constitution of The Commonwealth of
The Bahamas.

Hailbronner, Kay. 2003. "Nationality." In Migration and International Legal
Norms, edited by T. Alexander Aleinikoff and Vincent Chetail, 75–85. The
Hague: T. M. C. Asser Press.

Inter-American Court of Human Rights. 2005. Case of the Girls Yean and Bosico
v. Dominican Republic. http://www.corteidh.or.cr/docs/casos/articulos/
seriec_130_%20ing.pdf, accessed March 4, 2015.

International Organization for Migration. 2005. "Haitian Migrants in the
Bahamas 2005." http://www.iom.int/jahia/webdav/site/myjahiasite/shared/
shared/mainsite/published_docs/books/Haitian_Migrants_Report.pdf,
accessed March 4, 2015.

Jackson, Vicki C. 2009. "Citizenships, Federalisms, and Gender." In Migrations
and Mobilities: Citizenship, Borders, and Gender, edited by Seyla Benhabib
and Judith Resnik, 439–86. New York: New York University Press.

Jacobson, David. 1996. *Rights across Borders: Immigration and the Decline of Citizenship*. Baltimore: Johns Hopkins University Press.

Kostakopoulou, Theodora. 2008. *The Future Governance of Citizenship*. Cambridge: Cambridge University Press.

Kymlicka, Will. 1995. *Multicultural Citizenship: A Liberal Theory of Minority Rights*. Oxford: Oxford University Press.

Manly, Mark. 2007. "The Spirit of Geneva—Traditional and New Actors in the Field of Statelessness." *Refugee Survey Quarterly* 26 (4): 255–61.

MOSCTHA. 2012. "Statelessness in the Dominican Republic." https://vimeo.com/60862831, accessed March 4, 2015.

Murphy, Michael, and Siobhan Harty. 2003. "Post-Sovereign Citizenship." *Citizenship Studies* 7 (2): 181–97.

Nyamnjoh, Francis B. 2007. "From Bounded to Flexible Citizenship: Lessons from Africa." *Citizenship Studies* 11 (1): 73–82.

Ong, Aihwa. 1999. *Flexible Citizenship: The Cultural Logics of Transnationality*. Durham, NC: Duke University Press.

Open Society Justice Initiative and the Center for Justice and International Law. 2012. "Submission to the United Nations Human Rights Committee: Review of the Dominican Republic."

Republic of Haiti. 1987. "Haitian Constitution." http://pdba.georgetown.edu/constitutions/haiti/haiti1987.html, accessed March 4, 2015.

———. 2012. "Sommaire." *Journal le Moniteur* 96.

Rojas, Ricardo. 2013. "Dominican Court Ruling Renders Hundreds of Thousands Stateless." Reuters. www.reuters.com/article/2013/10/12/us-dominican-republic-citizenship-idUSBRE99B01Z20131012, accessed March 4, 2015.

Rolle, Krystel. 2012. "Ingraham: Haitian Leader 'Mistaken.'" *Nassau Guardian*. February 13. www.thenassauguardian.com/index.php?option=com_content&view=article&id=24004&Itemid=27, accessed March 4, 2015.

Sassen, Saskia. 2006. *Territory, Authority, Rights: From Medieval to Global Assemblages*. Princeton, NJ: Princeton University Press.

Somers, Margaret R. 2008. *Genealogies of Citizenship: Markets, Statelessness, and the Right to Have Rights*. Cambridge: Cambridge University Press.

Soysal, Yasemin Nuhoğlu. 1994. *Limits of Citizenship: Migrants and Postnational Membership in Europe*. Chicago: University of Chicago Press.

Teune, Henry. 2009. "Citizenship Deterritorialized: Global Citizenships." In *The Future of Citizenship*, edited by Jose V. Ciprut, 229–52. Cambridge, MA: MIT Press.

Turnquest, Ava. 2011. "Immigration Policy Set for Changes." *The Tribune.* June 10. 107 (163): 1, 9.

United Nations. 1948. *Universal Declaration of Human Rights.* www.un.org/en/documents/udhr/index.shtml, accessed March 4, 2015.

———. 1954. *Convention Relating to the Status of Stateless Persons.* www2.ohchr.org/english/law/stateless.htm, accessed March 4, 2015.

———. 1961. *The Convention on the Reduction of Statelessness.* www.unhcr.org/3bbb286d8.html, accessed March 4, 2015.

United Nations High Commissioner for Refugees. 2012a. "2012 Regional Operations Profiles—Americas." www.unhcr.org/pages/4a02da6e6.html, accessed May 23, 2012.

———. 2012b. "Guidelines on Statelessness No. 1." HCR/GS/12/01.

———. 2013a. "2013 UNHCR Country Operations Profile—Americas." www.unhcr.org/pages/4a02da6e6.html.

———. 2013b. "Searching for Citizenship." www.unhcr.org/pages/49c3646c155.html.

United Nations Human Rights Council. 2008. "Report of the Special Rapporteur on Contemporary Forms of Racism, Racial Discrimination, Xenophobia and Related Intolerances, Doudou Diene, and the Independent Expert on Minority Issues, Gay McDougall, Addendum: Mission to Dominican Republic." A/HRC/7/19/Add.5 and A/HRC/7/23/Add.3.

United States Department of State. 2010a. "2010 Human Rights Report: Bahamas." www.state.gov/documents/organization/160152.pdf, accessed May 23, 2012.

———. 2010b. "2010 Human Rights Report: Dominican Republic." www.state.gov/documents/organization/160162.pdf, accessed March 4, 2015.

Wooding, Bridget. 2009. "Contesting Discrimination and Statelessness in the Dominican Republic." *Forced Migration Review* 32: 23–25.

Wooding, Bridget, and Richard Moseley-Williams. 2004. "Inmigrantes haitianos y dominicanos de ascendencia haitiana en la República Dominica." Published in the Dominican Republic for Cooperación Internacional para el Desarollo y el Servicio Jesuita a Refugiados y Migrantes. http://espacinsular.org/IMG/_Inmigrantes_haitianos.pdf, accessed March 4, 2015.

7

"FREE" MEN AND AFRICAN COLONIZATION

· · · · · · · · · ·

The Difficulties of Defining Citizenship
in the Early American Republic

EUGENE VAN SICKLE

The opening decades of the nineteenth century proved turbulent ones in the United States as Americans struggled to shape their national political and cultural identity. As part of this process, the period witnessed the birth of competing movements designed to shape America to fit idealistic visions often informed by Jeffersonian thought. One of the most prominent movements of the period was African colonization. The African colonization movement addressed the overlooked theme of citizenship, a central element for understanding the democratic transformation of the early republic period of American history. Citizenship, Rogers Smith explains, is a socially and politically manufactured conception that evolves in a continual process of construction and destruction (Smith 2013, 3). Americans struggled to define citizenship in the decades before the Civil War, in part due to the presence of so many "free" men who were not fully citizens of the republic. Citizenship was a contentious subject because Americans had yet to reach consensus on its meaning at any political level—local, state, or federal. Americans did differentiate citizenship through formal and informal mechanisms, prohibiting men without property from voting while requiring African Americans to leave states when emancipated from slavery. Informally, discrimination in employment, hiring white workers over free African Americans for instance, kept second-class citizens from attaining an economic status that would likely bring entrance into full citizenship. The African colonization movement has been ignored in the process of constructing American citizenship in a period of intense change. This essay examines the role of African colonization in resolving the contested meaning of citizenship in the early republic and as a commentary on the final status of free African Americans in the United States.

The African colonization movement, initiated under the direction of the American Colonization Society (ACS) in December 1816, was the first truly national movement in United States history. Based in Washington, DC, the ACS claimed auxiliaries throughout the nation, enjoying its strongest support in the border states. In these states, citizenship was contested politically between the three levels of government, socially as immigrants vied with free African Americans for recognition from white males as more than second-class members, and economically for the material status that could open the doors to political inclusion. White Americans joined the colonization movement for myriad reasons, but nearly all were tied to the paradoxes associated with citizenship. Historians have generally ignored the colonization movement's commentary on the meaning of citizenship in the early republic in favor of exploring the ACS in relation to slavery. Debates over slavery helped define citizenship, and the fact that the colonization movement existed is acknowledgment that the subject troubled Americans struggling to define their identity. To be an American was to be "free," and the existence of any class of people labeled "free" yet denied nearly every benefit associated with that designation could not be ignored forever. Thus colonization emerged as a solution to that problem. Unfortunately, most interpret the movement only in relation to the ACS stance on slavery, when the movement offered a means to end a prominent form of second-class citizenship. Thomas Jefferson proclaimed that black Americans could be a nation unto themselves in the 1780s, but their inclusion in the United States was unpalatable for many white Americans. There was no place or "space (literally) for the emancipation and amalgamation of freedpeople into a more inclusive national identity." Agents of the African colonization movement recognized this reality in the aftermath of the War of 1812 and acted on the principles Jefferson identi-fied. Indeed, many colonizationists believed that they would save the United States and make citizenship universal by removing Jefferson's "captive nation" of black Americans (Onuf 2000, 161).

Black commentators on the American condition confirmed the obvi-ous contradictions that colonizationists saw in society. They lived in a nation where skin color alone was grounds for differentiated status; African Ameri-cans' skin tone overruled character and consigned them to second-class sta-tus despite being "free." Free African Americans also understood that they were not the ones to define freedom in the United States, try as they might. Reverend Samuel Cornish provided poignant documentation on the reality African Americans faced every day in the United States. Cornish was the editor of the first African American owned and operated newspaper in the United States, along with his colleague John B. Russwurm. In the *Weekly Advocate* he described "free black" with clear contempt, mocking the spirit ingrained in the American identity. Although the United States was pro-fessedly the home of a free people, Cornish boldly declared, America "righ-teously deprived" African Americans "of every civil and political privilege." "Free indeed," he taunted, "When almost every honorable incentive to the pursuit of happiness, so largely and freely held out to his fairer brother is withheld from him. . . . Too often the virtuous and intelligent man of color, must drag out an ignoble life, the victim of poverty and sorrow" (quoted in Kinshasa 1988, 7). This was America. The free black American was no citizen; he had no claim to nationality, nor could he count on the same legal protec-tions a white man took for granted in the United States. Cornish loudly proclaimed that rhetoric be damned, citizenship in the United States was hardly an equal or uniform proposition. American citizenship depended on hue; Cornish and those like him were clear proof of a class of people enjoy-ing a state of semicitizenship in the United States (Smith 2013, 9).

In the aftermath of the American Revolution, the free black popula-tion in the United States experienced explosive growth—statistically one of the fastest-growing segments of society by the 1820s. Driven by a wave of post-Revolution emancipations, African Americans flocked to urban areas seeking opportunities to elevate their economic status in hopes that it could be translated into political equality. The growth of cities such as Baltimore and Philadelphia concerned white Americans who failed to realize the full range of factors driving this internal migration. Many openly speculated on the character of black Americans as this process raced ahead, combining it with the Jeffersonian belief that two free races harmoniously coexisting and enjoying the rights and privileges of the American system was anathema; such a world was unbearable to contemplate, and a solution needed to be found before war came in the struggle for equality. A nascent industrialization magnified the paradox free African Americans exposed by adding thousands of landless workers who also flocked to cities looking for work. The growing classes of wage workers, white and black, made citizenship an imperative goal. Economic transformation, fear of a rapidly growing population of free second-class Americans, and angst over a burgeoning class of landless industrial workers merged in the psyche of Jeffersonian republicans to convince many colonizationists that America faced a calamitous situation; the United States would disintegrate in a cataclysmic race war. This context birthed the ACS, and its members sought to solve every issue and save the nation by creating a homogeneous society—one where it was possible to define citizenship as equal and uniform for every American (*African Repository* n.d., vol. 15, no. 16, 268; Kennedy 2003, 36–37, 177; Onuf 2000, 161, 175; Staudenraus, 1961, viii, 17–20).[1]

Colonization interestingly implied something that African Americans repeatedly demonstrated but most whites sought to ignore: a free people, denied full citizenship, would not hold their peace indefinitely. Colonization anticipated a day when no level of American government or society could exclude free African Americans from their rights as citizens. In the early republican period it became increasingly difficult to avoid the moral call for uniform citizenship inferred by democracy. Moreover, free African Americans demonstrated daily a willingness to earn citizenship. One of the reasons that black communities in the upper South and mid-Atlantic grew so quickly is that these urban areas offered institutions that could help African Americans meet the demands of citizenship. Through black schools and black churches, African Americans found ways for self-improvement to live better lives and to challenge white racial dominance all while raising their political and social condition to levels whites could recognize as worthy of citizenship (Kinshasa 1988, 6–7).

In its barest form, colonization under the ACS was a preemptive move made on a scale comparable to a national defense policy. African colonization anticipated the day when whites would no longer be able to withstand the moralizing onslaught in the demands of citizenship for African Americans.

The history of the mid-twentieth century illustrates just how prophetic the founders of the ACS were in their understanding of the power of freedom and the quest for inclusion as citizens. Colonizationists aimed at building a racially standardized society where a messy definition of citizenship was no longer required. Moreover, the developing democratic system that vaulted Andrew Jackson into the presidency seemed to demand a unitary definition of citizenship. Racism and slavery, said colonizationists, had so thoroughly complicated the status of African Americans that white minds could barely separate the free from the enslaved. Slavery had also built up significant barriers to citizenship and entrenched a general attitude that all black Americans were wretches, forever backward and incapable of civilization. The white race subordinated the black in nearly every way possible, ingraining "deep-rooted prejudices" that made a race war inevitable if they attempted to share citizenship. Lyman Trumbull, whose support was instrumental in adding the 13th Amendment to the Constitution, provides such an example of entrenched prejudgment. He noted early in his career that he wanted nothing to do with black Americans whether free or slave. Morally such distinctions, whether legal or social, contradicted the philosophy of American freedom and the power of American democracy. Colonization proposed a remedy for this particular dilemma (Kinshasa 1988, 103).

Robert G. Harper, one of the founders of the ACS, captured the essence of colonizationists' attitudes about free blacks. They were, he noted, "condemned to a state of hopeless inferiority and degradation, by their colour; which is an indelible mark of their origin and former condition, and establishes an impassible barrier between them and the whites." Citizenship was consequently "closed forever, by our habits and our feelings, which perhaps it would be more correct to call our prejudices, or a mixture of both." Harper was no progressive-thinking Yankee abolitionist when these words were published for public contemplation. Harper was a former South Carolina congressman living in Baltimore, Maryland, and married to the daughter of Charles Carroll. Charles Carroll of Carrollton owned thousands of acres of land and dozens of slaves in Maryland. He, as much as the man who married his daughter, had noticed the alarming changes in Baltimore—an industrializing city and home to one of the fastest-growing free black communities in the United States. Harper admitted such feelings "make us recoil with horror from the idea of an intimate union with the free blacks, and preclude the possibility of such a state of equality between them and us, as alone could make us one people" (A Letter from Gen. Robert Goodloe Harper 1818, 6). Harper clearly proves what Rogers Smith highlights in his own work: democracies never establish "uniform, unitary citizenship" (Smith 2013, 6). White Americans, regardless of their positions on slavery, refused to extend citizenship to people of African descent under any circumstances; the best Harper and those like him could tolerate was settling African Americans outside the boundaries of the United States where they could enjoy citizenship in their own nation.

Some African Americans recognized the obstacles racism placed before them and decided that emigration was their best option. Reverend Lott Cary was one of the first emigrants to the ACS colony of Liberia; he went as part of the founding group of colonists in 1821. When asked by a fellow minister why he was going, Cary answered, stating, "I am an African, and in this country, however meritorious my conduct, and respectable my character, I cannot receive the credit due to either. I wish to go to a country where I shall be estimated by my merits, not by my complexion; and I feel bound to labor for my suffering race" (Gurley 1835; Kinshasa 1988, 24). Unable to fully participate in the nation that gave him life, Cary chose to be a founder of a new one where men like him could be free. Cary further combined religious purpose with his own desire to enjoy liberty much like many white Americans. He shared a purpose in spreading freedom but also recognized the hurdles that democratic societies erected to limit full participation. Cary's perception of America and the role of colonization further mirrored white colonizationists' attitudes. Reverend Samuel Hopkins promoted colonization in combination with missionary efforts in the late eighteenth century. Even then, he noted that it was the only path to freedom open to free blacks. Free black Americans and white colonizationists at least shared this common ground—opportunities in the United States were intentionally limited for people of color, but they could add to the number of citizens on Earth and in Heaven through colonization (*African Repository* n.d., 201–3; Kinshasa 1988, 28).

Despite attitudes about race and the future prospects of free African Americans in the United States, the colonization movement faced serious opposition from many quarters even though the ACS marketed itself as a solution to uniquely American problems. That free African Americans rejected colonization overwhelmingly should come as no surprise. Yet colonization raised the ire of slaveholders as well, especially in the Deep South.

There colonization was synonymous with treason because some supporters thought it a means for ending slavery in the United States. More problematic was the society's recognition of free African Americans as potential citizens. In this sense colonizationists were heirs of Jefferson in seeing black Americans as eligible for membership in a nation of their own. But such notions undermined legal structures built to support slavery and social order, essential pillars of southern society. Nearly every possible approach to citizenship was closed to people of African descent in a slave society, and any suggestion that an obviously inferior race of men could be candidates for equal participation was the most profane type of subversion one could perpetrate. Colonizationists' nevertheless attempted to accommodate slave owners and reach a middle ground hoping people would see the pragmatism of their plan. If successful, colonization would open the gates of freedom to generations (Staudenraus 1961, 31, 39, 111).

Colonizationists in the border states generally argued that free blacks could attain citizenship outside the United States with their assistance. One colonizationist made this explicitly clear in chastising the white governor of the Maryland colony at Cape Palmas in 1835; Charles Howard, one of managers of Maryland's state colonization fund and a future president of the Maryland State Colonization Society, wrote that no matter how "confident [you] might be in the abilities of a coloured person as your representative in your absence yet some years must elapse before such an one will be viewed with the respect that is accorded to a white man" (*African Repository* n.d., vol. 15, no. 16, 28).[2] Colonization would show with firm examples that black Americans could be elevated to equal status, but it would take time and it required removal outside North America.

Howard's attitude was more common than one may think for the period. No matter what free blacks did to prove themselves worthy of participation or inclusion in American society, the baggage of slavery and racism clouded the vision of white Americans including ACS leaders to the point that they saw their plan as protecting an emerging American identity. They could conceive no "bonds of citizenship" as described by Rogers Smith that could join these communities together at any level (Smith 2013, 17). The work of William Stanton showed that Americans' views of race in the early nineteenth century were confused about the proper place of African Americans in society (Stanton 1960, 3–16). Americans had in fact debated the final status of African Americans for decades, even to the point of speculating on human origins all in an effort to rationalize varying degrees of inclusion or exclusion in the American experiment.

Samuel Stanhope Smith, a Presbyterian minister and president of the College of New Jersey, argued in his *Essay on the Causes of the Variety of Complexion and Figure in the Human Species* (1787) that the human species descended from a common remote ancestor. Human differences, continued Smith, originated from environmental conditions and the habits of life—especially the states of savagery and civilization. In essence, Smith's treatise implied that anyone could be civilized in the right environment, a point colonizationists made in arguing that slavery had irrevocably marked African Americans as inferior beings. Richard Harlan, founder of vertebrate paleontology in the United States, reinforced Smith's position by arguing that humans had common (read shared) origins. Harlan cited history in declaring Africans were the least civilized peoples; thus, they had the weakest claims to citizenship, but it did not mean they were perpetually excluded from it. From these roots, white society concluded that African Americans would likely never attain equal levels of civilization even if they had a shared heritage (Stanton 1960, 10). Prominent scholars and philosophers Alexander Pope, David Hume, and Georges Cuvier reinforced white attitudes of superiority along these same lines (Gould 1996, 62–63, 66, 71). While definitions of citizenship remained fluid, few found evidence to upset "the propriety of racial ranking during the eighteenth and nineteenth centuries," even though colonizationists anticipated a day when it would be required because blacks constituted a nation (Gould 1996, 66).

Thomas Jefferson claimed black inferiority as well in his early commentaries about America. His suggestions that black Americans were biologically different combined with his plan to end slavery profoundly shaped the colonization experiment and informed the argument over citizenship (Jefferson 1999, 144–46). He suggested that his own slaves were capable of improvement, but the system of slavery made it nearly impossible for them to be accepted as equals in the United States, even by himself. Moreover, as Peter Onuf argues, Jefferson envisioned African Americans as a separate nation. The significance of such descriptors is underappreciated and dismissed as Jeffersonian hypocrisy because he admitted that all men were capable of equality while steadfastly holding them in bondage. Yet Thomas Jefferson understood the root problem: "Whatever be their degree of talents, it is no measure of their rights" and no amount of reasoning or moralizing could dismiss this simple fact by one of the designers of American rights! (Onuf 2000, 161; Jefferson 1999, 63). An inclusive citizenship would not have been a problem in an earlier age or if there were not more than a million slaves in America, but in the 1820s it had become a significant concern, as the nation grappled with its own identity and destiny. Slave masters searched far and wide to justify the continued enslavement of African peoples, while white society barred free African Americans' entry to citizenship status.

Henry Clay noted that the uniformity needed for the republic to survive required colonization. It always had. Clay, another ACS founder and prominent politician, echoed the observations of both Harper and Jefferson. What he added was the crucial question of political status for African Americans. "Emancipation in the farming states," said Clay "is one whose solution depends upon the relative numbers of the two races, in any given state" (Clay 1904, 216). Free blacks were "peculiarly situated," Clay pronounced, because they had neither "the immunities of freemen [citizenship], nor [were they] subject to the incapacities of slaves." African Americans shared in "the qualities of both"; thus, the danger of the population (Clay 1961, 2: 263). Thomas Jefferson, Robert and Charles Harper, and Henry Clay all recognized that black men could experience the unalienable rights that formed the core of the American system. Nevertheless, Clay's comments finally made clear the real problem in America: worthiness as citizens was less important than the potential political power African Americans might exert in areas where they made up a significant percentage of the population. It was easily conceivable that free African Americans, if made citizens, could control local governments, and this was the future that was intolerable even for a "nationalist" like Henry Clay. Clay made it clear why the ACS existed for him (Staudenraus 1961, 28).

Colonizationists' insistence that their work begin with free African Americans has made it easy for scholars to view colonization as nothing more than a racist movement feigning humanitarian and Christian concern for Africans and their descendants. Others have argued that the movement was antislavery in substance because it recognized the role of slavery in hindering the expansion of freedom in the United States. Abolitionists reached the opposite conclusion, identifying the ACS as a proslavery agent seeking to strengthen the bonds of slavery (Staudenraus 1961, 29). All of these interpretations miss a key point Clay identified, in that ending slavery was only part of the issue at stake. There was the final question of what to do with the "captive nation?" Charles C. Harper invoked Jefferson when he declared that African Americans had been ascribed an "inferiority so dejected, that even their complexion has become a badge of it." Harper's "badge" could never be taken off, and every American knew it. He unequivocally linked that "badge" with permanent second-class status; if African Americans "remain among us here their condition cannot be materially improved ... above the level to which your [American] injustice had reduced him."[3] Freedmen would remain a "captive nation" even if the law no longer bound them to subservience.

Certainly, Harper hoped his audacity would win the support of African Americans who passionately opposed the movement. Yet the oddity of the speech no doubt offended many white supporters. Outside of the black press or radical abolitionist pamphlets, such scathing statements were virtually nonexistent. Thus to dismiss colonization as simply racist ignores the complexity of both the movement and the question of citizenship in an era of expansive North American democracy. The colonization movement originated with individuals who thought the injuries slavery caused were so great that they would prevent, for all time, the development of a homogeneous population that shared an easy yet uniform citizenship. Free blacks were the focal point of colonization because they were the most hazardous to this vision for the American republic—they were free people in a nation boasting of having the freest government in history yet they were denied, by every possible means, the enjoyment of the rights entailed in freedom (*African Repository* n.d., vol. 17, no. 19 [1841], 294–96).

The breadth of the argument over the place of African Americans went far beyond the philosophical. Dr. Charles Caldwell, a Philadelphia physician, founder of at least two medical schools, and an ardent racist, chimed in with his *Thoughts on the Original Unity of the Human Race* in 1830. Caldwell argued that multiple creations had birthed distinct human species. He posited that it was impossible that a single species could hold such wide variation in physical appearances. If Caldwell's speculation was right, two races of free people in the United States could never become true equals.[4] Stephen Jay Gould notes in his *Mismeasure of Man* that scientific explanations of racial differences like Caldwell's mirrored the social atmosphere of the nineteenth century; frequently, the issue at stake was the "place" or station open to nonwhites in society (Gould 1996, 54). African colonization mirrored American society too as one of the many movements seeking to alter the fabric of

American society to remove the legal, social, and economic mechanisms that differentiated America's citizenry.

Samuel George Morton joined Caldwell before the decade closed, providing the "hard" scientific evidence proslavery apologists needed to deny black Americans any claim to citizenship while entrenching slavery deeper in the American mind. Morton published his *Crania Americana* in 1839. Respected as a scientist and the head of the American School of Ethnology, Morton had built a grisly collection of human skulls for his study. His examination of American crania formed the bedrock of the argument for racial inferiority and consequently exclusion from citizen status in the United States as tensions rose over slavery. While Morton himself did not suggest his analyses implied intelligence level or inferiority, his work nevertheless gave scientific weight to those who rejected arguments for any form of equality. *Crania Americana* revived eighteenth-century arguments about human origins and, through its quantitative analysis, suggested it was possible to distinguish, precisely, a natural hierarchy through science. Science provided a means to differentiate citizenship in ways that no amount of moralizing could revoke, while removing the need to rationalize discriminatory laws that relegated human beings to second-class status (Lowance, 2003, 256; Stanton 1960, 33).

Morton's collection of skulls continued to grow thanks to his friendship with George R. Gliddon. Serving as the American proconsul in Cairo, Egypt, Gliddon used his position to procure Egyptian artifacts, which he sent back to the United States. Capitalizing on the peculiar American fascination with Africa, Gliddon provided Morton with dozens of African skulls. He also arranged tours for himself where he personally unveiled Egyptian mummies to the American public for a small entrance fee. Americans in the 1830s and 1840s in spite of their claims to abhor all things African were clearly fascinated by Africa. Americans read with great interest the tales of explorers trekking into the Dark Continent. The skulls Gliddon contributed became the foundation of Morton's 1844 work, *Crania Aegyptiaca*. Two important conclusions came from Morton's second study that proslavery advocates latched on to in defending their calls for black inferiority. First, Morton seemingly resolved a burning question about who built the Egyptian pyramids; Caucasians and Negroes built this fascinating civilization known as Egypt. He continued with his second proposition, explaining that Negroes were numerous in Egypt, and they were servants and slaves, just like they were in nineteenth- century America (Gould 1996, 85; Stanton 1960, 51–52).

Morton's second work had far-reaching consequences in the United States. Those who argued that free blacks were incapable of civilization now had scientific proof to support their exclusion and, worse, to recommend their enslavement. Morton's studies implied that all Negroes were biologically inferior and had always known a condition of servitude. While Morton's obviously flawed methodology and conclusions have been dismissed, his work proved important at the time because of its application in the proslavery arguments of Josiah Nott, H. "Ariel" Payne Buckner, and George Fitzhugh; all three maintained that African descended peoples were biologically inferior to Caucasians (Nott and Gliddon 1854; Payne 1867; Fitzhugh 1857). However, as Gould notes, the support Morton's studies gave to race-based arguments placed Americans in a severe bind. Scientific data that "proved" racial inequality resolved the dilemma created by the American paradox of slavery and freedom on the one hand; on the other hand, it did nothing to contradict evidence in their own communities where free blacks worked for self-improvement by creating their own schools, churches, and community organizations. It did nothing to counter the examples of Cornish, David Walker, or Frederick Douglass (Gould 1996, 101–3; Kinshasa 1988, 22).

A closer look at Josiah Nott illustrates the ways proslavery apologists fought for the peculiar institution while demonstrating how scientific racism undermined arguments for citizenship. Born in South Carolina, Nott became a physician and ardent supporter of slavery. Nott praised Morton's work for establishing as indisputable fact, the inferiority of all nonwhite races and for demonstrating that biology would not permit the "mental cultivation" needed to "elevate an inferior to the level of a superior race" (McCardell 1979, 80). Nature, Nott argued, had permanently fixed the status of black Americans. Morton's science obviously supported what Josiah Nott already believed, as he became one of the most outspoken advocates of African inferiority and the positive good of slavery, all of which combined to mute arguments for citizenship.

Nott eventually combined his efforts with those of George R. Gliddon to resurrect the diversity of creation argument as the final word on the status of African Americans and the rationale for subordination. Polygenesis, as it was termed, was a theory Swiss naturalist and Harvard University professor of natural history Louis Agassiz promoted. Agassiz immigrated to the United States in the early 1840s. After a visit to Philadelphia, Agassiz immediately argued that the presence of free blacks in the South would cause the downfall of the United States, and he set out to prove black inferiority through scientific inquiry. The result of his study was the theory of poly-genesis, which Nott and Gliddon claimed, in 1854, was a notion never "con-ceived by any primitive nations, such as Egypt or China. Neither does the idea appear to have occurred to the author of *Genesis*" (Lowance 2003, 316; Stanton 1960, 103). History itself, Nott later stated, gave undeniable proof that the white race was superior and that black and white could only coex-ist as master and slave. Short of that relationship, the only other option was expulsion or extermination (Nott, "The Negro Race: Its Ethnology and His-tory," in Lowance 2003, 320). Ironically, the suggestion that a decimating race war loomed in America's future reflected what so many colonization-ists believed; thus, the need to remove African Americans to the place God intended for them—Africa. Slavery, Nott concluded, was the "normal condi-tion of the negro, the most advantageous to him, and the most ruinous, in the end to a white nation" (ibid., 326). Only the effort to incorporate them as equals would be worse. Nott oddly embraced the idea of colonization even though it was a useless experiment. Liberia was, he said, the "last hope of the Negro as an independent race" even though it was "a vain struggle against fixed laws of nature" (quoted in Stanton 1960, 148).

Scientific racism forced colonizationists to respond in ways that surely made them uncomfortable as they pushed the boundaries of what white society could tolerate. Consistency required it however, as colonizationists had publicly declared free African Americans capable of attaining equality with white nations, albeit outside US borders. Colonizationists challenged scientific racists like Nott who jeopardized their efforts to colonize Africa and make the United States into a homogeneous nation. Moreover, Nott's contention that colonization was pointless suggested that more than two decades of effort had been for naught, a proposition they flatly rejected. In 1847, the colonies started by the ACS merged into an independent republic called Liberia—derived from the word *liberty*. If Morton was correct and nature itself was against the improvement of African Americans, why should anyone support the colonization of Africa? Why should the issue of citizen-ship be discussed any longer? Colonizationists argued that colonists exer-cised their own rights while bringing civilization and salvation to the "Dark Continent." If apologists for slavery, bolstered by this new data, were correct, colonizationists used the least qualified agents of American society to spread both the gospel and American-style liberty to parts of the world that would never be able to truly enjoy them.

Colonizationists vigorously disagreed with racists like Nott, refusing to accept the validity of the science he embraced. The irony of it all was unfortunately lost on colonizationists; white men who had spent decades trying to rid the nation of free African Americans found themselves ardently defending black humanity and their suitability to be part of the family of nations but not part of the bonds that tied the citizenry of America together. From the beginning of the movement, supporters of colonization maintained that settling African Americans in Africa not only saved them from a life of degradation in the United States, it also allowed them to partake in the natural rights Jefferson helped define in the eighteenth century. Moreover, free black Americans could participate in the grand design the almighty had for the American republic to spread an empire of liberty (see Crapol 1997, 470).[5] American colonization of Africa would save the Dark Continent from its floundering existence by bringing the light of Christianity and the saving graces of western civilization to people left behind by history and injured by slavery. Even after the national colonization society splintered, state colonization societies continued to argue that the scheme was the only way to save the American republic and do justice to an injured race, fully human and descended from the same ancestors as whites (*African Repository*, vol. 15, no. 8 [October 1839]; vol. 17, no. 19 [October 1841], 294–95; vol. 22, no. 9 [June 1847], 166).

The Maryland State Colonization Society (MSCS) was one of the most consistent in defending black humanity and condemning white prejudice, though its members certainly were not abolitionists in the vein of William Lloyd Garrison. The MSCS broke with its sister societies and established its own colony in Africa in 1834. The society was a trailblazer of sorts, appointing expatriate John B. Russwurm as the first black governor of any Liberian colony in 1836. Perhaps more convincing, however, of how seriously the members of the MSCS pursued their task was the education of Samuel F. McGill. McGill was the son of an African American from Baltimore who left Maryland for Africa in 1827. Like many who chose emigration over semicitizenship in Maryland, McGill went specifically so his children could be free; he doubted they would ever experience true freedom in the United States, at least as long as slavery existed. The Maryland society offered to educate Samuel as a physician (it is worth noting that the MSCS also wanted him to be its colonial physician). McGill agreed and returned to the United States for medical training at MSCS expense. Samuel McGill arrived in 1836 no doubt excited about beginning education for a professional career only to be reminded of the reality of his status in America. One of the most influential members of the MSCS in Baltimore, cautioned the lad; it is necessary, began Moses Sheppard, "to apprise you that it [your race] will preclude you from associating with the whites, and place you in the degraded class of the blacks. You must not expect to hear the term Mr. McGill from a white man. In the college you must appear as a servant; there is not a medical school in the United States into which you could be admitted in any other character, but you will have all the means of improvement and the same instruction as the other students, and in proportion as you waive the claim of equality it will be conceded to you, in proportion as you claim it, it will be denied."[6] In a moment of brutal honesty, Sheppard captured the essence of nineteenth-century America for every free African American—they could enjoy some of what the United States offered, but they would always be second-class Americans.

Maryland colonizationists were not the only ones who acknowledged the reality Sheppard described to young McGill. Expressing rhetoric that could just have easily been read in a 1776 manifesto, the ACS printed the following in its journal in 1839: "all men are born equally free and independent, and have the same right to their freedom which they have to property, or life" (*African Repository*, vol. 15, no. 16 [September 1839], 268). It seems that colonizationists, even when they failed to see their own hypocrisy, were the only ones in the white community willing to see things as they really were in the United States. In 1844 the ACS reasserted human unity and rights. In May, the *African Repository and Colonial Journal* carried an editorial calling on Americans to fulfill their destiny. "We are bound," said this edition, "to do good and communicate unto all men, as we have opportunity, *because they are men* possessing a common nature." The writer continued: "They [free blacks] are embarrassed in that natural pursuit of happiness which is *the birthright* of MAN, by the shackles of an arbitrary and iron caste, and by the potency of a popular opinion at present irresistible" (*African Repository*, vol. 20, no. 5 [May 1844], 150). It was time for all Americans to see and hear—African Americans could not be denied their rights forever; colonizationists had a plan in place to fulfill America's destiny as a beacon of human liberty and solve the issues arising from the presence of slavery in a democratic republic.

In the same article that declared black entitlement to natural rights, the ACS noted that the physical attributes of African peoples was an adaptation, divinely inspired, to the physical and natural instincts needed for survival in tropical Africa. Because environment forced humans to adapt, it was logical to assert that slavery was the sole factor that made blacks inferior in the United States. African colonization, because it sought to improve the condition of black men through repatriation, was legitimate, the ACS contended, because it placed the natural rights of man within reach of the colored race without upsetting the quest for unitary citizenship in the United States (*African Repository*, vol. 20, no. 5 [May 1844], 152). In September 1846, the ACS again refuted the conclusions of a scientist studying the "Bushmen" of South Africa. Identified only as Mr. Hope, the author alleged that the Bushmen were less intelligent than slaves and behaved like monkeys. Hope suggested that his observations were proof enough that there were different species of unrelated humans. Negroes were good for little more than the tasks assigned them at creation—"to be hewers of wood and drawers of water, and renders it impossible for them even to rise above these menial occupations" (*African Repository*, vol. 22, no. 9 [September 1846], 265).[7] ACS members responded, "to remove this prejudice and correct these false ideas." Liberia alone provided sufficient proof that Hope's assertions were beyond the absurd. "The present degraded *character* of the colored people, is the legitimate consequence of their degraded *condition*" in America! (ibid., 266).

Colonizationists went on to challenge the inferences about race in the works of Hope, Morton, and Nott. While the author is unknown, an article titled "Unity and Diversity" ran in several colonization journals. Colonizationists slammed southern whites for accepting the "doctrine of original *diversity* in the human family" under the guise of a rational defense of slavery and for its clear meaning for citizenship. Colonizationists sarcastically asserted that there was a better defense for slavery. Polygenesis was an idea "entirely erroneous ... the human race is really one family, from a common ancestry, (and therefore the total fallacy and feebleness of any system which assumes the contrary,) we are well persuaded that the sanction, which the South receives from the Bible, to her inherited institutions, is the true and the unanswerable reply to all the appeals of a spurious philanthropy, and all the ravings of an insane fanaticism, on this subject." Recognizing the importance of consistency in their argument, colonizationists opined that, "To shift our position from this substantial ground of sacred truth, and to place ourselves on the shifting quicksand of an untenable infidel theory, is at once to become embarrassed with a great scientific error, and, by outraging the common conscience of Christendom, to incur the odium of inhumanity and irreligion. If the diversity theory be true, if the dark-skinned African be in origin different from ourselves, not of the same human family, and therefore not comprehended in the provisions of God's laws and Christ's redemption as conveyed in the Bible, then it is plain we sustain to that race no such relations as those which the Colonization movement supposes. Negroes, in such case, can only be looked upon as a higher order of cattle, not to be dealt with on rational or religious principles; not to be trained and Christianized, toward ultimate elevation and self-government in their own dark continent, or any where else; but to be treated merely as interest of convenience may dictate."[8] It would be nonsensical to allow slaves in church if they were not fully human and capable of receiving the long-lost rights endowed in all mankind by the creator. In its boldest statement, the ACS definitively declared not only that African Americans were human beings, but also that they were entitled to the natural rights of man as dictated by the God of nature.

For those doubting the right of colonizationists to lecture on the subject, the *Maryland Colonization Journal* picked up the thread. "We are not going beyond our special province in entering upon this question. On the contrary, agitated as the question is, and liable to be misled as the uninformed are, it is due to ourselves, and to the important interest we represent, that we should at least indicate (our limits forbid more) the chief considerations which establish the unity of the human race, and consequently, the family relationship between the sablest native of Guinea, and the fairest inheritor of noble Saxon blood."[9] Morton's shortcoming was in dwelling on the "marked peculiarities" of the races of men, an unsound practice in their opinion. Colonizationists pointed out that the Finns, Hungarians, and Turcomans—widely differing people in physical appearances—could still be traced to "the same stock." Moreover, they appealed to linguistic evidence for proof of the common origins of all humanity by noting the connections in languages between India and Europe while the physical appearance was as different as those between African and Caucasian.[10]

Agassiz was mistaken as well in advocating polygenesis. Gould describes Agassiz as a splitter; that is, he made distinctions between species based upon intricate peculiarities in their design (Gould 1996, 76). Colonizationists noted this quality in Agassiz's work as well, disputing his insistence that minute differences were evidence of distinct species. "The *Physical corre-spondencies*" of men, regardless of climate showed all races were part of the same species; "all men have an upright attitude, and the omni-versel hand, the one giving them practical control of the earth, the other directing them heaven-ward." There were physiological associations too that colonizationists argued proved their case. Immutable natural laws governing sex, generation, growth, maturation, and death applied to all races. "Newton and the negro, are indeed far apart in mental elevation," but this could also be said of any and every infant regardless of pedigree.[11] Colonizationists concluded by noting that societies, regardless of location and history, shared the monumental tokens of a common ancestry. Similar social and religious customs are found among peoples separated by vast distances. People were citizens of civilizations, kingdoms, and empires. Human beings shared an instinctive nature; no matter the race, location, or the environment, there were certain things humans created in every society. Why should black Americans not be citizens of their own nation?[12]

The Civil War ultimately ended the Jeffersonian vision for American development, dooming the colonization movement to the dustbin, judged a failure by historians. As such, the public discourse on the place of black Americans goes largely unnoticed insofar as the colonization movement is concerned. It continues, despite the passionate discourse flowing from ACS supporters, to be overshadowed by the insistence of viewing colonization only in relation to its effectiveness as a means to end slavery. We should consider the movement and its place in the larger narrative of nineteenth-century citizenship struggles. Surely, supporters of colonization had pragmatic motives for taking the stances they did, informed by their own struggle to come to terms with adopting Jeffersonian notions about the relationship of two free races in a republic. However, if we consider African colonization as a commentary on citizenship in the early republic, the movement provides remarkable insight into what the first generations of Americans thought in constructing their own meaning of citizenship in a new nation. Colonization illustrates the degree to which notions of belonging are constructed and should remind us that inclusion as citizens is not an automatic function of presence. The colonization movement gave voice to those concerned about the direction of the republic and who was eligible to participate in the process in a period characterized by the idea of the "common man." The study of the colonization movement also provides a practical example of Rogers

Smith's assertion about the difficulties democratic societies face in form-ing a unified version of citizenship. In the final analysis, the colonization movement should make us appreciate that nineteenth-century Americans understood the importance of reaching consensus on an American definition of citizenship, and that citizenship is often a negotiated status that needs to be guarded every day.

NOTES

1. See also "Colonization of the Free Colored Population of Maryland and of Such Slaves as May Hereafter Become Free," reel 31, the Maryland State Colonization Society Papers (hereafter *MSCS Papers*).
2. Quoted from *MSCS Papers*, 2. Correspondence Sent, Latrobe Letter Book, reel 16. Charles Howard to James Hall, May 30, 1835; "An address Delivered at the Annual Meeting of the Maryland State Colonization Society, in the City of Annapolis," January 23, 1835. By Charles C. Harper, *MSCS Papers*, 15. Pamphlets (not in the original collection).
3. *MSCS Papers*, 15. Pamphlets (not in original collection), 4. "An Address deliv-ered at the Annual Meeting of the Maryland State Society by C. C. Harper," January 23, 1835.
4. http://books.google.com/books?id=nBXjonLvlıMC&pg=PAı&lpg=PAı&d q=Thoughts+on+the+Original+Unity+of+the+Human+Race&source=bl&o ts=Dk26be6yoZ&sig=u2jtie799ANUWO7Qduwl7KxMdqE&hl=en&sa=X &ei=23IMT7ixIITctwerucS7BQ&ved=0CB4Q6AEwAA#v=onepage&q=T houghts%20on%20the%20Original%20Unity%20of%20the%20Human%20 Race&f=false, accessed January 10, 2012.
5. The notion of America as an empire of liberty stems from a letter Jefferson wrote to James Madison, April 27, 1809. The idea continued to be part of the American vision of later presidents.
6. *MSCS Papers*, Correspondence Received, A. Letter Books, reel 2. Moses Sheppard to Samuel Ford McGill, January 12, 1836.
7. *African Repository*, Vol. 22, No. 9, September 1846, 265.
8. *MSCS Papers*, reel 29, *Maryland Colonization Journal*, March 1856, vol. 8, no. 10, 157.
9. Ibid.
10. Ibid., 158.
11. *MSCS Papers*, reel 29, *Maryland Colonization Journal*, March 1856, vol. 8, no. 10, 158.
12. Ibid.

WORKS CITED

A Letter from Gen. Robert Goodloe Harper, of Maryland, to Elias B. Caldwell, ESQ. Secretary of the American Society for Colonizing the Free People of Colour, in the United States, with their own consent. 1818. Baltimore: Printed for E. J. Cole, by R. J. Matchett, West Virginia University Wise Library.

African Repository and Colonial Journal. n.d. West Virginia University Wise Library.

Caldwell, Charles. 1830. *Thoughts on the Original Unity of the Human Race.* http://books.google.com/books?id=nBXjonLvlɪMC&pg=PAɪ&lpg=PAɪ&dq=Thoughts+on+the+Original+Unity+of+the+Human+Race&source=bl&ots=Dk26be6yoZ&sig=u2jtie799ANUWO7Qduwl7KxMdqE&hl=en&sa=X&ei=23IMT7ixIITctwerucS7BQ&ved=0CB4Q6AEwAA#v=onepage&q=Thoughts%20on%20the%20Original%20Unity%20of%20the%20Human%20Race&f=false.

Clay, Henry. 1904. *The Works of Henry Clay in Ten Volumes, Federal Edition Comprising His Life, Correspondence, and Speeches.* Edited by Calvin Colton. New York: G. P. Putnam's Sons.

———. 1961. *The Papers of Henry Clay.* Edited by James F. Hopkins. Vol. 2, *The Rising Statesman, 1815–1820.* Lexington: University Press of Kentucky.

Crapol, Edward P. 1997. "John Tyler and the Pursuit of National Destiny." *Journal of the Early Republic* 17 (3): 467–91.

Fitzhugh, George. 1857. *Cannibals All!* Reprint, Cambridge, MA: Harvard University Press, 2009. http://books.google.com/books?id=ECdb7EjiBnEC&printsec=frontcover&dq=george+fitzhugh&hl=en&sa=X&ei=-YgNT_C8GpCctwfnsPXABQ&ved=0CDAQ6AEwAA#v=onepage&q=george%20fitzhugh&f=false.

Gould, Stephen Jay. 1996. *The Mismeasure of Man.* New York: Norton.

Gurley, Ralph Randolph. 1835. *Sketch of the Life of the Rev. Lott Cary in "Life of Jehudi Ashmun, Late Colonial Agent in Liberia. With An Appendix, Containing Extracts from His Journal and Other Writings; With a Brief Sketch of the Life of The Rev. Lott Cary."* Electronic edition, Chapel Hill: University of North Carolina, 1999. http://docsouth.unc.edu/neh/gurley/gurley.html.

Jefferson, Thomas. 1999. *Notes of the State of Virginia.* New York: Penguin.

Kennedy, Roger G. 2003. *Mr. Jefferson's Lost Cause: Land, Farmers, and the Louisiana Purchase.* Oxford: Oxford University Press.

Kinshasa, Kwando M. 1988. *Emigration vs. Assimilation: The Debates in the African American Press, 1827–1861.* Jefferson, NC: McFarland.

Lowance, Mason I., Jr. 2003. *A House Divided: The Antebellum Slavery Debates in America, 1776–1865.* Princeton, NJ: Princeton University Press.

The Maryland State Colonization Society Papers. n.d. West Virginia University Wise Library.

McCardell, John. 1979. *The Idea of a Southern Nation: Southern Nationalists and Southern Nationalism, 1830–1860.* New York: Norton.

Nott, Josiah Clark, and George Robins Gliddon. 1854. *Types of Mankind; or, Ethnological researches, based upon the ancient monuments, paintings, sculptures, and crania of races, and upon their natural, geographical, philological and Biblical history: / illustrated by selections from the inedited papers of Samuel George Morton . . . and by additional contributions from Prof. L. Agassiz, LL. D., W. Usher, M. D., and Prof. H. S. Patterson, M. D. By J. C. and Geo. R. Gliddon.* Philadelphia: Lippincott, Grambo. http://books.google.com/books?id=woc OAQAAMAAJ&printsec=frontcover&dq=Josiah+Nott&hl=en&sa=X&ei=i okNT_6UDoS3twfZlZWlBQ&ved=0CDAQ6AEwAA#v=onepage&q=Jos iah%20Nott&f=false.

Onuf, Peter S. 2000. *Jefferson's Empire: The Language of American Nationhood.* Charlottesville: University of Virginia Press.

Payne, Buckner H. "Ariel." 1867. *The Negro: What Is His Ethnological Status?* 2nd ed. Project Gutenberg. www.gutenberg.org/files/31302/31302-h/31302-h.htm.

Smith, Rogers. 2013. "The Questions Facing Citizenship in the 21st Century." Keynote lecture at "The Meaning of Citizenship" conference, Wayne State University, Detroit, Michigan, March 21, 2013.

Stanton, William. 1960. *The Leopard's Spots: Scientific Attitudes toward Race in America, 1815–1859.* Chicago: University of Chicago Press.

Staudenraus, Philip J. 1961. *The African Colonization Movement, 1816–1865.* New York: Columbia University Press.

8

JUSTICE FOR
BORDER-CROSSING PEOPLES

· · · · · · · · · ·

DAVID WATKINS

INTRODUCTION

Citizenship, as a legal and normative concept, defines the condition of full membership in a sovereign, self-governing national community. Understood in these terms, citizenship produces remainders: individuals, groups, and ways of life that do not fit in the legal-normative model of equal citizenship in a single, unified national community. Many of these remainders are produced by the ancient and venerable practice of human migration, a social practice often found at or near the center of human societies and cultures for many thousands of years. States have claimed a right to exercise control of border-crossing activities as central to their understanding of their sovereign power, and the logic of the status of citizenship only bolsters that claim. If the state is to treat her citizens as full, equal rights-holding members of society, it must keep track of who those citizens are; migration must be tracked, and noncitizens permitted to be present in the polity's territory must be marked with a status of their own, in part to distinguish them from citizens.

For tourists, business travelers, and many other border crossers, this arrangement, at least when functioning reasonably well, raises few concerns. Many countries provide a status for such visitors consistent with some of the rights of citizenship—protection from crime, due process, access to infra-structure, and so on—that are necessary for their purposes, but not those ele-ments of citizenship that seem irrelevant or inappropriate for them (such as the right to vote or access to social welfare programs). But for a large group of border crossers, the norms of citizenship present a greater challenge. The secondary statuses available to them and their access to borders do not obvi-ously fulfill the requirements of justice. While they are not the only group of people for whom citizenship as membership produces legal and normative remainders, I will focus here on a group I call "border-crossing peoples." I define border-crossing peoples as a distinct group whose historical cultural, religious, and socioeconomic way of life requires regular and routine access to the crossing of an international border. Border-crossing peoples gener-ally have a long-standing history of participating in the cultural/social/economic pattern that necessitates that border crossing; sometimes predat-ing the existence of the border itself, or predating any significant efforts to control or restrict the border. Just as the control of borders is presumably a tool a national community uses to maintain and shape its identity, the crossing of the border is crucial to the shaped identities of border-crossing peoples. In the now-vast literature on migrants and migration, in which migrants are divided into a variety of analytic categories, this general cate-gory has not (to my knowledge) been identified. The most similar analytic category I'm aware of is "border-straddling nations," a category identified recently by Margaret Moore (2013). My conception of "border-crossing peoples" differs from Moore's "border-straddling nations" in two significant ways. First, I do not restrict this category to groups that constitute a distinct nation, with all that that entails. Some border-crossing peoples may be a small slice of a nation; others may be identified as a distinct group by a set of markers—perhaps ethnic, regional, or religious—that fall short of approach-ing the status of "nationhood." Second, a border-crossing people need not "straddle" the border territorially. One quintessential example of a border-crossing people, whose border-crossing rights are discussed in detail below, is the Kickapoo tribe. Their primary territorial locations do not straddle the US-Mexico border—their reservations in Oklahoma and Kansas and their settlement in Nacimiento, Mexico, are all several hours' travel from the US-Mexico border, and yet they are properly characterized as a border-crossing people because of the historical nature of the social, cultural, familial, and economic ties between the Kickapoo settlements in Mexico and the United

States. Whatever the reason border-crossing peoples has been ignored in the literature on immigration, it is unfortunate, as they have a distinct claim for accommodation. Indeed, much of the literature on citizenship and migration focuses on one-way, permanent migration, not on the kind of back-and-forth border crossing that characterize the lives of border-crossing peoples (Hampshire 2013). At the same time, the vast majority of the literature on migration focuses on the on question of the scope and limits of justifiable migration policies for abstract "liberal-democratic states" or "national communities" with little attention to the particular histories, practices, sins, or commitments of actually existing states.[1] This chapter attempts to overcome these two shortcomings in the existing literature by developing and exploring an analytical resource, in the form of a normative-legal concept, to articulate, justify, and defend claims of border-crossing rights for border-crossing peoples.

My aim here is to go beyond standard approaches to thinking about the boundaries of citizenship in order to solve the problem of one of citizenship's remainders. In a sense, I see the argument presented here as a way of supplementing citizenship in theory and practice, by stepping outside of standard citizenship thinking and drawing from resources in property and international law to provide a theory of the rights of border-crossing peoples. One approach to the remainders of citizenship is the "semicitizenship" approach advocated by Elizabeth Cohen (2009), or what Rogers Smith (2015) in this volume calls "appropriately differentiated citizenship." This approach seeks to recognize the universality and apparent unavoidability of the practice of granting semicitizenship status to some citizens, and investigates the plausibility of different approaches to partial citizenship statuses (Cohen 2009). The argument fits within this approach, as I seek to establish why some members of particular groups might have a justified demand for a specific set of (partial) citizenship rights in a country other than their primary citizenship home. This may be a demand for full dual citizenship, or may be limited to a demand for a much less comprehensive partial citizenship narrowly construed as a right of passage to the second state.

The first section of this chapter considers what it might mean to deny a would-be border-crosser passage in the most general and abstract terms: is such a refusal best understood as an act of coercion or an act of prevention? Even if we assume it is (merely) an act of prevention, it still requires justification, and the way in which we define the right to exclude will shape the contours and boundaries of that right. The second section of this chapter considers the national territorial rights thesis as a foundation for the justified right to exclude. This approach relies, crucially, on an analogy with an individual's right to exclude others from her private property. In the third section, I argue David Miller has ignored an important dimension of this analogy. If (individual) private property rights are appropriately analogized to the act of migrant exclusion by national communities, we must consider other dimensions of property law that might press in the other policy direction, identifying cases where migrant inclusion is demanded. The law of easements suggests one such way. In particular, I will consider the ways in which easements by prescription and easements by necessity can come to be created in individual property arrangements. In the fourth section I'll discuss actually existing arrangements for border-crossing rules that suggest that something akin to border-crossing easements do exist, incompletely, in existing law and custom. In the fifth section, I will use two cases of historically grounded patterns and cultures of labor migration—from Mexico to the United States and Lesotho to South Africa—to argue that the general conditions for easements in property might also apply to patterns of migration, thus expanding the conception of what constitutes a border-crossing people that we might plausibly derive from existing practice. Actually existing border-crossing easements, I will argue, should not categorically exclude border crossing for the purposes of labor. I conclude with a brief reconsideration of Miller's arguments regarding immigration, and examine the exceptions to the right to exclude that appear in his account. Miller's theory can potentially make room for border-crossing easements by necessity, but not border-crossing easements by prescription. I will close by reflecting on Miller's failure to recognize the possibility of border-crossing easements by prescription, and what it might mean for his theory.

I. BORDER EXCLUSION: PREVENTION OR COERCION?

Normative dimensions of immigration policy have garnered significant attention from political theorists and philosophers recently. A central focus of this literature regards the justification of restrictive immigration policies—can they be justified, and if so, how, and to what extent? A number of scholars have emphasized just how difficult it is to justify border exclusions. In his now-classic treatment of this issue, Joseph Carens emphasizes the challenge for justified migrant exclusion:

Perhaps borders and guards can be justified as a way of keeping out criminals, subversives, or armed invaders. But most of those trying to get in are not like that. They are ordinary, peaceful people, seeking only the opportunity to build decent, secure lives for themselves and their families. On what moral grounds can these sorts of people be kept out? What gives anyone the right to point guns at them? (Carens 1987, 251)

Carens is not alone in characterizing such restrictions as difficult to justify (Abizadeh 2008; Child 2011; Cole 2000; Dummett 2001; Hidalgo 2014; Kukathas 2005; 2012; see also Carens 2013). While stopping short of an all-things-considered defense of a fully open borders policy, theorists such as Carens demonstrate the power of the case against border restrictions and set the threshold for exclusion quite high. In response, David Miller makes two arguments in an effort to justify most immigration restrictions (Miller 2005; 2007, 201–30; 2010; 2011; 2012). First, he argues theorists such as Carens and Arash Abizadeh (2008) have mischaracterized the act of migrant exclusion in a way that exaggerates the threshold for justification. Second, he affirms a collectivist Lockean right of national communities to craft restrictive immigration policies as an act of democratic self-determination. In this chapter, I will not directly challenge either of these positions. I will instead examine the foundations of Miller's "national territorial rights" position and its implications. On his own terms properly understood, he has exaggerated the scope of just exclusion in at least one important way.

In a recent essay Miller concluded that "even if the United States is the favored destination of the vast majority of Mexican immigrants, that fact alone does not give them a special right to be represented in the making of US Border policy. The United States is not coercing the Mexicans; nor is it single-handedly depriving them of the chance to lead autonomous lives" (Miller 2010, 118). This observation came in the context of a debate between Miller and Abizadeh regarding the appropriate way to characterize the act of refusing admittance to a prospective migrant (Abizadeh 2010; Miller 2010). Abizadeh insists that such an act is an act of coercion in the classic sense of the term: those denied entry by a restrictive border enforcement regime have been subjected to autonomy-invading coercive state action, which triggers a demand for democratic legitimation (Abizadeh 2008). Miller contends that under normal circumstances, the act of exclusion at the border is not an act of coercion but an act of prevention (Miller 2010). Prevention still requires justification, but at a considerably lower threshold—the demand for *democratic* justification, according to Miller, isn't applicable in this situation. Miller reaches this conclusion via an analogy between the private property rights of individuals in possession of land or other real property, on the one hand, and national communities in possession of a sovereign national territory, on the other. The right to prevent entry into a territory by a national community (acting through her representative government) is treated as analogous to a property owner refusing access to her property. As I will argue in the next section, this analogy is central to Miller's theory of national rights.

Miller's position on Mexican migration to the United States, as stated above, does not explicitly rule out the possibility of other reasons limiting the right to exclude in this case. However, his other recent writings on immigration suggest he is likely to be skeptical. Miller has elsewhere defended the right of national communities to restrict immigration, potentially quite severely, in service of their legitimate, reasonable, and democratic quest to control and shape "the way that their nation develops, including the values that are contained in the public culture" (Miller 2005, 200). Miller notes that the right to exclude is not absolute: "claims of material necessity—or more generally claims based on human rights—can sometimes place limits on their exercise" (Miller 2007, 221). Preferences and desires of prospective migrants aside, the "real question . . . is whether a decision to restrict immigration violates the *human rights* of those who are excluded" (Miller 2011, 2033). Miller's primary recognized exception to the right to exclude follows the general international legal and moral consensus regarding legitimate asylum seekers (while keeping open the possibility of recognition of economic refugees, a shift that has the potential to expand the scope of legitimate asylees considerably). While this might seem to be a significant exception, Miller contends that its moral force cannot simply be wielded against the country of the would-be migrants' choice, as "the claimant cannot choose who bears the specific remedial responsibility in his case" (Miller 2007, 221). Except for special cases of emergency (such as someone adrift at sea, arriving in national waters, or fleeing immediate political violence across a land border), it is up to each national community how to discharge their fair share of remedial responsibilities with respect to refugees and asylum seekers. In other words, the moral demand on national communities here contains a significant amount of discretion in how "fair share" requirements are understood, and for whom asylum is granted. Should no national community choose to accept a migrant with a legitimate asylum claim, they may well have no recourse—they may simply have fallen through the "justice gap" between "what people in poor countries can legitimately claim as a matter of justice (protection of their human rights, especially) and what the citizens of rich countries are obliged, as a matter of justice, to sacrifice to fulfill these claims" (Miller 2007, 274). In the absence of an effective international regime governing refugee policy, states can violate their "fair share" obligations without fear of effective recourse from excluded asylum seekers (Miller 2011; Owen 2010).

Rather than challenge Miller's claim that a "mere" act of prevention does not trigger democratic justification, I will argue that the reasoning that prompts Miller to classify exclusion as "mere" prevention may be less amenable to the justification of restrictive immigration policies than Miller currently suggests it is. Miller's case ultimately rests on an analogy between private property rights for individuals and territorial rights for nation-states. A more thorough consideration of the implications of this analogy identifies potential limits on just exclusion that Miller does not consider. Examining Miller's position on its own terms, I argue specifically that the national territorial rights thesis he defends may not justify his conclusion about the right to exclude Mexican labor migrants from the United States and other similar acts of exclusion.

II. TERRITORY AS A FORM OF PROPERTY

The case that the exclusion by force of a would-be border crosser is an act of prevention is easy to make. Insofar as this claim is controversial, it is not in the claim that prevention is taking place, but in the claim that the relevant act is "mere" prevention, and not a greater imposition. In order to make the case that this is the proper register to understand such exclusions, Miller relies heavily on the metaphor of the property owner, excluding others from access to her property. He analogizes border control to a hypothetical Scottish landowner who warns all who might attempt to access his private island that they would be met with violence, and to a homeowner who refuses to grant his obnoxious and persistent neighbor access to his house (Miller 2010, 114–16). But Miller does not solely rely on property analogies. He includes the following scenario: "Suppose that Peter, very much wants Jane to have dinner with him, and proposes that they should go to a nearby Thai restaurant. Jane, however, hates Thai food and makes it clear to Peter that if he goes to the Thai [restaurant], she will not be joining him—a threat sufficiently grave that Peter immediately drops his proposal" (Miller 2010, 113). It is clear, Miller argues, in this case, that Jane does not invade Peter's autonomy or coerce him through her act of refusal in this scenario. For Miller's purposes this analogy works if there are sufficient options beyond Thai food to meet Peter's basic needs (thus anticipating a potential exception for refugees in the general right to exclude). But as Abizadeh notes, this analogy has a flaw: in the case of denying someone a particular option they prefer in the course of a friendship, one is not backing up that threat with the kind of coercive measures we associate with a state—"imprisonment, death, and so on" (Abizadeh 2010, 126). Insofar as the illustrative examples Miller uses to establish the noncoercive nature of territorial exclusion are apt, they rest, exclusively, on the private property analogy.

Of course, this does not require that the territorial rights of peoples are in every sense identical to private property rights. Tamar Meisels, a fellow national territorial rights theorist and territorial collectivist Lockean,[2] gives an account of the important differences between individual property and collective territorial rights: "property and sovereignty are two forms, or two aspects, of ownership rights. Property in our connection refers to the ownership of land, while sovereignty includes inter alia the right to make the laws concerning real estate (as well as other) property" (Meisels 2009, 23; see also Meisels 2005, 5–8; Nine 2012, 11–13). The analogy between (individual) private property and (collective) territorial sovereignty can survive the obvious differences between the privileges that adhere to those rights, as they both generate the kind of ownership rights appropriate to that particular kind of agent as well as the principles that justify the type of ownership claim. For individual property owners, this means a collection of rights geared toward productive economic activity, "quiet enjoyment," and significantly, the exclusion of other individuals in most cases (the latter may be limited in certain ways if the property is used for commercial purposes in some jurisdictions, but for property used for dwelling or other private purposes, the right to exclude remains robust under normal circumstances). Territorial rights, adhering in national communities via the state as an institutional proxy,[3] produce jurisdictional and metajurisdictional powers,[4] and other powers and duties associated with norms of sovereignty. The difference between the specific content and contours of rights that attach to these different forms of ownership is explained by a logic of appropriateness or fit. The concrete nature of the rights and privileges that attach to each form of ownership differ due to the different purposes of each form of ownership, and what is needed to achieve that purpose. Individual ownership rights are shaped by what individuals do with land—primarily, to live and engage in economic activity (as noted earlier, the right to exclude may differ somewhat for these two kinds of ownership in ways that reflect the difference between their purposes). Limits are placed on those rights insofar as those limits are necessary to make property rights consistent with other important values and goals; for example, antipollution laws and "takings" legislation may prove necessary to protect the health of the environment (and, as such, the value and usefulness of other people's property) and to provide for adequate infrastructure, respectively.

Similarly, the scope and limits of national communities' territorial rights should fit with the nature and purpose of those rights. One of the central purposes of national territories is self-governance, and as such the territorial rights of states include jurisdictional and metajurisdictional rights over subjects and rights over territory (Nine 2008; Simmons 2001).[5] It is also argued that they contain what Simmons calls "rights against aliens" and what Miller classifies at the right to exclude would-be immigrants (Miller 2005; 2007, 201–30; 2012; Simmons 2001, 301). This, Miller argues, is necessary to fulfill at least one central purpose of national territory—the right of national communities to attempt to shape and control the development of their culture and economy (2005, 201). As with Lockean accounts of individual property rights, the justification for this mode of ownership is bolstered by transformation. A national community's right to claim ownership of a particular territory (with the attendant right to exclude) grows as the occupation and settlement leads to a physical transformation of that territory (Kolers 2002, 34; Meisels 2005, 75–96; Miller 2007, 217–20). Just as a Lockean individual property owner's claim strengthens as he transforms the land (and renders it economically efficient) through his labor, so does a national community gain a stronger claim via transformation. In the case of a national community this process is transformative in a dialectical fashion. National cultures shape the transformations of the land, but the physical and environmental features of the land, and the limitations and opportunities they provide, play a role in shaping the national culture as well, such that the character of the land and the character of the national community are deeply intertwined.

Occupation, settlement, and transformation justify a national communities' territorial claim in both backward-looking and forward-looking ways. Looking backward, it bolsters the territorial claim against other potential claimants. Looking forward, it demonstrates an important practical reason to recognize territorial rights claims of national communities—they are particularly well positioned to benefit from this particular piece of territory, due to the connection that now exists between the people and the land. This mutual connection between national communities and the land they occupy equips Miller with a ready response to the argument that it is difficult to make a national territory claim persuasively because most national communities occupy territories obtained originally through conquest, occupation, or otherwise problematic means. The territorial rights of national communities are not tied to a just initial acquisition. While a national community that violently dispossesses other occupants for a piece of land does not automatically acquire a right to that territory, they may do so over time, as multiple generations live, settle, and transform the land. Past sins of acquisition are still potentially morally relevant to the present-day community, but they may take the form of (unspecified) national responsibilities for past wrongs, which are best discharged in ways that don't directly interfere with that national community's existing territorial rights. The "transformation" feature of territorial rights claims also provides a tool to evaluate the relative strengths of competing claims, which are necessary in a world in which "unblemished title" is an impossible standard (Miller 2007, 219–20).

III. EXTENDING THE ANALOGY: BORDER-CROSSING EASEMENTS

Whatever the shortcomings of the national territorial rights thesis and the analogy on which it rests, it clearly captures something important about national communities and the territories they occupy and govern. However, in the hands of national territorial rights theorists, the analogy is applied in an overwhelmingly one-sided manner. It is deployed almost exclusively in ways that serve to bolster the territorial rights of national communities to exclude. Miller does recognize exceptions to exclusion, but as noted in part I they are significantly limited in scope and application. I will return to a discussion of his limited exceptions in the final section. In this section, I'll identify a way in which the underlying logic of the property analogy might suggest significant limitations on the right to exclude migrants, including Mexican labor immigrants to the United States.

One way in which the property analogy has generated an argument against territorial privileges of national communities has been through a critique of inherited birthright citizenship. This inheritance, it is argued, is an illiberal form of privilege that troublingly resembles feudal birthright, and as such presents a substantial challenge to those national communities that have ostensibly liberal characters and commitments (Carens 1992; Shachar 2009; Stevens 2010).[6] This is certainly a way in which a property analogy could work against a strong right to exclude. Whatever the merits of this argument, from a national territorial rights perspective it appears to be a category error. It focuses on the rights of individual citizens rather than the rights of the national community as such. By reducing this collective right to an individual right, this critique of birthright citizenship fails to engage the national territorial rights claim on its own terms. As such is it not likely to be persuasive to those committed to a collective territorial right for national communities that cannot be reduced to the sum of its parts.

Can Miller's robust account of just exclusion be challenged if we remain in the sphere of collective territorial rights analogous to, but not reducible to, individual property rights? I believe it can. In order to do so, I will explore one way in which individual property rights are limited by convention and law, and the purpose of that limitation, and argue that something similar should be applied to the territorial rights claims of national communities. I refer here to the law of easements. An easement is a specific legal limitation that restricts a property owner in a particular way.[7] A common form of easement, for example, is the requirement to maintain a route of access to another piece of property for its owners. In property law, the "dominant tenement" holds an easement that restricts some aspect of the property use of the holder of a particular piece of property (the "servient tenement").

One way easements are created is by agreement, in other words, by contract. In legal terms this is an express easement. In addition to basic contractual easements, however, there are easements by prescription, easements by prior use, and easements by necessity. These are of particular interest for the purposes of this analogy. This is but one example: "Besides right of way, the law of easements included the right to place clothes on lines over neighboring land, the right to nail fruit trees on a neighbor's wall, and the rights to water cattle at a pond and take water for domestic purposes" (Dukenminier et al. 2006, 670–71). Also included in the law of easements are negative privileges— preventing a particular development or activity on a particular parcel of land.

Easements by necessity come into existence in a situation in which a parcel of property would be significantly diminished in value without the use or access the easement protects. For example, if I were to sell a piece of my property with no independent access to public roads except through another section of my property, an easement would be necessary to allow access to this new parcel. Insofar as it can be shown that a particular restriction on parcel A is necessary for the enjoyment or use of parcel B, parcel A may be subject to an easement restriction. Easements by necessity are usually created through lawsuits, in which the claim of necessity is scrutinized and the costs of granting the easement are weighed against the costs that would be borne by the servient tenement, should the easement be granted. While the standard of necessity is generally quite high, easements by necessity are not strictly limited to questions of the economic use value of the land. For example, many states grant easements by necessity to descendants of those buried in private cemeteries to visit the grave of their ancestor.

Of even greater interest for my purposes are easements by prior use and easements by prescription. These forms of easements do not rest on claims of necessity or prior agreement. The specific rules of such easements vary by jurisdiction, but the idea is that an easement can be created through the continued, specific use of a piece of property for a particular purpose over a significant period of time. For example, under Kentucky law, "an easement, such as a right of way, is created when the owner of a tenement to which the right is claimed to be appurtenant, or those under whom he claims title, have openly, peaceably, continuously, under a claim of right adverse to owners of the soil, and with his knowledge and acquiescence, used a way over the lands of another for as much as 13 years" (Dukenminier et al. 2006, 677). The strength of a claim to an easement is increased by a demonstrable improvement of an accessway (such as paving a road) by those who are claiming the easement. In other words, the extent to which the prospective dominant tenement has invested in or improved a particular land use increases the strength of their legal claim to continued use via an easement.

Easements by prescription can be created in two ways. The first is described in the preceding paragraph. The second, a combination of the logic of necessity and the logic of prescription, is also of potential relevance to the idea of border-crossing easements: "the easement is implied when the court finds the claimed easement is necessary to the enjoyment of the claimant's land and that the necessity arose when the claimed dominant parcel was severed from the claimed servient parcel" (Dukenminier et al. 2006, 688). In other words, when a particular property border is created through a division of a parcel in such a way that creates the necessity of a particular use of the servient tenement by the dominant tenement, this may produce a claim of easement by necessity.

The law of easements discussed here draws from US law, but easements as a legal category of property law is both older and broader than its current American application. Modern easement law is a product of the common law tradition, but the genealogy goes back quite a bit further: easements have been characterized as "the most Roman part of English law" (Dukenminier et al. 2006, 668n2). The specific history of easements in the common law tradition dates back to the breakup of the feudal order and the enclosure of the commons. As common fields were becoming patchwork-private plots, the need for owners of particular plots to have access to them became encoded in property law. While the specific content and purpose of easement law has changed over time, a consistent theme of easement law has been recognition that property rights are imbedded in a social, ecological, geographical, and historical context that cannot, in some cases, be entirely escaped by the current title holder. Medieval property law contained extraordinary complexities that have since been substantially simplified. These simplifications have been useful—indeed, probably necessary—for the flourishing of commercial and industrial society. But as useful as they are, they remain useful fictions. The persistence of easement law demonstrates a limit of this useful fiction, as they directly confront the specific costs to others of unfettered freedom of property and resolve those claims in ways that acknowledge the legal/moral significance of existing historical practices over unlimited freedom to dispose of one's own property. With property easements, this historical sequence has been completed; with border-crossing easements the third step has so far proceeded in an ad hoc manner, limited to a handful of cases discussed in section V below.

The next two sections examine empirical examples of laws, practices, and customs that take the form of border-crossing easements, and the normative case for granting easements in cases of long-standing, economically and culturally embedded labor migration, respectively. Before turning to these examples, I want to briefly consider some ways in which some existing logics of citizenship and immigration law and practice are similar to the logic of border-crossing easements offered here. The factors that should motivate the recognition of border-crossing easements are also present in migration and citizenship law in a variety of other ways. Obviously, time is significant to easements. An easement by prescription is based on the length of time of a particular use or practice. There is historical precedent to a temporal dimension to United States citizenship law as well. Prior to the 14th Amendment, "there is very strong evidence that a temporally based principle of citizenship . . . was treated as decisive when, following the founding, the U.S. Supreme Court and many state courts issued their decisions about the status of the first U.S. residence to whom irregular citizenship status was ascribed" (Cohen 2011, 575–76). Prior to the restrictive turn in immigration policy in the 1920s, there were a number of provisions limiting the government's prerogative to deport settled, long-term residents, and "discretionary mechanisms" for such individuals to adjust their status (Shachar 2013, 136; Ngai 2004, 59–90). In a host of nineteenth-century court decisions, the duration of residency was a crucial factor in determining citizenship status of residents.[8] Indeed, the earliest federal deportation laws were limited to those who had been residing in the United States up to only one year (later changed to five years). In the 1940s and 1950s, Congress created legal mechanisms to avoid deportation for long-term residents (Ngai 2010, 58–60). Such arrangements exist in other countries as well. In France, until 2003, legal resident status was available to anyone who could demonstrate ten years of residence (Carens 2010, 21). In addition to the relevance of time to citizenship law, changing definitions of family have played an important role. Time is not the only familiar dimension of the logic of easements in existing citizenship law. During World War II, a number of American soldiers married while serving abroad. For the majority of the "war brides" from Europe, this presented no legal challenges based on current immigration law. But for the approximately 25 percent of the brides who were from Asia (primarily China), the situation was quite different. Their admission to the United States, even as spouses of current citizens, would be in direct conflict with the notoriously racist laws that had severely restricted Asian immigration over the previous several decades. This was initially dealt with in a fairly ad hoc fashion—via a hastily passed "War Brides Act" in 1945, designed to "cut the red tape" and otherwise circumvent long-standing immigration law and practice (Wolgin and Bloemraad 2010, 35).

How do these stories from the history of immigration and citizenship laws relate to the concept of border-crossing easements? In the first case, I merely seek to demonstrate that the temporal principle that underlies the concepts of easements by prescription has long had a place—sometimes a prominent one—in our thinking and adjudication about citizenship. I raise the issue of the Asian war brides and their legal accommodation to make the following point: it is not unprecedented to grant exceptions to general rules and laws regarding immigration if doing so is necessary to meet some other broadly agreed-upon value or goal. The flourishing of intimate family life required such an exception.[9] Border-crossing easements, as I'll show in the following sections, are also necessary for the flourishing of long-standing economic and cultural arrangements. In both cases, respecting autonomy means granting exceptions, and easements is one form these exceptions can take.

Consider the logic of the centrality of family reunification in contemporary immigration law. As long as legal immigration routes to developed countries remain a scarce resource, a strong case could be made for placing refugees on a par with, or higher than, family reunification in immigration (Gibney 2004; Honohan 2009). Why does family reunification continue to occupy a central place in current immigration law?[10] Why should this particularistic consideration take precedence over more universal measures of desert, or fairness? One possible answer is that migration regimes should be constructed so as to make current migration practices consistent with the development of one's intimate family life and culture. In this sense, the impetus behind family reunification as a top priority in immigration could, arguably, be leveraged to support border-crossing easements as well.

Obviously, there is currently no law, national or international, designed to provide specific guidance for granting or recognizing border-crossing easements in the sense that there does exist for property easements. But this is not a reason to abandon the idea. Recall the common law origins of easement law: easements emerged from changes in the practice of property ownership and allocation that took place during the breakdown of the feudal order. Changes in actual practices rendered a new legal category necessary, and it was developed in a bottom-up, ad hoc manner to respond to that challenge before it became a body of codified and general law. As James Scott recently noted, "The movement from practice to custom to rights inscribed in law is an accepted pattern in both common and positive law" (Scott 2012, 16). A case could certainly be made that past and current practices of migration, in light of an increasing trend to monitor, police, and restrict national borders by nation-states, represent analogous conditions to generate border-crossing easements, and existing legal arrangements of the sort discussed in this section could be seen as the early stages of ad hoc development of border-crossing easements, not yet identified as such.

IV. ACTUALLY EXISTING BORDER-CROSSING EASEMENTS

Easements are a form of servitude in property law, so the first place to look for such arrangements is the law of international servitudes, in particular those servitudes that relate to a right of free passage across sovereign territory.[11] One area in which such an arrangement has frequently come up is for enclaves—pockets of sovereign territory entirely surrounded by another country. In such cases, it is common for a right of passage from the enclave to the main body of territory of the state to which it belongs. A good example here is Llivia—a small Spanish town in the Pyrenees, removed from the main border by several miles and entirely surrounded by French sovereign territory. While the Schengen agreement has rendered the right of free passage to this enclave redundant, it existed for many centuries—from the creation of the modern border in 1659, which intended to cede Llivia to France but failed to do so through "defective wording in the Treaty of the Pyrenees" (Catudal 1974, 123; see also Krenz 1961, 65–70; Sahlins 1989) until the late twentieth century. The road from the border to Llivia, known as the *chemin neutre* ("Neutral Road") was open to Llivia residents on a permanent basis (Catudal 1974, 120). Even as both French and Spanish authorities chafed at the cost of this arrangement—"This enclave provides a livelihood for a Corps of French and Spanish customs officials almost as numerous as the rest of its inhabitants" (Farran 1955, 298)—the right of free passage persisted as an obligation for both states for hundreds of years. Llivia is not unique among enclaves in this respect. According to a number of scholars of enclaves in international law, there is a right of access for enclave residents, as well as a variety of state officials, that while not absolute, should be understood as a requirement of customary international law (Catudal 1974, 130–31; Farran 1955, 304; Krenz 1961, 138–46). When India denied Portugal access from the coastal colony of Daman to the interior enclaves of Dadra and Nagar Evili in 1954, the International Court of Justice responded with the finding that "Portugal possessed a right of transit for goods, private persons, and officials" between the coastal territory and interior enclaves, and India was required to permit access under international law (Krenz 1961, 64–65).[12] The customary international law surrounding access to enclaves appears to be the most obvious international analogy for easement law. But there are other examples: international law has long recognized a number of transit rights and usage rights that fall under the category of international servitudes.[13] Furthermore, it is not uncommon for specific subnational groups for whom international border restrictions impose a significant hardship to have some form of special border-crossing rights. De facto and de jure border-crossing privileges have been granted for reasons conceptually similar to the logic of easements suggested here. The remainder of this section identifies and explores examples of such "border-crossing easements."

Legal border-crossing privileges on the US-Canada border for indigenous peoples date back to the Jay Treaty of 1794, in which the United States and Great Britain agreed that "Indians dwelling on either side of said boundary line, freely to pass and re-pass by land or inland navigation, into the respective territories and countries of the two parties, on the continent of America" (Osburn 1999, 472). These border-crossing rights were reaffirmed explicitly after the War of 1812 in the Treaty of Ghent and went largely unchallenged until the anti-immigration movement of the 1920s. They were severely curtailed in the 1924 Immigration and Naturalization Act. However, the Supreme Court effectively reinstated native treaty rights just four years later in *U.S. ex rel. Diablo v. McCandless*. In 1952 a 50 percent blood quantum requirement was added, but this was again replaced by simple possession of tribal identity cards by the 1980s, returning determination of tribal membership to the tribes (Luna-Firebaugh 2002, 162–63; Osburn 1999, 474–79). In the case of the United States' northern border, the analogous type of easement is an express easement; these border-crossing rights, while reflecting long-standing cultural and historic practices, are based on treaty law.[14] A similar express easement was negotiated on behalf of indigenous residents of western Alaska and northeastern Russia in the early 1990s, shortly after relations between the United States and Russia improved following the collapse of the Soviet Union (Osburn 1999, 481–82).

On the southern US border, the situation is more complex and tenuous, and existing border-crossing rights for indigenous peoples have deteriorated in recent years (Singleton 2008). Some indigenous groups have received express easements through law, others have been granted border-crossing rights via ad hoc administrative rules, and others have no border-crossing rights at all. The clearest case of a recognized border-crossing easement can be found with the Kickapoo. Originally from the Great Lakes region, the

Kickapoo tribe moved around considerably beginning early in the nineteenth century "as a result of broken land treaties and a desire to resist the forces of colonization" (Luna-Firebaugh 2002, 168). Some subgroups of the Kickapoo briefly settled in Texas, but due to local hostilities moved south to Mexico, where they were granted land and citizenship by the Mexican government, in exchange for military service (Osburn 1999, 480). Meanwhile, the US government established a Kickapoo reservation in Indian Territory (present-day Oklahoma) in 1883. The two branches of the Kickapoo tribe subsequently "maintained close relations through intermarriage and frequent visitation" (Osburn 1999). The Mexican Kickapoo lived year-round in Mexico until the 1950s, when a series of droughts forced an annual labor migration to Eagle Pass, Texas. The centrality of free passage across the US-Mexico border for the economy and culture of the Kickapoo tribe was acknowledged by the INS, which issued tribal identity cards that enabled free passage for all tribal members (of Mexican and US citizenship) in the 1950s. This administrative easement was formalized into law in 1983, when the Texas Band of Kickapoo Act was passed, which granted free and unlimited passage of the US-Mexico border for all tribal members. The cultural necessity of continued free passage was explicitly noted in this legislation (Osburn 1999, 480–81).

This is the most clear-cut present border crossing easement on the US-Mexico border, and while it became an express easement in 1983, it was clearly recognized as an easement right prior to that, as that legislation codified existing informal INS privileges. Other groups have had similar arrangements. The Cocopah peoples' traditional lands were separated by the Gadsden Purchase, but they continued to cross freely until the 1930s. After an initial crackdown, the Cocopah "developed an unofficial agreement with the INS that allowed for freedom of passage of Mexican Cocopah into the U.S." (Luna-Firebaugh 2002, 167). The Yaqui's homeland was not directly split by the border, but Yaqui subgroups resided on both sides. Furthermore, the Yaqui practice religious ceremonies that require the presence of religious leaders from other regions, often across the border. The Yaqui came to an agreement with the INS Arizona regional office in 1997, which allowed Yaqui leaders to identify and sponsor religious leaders from Mexican Yaqui communities to cross the border for these ceremonies (Luna-Firebaugh 2002, 174). The Tohono O'odham, whose territory in southern Arizona extends into the state of Sonora, have long sought recognition for a border-crossing easement, which is particularly urgent in their case since about 10 percent of registered tribal members are Mexican nationals (making them the only US tribe to grant full tribal membership to non-US citizens). A traditional unofficial border-crossing location for O'odham members was quietly ignored by the INS for decades. Recent border enforcement strategies have complicated this arrangement, as nonindigenous illicit border crossings have been pushed farther away from population centers and brought disruption, crime, and border guards to O'odham territory (Cadava 2011; Luna-Firebaugh 2002, 166). As a result, the nonofficial border has been closed, imposing a significant hardship on the Mexican tribal members, who are now forced to make a several hour trip to visit friends or relatives, receive medical care, or otherwise participate in tribal activities just a few miles away from their home (Ellingham 2004, 122–36). O'odham leaders continue to negotiate special "laser visas" for tribal members, which would presumably ensure their members are permitted by immigration officials to cross the border, but not address the geographical problem (Luna-Firebaugh 2002, 170–73).

An argument could be made that the Tohono O'odham have a uniquely strong case for border crossing rights (Ozer 2002). Their presence on the border substantially predates the Kickapoo (and, of course, the border itself). While the Kickapoo's border crossing dates back to the early 1800s, the Tohono O'odham have been crossing the present-day border for, at a minimum, several hundred years before contact with European settlers. The Kickapoo must cross the border to get from one territory to another, whereas the border split the Tohono O'odham's homeland. So why was the Kickapoo border-crossing easement legislatively successful, whereas the Tohono O'odham not? The details of the failed legislation are important here. In both cases in which a legislative border passage right was pursued, there was broad agreement between the tribe and the US government regarding the need for and justice of a border-crossing right for tribal members. In both cases, the sticking point became how the border would be crossed. In both cases the US and Mexican governments insisted that border crossing could only take place at officially recognized border crossings, whereas the Tohono O'odham insisted on being permitted to cross the border on their own land, via customary migration paths (Luna-Firebaugh 2002, 170–71).[15] This was a cultural necessity, but also a practical matter, as crossing at an official border checkpoint would force a 120-mile trip to visit a village a few miles away (Osburn 1999, 149). Indeed, the traditional migratory routes had been used: "The O'odham maintain an unofficial border crossing on tribal lands that, while known to U.S. customs, is not regulated by the U.S. government" (Luna-Firebaugh 2002, 166). However, this arrangement became untenable as new restrictive border enforcement efforts pushed other border crossers and smugglers into more remote territory, bringing law enforcement with them and severely disrupting life in the Tohono O'odham's territory (Madsen 2007; 2014). In other words, the idea that a border-crossing easement for the O'odham is both needed and deserved was never in doubt—the easement failed for reasons related to the challenge of implementation, especially insofar as it might conflict with the US government's renewed and reinvigorated effort to aggressively police the border. Prior to the significant increase in border enforcement, the O'odham's informal crossing was tolerated by various agents of the US government because there was no reason to believe anyone else might seek to take advantage of it, given its remote location. With the militarization of less remote sections of the border, this was increasingly not the case. This easement fell apart because it conflicted with a higher priority for the state, not because the force of the claim was rejected.

It might be argued that indigenous peoples are a special case, because their status as (a) sociopolitical forms that predate the state that were also (b) subjected to all manner of indignities by those states that now separate them, they might have a different and much more substantial case to make for border-crossing easements. In particular, one could argue their status as sociopolitical entities that predate the settlement of modern states imbues them with a claim for accommodations and rights that is qualitatively different, and more demanding, than any other sort of plausible subnational group claim. Indigenous peoples can point to the United Nations Declaration on the Rights of Indigenous Peoples, which includes a statement of support for indigenous border-crossing rights in Article 36.[16] I would certainly grant that indigenous border-crossing easements may be among the most morally and politically compelling. Such claims are not, however, irreducibly unique. The justification for indigenous border-crossing easements and those of nonindigenous labor migrants are based on broadly similar principles. First, the length of time the border has been crossed (and the length of time the geography of the community has necessitated border crossing); second, the cultural and economic importance of the border crossing; third, the hardship or harm done through the act of border creation and the ongoing policies of restricted access. For each of these criteria, the indigenous claims to border-crossing easements, while often quite strong, are not qualitatively unique.

I have focused here on border-crossing easement-like arrangements at US borders. There are many non-US border examples of such arrangements, however, including the legal recognition of border-crossing rights of the Sami people in northern Scandinavia, which date back to at least 1751, when the Lapp Codicil was added to the Stromstrad border treaty between Sweden and Norway. This granted the "Lapp people" the formal right to cross the border between these two countries to continue their long-standing practice of nomadic reindeer herding (Henrikson 2008, 28; Hannum 1990, 247–62; Lantto 2010). Under provisions of the Torres Strait Treaty of 1985, residents of certain villages in the Torres Strait islands have legal permission to cross the maritime border between Australia and Papua New Guinea "to visit and trade with one another without having to go through formal customs inspection, passport control or other formalities" (Arthur 2001, 219). Since 1967, the Druze people of the Golan Heights have found themselves separated by a new international border from the rest of their people. Even as tense relations have led to a closed border for most Israelis and Syrians, the Qunietra Crossing has been open to residents of four Druze villages in the northern Golan Heights only, for the purposes of attending school, family events, visiting significant religious sites, and commerce (in the form of apple sales) in Syria (Ashkenazi and Khoury 2013; Einav 2010). Examples of easement-like arrangements for border-crossing peoples are, if not routine, not entirely unusual.

V. SEARCHING FOR BORDER-CROSSING EASEMENTS: MEXICO–UNITED STATES AND LESOTHO–SOUTH AFRICA

The previous section establishes that "border-crossing easements" do, in fact, exist. But which groups should be granted border-crossing easements? Most of the examples of successful border-crossing easements identified in the previous section fall under two categories—indigenous peoples and residents of enclaves. These are perhaps two of the easiest cases for border-crossing easements, but the case for expanding the concept beyond them is strong. In this section, I want to explore two cases I believe are eligible for a border-crossing easement, due to the central role a pattern of labor migration plays in the society, culture, and identities of the would-be dominant tenement. The two cases are Mexican labor migration to the United States (particularly from parts of Mexico with a robust and long-standing culture of labor migration, such as many rural Oaxacan villages) and Lesothan labor migration to

South Africa.[17] I will give an account of some of the salient features of these two cases for our purposes before making the case that they may qualify as border-crossing easements.

First, the specific location of both of these borders has historical origins in the prerogative of the wealthier and more powerful country. In this case "both borders were established through a process of war, resistance, and domination" and "the conquered local people were not consulted as to where the border would inevitably run" (Coplan 2010, 55). The US-Mexico border was the product of a protracted nineteenth-century struggle in which the United States effectively seized a considerable portion of Mexican territory, in which itinerant labor had (and continued to) moved freely. At the time of the Treaty of Guadalupe Hidalgo approximately 100,000 Mexican citizens (as well as twice as many Native Americans) resided in the territory ceded to the United States (Nevins 2002, 19). The present-day American Southwest was severed from Mexico politically, but the social, cultural, and economic ties between these territories were not. The border remained unstable and virtually unpoliced for many decades, as the initial boundary between America and Mexico in this newly acquired territory was racial rather than geographic.

Similarly, Lesotho's current border with the South African Free State to the west was shaped through conflict with the Orange Free State Republic in the mid-nineteenth century, in which virtually all of the Lesothan western lowlands were ultimately lost to the Boer Republic (which later merged with South Africa after the second Boer war). The borders of modern Lesotho were settled when the British agreed to make what was left of Lesotho a protectorate in 1868, after nearly two decades of fighting a losing war of attrition, thus preventing any territorial concessions to the Orange Free State. At its founding, Lesotho became, effectively, a labor reserve for the rest of South Africa—the agriculturally productive lowland region of the country was now almost entirely gone, leaving scarce options for domestic employment (Coplan 2001; Mensah and Naidoo 2011). The country that was once known as the "granary of the Orange Free State" (Ferguson 1994, 65) saw its status as a major agricultural exporter decline rapidly, to the point that it was no longer close to agricultural self-sufficiency. This decline has multiple causes—the disruptions of the Orange Free State wars in the 1850s and '60s and the aforementioned loss of fertile agricultural land in 1868 to the Orange Free State, but also the development of a system of labor migration in which investment in agricultural activity and capacity declined precipitously

(Coplan 2001). While the inequality in *drawing* the border is historical, the inequality in *defining* the border is contemporary. In both cases discussed here it is the more powerful, wealthier state, the United States and South Africa, that has attempted to create a highly restrictive border regime where a largely open border had once existed. In both cases, the present-day character of the border is not defined by the policies and enforcement regimes of the Mexican and Lesothan governments to any significant degree.

Also, in both of these cases labor migration has a deep and long history, dating back approximately one and a half centuries. This practice has long contained a great deal of exploitation and unfair treatment of workers, but it could also be characterized as beneficial to both sides.[18] Economic development on both sides of each of these borders has been shaped and driven by these migratory practices for some time. But these long-standing patterns and practices of migration have not merely shaped the economic path of both nations, they have shaped (and been shaped by) a culture of migration that has taken hold in virtually all of Lesotho and a number of regions in Mexico. As Miller (2007, 218–21) argues, just as a national community transforms and is transformed by the land such that they become a fit for each other, so too do long-standing migratory patterns and practices.

Lesotho "has served as a labor reserve supplying migrant wage labor to South African mines, farms and industry for more than a century" (Ferguson 1994, 26; Murray 1981). The centrality of labor migration in Lesotho dates back to the period of the Orange Free State wars, during which time Basothan[19] men sought work in Natal and the Cape to escape the war. After the settlement of the boundary, two facts drove the practice of labor migration to become widespread and permanent: the aforementioned loss of the fertile agricultural portion of the Basothan homeland in the west, and the opening of labor-intensive diamond mines in nearby Kimberley. Basothan labor migrants were pushed, but also pulled, across the border. By the end of the nineteenth century, the vast majority of men of working age sought passes for work outside the territory (Murray 1981). The agricultural productivity of Lesotho continued to decline as much of the labor force spent their working years in South Africa—for many years, in the mines, and more recently on Free State and Transvaal farms (Coplan 2010; Ulicki and Crush 2007). The particular pattern of migration in which men of working age spent between six and ten months a year or more working abroad, but women were not allowed to take work in South Africa, had a profound impact on gender roles, the nature of marriage, and the structure of family relations in Lesotho (Coplan and Thoahlane 1995; Modo 2001; Murray 1981, 110–19). The relationship between family, work, and conceptions of masculinity in Lesotho are now such that "men in rural areas of Lesotho generally do not consider work on one's family farm as legitimate work" (Mensah and Naidoo 2011, 1030). South Africa's development was also shaped by these migratory patterns and their malleability. When NUM, the primary mineworkers union, became too militant in the view of the South African state, the presence of foreign workers (primarily Basothan, who were often among the most skilled miners and the most militant union leaders) became a valuable tool in undermining union power, as they could be deported and sent to other locations when they reapplied for work. Migratory patterns became a useful tool for the manipulation of labor relations for the South African regime (Coplan 2001, 96–98). The migratory pattern has even been politically useful—in 1994 a significant number of Basothans in South Africa were promised permanent resident documents in exchange for their vote for the ANC. The following year, South African president Nelson Mandela made a public pledge that Basothan migrant workers would not be denied access to work in mines (Mensah and Naidoo 2011, 1018–19). In sum—the migratory practices of Basothans have, over time, played a significant role in shaping and reshaping the economy, society, politics, and culture of South Africa. Furthermore, a culture of labor migration for virtually all competent working-age men has been central to Lesothan society for much of the same time.

As with Lesotho, Mexican labor migration to the United States has been a feature of life since the boundary was established in the nineteenth century. As the new American territories seized at the conclusion of the Mexican-American War were settled and developed, Mexican labor migration played an important role. In particular, the agricultural economy of the American West came to rely on a shifting, itinerant population of workers at certain times of the year; the manpower to complete the harvest would have otherwise been impossible given the scarcity of local available labor. Temporary Mexican labor migration, from regions near the border but also from southern Mexican regions such as Oaxaca (Cohen 2003), became central to the development of the economy of the US Southwest, providing labor flexibility that intra-American migratory practices did not. The economy of the American West could not have developed as it did without Mexican labor migration. This long-standing pattern of migration has, predictably, deeply shaped Mexican communities as well. The practice of labor migration has been a central feature of cultural and family life in many parts of Mexico for over one hundred years (Cohen 2003; Coplan 2010; Kandel and Massey 2002; Wilson 2010). The social dynamic of (mostly male) long-term migration and (mostly female) migratory communities in parts of rural Mexico has had a profound role in shaping gender norms, relations, and expectations as well as family patterns. On the economic front, recent evidence suggests that remittances from US-employed labor migrants are a major engine of economic development in parts of Mexico where labor migration is common (Orrenius et al. 2012). The culture of temporary, cyclical out-migration can be seen as "a set of interrelated perceptions, attitudinal orientations, transnational social networks, growing out of the international migratory experience, which constantly encourage, validate, and facilitate participation in this movement" (Cornelius 1990, 24).

The legal status of these migratory practices has changed considerably over time. That said, their status as licit (if not necessarily legal) practices remained largely unchanged—in both societies; the practice of labor migration (including, at times, labor migration outside the law) was both expected and normal on both sides of the border. Changes in the legal status of migration (and the relevance of that legal status to the actual experiences of migrants) have remained largely in the hands of the more powerful country in each pair, the United States and South Africa. For both countries, the manipulable nature of the legal status of migrants from the other country has served as an economic and political resource, to be altered to meet the different and changing needs (as previously noted with respect to labor organizing in South African mines). In the case of the United States, policies and enforcement have shifted over time as well, with a similar dynamic. Initially, there was virtually no border enforcement. Between 1890 and 1930, the Mexican border became an object of concern, first as a circuitous route for unwanted and illegal Asian immigration, and later as part of a general turn against immigration in the 1920s, which would only intensify in the 1930s. During this time the US government also saw the Mexican border as a potential financial resource, offering "work permits" to would-be migrants at rates few could afford (Nevins 2002). Still, during this time enforcement was sufficient only to moderately disrupt or complicate labor migration for a few, rather than preventing or significantly altering the flow of migrants. By the early 1990s, however, the flow of migration from Mexico became another kind of political resource—namely, a stage for politicians to engage in a performance of sovereignty in the form of a "crackdown" on "illegal" immigration (Andreas 2009; Brown 2010; Nevins 2002). This may have been useful for the politicians engaged in it, but its consequences for the culture of migration was not to end it but to alter the flow; under the new regime of fences and expanded border enforcement, labor migrants shifted from temporary to permanent (as multiple border crossings became too risky). *Coyotes*—smugglers of labor immigrants—became more profitable and powerful, changing the demographics of who can afford to migrate, and border crossings became more deadly as they were pushed out into the harsher desert (Nevins 2002).

This historical account of these migratory patterns suggests several reasons why they might trigger a justified demand for an easement. One way to make the case for border-crossing easements would be to observe that the very idea of states "controlling borders" is a relatively recent imposition on the ancient and venerable practice of human migration, which has been a central feature of human civilization for far longer than national communities or states have existed, let alone the much more recent practice of attempted control of border crossings, and explains how our species came to occupy most of the habitable territory on the planet in the first place. On this perspective it is not migration that disrupts the nation-state but the nation-state that disrupts migration (Brubaker 2010). While this view has a certain appeal, the spirit of easement law is not so radical. It is, instead, a minor supplement to the system of private property rather than a radical challenge to it. I presume a similar scope for border-crossing easements.

The central purpose of easements is the continued use and enjoyment of property. Insofar as a particular pattern of property use/access has become central to the relevant parties' continued enjoyment of their property, restriction on one parcel can be created to facilitate that continued practice. Something similar could be said to exist with respect to these patterns of labor migration. First, the migratory patterns here are long-standing. Easements by prescription are developed over time, as patterns of use become embedded and habitual. While minor details have changed, both of these migratory patterns have persisted for well over a century. Second, the cultures and economies of the equivalent of the dominant tenement (Lesotho and Mexico) have been shaped and altered considerably by this practice. These migration patterns have been tolerated or even encouraged by the servient tenement (United States and South Africa), but have also played a role in "improving" the economy of servient tenement, through the provision of flexible, temporary labor whenever and wherever it is needed. Just as the claim for an easement is bolstered if the would-be dominant tenement has made improvements to the land, the border-crossing easement claim should also be similarly bolstered. For better or for worse, the local cultures and economies of the dominant tenement have been significantly shaped by the long-standing pattern of return migration. This has been done with the quiescence of the would-be servient tenements, who have, in fact, used these migratory patterns (and their own ability to manipulate them) in pursuit of their own political and economic projects. Third, the legal claim for an easement by prescription is bolstered when the initial severance of the two parcels of land placed the would-be dominant tenement in a difficult position without the easement. The moment of severance (the creation of the modern border—the Treaty of Guadalupe Hidalgo and the Gadsden Purchase in 1848 and 1853, respectively, and the creation of modern-day Lesotho as a British Protectorate in 1868) placed potentially significant limits on the continued enjoyment of the would-be dominant parcel without the easement. The basic ingredients for a justified easement claim are clearly present in both cases. If easements are good property law, and the law of individual property ownership serves as the metaphorical foundation of the territorial rights of national communities, should not those territorial rights be subject to claims of easements?

VI. ARE NATIONAL TERRITORIAL RIGHTS AND BORDER-CROSSING EASEMENTS COMPATIBLE?

In the final section of this chapter, I return to David Miller's theory of immigration and consider his account of exceptions to the right to exclude in light of the preceding discussion of border-crossing easements.[20] Miller's writing on immigration suggests he might accept border-crossing easements by necessity but reject border-crossing easements by prescription. I will attempt to explain why Miller might be inclined to make this distinction, given his larger commitments, and why it is nevertheless a mistake to do so.

No particular form of ownership automatically generates a general or absolute right to exclude. Identifying a person or collective as an "owner" is the beginning, rather than the end, of a discussion of the particular rights that resource ownership entails (Pevnick 2011, 43). Each form of ownership generates a specific set of legal exclusions that are tied to the purpose of that particular form of ownership. While ownership usually entails some exclusion rights, the contents of those exclusion rights vary considerably, based on the point of the kind of property right being claimed. For example, a racist who does not wish to associate with African Americans in any capacity has a right to categorically exclude them from her private residence, but not her restaurant. This reflects a legal distinction between the purpose of private residences and businesses shaped by civil rights legislation; the latter is public in a way that the former is not, and as such it is a form of property that is more subject to limitations based on the public value of racial equality. Or, to consider this from another angle, consider the exclusions generated by intellectual property. If you published a book, you would have no right whatsoever to exclude African Americans—or any other paying customer—from reading it. You do, however, retain a host of exclusion rights as an intellectual property holder in this case. Specifically, you (and/or your publisher) would have the right to exclude any reproductions or use of the copyrighted material beyond what relevant statutes determine is "fair use." Finally, consider the recent revolution in Australian constitutionalism. Since *Queensland v. Mabo* (1992), the founding doctrine of *terra nullius* (empty land) has been replaced by a system in which "native title" claims can be made, in which Australian Aboriginals' long-standing cultural and spiritual ties to the land can provide a kind of legal title. It isn't straightforward ownership, however, that they have been granted in most cases, but rather a combination of ceremonial rights, dwelling rights, and some light commercial rights. Pastoral rights and mineral extraction rights have generally remained in the hands of the pre-*Mabo* economic interests that own them. "Native title" is a particular form of ownership that entails some privileges but not others—presumably, the privileges that are historically and culturally relevant for traditional native land use (Glaskin 2003; Hinchman and Hinchman 1998).[21]

With this set of lessons in mind, it's important to note that, much like property easements, border-crossing easements are likely to take many different forms, and generate different sorts of "differentiated citizenship" statuses, relevant to the circumstances that lead to the justified claim for an easement. I initially formulated this concept as "migration easements," but this suggests a right to actual migration, which might attach in certain cases, but by no means all of them.[22] In some cases, a border-crossing easement may entail little more than an exception to administrative checkpoints (for the Tohono O'odham, for example, or Torres Strait Islanders traveling between Australia and Papua New Guinea). In other cases, border-crossing easements may entail permission to cross borders for the purposes of seasonal work or temporary migration. In some cases, border-crossing easements may entail political incorporation, with full citizenship for citizens of the dominant tenement in the servient tenement. During the years of South Africa's apartheid regime, Lesothan incorporation into South Africa was unthinkable. Since South Africa's democratization, however, ethnic Basothans from the South African side of the Free State border have played a significant role in Free State governance, and many nonelite Lesothans, who regard their own domestic political elites and institutions as an oppressive, extractive anachronism compared to South African democracy, regard political incorporation as an attractive option (Coplan 2001, 110–13). A case could plausibly be made that political incorporation, with Lesotho as a tenth South African state, would be the best way to fulfill the easement demands of Lesothan workers. The point I wish to make here is that there is not a preferred or ideal administrative or legal form of border-crossing easement rights; like easements in property law, they arise to address particular situations, and their form is determined by the nature of the border-crossing practices and the obstacles they now face. Furthermore, this argument is not meant to suggest that all border-crossing easements are absolute or permanent. Just as property easements can be brought to an end by negotiated arrangements or changes in use patterns, so too might border-crossing easements. And an easement might be trumped by another, more urgent consideration; for example, a particular individual who has a border-crossing easement right might be justly denied entry if he has demonstrated a pattern of violent criminal behavior. The precise conditions that might justifiably override a migration easement are beyond the scope of this chapter; I merely note here, drawing another parallel to conventional property easements, that such an override is conceivable and consistent with a fairly strong easement right.

If we are to accept the national community claim to territory as a form of property, we need an understanding of justified exclusion to fit the purpose of this particular property right. I have argued that border-crossing easements are analogous to easements in property law in several important respects such that they provide sufficient justification for an exception to the right to exclude outsiders. Miller's account of the right to exclude as a territorial-ownership right is not absolute; refugees and the truly desperate may have a justified right to demand an exception to a policy of exclusion. This would suggest he might be amenable to border-crossing easements by necessity, but not particularly welcoming to easements by prescription, since necessity for self-sufficiency is not a condition for the latter. But just as easements by prescription are consistent with our general enjoyment of private property rights, border-crossing easements by prescription, such as the cases considered here, can and should be understood as consistent with the general purpose and function of territorial rights of national communities. That purpose for Miller is to give a people the chance to build a way of life together, intentionally and democratically. That is certainly one way to describe the set of practices over the last century or more that created the claim to a border-crossing easement—if a national community is the kind of agent that Miller wants it to be, it should be considered the kind of agent capable of entering into practices and arrangements that create responsibilities and obligations going forward, such as the creation of easements.

One curious feature of Miller's argument is that when he describes the nature and value of national communities, his account is deeply sensitive to their status as specific and concrete historical entities, and to the claim that shared history has on those operating in the present. His account of national communities is very much grounded in their actual historical character, culture, and long-standing practices. But when he turns to considering the range of possible approaches to the question of migration and exclusion, the weight and power of historical practice has suddenly vanished. He does not mention how previous approaches to inclusion and exclusion might play a role in determining the boundaries of just inclusion. Miller argues that Mexican labor migrants have no special claim to gain admittance to the United States even if it is their "favored destination" (2010, 118). But it is their favored destination not as a simple matter of taste or even just as a matter of convenience. It is their "favored destination" due to a series of decisions made by a variety of actors on both sides of the border during the last 165 years that have shaped the cultures and economies that confront the individual and condition that "preference." Miller grants national communities a legitimate right to attempt to control and shape the development of a common culture through immigration policy. If we accept this we surely must also accept that some previous efforts to do just this may create limits on what we can do today, particularly in cases where our previous efforts have shaped not only our own national community but also that of a neighboring country (and a substantially weaker and less powerful one at that). The recognition of border-crossing easements by prescription would make the general right to exclude less robust, but it would make it more consistent with the purpose of exclusionary territorial rights for national communities. Indeed, it would better recognize national communities as moral agents, by recognizing their historical capacity to incur specific responsibilities via long-standing patterns of behavior and use. It would also entail recognition of an important fact about such communities—that, like plots of private property within a nation, they are not islands, and through ordinary historical practice may become entangled with each other in ways that create moral/legal obligations and restrictions.

NOTES

1. Exceptions to this trend include Smith (2008), Exdell (2009), and Blake (2013).
2. By "collectivist Lockean," I refer to those who argue that territorial rights ought to be granted to the collective entities. Generally, national communities, although Miller (2012) suggests indigenous groups may sometimes qualify as well for reasons similar to those Locke argues grant individual rights. Miller (2007; 2010; 2011; 2012), Meisels (2005; 2009) and Nine (2008; 2012) defend different variants of collectivist Lockean positions. This stands in contrast to an individualist Lockean justification for territorial rights. This position, defended by A. John Simmons (2001) and Hillel Steiner (1996), holds that territorial rights are justified by individual property rights, insofar as they are necessary to create an entity that can sufficiently protect such property. This chapter will not address the individualist Lockean territorial argument.
3. Miller insists that these rights belong first and foremost to the national communities, and are only contingently granted to "the state" as a placeholder for the national community. This position has been criticized by a number of theorists who see the state as a stronger candidate for holding territorial rights (Levy 2008; Laegaard 2007; Pevnick 2011; Stilz 2011). Recently Miller has explicitly considered the possibility that territorial rights might adhere to groups other than national communities, singling out indigenous groups as another promising candidate (Miller 2012).
4. On the importance of metajurisdictional rights for collectivist Lockean accounts, see Nine (2008).
5. Miller contends that jurisdictional rights are necessary for groups with a "repository of value" in a particular parcel of land, in order for their ownership

and control of that land to remain secure (Miller 2012, 263). For a skeptical assessment of that account, and an argument for collective private property rights in some cases, see Angell (2013).

6. For an argument that the feudal privilege analogy is inapt, see Pevnick (2011, 130–32).

7. My discussion of easements in the following paragraphs draws heavily from Dukenminier et al. (2006, 667–740).

8. For a forceful argument that the temporal dimension should play a role in adjudicating the fate of irregular migrants today, see Carens (2010). Mae Ngai (2003) has argued that allowing legal residence after a period of time in residence is simply to place a statute of limitations on the crime of illegal border crossing.

9. This exception shouldn't have been necessary, of course: the stated goal behind anti-Asian immigration laws at the time was explicitly and openly racist. But my point here regards merely the exception, rather than the general rule—an exception to a rule can be justified on its own terms, separately from any examination of the justifiability of the rule itself.

10. Family reunification is responsible for a majority of legal migration in the developed world. For a defense of family reunification–driven migration, see Lister (2010). For arguments that "family" should be rethought to consider a variety of nontraditional forms, see Lister (2007) and Holland (2008).

11. On international servitudes in general, see Reid (1932) and Vali ([1958] 1986). On the right of transit in general, see Lauterpacht (1958). On the right of transit as it relates to enclaves, see Catudal (1974), Farran (1955), and Krenz (1961).

12. By the time the ruling was issued in 1960, Portugal had effectively lost control of these colonies.

13. While dated, thorough accounts of such rights can be found in Reid (1932) and Vali (1986).

14. There is some question about whether the contemporary free passage rights are best understood as treaty rights or whether the relevant treaties have been entirely superseded by statute. The latter case is made by Yablon-Zug (2008), while the treaty rights case is made by Lewerenz (2010).

15. The O'odham operated an illegal shuttle across the border to bring their Mexican members to their medical clinic in 2001–2, but by 2004 they had abandoned this service, as both the increased presence of border guards, and the increased danger from criminal activity associated with border crossing had rendered the shuttle impractical (Ellingwood 2004, 122–36).

16. Article 36 of the Declaration of the Rights of Indigenous Peoples reads:

> 1. Indigenous peoples, in particular those divided by international borders, have the right to maintain and develop contacts, relations and cooperation, including activities for spiritual, cultural, political, economic and social purposes, with their own members as well as other peoples across borders.

> 2. States, in consultation and cooperation with indigenous peoples, shall take effective measures to facilitate the exercise and ensure the implementation of this right.

> The Declaration, adopted by the UN General Assembly in September 2007, can be found at www.un.org/esa/socdev/unpfii/documents/DRIPS_en.pdf. For a thoughtful assessment of the possibility of using this treaty to reassert and defend Jay Treaty rights for Native Americans at the US-Canada border, see Garrow (2012).

17. For an account of the important similarities between these borders see Coplan (2010).
18. Mutually beneficial but still highly exploitative cross-border cooperation is a common feature of highly unequal borders (More 2011).
19. Lesothan refers to the name of the country, while the people are known as Basothan (plural) and Mosothan (singular).
20. The method used in this chapter—drawing lessons from common law tradition with respect to individuals and applying those lessons to national communities—is one that Miller employs with respect to the inheritability of responsibility for harm. See Miller (2007, 148–50).
21. I am not making an argument here that native title under *Mabo* (and the subsequent Native Title Act of 1993) is sufficient in providing justice for Australian aboriginals. My point is merely that this arrangement is consistent with—indeed, based on—the notion that different forms of property rights entail different bundles of privileges based on the alleged purpose of that form of property rights. For compelling arguments that native title in Australia should be transformed into something more akin to alienable freeholder title, see Levy (1994) and Altman (2012). For an argument against such a plan, see Hepburn (2006).
22. I thank Robert Goodin for pointing this out.

WORKS CITED

Abizadeh, Arash. 2008. "Democratic Theory and Border Coercion: No Right to Unilaterally Control Your Own Borders." *Political Theory* 36 (1): 37–65.

————. 2010. "Democratic Legitimacy and State Coercion: A Reply to David Miller." *Political Theory* 38 (1): 121–30.

Altman, Jon. 2012. "Indigenous Rights, Mining Corporations, and the Australian State." In *The Politics of Resource Extraction: Indigenous Peoples, Multinational Corporations, and the State*, edited by Suzana Sawyer and Edmund Terrence Gomez, 46–74. Houndsmills: Palgrave Macmillan.

Andreas, Peter. 2009. *Border Games: Policing the US-Mexico Divide*. 2nd ed. Ithaca, NY: Cornell University Press.

Angell, Kim. 2013. "Do Insecure Property Rights Ground Rights to Jurisdiction? Miller on Territorial Justice." *Res Publica* 19 (2): 183–92.

Arthur, W. S. 2001. "Autonomy and Identity in the Torres Strait—A Borderline Case?" *Journal of Pacific History* 36 (2): 215–24.

Ashkenazi, E., and Jack Khoury. 2013. "Israeli Druze to Resume Apple Export to Syria." *Haaretz*, March 3, 2013. www.haaretz.com/news/national/israeli-druze-to-resume-apple-exports-to-syria.premium-1.506890, accessed April 10, 2013.

Blake, Michael. 2013. "Immigration, Causality, and Complicity." In *Varieties of Sovereignty and Citizenship*, edited by Sigal Ben-Porath and Rogers Smith, 111–24. Philadelphia: University of Pennsylvania Press.

Brown, Wendy. 2010. *Walled States, Waning Sovereignty*. New York: Zone Books.

Brubaker, Rogers. 2010. "Migration, Membership, and the Modern Nation-State: Internal and External Dimensions of the Politics of Belonging." *Journal of Interdisciplinary History* 39 (1): 61–78.

Cadava, Geraldo. 2011. "Borderlands of Modernity and Abandonment: The Lines within Ambos Nogales and the Tohono O'odham Nation." *Journal of American History* 98 (2): 362–83.

Carens, Joseph. 1987. "Aliens and Citizens: The Case for Open Borders." *Review of Politics* 49 (2): 251–73.

————. 1992. "Migration and Morality: An Egalitarian Perspective." In *Free Movement*, edited by Brian Barry and Robert Goodin, 25–47. University Park: Pennsylvania State University Press.

————. 2010. *Immigrants and the Right to Stay*. Cambridge, MA: MIT Press.

————. 2013. *The Ethics of Immigration*. Oxford: Oxford University Press.

Catudal, Honoré. 1974. "Exclaves." *Cahiers de Geographie du Quebec* 18 (43): 107–36.

Child, Richard. 2011. "Global Migratory Potential and the Scope of Justice." *Politics Philosophy and Economics* 10 (2): 282–300.

Cohen, Elizabeth. 2009. *Semi-Citizenship in Democratic Politics.* Cambridge: Cambridge University Press.

———. 2011. "Reconsidering US Immigration Reform: The Temporal Principle of Citizenship." *Perspectives on Politics* 9 (3): 575–83.

Cohen, Jeffrey. 2003. *The Culture of Migration in Southern Mexico.* Austin: University of Texas Press.

Cole, Philip. 2000. *Philosophies of Exclusion: Liberal Political Theory and Immigration.* Edinburgh: Edinburgh University Press.

Coplan, David. 2001. "A River Runs Through It: The Meaning of the Lesotho–Free State Border." *African Affairs* 100 (1): 81–116.

———. 2010. "First Meets Third: Analyzing Inequality along the US-Mexico and South Africa–Lesotho Borders." *Journal of Borderlands Studies* 25 (1): 53–64.

Coplan, David, and T. Thoahlane. 1995. "Motherless Households, Landless Farms: Employment Patterns among Lesotho Migrants." In *Crossing Boundaries: Mine Migrancy in Democratic Southern Africa*, edited by Jonathan Crush and Wilmot James, 139–50. Cape Town, South Africa: Institute for Democracy in South Africa.

Cornelius, Wayne. 1990. *Labor Migration to the United States: Development Outcomes and Alternatives in Mexican Sending Communities.* La Jolla, CA: Center for US-Mexican Studies, University of California at San Diego.

Dukenminier, Jesse, James Krier, Gregory Alexander, and Michael Schill. 2006. *Property.* 6th ed. New York: Aspen Publishers.

Dummett, Michael. 2001. *On Immigration and Refugees.* London: Routledge.

Einav, Hagai. 2010. "Israeli Druze Go on Historic Visit to Syria." *Israel News*, October 6, 2010. www.haaretz.com/news/national/israeli-druze-to-resume-apple-exports-to-syria.premium-1.506890, accessed April 10, 2013.

Ellingwood, Ken. 2004. *Hard Line: Life and Death on the U.S.-Mexico Border.* New York: Random House.

Exdell, John. 2009. "Immigration, Nationalism, and Human Rights." *Metaphilosophy* 40 (1): 131–46.

Farran, C. d'Oliver. 1955. "International Enclaves and the Question of State Servitudes." *Journal of International and Comparative Law* 4: 294–307.

Ferguson, James. 1994. *The Anti-Politics Machine: "Development," Depoliticization, and Bureaucratic Power in Lesotho.* Minneapolis: University of Minnesota Press.

Garrow, Carrie. 2012. "The Freedom to Pass and Repass: Can the UN Declaration on the Rights of Indigenous Peoples Keep the US-Canadian Border Ten Feet above Our Heads?" In *Indigenous Rights in the Age of the UN Declaration*, edited by Elvira Pulitano, 172–97. Cambridge: Cambridge University Press.

Gibney, Matthew. 2004. *The Ethics and Politics of Asylum*. New York: Cambridge University Press.

Glaskin, Katie. 2003. "Native Title and the 'Bundle of Rights' Model: Implications for the Recognition of Aboriginal Relations to Country." *Anthropological Forum* 13 (1): 67–88.

Hampshire, James. 2013. "Citizenship, Migration, and the Liberal State." *Migration and Citizenship Newsletter* 1 (1): 37–43.

Hannum, Hurst. 1990. *Autonomy, Sovereignty, and Self-Determination: The Accommodation of Conflicting Rights*. Philadelphia: University of Pennsylvania Press.

Henrikson, John. 2008. "The Continuous Process of Recognition and Implementation of the Sami People's Right to Self-Determination." *Cambridge Journal of International Affairs* 21 (1): 27–40.

Hepburn, Samantha. 2006. "Transforming Customary Title to Individual Title: Revisiting the Cathedral." *Deakin Law Review* 11 (1): 63–88.

Hidalgo, Javier. 2014. "Freedom, Immigration, and Adequate Options." *Critical Review of International Social and Political Philosophy* 17 (2): 232–54.

Hinchman, Lewis, and Sandra Hinchman. 1998. "Australia's Judicial Revolution: Aboriginal Land Rights and the Transformation of Liberalism." *Polity* 31 (1): 23–51.

Holland, Aubry. 2008. "The Modern Family Unit: Toward a More Inclusive Vision of the Family in Immigration Law." *California Law Review* 96 (2): 1049–91.

Honohan, Iseult. 2009. "Reconsidering the Claim to Family Reunification in Migration." *Political Studies* 57 (4): 768–87.

Kandel, William, and Douglas Massey. 2002. "The Culture of Mexican Migration: A Theoretical and Empirical Analysis." *Social Forces* 80 (3): 981–1004.

Kolers, Avery. 2002. "The Territorial State in Cosmopolitan Justice." *Social Theory and Practice* 28 (1): 29–50.

Krenz, Frank. 1961. "International Enclaves and Rights of Passage, with Special Reference to the Case concerning Right of Passage over Indian Territory." PhD diss., Graduate School of International Studies, Geneva, Switzerland.

Kukathas, Chandran. 2005. "The Case for Open Immigration." In *Contemporary Debates in Applied Ethics*, edited by Andrew Cohen and Christopher Wellman, 207–19. London: Blackwell.

———. 2012. "Why Open Borders?" *Ethical Perspectives* 19 (4): 649–75.

Laegaard, Sune. 2007. "David Miller on Immigration Policy and Nationality." *Journal of Applied Philosophy* 24 (3): 283–98.

Lantto, Patrik. 2010. "Borders, Citizenship, and Change: The Case of the Sami People, 1751–2008." *Citizenship Studies* 14 (5): 543–56.

Lauterpacht, Elihu. 1958. "Freedom of Transit in International Law." *Transactions of the Grotius Society* 44: 313–56.

Levy, Jacob. 1994. "Reconciliation and Resources: Mineral Rights and Aboriginal Land Rights as Property Rights." *Policy* 10 (1): 11–15.

———. 2008. "Nationalist and Statist Responsibility." *Critical Review of International Social and Political Philosophy* 11 (4): 485–99.

Lewerenz, Dan. 2010. "Historical Context and the Survival of the Jay Treaty Free Passage Rights: A Response to Marcia Yablon-Zug." *Arizona Journal of International and Comparative Law* 27 (1): 193–223.

Lister, Matthew. 2007. "A Rawlsian Argument for Extending Family-Based Immigration Benefits to Same-Sex Couples." *University of Memphis Law Review* 37: 745–80.

———. 2010. "Immigration, Association, and the Family." *Law and Philosophy* 27 (3): 717–45.

Luna-Firebaugh, Eileen. 2002. "The Border Crossed Us: Border Crossing Issues of the Indigenous Peoples of the Americas." *Wicazo Sa Review* 17 (1): 159–81.

Madsen, Kenneth. 2007. "Local Impacts of the Balloon Effect of Border Law Enforcement." *Geopolitics* 12 (2): 280–98.

———. 2014. "The Alignment of Local Borders." *Territory Politics Governance* 2 (1): 52–71.

Meisels, Tamar. 2005. *Territorial Rights*. Dordrecht: Springer.

———. 2009. "Global Justice and Territorial Rights." *Studies in Ethnicity and Nationalism* 9 (2): 231–51.

Mensah, Samuel, and Vannie Naidoo. 2011. "Migration Shocks: Integrating Lesotho's Retrenched Migration Miners." *International Migration Review* 45 (4): 1017–42.

Miller, David. 2005. "Immigration: The Case for Limits." In *Contemporary Debates in Applied Ethics*, edited by Andrew Cohen and Christopher Wellman, 191–206. Oxford: Blackwell.

———. 2007. *National Responsibility and Global Justice.* Oxford: Oxford University Press.

———. 2010. "Why Immigration Controls Are Not Coercive: A Reply to Arash Abizadeh." *Political Theory* 38 (1): 111–20.

———. 2011. "David Owen on Global Justice, National Responsibility, and Transnational Power: A Reply." *Review of International Studies* 37 (4): 2029–34.

———. 2012. "Territorial Rights: Concept and Justification." *Political Studies* 60 (2): 252–68.

Modo, I. V. O. 2001. "Migrant Culture and the Changing Face of Family Structure in Lesotho." *Journal of Comparative Family Studies* 32 (3): 443–52.

Moore, Margaret. 2013. "Divided Nations and the Challenges to Statist and Global Theories of Justice." In *Divided Nations and European Integration,* edited by Tristan Mabry, John Macgarry, Margaret Moore, and Brendan O'Leary, 33–51. Philadelphia: University of Pennsylvania Press.

More, Inigo. 2011. *The Borders of Inequality: Where Wealth and Poverty Collide.* Tucson: University of Arizona Press.

Murray, Colin. 1981. *Families Divided: The Impact of Migrant Labour in Lesotho.* Johannesburg, South Africa: Ravan Press.

Nevins, Joseph. 2002. *Operation Gatekeeper: The Rise of the "Illegal Alien" and the Making of the US-Mexico Boundary.* New York: Routledge.

Ngai, Mae. 2003. "The Strange Career of the Illegal Alien: Immigration Restriction and Deportation Policy, 1921–1965." *Law and History Review* 21 (1): 69–108.

———. 2010. "Reply." In *Immigrants and the Right to Stay,* by Joseph Carens, 55–64. Cambridge, MA: MIT Press.

Nine, Cara. 2008. "A Lockean Theory of Property." *Political Studies* 56 (1): 148–65.

———. 2012. *Global Justice and Territory.* Oxford: Oxford University Press.

Orrenius, Pia, Madeline Zavodny, Jesus Canas, and Roberto Coronado. 2012. "Remittances as an Economic Development Engine: Regional Evidence from Mexico." In *Migration and Remittances from Mexico: Trends, Impacts, and New Challenges,* edited by Alfredo Cuecuecha and Carla Pederzini, 187–202. Lanham, MD: Lexington.

Osburn, Richard. 1999. "Problems and Solutions Regarding Indigenous Peoples Split by International Borders." *American Indian Law Review* 24 (2): 471–85.

Owen, David. 2010. "National Responsibility, Global Justice, and Transnational Power." *Review of International Studies* 37 (1): 97–112.

Ozer, Courtney. 2002. "Make It Right: The Case for Granting Tohono O'odham Nation Members U.S. Citizenship." *Georgetown Immigration Law Journal* 16 (3): 705–23.

Pevnick, Ryan. 2011. *Immigration and the Constraints of Justice.* New York: Cambridge University Press.

Reid, Helen. 1932. *International Servitudes in Law and Practice.* Chicago: University of Chicago Press.

Sahlins, Peter. 1989. *Boundaries: The Making of France and Spain in the Pyrenees.* Berkeley: University of California Press.

Scott, James. 2012. *Two Cheers for Anarchism.* Princeton, NJ: Princeton University Press.

Shachar, Ayelet. 2009. *The Birthright Lottery: Citizenship and Global Inequality.* Cambridge, MA: Harvard University Press.

———. 2013. "The Missing Link: Rootedness as a Basis for Membership." In *Varieties of Sovereignty and Citizenship*, edited by Sigal Ben-Porath and Rogers Smith, 124–45. Philadelphia: University of Pennsylvania Press.

Simmons, A. John. 2001. "On the Territorial Rights of States." *Philosophical Issues* 11: 300–326.

Singleton, Sara. 2008. "'Not Our Borders': Indigenous People and the Struggle to Maintain Shared Cultures and Polities in the Post-9/11 United States." *Journal of Borderlands Studies* 23 (3): 39–54.

Smith, Rogers. 2008. "Constituted Identities and the Obligation to Include." *Ethics and Global Politics* 1 (2): 139–53.

———. 2015. "The Questions Facing Citizenship in the Twenty-First Century." This volume.

Steiner, Hillel. 1996. "Territorial Justice." In *National Rights, International Obligations*, edited by Simon Caney, David George, and Peter Jones, 139–48. Boulder, CO: Westview Press.

Stevens, Jacqueline. 2010. *States without Nations: Citizenship for Mortals.* New York: Columbia University Press.

Stilz, Anna. 2011. "Nations, States, and Territory." *Ethics* 121 (3): 572–601.

Ulicki, Theresa, and Jonathan Crush. 2007. "Poverty, Gender, and Migrancy: Lesotho's Migrant Farmworkers in South Africa." *Development Southern Africa* 24 (1): 155–73.

Vali, F. A. [1958] 1986. *Servitudes of International Law: A Study of Rights in Foreign Territory.* 2nd ed. London: Sweet and Maxwell.

Wilson, Tamar Diana. 2010. "The Culture of Mexican Migration." *Critique of Anthropology* 30 (4): 399–420.

Wolgin, Philip, and Irene Bloemraad. 2010. "'Our Gratitude to Our Soldiers': Military Spouses, Family Reunification, and Postwar Immigration Reform." *Journal of Interdisciplinary History* 39 (1): 27–60.

Yablon-Zug, Marcia. 2008. "Gone but Not Forgotten: The Strange Afterlife of the Jay Treaty's Indian Free Passage Right." *Queens University Law Journal* 33: 565–628.

III

. . . .

The Character of Politically Sustainable and Normatively Appropriate Civic Bonds

9

CITIZENSHIP AND THE AMBIGUITIES
OF JEWISH SELF-CONFIDENCE

··········

HOWARD N. LUPOVITCH

In the summer of 1865, amid the growing debate in the Hungarian State Diet over Jewish emancipation, Leopold Löw, the editor of the Jewish weekly *Ben Chananya, recalled the prevailing sense among Hungarian Jews—or, at least, among Hungarian Jewish intellectuals like himself—that Jewish emancipation in Hungary was long overdue, and that Hungarian Jewry's second-class status glaringly contradicted what was, in his mind, their deserving full citizenship:*

> Only we Israelites, we alone who have been excluded, must observe these events painfully as mere spectators, barred from participating in the election process though we be as intelligent and sympathetic to the cause. Truly a most sad and sorrowful state! In such moments one feels the bitter pain of rejection and exclusion; and so much more sensitively in our time, since previously, when only nobles had the vote, we were not alone in being excluded; while today the Jewish landholder, householder, manufacturer, wholesaler, teacher, and civil servant—men who have earned distinguished social standing—must calmly watch as a lowly intendant expresses the very right to vote that is denied to him. (Löw 1865, 593)

That Löw made this statement boldly, publicly, and unapologetically nearly a decade before Hungarian Jews were emancipated suggests a need to reconsider the dynamics of the path to Jewish emancipation and how Jews perceived and were affected by this path. Indeed, the voluminous scholarship on the history of Jewish emancipation during the last several decades of scholarship on Jewish emancipation—for better or worse, the colloquial term for the granting of citizenship to Jews—has produced several useful truisms. It is generally agreed, for example, that emancipation of Jews did not entail liberation from slavery, since, without exception, Jews had enjoyed certain rights along with obligations and restriction; rather, emancipation entailed Jews exchanging one set of rights and obligations for another.

There is also a broad consensus that while in most cases citizenship was granted to Jews through a single legislative act of legal emancipation, such legal acts generally punctuated a more protracted and tortuous process of social emancipation, in which Jews were gradually transformed from second-class to full citizens amid larger processes of social and political change. Thus while it is possible to list a series of dates of emancipation, each of those dates represents the culmination of a distinct decades-long series of local political, demographic, and cultural developments.

For this reason, using the legal emancipation of Hungarian Jewry in 1868 as a sharp line of demarcation between two mutually exclusive periods in Hungarian Jewish history simplifies a more complex picture. As will be seen presently, in certain ways, Hungarian Jews behaved as though they were emancipated a full generation before the emancipation act of 1868, reflected by the aforementioned statement of Leopold Löw; while, at the same time, certain rights of full citizenship continued to elude Hungarian Jewry for a full generation after 1868, most notably, Judaism was a second-class religion in Hungary long after Hungarian Jews were made full citizens. Accordingly, the mentality of preemancipated and emancipated Jews in Hungary cannot be contrasted in binary or Boolean terms, that is, between emancipated Jewish haves and not yet emancipated Jewish have-nots.

In light of this complexity, the self-confidence of Hungarian Jews during the decades that preceded and followed legal emancipation is a useful indicator of where Hungarian Jews were situated—or, at least, where they thought they were situated—along the path from second-class to full citizenship.[1] To this end, let us consider three episodes at various points before and after legal emancipation in which Hungarian Jewry demonstrated a measure of self-confidence and explore the roots of this confidence in a political and social context that provides a glimpse into the root of this self-confidence: the construction of the Dohány Street Synagogue in Budapest during the 1850s; the public debates and conflicts between Neolog and Orthodox Jews during the 1850s and 1860s; the surprisingly tenacious Jewishness of assimilated Hungarian Jews, specifically during the campaign by Hungarian Jews during the 1890s to place Judaism on equal footing with Christian denominations; and the unselfconscious willingness of assimilated Jews to maintain a connection with their Jewishness, even in the face of emancipation rhetoric that often discouraged and even precluded this very possibility.[2]

At the heart of the complexity of Jewish emancipation in Hungary is the broader complexity of Hungarian politics, and, in particular, the preeminent role of the Hungarian nobility in Hungarian politics and society. In Hungary, into the twentieth century, the nobility—which comprised approximately 5 percent of the population of Hungary—retained much of its power and influence into the twentieth century, as well as its perch atop the hierarchy of Hungarian society and politics. This meant that into the twentieth century, 95 percent of the population was in a position of social and civic inferiority to the other 5 percent. In addition, the nobility was the champion of Hungarian liberalism, and the driving force in the wedding of Magyar nationalism and Hungarian citizenship.[3]

For Hungarian Jews, this altered the notion of Jewish emancipation, since full citizenship for most people in Hungary did not preclude the superior status of nobles vis-à-vis non-nobles. Implicitly, the debate over Jewish emancipation was a debate over whether to place Jews on equal footing with other non-nobles. From 1790 to 1840, owing largely to the close commercial relationship between Jewry and nobility, the gap between Jews and non-noble Christians closed narrowed steadily—de facto though not de jure—as the patronage of a powerful noble made it easier for Jews to circumvent occupational and residential restrictions. These incremental changes were made official by Law XXIX, which was enacted by the National Diet. Among other things, Law XXIX removed residential restrictions on Jews and allowed Jews to join artisan guilds and to lease land. For all intents and purposes, this law placed Jews on equal footing with other non-nobles.

The improvement in the status of Jews was followed by the active participation of Hungarian Jews in the Hungarian Revolution of 1848 and the ensuing War of Independence. In addition to demonstrating beyond any reasonable doubt their loyalty to the Kingdom of Hungary, the nobility, and the Magyar nation, hundreds of Hungarian Jews joined the Honvéd (National Guard) and helped defend Hungary from its Habsburg invaders. The brief outburst of anti-Semitism that accompanied the outbreak of revolution in March 1848 did not deter Hungarian Jews from a powerful sense of solidarity with their Hungarian compatriots. On the contrary, this sense of solidarity persevered and then was compounded by an edict of emancipation the revolutionary government issued in the summer of 1849. Although short-lived, this legislative act acknowledged and affirmed the sense of solidarity that Hungarian Jews had sensed for nearly a decade. That this act was repealed not by a Hungarian government but by a Habsburg government ruling from Vienna further reinforced the belief among Jews in Hungary that they were now Magyars of the Jewish persuasion.

Nowhere were the impact of Law XXIX and the ethos of the revolution more keenly felt and expressed than in Pest. Three years after the end of the revolution, the Jews of Pest, now living under Habsburg Neo-Absolutist rule, began to plan the construction of a new, great synagogue on Dohány Street. Construction began in 1853 and, six years later, the Jews of Pest dedicated one of the largest synagogues in Europe—indeed, in the world. The dedication of this synagogue was a major event not only for Jews but also for the city of Pest. As a reporter for the local German-language weekly noted: "On the morning of May 6, the newly built Jewish house of worship (Izraelit Gotteshaus) was dedicated in a festive and dignified ceremony. The events, which included our Jewish fellow citizens and which did not pass without arousing the lively interest of broader circles, were witnessed also by, her ladyship, wife of the imperial and royal vice-lieutenant Sir Ede Cseh of the General Staff, and many leading figures from civic, spiritual, and military life. Already by eight a.m. the courtyard of the synagogue was filled with a crowd in a reverential mood" (quoted in Klein 2011, 281).

Similarly, another observer noted in the Hungarian-language weekly *Magyar Sajto:* "The celebration began at nine, but already by eight the immense synagogue was completely full, the balcony occupied by a ring of festively clad ladies, while the ground floor was filled with invited gentlemen, among whom were numerous Catholic, Orthodox, and Protestant clergy, many high-ranking soldiers and honoratiors, who sat in seats in by the sanctuary. In the area in front of the sanctuary, which was blocked by a gilded iron grate, were high-ranking civic and military authorities with pews, who made an official appearance for the ceremony" (quoted in Klein 2011, 282).

The fanfare that surrounded the completion of the synagogue exemplified the seismic shift in attitude among Jews in Pest. Less than two decades earlier, Pest Jewry did not officially exist. As late as 1833, more than 80 percent of the five thousand Jews living in Pest resided there illegally. While many of these illegal residents had been there for years or even decades, the periodic attempts by the city government to rid the city of illegals precluded any real sense of long-term security and connection with the city (Lupovitch 2005, 42–43; Silber 2010).

Only in 1833, moreover, were Jews in Pest defined by the city as a community rather than as an enclave of Jewish individuals who happen to live in the same town. None of the handful of synagogues in Pest were very large; most were small and middling edifices, not least of all because prior to the 1840s it was difficult for Jews in Pest to know with any certainty that they would still be living there a decade or two henceforth—long enough to make worthwhile a major investment in a permanent structure.

The events of the 1840s changed all of this. By the beginning of the 1850s, the vast majority of Jews in Pest, now numbering around 12,000, resided and worked there legally. There was a real sense among Pest Jews that they were part of Hungarian society and that they had a real future there.

It is this change in attitude that underscores the construction of the Dohány Street Synagogue. The capability to undertake this project reflected, first of all, the commercial success of Jews in Pest. The cost of constructing and maintaining this magnificent edifice was by far the largest Jewish communal expense during the 1850s and early 1860s, at times exceeding all other communal expenses combined.

Yet this project represented more than an accumulation of Jewish wealth. The willingness to construct so prominent and ostentatious a building in the heart of Pest would have been unthinkable to Jews who felt less than fully secure in their environment, that is, who felt that they were teetering on the brink of a riot or an expulsion. The project signaled a sense of confidence in the future growth, security, and permanence of Jewish communal life in Pest (indeed, a century and a half later, the synagogue still stands and is still the religious center of Budapest Jewry).

To be sure, the construction of this synagogue was not an isolated event in the architectural history of Pest. On the contrary, it was part of a broader rebuilding effort during the generation following the flooding of Buda and Pest in 1838 that aimed at transforming Pest and Buda into more impressive towns that would narrow the gap between the Hungarian twin capitals and Vienna (Lajos 1975, 290ff.). Even so, that Pest Jews eagerly immersed themselves in this municipal rebuilding project further reflected a sense of connection.

The location of the Dohány synagogue, moreover, further underlines this point. The decision to build this synagogue on Dohány Street was the result of practical considerations, such as available property. Yet this location, on the edge of Terézváros, the older, immigrant Jewish neighborhood, and Józsefváros, a home to upwardly mobile second- and third-generation Jewish denizens of Pest, expressed that the sense of belonging in Pest had expanded beyond the confines of the old neighborhood to include much more of the city. Even if some parts of the city were still largely off limits to Jews—such as the Belváros, or inner city—there were still new possibilities and opportunities to move into heretofore inaccessible neighborhoods—and all of this more than a decade before legal emancipation.

A similar sense of security and self-confidence was reflected by the heated public debate that raged between traditionalist and progressive Jews during the 1850s and 1860s and climaxed with the schism between Orthodox and non-Orthodox Jews at the end of the 1860s. Historically Jews in preemancipation Europe and elsewhere were generally loath to engage in religious disputes and conflicts publicly. Jewish communal leaders discouraged intracommunal contentious behavior over religious matters out of a concern that Christian missionaries might be encouraged to take advantage of such disputes. Any theological uncertainty ostensibly suggested by a disagreement over some essential Jewish belief, the fear was, could undermine the ability of Jews to refute the truth of Christianity and evade the pressures of Christian missionizing ("if you unable to agree among yourselves as to the truth of Judaism, how can you categorically deny the possible truth of Christian belief"). As such, the heated religious debates that consumed Hungarian Jewry during the decade and a half leading up to legal emancipation in 1868—whose complex origins and particular issues are beyond the scope of this paper—suggest a lack of concern among Jews on both sides regarding the potential civic consequences for Hungarian Jewry (see Katz 1998). Indeed, this lack of concern was well founded and consistent with the way that the expectations associated with Jewish emancipation—often referred to as the price of emancipation—had changed during this period.

The price of emancipation was a common feature in the debates over Jewish emancipation, in Hungary and elsewhere in Europe. Typically, these expectations boiled down to Jews assimilating into mainstream society. The degree to which Jews were expected to assimilate varied widely from country to country. Jews everywhere in Europe were expected to adopt the local vernacular as their spoken language and the local dress and manners in place of particular Jewish dress and manners; in other words, Jews were generally expected to acculturate.

Beyond this point, though, expectations varied widely from country to country, and even among proponents of emancipation in each country. Initially in Hungary, the two most outspoken political and social reformers—Istvan Széchenyi and Lajos Kossuth—contended that full Jewish assimilation was not only an expectation but also a prerequisite to attaining citizenship. Széchenyi contrasted the difficulty of Hungarian society absorbing a quarter of a million mostly unacculturated, Yiddish-speaking Jews without undermining the development of the still nascent Magyar nationalism, language, and culture, with the relative ease with which English society and a well-developed English culture absorbed a much smaller number of Anglicized Jews: "The English lake can easily absorb a bottle of Jewish ink; but the same bottle would ruin the Hungarian soup" (quoted in Barany 1974, 53).[4] Along similar lines, Kossuth personified Hungarian Jews as the small town, tavern keeper who exploited peasants and was far removed from Hungarian state building and Magyar nation building.

For both Széchenyi and Kossuth, the concern regarding the difficulty of absorbing an emancipated Jewry was part of a broader problem of asserting the dominance of Magyar nationalism over non-Magyar minorities and transforming Hungary into a Magyar-dominated state and society. Kossuth, in particular, reared in a predominantly Slovak region in northeastern Hungary, was especially sensitive to the deleterious impact of unacculturated minorities and foreigners. Kossuth thus demanded of Jews not only extensive acculturation but also far-reaching reform of Judaism itself, which, he believed, was at the heart of the foreignness of the Jews. Until the end of the 1840s, this was the prevailing attitude toward Jews and, more generally, toward immigrants and foreign elements. Not surprisingly, disputes between Hungarian Jewish leaders over the acceptability and extent of religious reform were largely muted until the end of the 1840s.

Following Széchenyi's retreat from politics and death, and Kossuth's flight from Hungary after the defeat of the revolution in 1849, there emerged a different attitude toward Jewish emancipation and its relationship to Magyar nationalism, particularly in the influential writings and liberal leadership of Baron Joseph Eötvös and Bertalan Szemere. Eötvös and Szemere, more confident in the vitality of Magyar nationalism, believed that a strong affinity for Magyar language and culture could be cultivated among the non-Magyar minorities through state-sponsored education and other cultural programs. Thus they were far less concerned with the religious behavior of Hungarian Jews—or any religious group, for that matter—than with Jews adopting the Magyar language over Yiddish and German and embracing other features of Magyar culture—all of which were nonnegotiable prerequisites for Jewish emancipation. This meant that, for Eötvös and Szemere, a Magyar-speaking Orthodox Jew was no better and no worse than a Magyar-speaking Neolog (progressive) Jew. This divorcing of acculturation from religious practice became a core element in the path to Jewish emancipation from the 1850s onward.

The diminishing importance of religious observance and belief as factors for obtaining citizenship emboldened traditionalist and progressive Jews alike to champion their respective, contrasting beliefs more proactively. There were, of course, other factors that intensified this conflict and contributed to the schism within Hungarian Jewry—the availability of public schooling for Jews, for example (see Silber 1992, 24–25). Yet the public nature of this conflict reflected in no small part the sense of self-confidence among Hungarian Jews that, no matter how deep the rift, the conflict would not preclude the attainment of full citizenship. This assumption was borne out at the end of the 1860s when Eötvös, now minister of education and culture, recognized three separate denominations within the recently emancipated Hungarian Jewry with absolutely no change in the legal or civic status of Hungarian Jewry. Internal religious disputes had no bearing on the relationship between Hungarian Jewry and the Hungarian state, or on the admissibility of Hungarian Jews into the ranks of the Magyar nation.

The attainment of legal emancipation in 1868, though hailed by Jews and non-Jews alike as the culmination of decades of struggle, was an important step, but not the end of the path to full Jewish equality. As individuals, Jews enjoyed all the same rights of citizenship as other non-nobles.

What's more, more than three hundred Jewish families attained patents of nobility between the 1860s and 1914, thus entering the ranks of the social and political elite.

Yet despite these important individual gains, Judaism was still a second-class religion. That is, Judaism, like Protestant and Eastern Christian denominations, was still classified as a recognized religion, while Catholicism was a received religion. In practice, this had little practical impact, with one important exception: if a member of a received religion and a member of a recognized religion wanted to wed, the latter was require to embrace the religion of the former. The illiberal nature of this disparity became a matter of national debate during the 1890s in an episode known as the Recepcio Crisis. Once the Calvinist and Lutheran denominations were elevated to received religions, leading Hungarian Jews began to lobby on behalf of Judaism. In 1895, this campaign succeeded and Judaism, too, was placed on equal footing with the Christian denominations (see Katzburg 1957).

This campaign was not without its oddities. In particular, among the Jews who lobbied most vehemently on behalf of Judaism were those Jews who wanted the right to marry a Christian without having to convert to Christianity. In other words, the Recepcio debate created a situation in which Jews who were marginally connected to Judaism argued passionately on behalf of a religious faith they had largely abandoned.

And yet the unwillingness of these Jews who were marginally Jewish from a religious standpoint to abandon their Jewishness suggests an important dimension of Jewish identity in Hungary more generally. For Hungarian Jews, the degree to which one was religiously observant or nonobservant, no less the degree to which one maintained any sense of Jewishness, was generally not arrived at via a self-conscious decision in response to the pressures of proving oneself worthy of citizenship or demonstrating one's Magyar-ness. Such pressures had been substantially diminished by the attainment of individual rights and by the equating of Magyar-ness with Magyar-speaking. Thus Jews who lived on or near the boundary between Jewish and non-Jewish identity were able to immerse themselves in the latter without feeling pressured to abandon the former. To be sure, there were many Hungarian Jews who intermarried and for whom being Jewish meant very little. Even in such cases, though, often immersing in non-Jewish culture and even marrying a non-Jew did not necessarily entail abandoning one's Jewishness. A telling example of this blurred boundary between Jewishness and non-Jewishness was a phenomenon known as "the Siddur [prayer book] under the Christmas tree," that is, the not-infrequent occurrence of Jews celebrating Christmas but still valuing things Jewish (Konrád 2010, 175ff.).

That the two could coexist seamlessly was facilitated by the degree to which Hungarian Jews regarded themselves and were regarded by their non-Jewish neighbors, as Magyars. This powerful connection was reinforced by the tenuous position of the ethnic Magyars in Hungary. At a time when being a national or ethnic majority was a matter of great significance in political and cultural discourse, ethnic Magyars made up about 45 percent of the total population. Hungarian Jews made up around 8 percent of the total. This led to a simple mathematical conclusion: that defining Jews as Magyars meant an ethnic majority for Magyars.

In addition, Magyarized Jews, particularly in the outlying parts of the Kingdom of Hungary, were regarded as effective "Magyarizing agents" who would accelerate the magyarization of other, more menacing national minorities such as Slovaks, Croats, Germans, and Romanians. The more the Magyar-ness Jews in Hungary was a foregone conclusion, the more confidently assimilated Hungarian Jews could unself-consciously navigate the boundaries of their Jewishness, and the more the boundary between Jewish and non-Jewish became blurred.

The aftermath of the First World War, and the postwar truncating of Hungary, would fundamentally alter the situation of Jews in Hungary, no less than refashioning Hungarian society and politics as a whole from top to bottom. As they confronted the new and far more difficult realities of post-Trianon Hungary, the singular self-confidence that had characterized prewar Hungarian Jewry would begin to fray, though incrementally. During the interwar years, the Dohány synagogue would remain as impressive as ever, Orthodox and Neolog Jews would continue to spar, and assimilated Jews would continue to navigate a boundary between Jewish and non-Jewish life that was becoming less permeable. Yet the difficulties and setbacks of the interwar years do not belie the powerful sense of belonging and self-confidence that defined Jewish life in Hungary during an earlier period.

NOTES

1. I am using "self-confident" to refer to a demeanor that is minimally affected by a concern for what others may think.

2. The Dohány Street Synagogue is the largest synagogue in Budapest and one of the largest in Central Europe; see Klein (2010, 117ff.). Neolog is the progressive religious wing of Hungarian Jewry. Often mistaken for the "Hungarian branch" of Reform Judaism, the Neolog movement affiliated with the Conservative movement during the second half of the twentieth century; for a succinct overview in English, see Frojimovies (2007, 144–45). On the reception debate of the 1890s and the difference between received, recognized, and tolerated religious denominations in Hungary, see Prepuk (2010).

3. Although the nobility was a complex a variegated political and social entity, for brevity's sake, I am using the term to refer to all nobles collectively.

4. A similar sentiment was by Széchenyi's contemporary and fellow liberal Ferenc Deák, who noted that "Jews are like salt—everything needs a pinch, but too much ruins the food."

WORKS CITED

Barany, George. 1974. "'Magyar Jew or Jewish Magyar?' Reflections on the Question of Assimilation." In *Jews and Non-Jews in Eastern Europe, 1918–1945*, edited by Béla Vago and George L. Mosse, 53. New York: Wiley.

Frojimovics, Kings. 2007. "Who Were They?: Characteristics of the Religious Streams within Hungarian Jewry on the Eve of the Community's Extermination." *Yad Vashem Studies* 35 (1): 144–45.

Katz, Jacob. 1998. *A House Divided: Orthodoxy and Schism in Nineteenth-Century Central European Jewry.* Hanover, NH: University Press of New England.

Katzburg, Nethaniel. 1957. "Hungarian Jewry's Struggle for Religious Equality during the 1890s" (Hebrew). *Zion* 21–22: 119–48.

Klein, Rudolf. 2010. "Nineteenth-Century Synagogue Typology in Historic Hungary." In *Jewish Architecture in Europe*, edited by Aliza Cohen-Mushlin and Harmen H. Thies, 117ff. Petersberg: M. Imhof.

———. 2011. *Magyar Zsinagógák Magyarországon: Fejlődéstörténet, tipológia, és építészeti jelentőség, 1782–1918* (*Synagogues in Hungary, 1782–1918: Genealogy, Typology, and Architectural Significance*). Budapest: TERC Publishing.

Kőbányai, János, ed. 2000. *Zsidó reformkor* (The Age of Jewish Reform). Budapest: Múlt és Jövő Kiadó.

Konrád, Miklós. 2010. "'Szidur a karácsonyfa alatt!' Karácsonyi ünnepek és zsidó identitás a dualizmus korában" (Siddur under the Christmas Tree! Christmas Holidays and Jewish Identity in the Dualist Period). In *Képkeret: Az identitás konstrukciói*, edited by Gantner B. Eszter, Schweitzer Gábor, and Varga Péter, 175ff. Budapest: Nyitott könyvműhely.

Lajos, Nagy. 1975. *Budapest története III: A török kiűzésétől a márciusi forradalomig* (A History of Budapest III: From the Expulsion of the Turks through the March Revolution). Budapest: Akadémiai kiadó.

Löw, Leopold. 1865. "Pester Reminiscenzen aus dem Jahre 1861.» *Ben Chananja: Wochenblatt für jüdische Theologie* 5 (34): 593.

Lupovitch, Howard N. 2005. "Beyond the Walls: The Beginnings of Pest Jewry." *Austrian History Yearbook* 36 (January): 40–64.

Prepuk, Anikó. 2010. "Law of Reception." In *The YIVO Encyclopedia of Jews in Eastern Europe,* ed. Gershon Hundert. www.yivoencyclopedia.org/article. aspx/Reception_Law_of.

Silber, Michael K. 1992. "The Emergence of Ultra-Orthodoxy: The Invention of a Tradition." In *The Uses of Tradition: Jewish Continuity in the Modern Era,* edited by Jack Wertheimer, 24–25. New York: Jewish Theological Seminary of America.

———. 2010. "Budapest." In the *YIVO Encyclopedia of the Jews in Eastern Europe,* vol. 1, edited by Gershon Hundert. www.yivoencyclopedia.org/ article.aspx/Budapest.

10

SEARCHING FOR THE CIVIC SOUL
OF THE UNIVERSITY

· · · · · · · · · ·

Higher Education, Citizenship, and the Debate
over Military Training in the Interwar Period

CANDICE BREDBENNER

The vast body of American literature on the democratic purposes of education can be read as a historical narrative of the successive hopes and aspirations pinned on each rising generation of citizens. Until the beginning of
the last century, those wishes and ambitions were directed largely toward
the work of the country's primary and secondary schools. But by the early
twentieth century, as the public contributions of formally trained professionals became more apparent and enrollments at universities grew exponen-
tially, institutions of higher learning achieved recognition as "a major arbiter
of success in modern America" (Marsden, 1994, 339). Social commentators'
broad-ranging explorations of the impact of modern life on democratic citizenship, national character, and social cohesiveness also encouraged closer
examination of the country's system of higher education. Progressive reformers' emphasis on the importance of an educated citizenry and the country's
intervention in the Great War both elevated expectations about the roles of
colleges and universities in securing not just a bright economic future for the

country but a revitalized civil society. According to many of the period's most prominent educational reformers, one of the school's most critical functions was to promote the reinvigoration of those traditional social and civic bonds weakened by modern society's increasingly secular, individualistic, and culturally pluralistic character.[1]

When the United States entered the First World War the federal government relied heavily on educational institutions and agencies to help promote national unity by encouraging patriotic pride in the country's children, training young adults to serve in the army or other vital areas of national service, monitoring dissent, and "Americanizing" immigrants. The wartime government also deployed an ambitious propaganda campaign to reconcile a divided public to the military mobilization effort, hoping to inspire both citizen and noncitizen residents with the message that the strength of national character found its most powerful expression in voluntary acts of solidarity and cooperation. In reality, this vision of unity could not be achieved without coercion. Civil liberties suffered badly, but ostensibly for the purpose of not only ensuring victory for the Allies but also reminding the people that protecting democracy required vigilance and shared sacrifices.

Social and political commentators reflecting on the war's less inspiring domestic revelations often lamented that the demands of war-related service had exposed too many Americans' inability or reluctance to meet some of the basic obligations of citizenship. Thousands of men had failed the physical examinations administered by the Selective Service Administration and were thus ineligible for military service. Many others, though drafted, entered the army barely able to read and write—news that prompted some postwar discussion about the value of literacy tests for voting. And men who had resisted being drafted either because they were conscientious objectors, citizens of another country, or both, were denounced as poor material for citizenship. Some outraged members of Congress even called for the deportation of those aliens who had secured legal exemption from the draft.

There was also anxious speculation on the political implications of the country's return to "normalcy." Peaceful times, though always to be preferred over the alternative, allowed avoidance of some of the most demanding duties associated with patriotic citizenship. There was ample cultural evidence confirming young Americans' affection for their country's heritage of individual liberties, but a thriving democracy required the maintenance of a healthy balance between the exercise of those personal freedoms and their complementary duties. Thus the neglect of civic obligations, particularly the responsibilities of self-governance and self-defense, could be interpreted as a weakening of national character and a dangerous contraction in the purposefulness of citizenship. Cautionary reports that such political afflictions threatened the postwar public escalated with news that voter turnout for the 1920 elections had sunk to a low not seen for nearly a century.

The war and interwar periods showcased several signature efforts to invigorate and elevate the performative elements of citizenship. In the last stages of their campaign for the 19th Amendment, women's suffragists were able to draw advantageously on popular themes emphasizing citizenship's obligations. Advocates of stricter naturalization standards defended their agenda as a means of reaffirming the civic duties of US citizenship. The country's involvement in a world war generated an outpouring of patriotic propaganda directed at inspiring Americans, both draftees and civilians, to demonstrate their allegiance by actively contributing to the war effort. Both civilians and federal officials treated civil liberties as temporarily dispensable while harshly punishing alleged acts of rebellion against wartime obligations. The government awarded alien men who served honorably in the United States military forces during the war with citizenship and subsequently withheld it from those who chose to take the alien exemption from the draft. And, after the war, the peacetime preparedness movement regrouped to resume its vigorous promotion of universal military training for men—not just as a national defense imperative but also as an ideal means of promoting physical fitness, personal discipline, and service-mindedness among the country's youth.

Educators also offered to tackle the challenges to civic readiness revealed by the draft and other war-borne service demands. The editor of *School* offered a stock description of the situation when he challenged readers to consider whether, "If the revelations of illiteracy, physical disability, disease, luke-warm patriotism, not to say disloyalty, occasioned by the draft shocked the country[,] will it be willing to permit the continuation of conditions which have produced such disgraceful results?" ("Corporal Punishment" 1918, 128). All of these deficiencies were cast as serious drags on national character as well as the country's global ambitions, but also as problems that could be remedied by strategic educational reform. As one educator posited, "Not only has the disillusionment of America regarding Germany stimulated us to a realization of our great responsibility as a leading nation, but the war has served to impress upon us that certain fundamental weaknesses in our

American citizenry must be corrected in the oncoming citizens, through an improved educational system" (Wilson 1918, 505). President G. Stanley Hall of Clark University, contributing to this common postwar refrain, also directly linked the continued ascendency of the United States as a world power to the strength of its schools. The United States' new responsibilities as guarantor of democracy and peace depended heavily on the work of the country's educators, who would prepare the country's youth to either "win or lose the great war, after the war" (Hall 1918, 313, 314).

Many contributors to this theme also praised the federal government's wartime partnerships with education for grooming institutions of higher learning for this critical work. In the final months of the war, hundreds of colleges and universities had surrendered control over significant portions of their facilities and academic routines to serve several military mobilization programs. The operations of the War Department's Students' Army Training Corps (SATC) had effectively transformed these campuses into temporary military training complexes. Without access to the facilities and instructors of the many educational institutions hosting the program, the government could not have delivered either vocational or military training on such a large scale or as quickly. Colleges and universities, many of which were facing dropping enrollments, had quickly recognized that they could stem this exodus of students if they worked with the War Department as a partner rather than competitor for young men (Committee on Education and Special Training [1919], 18).[2] As President Charles F. Thwing of Western Reserve University noted with satisfaction, after the establishment of the SATC, the slogan "It's patriotic to go to college" became a popular "war-cry" (Thwing 1920, 65).[3]

Leaders of SATC campuses had generally responded enthusiastically to the federal government's call for their assistance, although candid postwar analyses revealed some frustration with the hastily constructed and very disruptive collaboration. One college president greeted the SATC's demobilization as "the end of the nightmare" ("The SATC—A Comedy 1919, 228). President Alexander Meiklejohn of Amherst College likely spoke for many weary campus leaders when he reported, "It is over, and I come from a tired, a very tired, college" (Smith 1920, 401). James Edwin Creighton, dean of Cornell's graduate school, acknowledged the SATC's considerable inconveniences but believed that the potential long-term impact of the program was beneficial. If academia had shed some of its "narrow pedantry" during this close encounter with wartime preparedness, then "the loss of a few academic hours is trifling in comparison with that great gain" (Association of American Universities n.d., 128).[4]

With the restoration of peace, the country's civilian college and university campuses resumed their normal routines, reintegrating those social and academic features of their communities suspended during the war. While most of the physical reminders of the SATC receded quickly, the short-lived program managed to reset many key observers' general assumptions about the social utility of higher education. Before the war, criticism of academia seemed sharper, rising, and eager to reinforce the public's suspicions that college students lacked discipline, generally found their academic studies boring, and demonstrated limited interest in important political issues. Unflattering descriptions of student and professorial personalities sowed a rather reproachful outlook on colleges' ability to cultivate self-reflective and engaged citizens (Thelin 2011, 190–91). But when the United States entered the Great War, a much different portrait of campus life emerged with news that college men were eager to join the army and their academic institutions were embracing the SATC.

The war only temporarily dampened criticism of academe, but some of the postarmistice commentary seemed infused with a fresh optimism and a renewed faith in the potential societal contributions of college-trained citizens (see, for example, Battle 1919, 260–61; Moore 1919, 235). Predictably, educators were among the most active and enthusiastic correspondents in those dialogues. Some observers reflected that the demands of mobilization had raised awareness of the importance of universities' delivery of professional and vocational programs. After the war, many institutions continued to refashion themselves along the latter lines, as even some of the most traditional schools had done (albeit under some duress) during the crisis. Educators, politicians, government bureaucrats, and social critics also praised the universities for demonstrating a capacity for developing more meaningful town and gown relations. Some contributors lavishly described the war as an epiphanic event, a powerful intervention that had infused higher education with new energy and purpose. While most postwar assessments were somewhat less dramatic than this description, many reflected hope that universities were now primed to embrace a larger public calling.

Many of the country's colleges and universities signaled strong interest in sustaining this era of good feeling toward higher education. One educator reflecting on this period characterized campuses' early postwar mindset as a paradigmatic crisis in which institutions grappled with a re-visioning of themselves as one of society's critical "watchtowers" rather than the historically insular "ivory tower" (Butts 1939, 330–57). Another faculty member described this conversion in more prosaic terms but still conveyed its larger significance: higher education's continued relevance required completing its historic turn "from private to public responsibility" (Hedges 1918, 350).[5] President Parke R. Kolbe of the University of Akron observed that postwar campuses seemed "infinitely removed from the colleges that 'yesterday' before the war" (Kolbe 1919, 4–5). Kolbe credited the advanced public role for universities and colleges affected by the war as the beneficial result of a longer process of "nationalization" that was enlarging the scope of institutional missions (Kolbe 1919, 185). He also praised higher education for emerging from the war having dramatically demonstrated its unique and invaluable strengths. "The ideas and teachings of college men led us into war, college men thought through the issues, and college men have directed its course to a successful conclusion," he boasted. But Kolbe also wondered whether institutions of higher learning would "collapse like a pricked balloon" once the wartime demands of public service and innovation had eased, or, as he hoped, might they continue to flourish "with renewed vigor from the social forces which even before the war were beginning to inspire it with new ideals" (Kolbe 1919, 184).

President Thwing of Western Reserve credited the SATC with encouraging democratizing changes on campuses by diminishing the relevance of traditional social distinctions and practices. The transformation was evident at all levels of collegiate life. Students, he reported, had acquired better manners and self-discipline, professors had demonstrated that they were not all resistant to change, and universities in general had unseated popular assumptions that they were disengaged from the common affairs of society (Thwing 1920, 72–78). Yet Thwing's reflections also highlighted a major source of educators' ambivalence toward their recent partnership with the federal government. While the war had boosted popular confidence in universities' readiness to provide vital assistance to the country in crisis, the resulting "academic revolution" had stripped universities temporarily of some of their most essential attributes. "It was the loss of the higher education itself," Thwing lamented. "It was the loss of culture; it was the loss of intellectual breadth; it was the loss of liberal learning" (Thwing 1920, 78).[6] Academe had become dangerously narrow in its pursuits, its work nearly reduced to the study of one deadly subject—the business of war. The lesson drawn from this cooperative endeavor between the state and higher learning, then, seemed ultimately a cautionary one for universities.

While opinions on the general benefits of SATC varied among firsthand observers of its operations, many exhibited a strong feeling that the recent experience of a world war should guide some kind of systemic peacetime response from higher education. George Gordon Battle, invited to speak at the University of Virginia's Founder's Day and centennial celebration in 1919, used the occasion to offer his academic audience an inspirational message on the legacy of the war. Battle, like the founder of the university, was not an educator, but if his speech on the future of the institution was a fair guide to his views concerning this subject, he also shared Thomas Jefferson's deep faith in education's vital role in sustaining a democratic nation. While public expressions of disillusionment with the outcome of the war would become plentiful enough, Battle chose not to comment on its terrible human and economic costs. Instead, he shared his conviction that the experiences of the war had moved the world closer to a more comprehensive vision of human rights—one that encompassed more than the achievement of political liberty, and also of economic justice and the cultivation of "fraternity." From the "hell and hatred of war" had emerged "a sense of brotherhood such as the world has never known," and this new passion for justice "must bring about the strongest resolution on the part of students and teachers alike to strive for higher things both within and without the walls of the university" (Battle 1919, 263–64, 271).

Philosophy professor Frederick Henke agreed that the war years had offered important political and social lessons to educators. Successful democracies, he advised, focused on the advancement of human welfare and the creation of governments that served the interests of all their people. This achievement also required that citizens be properly educated to seek more than just the promotion of personal liberty. They had to be motivated by "a genuine love of fellow-men, the spirit of brotherhood." It was the responsibility of the schools to cultivate such empathetic citizens who could also place national interests ahead of selfish pursuits (Henke 1919, 207–9).

Battle and Henke delivered these interpretations of the war's lessons to audiences in a country that had not only been spared the serious economic and political disruptions suffered by most of the belligerents but that had enthusiastically propagandized its citizens' voluntary demonstrations of civic cohesiveness and patriotism. These men could thus envision the war as an experience that had imparted new truths, gave new luster to old ones, and restored faith in the power of humanity's virtues. In their view, the war had also given Americans an opportunity to reaffirm the global significance of preserving democracy at home and abroad, to strengthen the civic bonds that united them, and to recommit themselves to the duties of self-government. It had tested the public's allegiances, but left a deeper understanding of the meaning of government by and for the people.

Yet the postwar project of revitalizing citizenship demanded more work from the citizenry, government, and the educational establishment. How the educators would cultivate such mindfulness toward the obligations of democratic citizenship provoked considerable internal negotiation as well as external interrogation of the purposes of a college education. The articulation of these concerns assumed their most vivid and divisive forms in the interwar debates over colleges' and universities' hosting of the Reserve Officers Training Corps (ROTC). Created by the National Defense Act of 1916, the ROTC had barely begun to operate when overshadowed by the more ambitiously scaled and resourced SATC.[7] But authorization to resume the ROTC came swiftly after the war, and the Committee on Education and Special Training, which had been responsible for the administration of the SATC, immediately sought to secure agreements from colleges and universities for the establishment of new ROTC units. While President Woodrow Wilson awaited the opening of the peace conference in Paris, his secretary of war, Newton Baker, announced that of the 115 ROTC units in operation before the war, about one hundred would be reestablished. Additionally, his staff was reviewing applications for approximately two hundred new units (Kolbe 1919, 81).

For its advocates within academia, the ROTC's emphases on practical skill building, leadership, public service, and civic engagement seemed an ideal enhancement to a postwar collegiate curriculum. Yet for other educational leaders, the peacetime presence of compulsory military training programs on college and university campuses undermined the core functions of a liberal education. As scrutiny of the ROTC intensified and commentary on its civic benefits and efficacy became familiar fare in educational journals as well as popular magazines, it also became increasingly difficult for the observing public to view it simply as a program that furnished military officers for the country's reserve forces—particularly when its most active supporters and detractors chose to associate it with explicitly political agendas.

Most of these ROTC programs were compulsory, a trend that in the minds of many peace advocates transformed this postwar collaboration between educational and military establishments into the leading edge of a movement to militarize America. There were, however, less conspiratorial explanations for this curricular decision. The federal government required ROTC programs to maintain a minimum enrollment in each unit. In order to comfortably meet their quota, many colleges and universities required male students to participate in the ROTC program during their first two years on campus but left the advanced course voluntary. However, as criticism of the program gained momentum, some universities ended their institutions' ROTC programs or chose to make the training optional. Between 1923 and 1937, sixteen colleges and universities took those actions.[8] The great majority, however, continued to maintain their compulsory programs despite diminishing support nationally from students and faculty. While students at many of these institutions became increasingly restive under this training requirement, the support of faculty and state legislators varied among campuses and states. Governing boards at public universities tended to be more conservative, unlikely to support a move to a voluntary program, and even less likely to agree to the termination of the training on campus.

The ROTC units at land grant universities trained the majority of students throughout the interwar years and boasted some of the best programs.[9] When the University of Wisconsin became the first university and first land grant university to end mandatory ROTC enrollment in 1923, its action unleashed a debate that had been kept in check by the prevailing assumption that the Morrill Land Grant Act required all land grant colleges to establish compulsory military training.[10] When the War Department declined to publicly challenge the university's new policy, the federal government effectively signaled that future responsibility for the continuation of mandatory military training at the country's land grant colleges and universities rested with the states. Yet in the interwar period, only two other land grant institutions abandoned compulsory training: the University of Minnesota in 1934 and North Dakota Agricultural College in 1937.[11] One significant deterrent to shifting policy, particularly during the Depression years, was the potential risk of losing federal revenue. When the University of Minnesota's ROTC program became voluntary, the federal government responded by reducing its funding of the unit. The university president's office greeted this as an unwelcome adjustment in the relationship, but its financial responsibilities could have risen even higher if the War Department had chosen to withdraw the unit. As a land grant institution, the campus had to offer studies in military tactics regardless of the level of federal support.[12]

The small number of defections from compulsory delivery of ROTC was testament to the strength of many host schools' commitment to the program, but, across the country, the questions mandatory training raised revealed a schism within higher education's establishment over how engaged citizenship should be properly promoted by colleges and universities. Should a college education include instruction designed to cultivate young Americans' "devotion to duty," "discipline," and "loyalty"? Should it offer students' practical training in meeting the needs of national defense?[13] As their policy decisions, public remarks, and private correspondence revealed, the interwar generation of higher education leaders would fall far short of offering a unified response to these questions.

Grasping the historical context in which these interwar debates over military training formed requires some familiarity with certain features of the country's history of civil-military relations at the turn to the twentieth century, particularly the emphases on civilian control of the military and the civic elevation of the volunteer citizen-soldier. Since the American Revolution, the citizen-soldier (consider, for example, the iconic Minuteman) had largely retained his status as the country's most compelling symbol of republican virtue—that patriotic American who unhesitatingly left his peaceful domestic duties to fight and perhaps sacrifice his life for home and country. Politically, an army composed of such civilian-soldiers, raised after a declaration of war but quickly demobilized upon the restoration of peace, seemed the proper defense force for a democratic republic. In peacetime, the states, not federal government, maintained the militia-based civilian reserves. Allowing the War Department to retaining anything more than a small professional army during peacetime was generally dismissed as a dangerous and un-American proposition as well as an unnecessary public expense. Throughout the nineteenth century, this remained the country's basic land force defense model. Even President Abraham Lincoln's decision to introduce a draft during the Civil War could not be interpreted as a rejection of this tradition of volunteerism, but rather as a strategy to encourage it. For many men of the era, joining the army as a volunteer was far preferable to enduring the ignominy of entering it as a draftee. The draft during World War I did mark a more intentional departure from the voluntarist model, but the new selective service system was presented persuasively to the American public as a democratic alternative because it reminded all able-bodied American men (at least those between the ages of eighteen and forty-five) that the basic principle of universal military obligation demanded their active contribution to the war effort.

Although the country's preference for a modest defense preparedness plan attracted some prominent critics over the decades, including George Washington, no significant proposal for expanding peacetime military training offered by the first president, his secretary of war, or several subsequent administrations gained sufficient political traction and public enthusiasm to become policy.[14] But by the early twentieth century, public anxieties the awful specter of world war generated furnished a more receptive political environment for some proposals aimed at strengthening the peacetime national defense system. Well-organized, affluent, and politically well connected, the preparedness leaders of that generation argued insistently that the scale and methods of modern warfare had fully exposed the danger of continued reliance on a hastily trained civilian volunteer army to defend its borders.[15] They were particularly scornful of their opponents in the "ground-springer" school, which included President Woodrow Wilson's secretary of state, William Jennings Bryan. The "Great Commoner" had reputedly declared that if the United States was drawn into the world war, a ready civilian force of a million men would "spring to arms" in a day. Preparedness advocates were quick to add that although they shared his faith in the volunteering spirit of American men, those eager new recruits would be rushed to the battlefront before they had acquired the skills to defend themselves. As one preparedness voice ominously warned, a hurriedly mobilized citizen army would tragically result in "the wanton sacrifice of volunteers in the first shock of battle" (Menkel 1915, 308).

The ROTC's introduction as part of the National Defense Act of 1916 came at the height of this defense preparedness campaign. This legislation did not authorize the general mobilization plan that the War Department had advocated and secretary of war Lindley Garrison would resign in protest over its passage. Yet the addition of the ROTC and provisions to federalize and increase the National Guard were important steps toward creating a larger and better-trained federal reserve. As intended, the introduction of the ROTC improved the overall quality and funding of the peacetime military training offered at the country's colleges and universities. Predictably, the presidents of the country's land grant universities, who were required by federal law to offer curricula that included military tactics, welcomed these benefits proffered by the new program. Preparedness apostles were able to coax further reforms from Congress shortly after the war in the form of the Defense Act of June 4, 1920, which created a funding support system for the ROTC and the Citizens' Military Training Camps (CMTC)—those components of the organized reserves that could furnish the bulk of future reserve officers.[16] Fifteen years later, the secretary of war boasted that contrary to the predictions of their critics, the peacetime civilian training programs supported by the National Defense Acts of 1916 and 1920 were not incubators of militarism and warmongering but of good citizenship practices. Indeed, their purposes harmonized with the aspirations of "the most idealistic lover of peace."[17]

The ROTC thus operated within a federalized military reserve structure that represented a significant improvement over the prewar model. The supporters of the ROTC greeted it as a successful example of the adaptation of time-honored civil-military traditions to meet the defense demands of the new century. Members of Congress had voted for the program as a palatable alternative to compulsory universal military training or the expansion of the regular army. The ROTC also promised to contribute to defense readiness, but within the conventions of military amateurism. The ROTC cadet was a student and a civilian, not a professional soldier. Nor did the program challenge the public's strong partiality toward voluntarism over compulsion insofar as the students who chose to attend the ROTC's host institutions made that choice freely. At the same time, it could be marketed as an invitation to the country's brightest young men to enhance their value as citizens while pursuing a college degree. And, despite the growing presence of female students on college campuses as well as their admission to the national electorate by the 19th Amendment, the ROTC's male-only membership quieted any fears that women would invade this deeply masculinized arena of public service. The weighty responsibility for, and privileges that could accrue from, armed defense of the United States remained monopolized by the men of the country.

Those university leaders who supported mandatory military training in the form of the ROTC felt the most pressure to defend their position publicly, forced by open challenges to their policies in the form of campus protests, petitions, student newspaper campaigns, and, eventually, lawsuits. Administrators' reactions to these events ranged from the issuing of polite statements acknowledging students' and faculties' interest in the subject to authorizing student expulsions or suspensions for refusing to participate in ROTC or otherwise defying university authority on the matter.[18] Students' claims that suppression or punishment of their communications violated their academic freedom were often ignored. Some institutions were more sympathetic to individual students' requests to be excused from military training for reasons of religious conscience, but efforts to force schools to offer such exemptions were frustrated by state and federal rulings in the case of *Hamilton v. Regents of the University of California*.[19]

Interest in bringing such a legal challenge had begun to emerge by the beginning of the 1930s, with the formation of a well-organized student campaign to end the compulsory military programs at California's public universities.[20] Earlier that year, support for modifying the policy had come from another high-profile source when the state governor, James Rolph Jr., had requested that the board of regents consider exempting those students from the ROTC whose religious convictions did not allow participation in war in any form. The regents declined to adopt this proposal.[21] Their resistance to these entreaties only produced more discontent in the form of student protests at the Los Angeles (UCLA) and Berkeley campuses. UCLA's suspension of Albert Hamilton and Alonzo Reynolds in 1933 for refusing to participate in the ROTC program for reasons of religious conscience further energized the antidrill campaign.

In the 1930s, widely publicized suspensions of conscientious objectors at several large universities helped fuel another outpouring of commentary on the social consequences of compulsory military training. Its contents confirmed that rifts within higher education over the subject had not mended.

State university presidents who publicly endorsed mandatory training did so for various reasons. They feared the loss of federal funding that could result from putting ROTC on an optional track, were under some pressure to satisfy their state's propreparedness legislatures, or believed strongly in the merits of the program. As Michael Neiberg observed of this and later generations of university administrators, many of them viewed the ROTC "not as an example of the military in the university but as an example of the university in the military" (Neiberg 2000, 4). They energetically disputed the claim that the ROTC encouraged a militarist spirit on campuses, offering the counter-argument that the program played the important role of reinforcing a civilian influence over national defense. The ROTC trainee was not a soldier; he was a student, a civilian, and, most importantly, a citizen fulfilling a fundamental duty to be prepared to defend his country in a time of national crisis.

Charles Wesley Flint, chancellor of Syracuse University, avowed that "I know of no way in which a semi-ready preparedness can be developed with less militarizing effect than when it is mixed with all the forces of a curriculum on a university campus" ("Flint Defends" 1936). President David Kinley of the University of Illinois added reassuringly that this preparedness training was given "in a civilian institution, from a civilian point of view, with emphasis upon citizenship . . . and under the inspiration of university ideals" (Kinley 1927, 32).[22] Militarist tendencies would be unable to flourish in such an environment. Lemuel Murlin, president of DePauw University and a Methodist minister, was less successful in turning back the movement on his campus to eliminate compulsory training. But he stalwartly defended the ROTC, dismissing predictions that universities were creating a generation of young men who could be "swash-buckled into war." He was confident that the ROTC graduate would go to war only "as the true surgeon goes to the operation . . . when he knows that all curative measures have been tried and have failed."[23]

University of Maryland's president Harry C. Byrd rallied support for the training by directly linking the country's political survival with the university's fulfillment of its civic responsibilities. He reminded his radio audience that the nation depended on colleges and universities to define "the kind of citizenship that shall be the America of the future. . . . In this way, and this way only, can we perpetuate ourselves as a people and as nation."[24] Ultimately, it was the citizenry who had to assume responsibility for ensuring its self-preservation. President Raymond Bressler of Rhode Island State College warned that higher education could not neglect its unique contribution to that cause. When an institution abandons compulsory military training, "it fails by just that much in meeting its full obligation to the nation."[25] Everett Lord, a dean at Boston University, bluntly averred that the country's inadequate military preparation for the Great War had cost the lives of too many American soldiers. But if another crisis arose, and if universities remained steadfast in their support of ROTC, they would have done their part to prepare young men to lead "with sufficient skill to avoid such needless slaughter."[26]

This interest in training service-ready and responsible citizens also reflected university educators' willingness to encourage activities they perceived as character- and confidence-building experiences. Julie Reuben noted that while many collegiate educators had lost faith and interest in formal moral training, they had not abandoned their general regard for promoting character development. Indeed, the evaluation processes of many schools' admissions offices indicated that factors of personality and character were becoming more rather than less important to university gatekeepers in this period (Reuben 1996, 255–65). Thus, as Michael Pearlman suggested, some college and university presidents likely welcomed military training to their campuses because it presented "a new opportunity to perform their old mission—to teach virtue and build character" (Pearlman 1984, 87).

Educators who strenuously opposed these administrators' decisions could still—and often did—share their sense of responsibility for setting the moral bearings of the country's young citizens. Yet a mutual interest in developing students' character as well as intellect was insufficient to override their clashing opinions on the habits of mind encouraged by military training. Some college and university presidents, their conclusions formed from close observation or ethical conviction, believed that the ROTC was not essential and perhaps detrimental to their institutions' cultivation of civic-minded young Americans. President Daniel L. Marsh of Boston University explained why he abolished compulsory training on his campus: "Because I am an American . . . I am opposed to Russianizing, Prussianizing, or Europeanizing America. Compulsory military drill is foreign to the genius of America."[27] Military training required the regimentation of mind and body. The habits of "obedience, promptness, and order" cultivated in such an environment demanded strict conformity, not the kind of critical reflection required of engaged citizens. David Starr Jordan, chancellor of Stanford University and a critic of the programs even before the war, offered the sweeping declaration that "no nation with compulsory military service can long retain its sanity or its freedom." Such training could not produce citizens more capable of self-government, he argued, because it methodically weakened their defenses against exploitation and indoctrination.[28]

While some university administrators acknowledged that their institution had an obligation to support national policies that would discourage the country's enemies from disturbing its peace and prosperity, they reserved the discretion to conclude that compulsory military drill was a misguided approach to meeting that objective. Demonstrating a commitment to the cultivation of a more peace-minded "enlightened citizenship" seemed to better reflect the intellectual and civic purposes of higher education.[29] As one college administrative body that elected to terminate its campus military training program clarified, "We recognize the many virtues of the soldier and appreciate the soldierly ideal of manhood. . . . But there is a better way of carrying on the nation's business than the way of force."[30] The country's declaration of war had given conscriptive military service a clear and finite purpose, but once that end had been achieved, the peacetime goal of "preparedness" seemed too vague and unbounded to continue to justify imposing involuntary training programs on freedom-loving Americans.

Until the institution of a peacetime draft in 1940, the expansion of compulsory military training programs at interwar civilian colleges and universities stood as one of the most visible achievements of a national preparedness movement whose ultimate but unrealized goal was the establishment of universal military training. For antimilitarists and pacifists, the ROTC represented the proverbial camel nose in the tent, the first step toward the forced militarization of American youth. While they spent a great deal of ink blaming the War Department for this maneuver, it was not a situation orchestrated primarily by the federal government. State laws and policy makers, college and university governing boards, chancellors and presidents were the major creators and enforcers of their mandatory military training programs. Thus the campaign against military training had to take its fight ultimately to the country's campuses and courts. It is worth noting that leaders committed to fighting militarism in the schools did not fault higher education for having assumed a political role, but rather for adopting the wrong one—for preparing students to serve a world at war rather than one at peace.

For those deeply invested in the outcome of this debate, the establishment of the ROTC signaled a move forward or backward in the evolution of higher education as an agent of positive social change. Faithful adherents to both interpretations imagined the early postwar period as a watershed for the country and its institutions, one in which even a curricular decision by the country's major universities could redirect the fate of the nation. Ernest Carroll Moore of UCLA reflected the faith of many progressive members in these sparring parties when he asserted that government created public education "to consciously unify people" and "to consciously shape the instinctive desires and attitudes of the young to social ends" (Moore 1919, 214). Inspired by the domestic displays of national unity and sense of shared purpose the war evoked, some university leaders energetically welcomed the ROTC as one means of sustaining that orientation toward national service. Some educators, disturbed by the military draft's exposure of what they perceived as serious weaknesses in the physical and patriotic robustness of the country's citizenry, promoted military training as the proven antidote to those deficiencies. Pacifist educators, repelled by the idea of any educational program harboring a military element, could find no justification for the existence of the ROTC. Others who denounced compulsory ROTC programs as threats to American democracy were highly skeptical that any citizenship training imposed coercively could cultivate authentic civic allegiances and promote healthy political behavior. Ultimately, neither subsequent generations of university presidents nor the federal government would choose to sustain the defense of compulsory ROTC.

When prominent leaders in higher education broadcast the virtues of military training offered under the moderating influence of a civilian administration, and when they defended the ROTC as an expression of universities' fundamental moral and civic commitments to the people, they provided an unofficial yet invaluable service to the federal government. At the turn of the century, some institutions of higher education had already begun to demonstrate their capacity to work with government to tackle major national problems. By the Progressive Era, as Mark Nemec observed, prominent universities had developed "intellectual and institutional apparatuses that legitimized and formalized national state authority" (Nemec 2006, 20).[31] World War I and the interwar years saw the continued maturation of that state-building role. In his history of modern American higher education, Christopher Loss has described universities in this period as "parastates," institutional intermediaries between the state and its citizens. As Loss explained, "In a polity afraid of big government, state builders used intermediaries to mete out federal authority at the local level. What they discovered . . . was that the federal government worked best when it operated by proxy" (Loss 2012, 2).[32] This model of state building is useful in grasping the larger importance of colleges' and universities' role as interwar administrators and advocates of the ROTC. It was an arrangement that deployed educational leaders to do what the federal government could not: convincingly represent a top-down governmental agenda as a bottom-up, citizen-building mission. Assuming this role as intermediary also meant higher education had to tolerate more critical scrutiny of its policies and curricula, a condition confirmed by the intense criticism institutions received for turning a small portion of their instruction of male college students over to the War Department.

As the divisions within the educational establishment over ROTC illustrated, the heart of the debate was not about what virtues of American citizenship were most desirable, but rather how the country's institutions should nurture and sustain them. In post–World War II academe, the perspective that ultimately prevailed left higher education's role in promoting responsible citizenship at least rhetorically intact, but entrusted more students with the liberty of crafting civic identities for themselves. Compulsory ROTC survived the interwar assaults, but by midcentury the program had begun its transition to optional curriculum status on most campuses.

Higher education's interwar leaders entered the ROTC fracas prepared to defend their policies and convictions, and, for the most part, they resisted parroting the false choices too often embraced by stalwart pacifists and militarists. The reasoned dialogue and flexible policies university leaders offered provided a contrast to the hyperbolic rhetoric on military preparedness that urged uncompromising solutions. This generation of educational leaders could not, however, resolve the ambivalence within their own ranks over the unprecedented political role that the ROTC had cast for them—that of brokering the obligational commitments of the citizen to the state. Yet it was a challenge they were largely responsible for creating and were reluctant to abandon. Despite their disparate views on the effects of the ROTC, members of the interwar educational establishment heralded its operation as confirmation of higher education's arrival as a vital force in the shaping of the nation's civic ideals and aspirations.

NOTES

1. Progressive educators saw the schools as critical contributors to the orderly management of a dynamic society. John Dewey described the best forms of education as those that encouraged the individual to develop "a personal interest in social relationships and control, and the habits of mind which secure social changes without introducing disorder" (Dewey 1916, 115).

2. Despite the brevity of SATC's existence, by the signing of the armistice agreement, the program had supported the training of 130,000 men, 100,000 of whom had transferred to the army. Before the SATC demobilized, the

War Department contracted for the training of 200,000 additional men to be distributed between 127 schools.

3. The federal government, colleges, and universities encouraged students to remain in school and enroll in the SATC program. See, for example, the wartime pamphlet, "Are You Going to Quit Now?" (Chapel Hill, NC: University of North Carolina, [1918]), urging students to stay at the university and train for the war while continuing their academic studies. Also, *Uncle Sam Is Alive: Are You? A Message from Harold Whitehead to American Youth* (Washington, DC: American Council on Education, [1918]).

4. Creighton was the first president of the American Philosophical Association.

5. A year later Hedges published his novel, *The Iron City*, which the *New York Times* described as a "scorching criticism of American methods of higher education." Shortly thereafter he ended his academic employment at Beloit College, moving on to careers as a reporter and a labor organizer.

6. For another assessment that acknowledged both strengths and weaknesses of the program, see Smith (1920, 401–19).

7. Act of June 3, 1916, 39 Stat. 166.

8. In chronological order, the University of Wisconsin, Pomona College, Boston University, City College of New York, DePauw University, Georgetown University, California Institute of Technology, Northwestern University (Dental College), Emory University, University of Cincinnati, Rose Polytechnic Institute, University of Utah, University of Minnesota, New York University, North Dakota Agricultural College, and the University of North Dakota.

9. The first Morrill Act (1862) stipulated that in exchange for federal funds or land, the new land-grant colleges must provide training in agriculture, the mechanical arts, and military tactics. Act of July 2, 1862, 12 Stat. 503.

10. The US Interior Department issued an opinion clarifying that colleges and universities subject to the law were obligated to offer training in "military tactics," but that their students' participation in the program could be voluntary. Department of the Interior, *Ruling in regard to compulsory military training for students in the land-grant* colleges, July 19, 1923. Also, 36 Op. Att'y Gen. 297, June 29, 1930. The chancellor of the University of Nebraska offered an alternative interpretation of the law. [Samuel] Avery, "The University's Obligation. Institution Morally Bound to Offer Compulsory Military Training to Its Male Students Because of Morrill Land Grant and Contract of 1916," *Nebraska Alumnus* (April 1926): 198–99. See also Sveinjborn Johnson,

"Military Training in the Land Grant Colleges: Is It Optional or Mandatory?" *Illinois Law Review* 24 (November 1929): 271–95.

11. At this time, both Minnesota and North Dakota had members of Congress who were strong critics of compulsory military training. Rep. Paul J. Kvale of Minnesota and Sen. Gerald P. Nye of North Dakota sponsored federal bills to prohibit compulsory ROTC units in schools and universities. See S. 3309 and H. R. 8950 (74:1). And, Senate Subcommittee of the Committee on Military Affairs, *Hearing on S. 3309*, June 2, 3, and 4, 1936. The major organizations that testified in favor of the legislation included the National Education Association, Progressive Education Association, American Federation of Teachers, United Parents Associations, American Civil Liberties Union, National Student Federation of America, American Student Union, Women's International League for Peace and Freedom, National Council of Jewish Women, National Women's Trade Union League of the Americas, Woman's Christian Temperance Union, YWCA, YMCA, and the National Council on the Prevention of War.

12. The secretary of war presented this scenario in correspondence with Sen. Henrik Shipstead of Minnesota. Letter from Secr. George Dern to Shipstead, April 16, 1935, reel 45, Records of the Committee on Militarism in Education, 1925–1940, Swarthmore College Peace Collection, Scholarly Resources microfilm edition.

13. In 1934, Willard Nash of Columbia University published a study of military science at the land grant colleges. Surveying the schools' general catalogs, he tabulated the most commonly described aims of the military science programs. "Leadership" ranked highest, along with the training of reserve officers. Among the other top scorers were "preparation for national emergency," "discipline," and physical and career training. "Respect for authority" was the next most commonly stated program objective, but it appeared in less than a third of the catalogs. Nash (1934, table XI).

14. But even George Washington, whose frustrations with the performance of the militia during the war were well documented, declared that it must remain "the palladium of our security." "Circular Letter to the Governors of Each of the States," 18 June 1783, reprinted in *Principles and Acts of the Revolution in America*, ed. Hezekiah Niles (Baltimore, 1822), 358.

15. See also the general remarks of secretary of war Newton Baker on the subject of preparedness in Baker (1916, 550–52).

16. 41 Stat. at L. 759 (1920).

17. Report of the Secretary of the War to the President, 1935, 13.

18. Faculties at these campuses appeared more inclined to support a voluntary program, for reasons that were curricular and ethical. Although many of its members had faced the issue on their campuses, the American Association of University Professors did not issue an opinion during this period. H. W. Tyler, Acting General Secretary of the AAUP, to Sen. Gerald P. Nye, April 4, 1936, reel 59, Records of the Committee on Militarism in Education.

19. 219 Cal. 663 (1934), 293 U. S. 245 (1934). The previous year, the US Supreme Court had declined to hear an almost identical case involving a student at the University of Maryland who contested his suspension for refusing to participate in ROTC. University of Maryland v. Coale, 165 Md. 224 (1933). In this case, university officials successfully challenged a ruling by the Superior Court of Baltimore denying their right to suspend Ennis Coale.

20. Copy of text of a petition signed by 1,900 UCLA students and outlining reasons for requesting a voluntary program is available in folder 1931:579, Records of the President of the University of California, Series 2, CU-5, Bancroft Library, University of California at Berkeley.

21. Letter from Rolph to the Board of Regents, February 14, 1931, Box 1931, folder 579(1), Records of the President of the University of California.

22. See similar comments by former University of Illinois dean, E. Davenport, "In Support of the R.O.T.C.," letter to the editor, *Christian Century* (June 9, 1937): 749–50.

23. Murlin to members of the DePauw Committee on Educational Policy, n.d., reel 39, Records of the Committee on Militarism in Education.

24. Transcript of radio address before the DC Chapter of the Daughters of the American Revolution, April 27, 1938, Box M15, folder "Military Dept. 1938," Papers of the President's Office, Series VIII, Special Collections, University of Maryland, College Park.

25. "Bressler Favors Military Training," *Providence Bulletin*, October 24, 1935. For statements supporting the ROTC by sixty-six other college and university presidents, *Statements by Presidents* (1935).

26. "The Benefits of Military Training," in *Military Training Compulsory in Schools and Colleges* (1926, 73).

27. Quoted in "Boston U. Head Explains Optional R.O.T.C. Stand," Committee on Militarism in Education, *Newsletter* (November 26, 1926), 1, 4. The article first appeared in the *New York Herald Tribune* on November 12.

28. "Military Training in American High Schools," *Advocate of Peace* 78 (October 1916): 267.

29. Comments of Harry A. Garfield, "Out of Harmony with Aims of College," Committee on Militarism in Education, *Newsletter*, 1. Garfield was president of Williams College.

30. Copy of letter from the Pomona College Administration Committee to Major General Charles E. Menoher, January 20, 1926, Box 25, folder 000.862 Pomona College, Office of the Adjutant General Files, 1926–1939, RG 407, National Archives and Records Administration, College Park, MD.

31. Nemec sees this relationship as a mutually beneficial one in which entrepreneurial presidents were able to effectively promote the societal and civic value of their institutions.

32. Brian Balogh's study of nineteenth-century Americans' attitudes toward federal authority explores this insight more fully. As Balogh concluded, the public preferred that the national government "enable rather than command." Balogh (2009).

WORKS CITED

Association of American Universities. n.d. *Journal of Proceedings and Addresses of the Twentieth Annual Conference* . . . December 4 and 5, 1918.

Baker, Newton D. 1916. "Our Military Situation," *The Outlook* 113: 550–52.

Balogh, Brian. 2009. *A Government Out of Sight: The Mystery of National Authority in Nineteenth-Century America*. New York: Cambridge University Press.

Battle, George Gordon. 1919. "What Will Be the Effects of the War upon University Education in America?" *Alumni Bulletin of the University of Virginia*, 260–73.

"Bressler Favors Military Training." 1935. *Providence Bulletin* (October 24).

Butts, R. Freeman. 1939. *The College Charts Its Course: Historical Conceptions and Current Proposals*. New York: McGraw-Hill.

Committee on Education and Special Training: A Review of Its Work during 1918 by the Advisory Board. [1919]. Washington, DC: War Department.

Committee on Militarism in Education. 1926. "Boston U. Head Explains Optional R.O.T.C. Stand." *Newsletter* (November 26): 1, 4.

"Corporal Punishment." 1918. *School* 30: 128.

Dewey, John. 1916. *Democracy and Education: An Introduction to the Philosophy of Education*. New York: Macmillan.

"Flint Defends the R. O. T. C. in Syracuse Talk." 1936. *New York Herald Tribune*. June 1.

Hall, G. Stanley. 1918. "Some Educational Values of War." *Educational Administration and Supervision* 4 (May): 312–16.

Hedges, M. H. 1918. "A War Basis for Colleges." *School and Society* 8: 349–51.

Henke, Frederick G. 1919. "The Ethical Bases of Democracy." *American Journal of Sociology* 25: 207–14

Jordan, David Starr. 1916. "Military Training in American High Schools." *Advocate of Peace* 78: 266–67.

Kinley, David. 1927. "Military Training at the University of Illinois." *National Defense Magazine* 1 (3–4): 32.

Kolbe, Parke Rexford. 1919. *The Colleges in War Time and After: A Contemporary Account of the Effect of the War upon Higher Education in America.* New York: D. Appleton.

Loss, Christopher P. 2012. *Between Citizens and the State. The Politics of American Higher Education in the 20th Century.* Princeton, NJ: Princeton University Press.

Marsden, George M. 1994. *The Soul of the American University: From Protestant Establishment to Established Nonbelief.* New York: Oxford University Press.

Menkel, William. 1915. "The Plattsburg Response: A Citizens' Movement toward Military Preparedness." *American Review of Reviews* 52: 301–8.

Military Training Compulsory in Schools and Colleges. 1926. Compiled by Lamar T. Beman. New York: H. W. Wilson.

Moore, Ernest Carroll. 1919. *What the War Teaches about Education and Other Papers and Addresses.* New York: Macmillan.

Nash, Willard S. 1934. *A Study of the Stated Aims and Purposes of the Departments of Military Science and Tactics and Physical Education in the Land-Grant Colleges of the United States.* New York: Columbia University Teachers College.

Neiberg, Michael S. 2000. *Making Citizen-Soldiers: ROTC and the Ideology of American Military Service.* Cambridge, MA: Harvard University Press.

Nemec, Mark R. 2006. *Ivory Towers and Nationalist Minds: Universities, Leadership, and the Development of the American State.* Ann Arbor: University of Michigan Press.

Office of the Adjutant General Files, 1926–1939. RG 407. National Archives and Records Administration, College Park, MD.

Papers of the President's Office. Series VIII. Special Collections, College Park, University of Maryland.

Pearlman, Michael. 1984. *To Make Democracy Safe for America: Patricians and Preparedness in the Progressive Era.* Urbana: University of Illinois Press.

Records of the Committee on Militarism in Education. 1925–40. Swarthmore College Peace Collection, Scholarly Resources microfilm edition.

Records of the President of the University of California. Series 2, CU-5. Bancroft Library, Berkeley, University of California at Berkeley.

Reuben, Julie A. 1996. *The Making of the Modern University: Intellectual Transformation and the Marginalization of Morality*. Chicago: University of Chicago Press.

Smith, Edward C. 1920. "The SATC from the Military Viewpoint." *Educational Review* 59: 401–19.

Statements by Presidents of Universities and Colleges on the Educational Value of Military Training. 1935. Washington, DC: Civilian Military Education Fund.

"The SATC—A Comedy. By a College President." 1919. *The Outlook* 121: 228–29.

Thelin, John R. 2011. *A History of American Higher Education*. 2nd ed. Baltimore: Johns Hopkins University Press.

Thwing, Charles Franklin. 1920. *The American Colleges and Universities in the Great War, 1914–1919*. New York: Macmillan.

Wilson, H. B. 1918. "The Americanization of Education." *Educational Administration and Supervision* 4: 501–9.

11

VOICES FROM THE PERIPHERY

· · · · · · · · · ·

Participatory Budgeting and the Remaking of Citizenship
in Porto Alegre, Brazil

TERESA R. MELGAR

INTRODUCTION

In the 1990s, the city of Porto Alegre in southern Brazil became the site
of a radical experiment to democratize public spending decisions through
the participatory budget (PB) process. Consisting of year-round community
assemblies to determine public spending priorities, the PB process eventually became the locus for asserting grassroots citizenship—one that insists
on deeper democratic participation in politics as a tool for inclusion and a
mark of its substantive presence. Since then, the core ideas of participatory
budgeting have spread in Brazil and globally; civil society groups and governments have experimented with different ways to integrate citizens into
policy-making processes, often seeing this as a means to extend citizenship
to those traditionally politically excluded.

All translations from Portuguese to English are by the author, unless otherwise
indicated.

By demonstrating how ordinary citizens successfully reshaped the exclusionary character of Porto Alegre's politics, participatory budgeting has raised significant questions about the dynamics of deepening citizenship. How did the PB process come to play this role and with what consequences for social and political citizenship rights? More than two decades after it was first launched, what are some of the challenges faced by Porto Alegre's PB process? Finally, what insights can Porto Alegre's PB experiences offer about the sustainability of such mechanisms for fostering inclusion?

To examine these questions, I adopt a historical approach, tracing the evolution of participatory budgeting and its relationship to broad citizenship claims. I suggest that over time, ideas of citizenship provided a powerful lens for grassroots communities to contest their social exclusion, challenge the clientelistic distribution of public resources, and insist on their right to participate in policy making through the PB process. I first examine how participatory budgeting emerged, rooting it to community movements' campaigns for decent housing and urban services during Brazil's authoritarian years. I then show how the legacies of such citizenship struggles fed demands to participate in municipal budget making following Brazil's democratic transition. Dovetailing with local state reformers' electoral pledge to transform city governance, these efforts eventually produced participatory budgeting in Porto Alegre, and this article briefly examines how the process functions. Finally, I explore how participatory budgeting contributed to political and social inclusion and the challenges it has faced since 2004 amid the changing political configuration of the city. This paper is based on an eight-month field research in Porto Alegre in 2006–7, and a six-week follow-up research in April–May 2013.[1]

CITIZENSHIP AND THE POLITICS OF INCLUSION

Most scholarly writings define citizenship as membership in a political community, with the relevant political community here often understood in terms of the state (Janoski 1998). A key marker of such membership is the substantive enjoyment of certain rights; these include political ones, such as the right of citizens to participate meaningfully in political decisions that affect their lives, as well as social rights, such as access to public goods and services that enable people to live dignified lives, regardless of their market contributions (Castles and Davidson 2000; Somers 2008) or political allegiances. Membership also implies being politically, socially, culturally, and economically included, thus supporting a sense of belonging to a broader political community. In the context of the state as the relevant political community, such membership may be progressively accomplished through official policies, programs, or other institutionalized mechanisms that advance citizens' economic well-being, strengthen a sense of integration into their societies, and empower them to participate in shaping its direction.

As Rogers Smith (2013) notes, however, citizenship is socially and historically constructed: full membership in a political community and the substantive inclusion it signifies are often products of struggle and claims-making processes directed at state institutions, economic managers, and the various arenas in which public issues get debated. Social movements and advocacy groups, formed around issues of exclusion and marginalization, typically play pivotal roles in advancing such claims for rights, recognition, and inclusion. These claims-making processes, in turn, generate their own discourses that legitimate such demands and contest exclusionary practices, in the process further deepening the basis for extending citizenship to those systematically excluded from its rights and protections.

In the case of Brazil, notions of citizenship and rights to inclusion provided especially powerful frames around which social movements organized, initially to contest the exclusionary and repressive policies of the military regime in the 1980s, and afterward to deepen democratization processes following the transition to civilian rule (Hochstetler 2000). In the 1990s, participatory budgeting experiments crystallized these efforts to advance citizenship rights to inclusion especially in cities and municipalities. Although there were incipient participatory initiatives elsewhere in the country, Porto Alegre's PB produced some of the most significant accomplishments, even if it has been seriously challenged in recent years. Taking off from these initial ideas, I now examine the dynamics by which participatory budgeting became the locus for the remaking of citizenship in the city.

LAYING THE GROUND FOR CITIZENSHIP STRUGGLES

Although participatory budgeting became part of Porto Alegre's political landscape only in the 1990s, its emergence is better understood within the changing dynamics of the city's urban popular movements. Since the early twentieth century, the city has been the site of intense urban struggles: workers spearheaded strikes to demand lower rents and access to basic services, along with more traditional calls for an eight-hour workday and higher wages (Bodea 1973; Borges 1993; Menegat 1995, 40). By the 1940s, another wave of organizing took place as the period saw the explosive growth of slums and irregular settlements in the city, making housing and the provision of urban services a critical issue. Yet until the 1964 military coup, such organizing largely took place under the control of populist political parties in power (Baiocchi 2005, 27–28). While these activities enabled grassroots groups to obtain key services for their communities, populist state leaders also expected them to provide electoral support in exchange for such programs—thereby limiting their associational autonomy and a broader conception of state services as social rights.

With the rise to power of a military dictatorship in 1964, political organizing was severely restricted in Porto Alegre, as in many parts of Brazil. Successive city governments in Porto Alegre adopted a technocratic and authoritarian approach to urban problems, wherein "popular actors were neither recognized as bearers of rights nor legitimate interlocutors to negotiate their demands before the state" (Fedozzi 2000, 21). In contrast to the populist period, these governments aligned themselves primarily with the city's elites—including industrialists, real estate, and construction companies—investing heavily in the middle- and upper-class districts of the city, thus driving up their market value (Fedozzi 2000, 21; Baierle 1992, 60). They also began an aggressive program to demolish slums to make way for these projects, forcibly relocating their inhabitants to the city's peripheries where infrastructure, jobs, transportation, and other services were scarce or virtually nonexistent.

Such forcible relocation attempts often provoked resistance from affected communities. In response, local officials either tried to co-opt grassroots groups by selectively distributing material goods to those that cooperated with City Hall, or directly repressed them. For a time, these strategies succeeded, as some communities were content to obtain their needs through personal linkages with local officials (Baierle 1992; Fedozzi 2000).

Beginning in the mid-1970s, however, Porto Alegre witnessed increased mobilization by the urban poor, claiming their rights to decent housing, land, and basic services; calling an end to demolitions; and demanding to be consulted in government projects that affected their communities. At the heart of these mobilizations was a new, more "combative"[2] mode of organizing, which increasingly emphasized the notion of political and social inclusion as rights and not favors to be granted by political elites, and which sought greater organizational autonomy from the state. Community activists with ties to left political parties, such as the Partido dos Trabalhadores (PT) (Workers' Party), church workers, middle-class professionals, and nongovernmental organizations were largely at the core of such organizing.

The growing conception of citizenship at the heart of this new mode of organizing was perhaps best expressed by residents of Vila Respeito, a slum community, in an open letter to the mayor as they protested a court order for them to leave the area:

> We want you to see us and to know who we are. We are demanding our rights. Our parents and grandparents built this land: we want a piece of it. Do you want us to live under a bridge with our children in this International Year of the Child? We built this country and this Palace where you live with our work, and [yet] we do not have a place to stay. What we are asking of you is something called Justice. This land is ours, and here we will stay. We are not asking favors. We are demanding a right. These people are united and we will not give up. (Zero Hora, June 22, 1979, 33, quoted in and translated by Guareschi 1980, 202)

As the new, more "combative" mode of popular organizing took root among Porto Alegre's poor communities, it also opened spaces for strengthening the antidictatorship movement, which by then was gaining momentum in the city. Indeed, grassroots groups increasingly saw their campaigns for access to land, decent housing, and rights to the city as part of the broader struggle against the military regime. In 1983, this merging of urban campaigns with the antidictatorship movement gained further ground with the founding of the União das Associações de Moradores de Porto Alegre (UAMPA) (Union of Neighborhood Associations of Porto Alegre), an umbrella organization of grassroots groups, nongovernmental organizations (NGOs), middle-class professionals and left party activists (Menegat 1995).

UAMPA sought to provide a broader political framework for the myriad issues being raised in poor neighborhoods, connecting these to national campaigns. By the time of its first congress in 1985, however, UAMPA did not only raise demands linked to national politics, it also called for the democratization of local governments and popular participation in budget making as the lynchpin of such process (Menegat 1995, 107–9). Recalling some of the discussions during this period, Paulo Guarniéri, who headed

UAMPA in the late 1980s, explains why activists felt it crucial to have a voice in municipal budget making: "At UAMPA, we had arrived at the conclusion that we would not make progress in discussing the policies of the government without discussing as well the budget, because it is the concrete expression of these policies, and without a discussion of resources, there would not be real popular participation. Our idea was to create popular councils with a deliberative character for each policy area: one council for education, one for culture, one for the budget" (Organização Não-Governamental Solidariedade 2003, 42).

Thus, from the start, the construction of citizenship among the grass roots was embedded in social mobilization: urban popular movements in Porto Alegre were pivotal in developing a more expansive notion of citizenship as political and social inclusion, as well as direct participation in governance. These movements arose partly as legacies of earlier waves of organizing, and as a result of the deliberate efforts of grassroots activists to respond to emerging issues of social exclusion, political repression, and economic hardships. As these movements resisted exclusionary local state policies aligned with Brazil's national authoritarian rule, they manifested an evolving perspective on politics, insisting on citizenship and inclusion. Rejecting the clientelistic practices of traditional political elites, they demanded the right to participate meaningfully in political decision-making processes. This claim to citizenship—of being equal members of a political community who had rights to participate in decisions that directly affected them—would be elaborated further in the postdictatorship period via participatory budgeting.

THE MAKING OF PARTICIPATORY BUDGETING

The transition to civilian rule and the restoration of electoral processes throughout Brazil opened up significant spaces for further democratizing policy making in Porto Alegre. In the 1988 local elections, the emergent Workers' Party won the mayorship of the city, translating residents' palpable disenchantment with traditional center and left parties into victory at the polls. Buoyed by the victory of new political forces that seemed more open to their demands, grassroots movements vigorously reiterated their call to participate in budget making. The following year, the first Workers' Party administration of Olivio Dutra, partly in response to these demands, started citywide discussions on the budget.

Since neither the Dutra administration nor popular movements had any blueprint on how to democratize the budget, these initial steps to create what would eventually congeal into participatory budgeting were marked by a lot of experimentation and debates. The said citywide discussions on the budget, for instance, generated enormous expectations: grassroots communities raised pent-up demands for services such as sewage systems and road paving. But given the huge fiscal deficit the city inherited and a new law approved by the previous administration that granted a 100 percent wage hike to municipal employees, the new administrators had barely any resources left to implement these projects (Cassel and Verle 1994). The result was widespread disaffection, leading to a huge decline in attendance in the 1990 budget assemblies (Filho 1994; Abers 2000, 67–75). So frustrated were community activists that some began to question the viability of participating in these institutional spaces, suggesting that popular movements might do better to return to their well-honed tactics of mass mobilization and confrontation with the state (Silva 2001, 112).

The following year, however, a palpable resurgence of community interest in the incipient PB process reflected the changing fiscal picture of the municipal government, as a set of progressive tax reforms launched by the Dutra administration had begun to improve the city's financial picture (Cassel and Verle 1994; Filho 1997). This tax reform campaign, coupled with increased monetary transfers arising from Brazil's decentralization process, generated more funds for city coffers. With more resources and significantly improved coordination among municipal departments, the Dutra administration successfully carried out all PB projects in 1991 (CIDADE, 2009, 2) generating much-needed credibility for the incipient experiment.

From then until at least the early 2000s, the PB consistently drew thousands of people in attendance;[3] participation brought improved services to long-marginalized communities, fueling a greater sense of inclusion and prompting more grassroots interest in the process (Melgar 2014). But how did participatory budgeting function? Under the city's four Workers' Party administrations (1989–2004), the entire PB cycle took place in a year, across sixteen PB regions into which the city was divided and six thematic assemblies.[4] In any given year, the PB process started in March with "preparatory meetings" open to everyone in the smaller units within the sixteen regions. Here, participants initially discussed some of their demands, such as specific projects relevant to the PB's themes for investment—a particular street for paving, for instance—and assessed their "relative priority" (Santos 1998, 471). These preparatory meetings were followed by the first of two rounds of assemblies in each of the regions and thematic areas, usually held in March and April.[5]

As in the preparatory meetings, these regional assemblies were open to any individual or organization, but only residents of the region were allowed to vote should the need arise. In contrast, anyone from any region may participate and vote in the thematic assemblies, which convened to discuss broad policy issues concerning the entire city, such as health policy (Santos 2005, 331). These assemblies generally began with a *prestação de contas* (rendering of accounts) where the mayor discussed the status of projects in the previous year's PB, thus enabling citizens to demand some measure of transparency and accountability from government. Participants could also raise questions about existing projects or probe government compliance with the previous year's PB. Finally, participants elected a portion of the Forum of Delegates (Fóruns de Delegados) for the regions and thematic areas. The delegates were responsible for systematizing and finalizing the priorities of each region and monitoring the implementation of PB projects.[6]

From here, the sixteen PB regions and six thematic assemblies, in a yearlong process, deliberated and voted on their priorities, including specific services or infrastructure, using a set of objective and transparent criteria consensually developed by PB participants themselves over the years. Such criteria generally combined the level of priority given to a particular project or program, population size, and extent of need (PMPA 2005). Constructing these criteria was critical, for through them, PB participants sought to redress the clientelistic distribution of resources that had historically subordinated communities to local politicians. The Council of Participatory Budgeting (COP), a key representative body in the PB, then used these priorities and criteria to craft the final investment plan in weekly meetings with municipal officials for some three months. In its final form, the investment plan presented the specific projects or services that government planned to undertake, named the municipal department responsible, and specified a budget allocation for each project or service (Melgar 2014). Once finalized, the document also became a "social contract" (Pozzobon 1995, 4, cited by Baierle 1998, 133) between the executive and the PB. Published by the municipal government as a booklet and distributed widely in the communities, it served as an instrument that local activists could use to monitor the progress of specific projects. It was also the main mechanism the executive referred to when it rendered an accounting of government performance in the next PB cycle.

In addition to the investment plan, the COP could also review the entire budget proposal of the executive before it was sent to the city council (legislature) for approval in late September, to see if it had incorporated broad PB priorities, or examine other budgetary items (Melgar 2014). In the mid-1990s, for instance, persistent questioning by COP members on certain budgetary allocations such as personnel salaries and the hiring of additional municipal employees led to the opening up of more municipal spending areas to participation by budget activists.

NEW CONCEPTIONS OF CITIZENSHIP AND DEMOCRACY

What has been the impact of participatory budgeting under four Workers' Party administrations? While there are many ways to assess the effects of participatory budgeting, this article focuses on how it has contributed to the deepening of citizenship rights. To what extent has participatory budgeting enabled a reenvisioning of one's rights as citizens, thus encouraging further participation in political decision-making processes?

Several studies in Portuguese and English have explored the empowering effects of the PB process among its participants. Writing in Portuguese, Schmidt (1992) underscores the *desidiotização* of Porto Alegre's grassroots communities, underscoring how participation in the PB process helped them develop a sense of themselves as active, engaged subjects, able to reflect on their common problems as they shaped municipal budget priorities. The same themes are echoed in other works (e.g., Baierle 1998; Fedozzi 1997; Abers 2000; Baiocchi 2005; Fedozzi 2008) that investigate how communities came to demand access to services and political inclusion as rights and not favors granted by political elites, suggesting that this indicated a growing consciousness of citizenship rights.

This process of learning to engage more confidently with community issues within a framework of rights is also captured in various interviews of PB activists who have formed Solidariedade, a local nongovernmental organization. For example, Antônio Vieira de Carboneiro, a forty-five-year old *papeleiro*—one who collects scrap materials for a living—was elected a delegate by his community, the Vila dos Papeleiros[7] in 1999. This community is a slum settlement where most residents are *papeleiros* like Antonio, thus its name. Reflecting on his experiences in the PB, Antônio says: "I learned that a people united is strong. I learned that I could speak. The first time that I spoke in a meeting of the PB, the first time I stood in front of the microphone, I felt very small, like an ant in front of a huge herd of elephants. . . . But I knew the needs of my community, thus, I decided to put aside my timidity and began to speak. I spoke from the heart about life here [in Vila dos Papeleiros] where even a dog would not want to live. It had such a great impact" (Organização Não-Governamental Solidariedade 2003, 57–58).

A similar sentiment is expressed by Marco Aurelio, who in 2002 was elected as councilor[8] for the Nordeste region, one of the poorest of the sixteen PB regions. "I began to participate in 1996 because I did not have a place to live. We were a group of thirty families, in an emergency situation. The rents were too expensive, many of us were unemployed, and we did not have the means to buy a piece of land. Therefore, we decided to occupy an area that, fortunately, belonged to the municipal government. We negotiated with DEMHAB [municipal housing department] but to get infrastructure [in the area], we had to go to the PB" (Organização Não-Governamental Solidariedade 2003, 63).

After several years of engaging with the PB process, this community was able to obtain some infrastructure to improve their living conditions. When he was eventually elected as councilor for the region, Marco Aurelio claims, "My motivation totally changed. I could not leave the [PB] process. I went into it because of necessity, but the PB process becomes a part of you, so you continue to help build your region, your city, because you feel that you are a citizen, and that is good" (Organização Não-Governamental Solidariedade 2003, 63–64).

Another PB participant, Paulo Renato Machado from the region Centro, recalls his initial involvement with participatory budgeting at twenty-four years old, because he wanted to see if land ownership could be legalized in the slum area where his mother, a domestic worker, lived. "I thought that I could [then] guarantee the house of my mother," narrates Paulo. He was eventually elected as a delegate for the region, but as he acknowledges, his concerns then largely revolved around soccer, outdoor barbecues, and social gatherings: "I did not know anything about politics and each Friday I had to go to the meetings of the forum [of delegates]. When I got there, it was such a confusing experience for me. . . . But little by little, you end up understanding how things function" (Organização Não-Governamental Solidariedade 2003, 100–101). Paulo was later elected as a substitute councilor for the region, and he speaks of the time he spent with the PB process as a learning experience that considerably shaped his outlook on various issues:

> Before, I would watch television without understanding. I would watch, for example, the films of Chaplin only because they were funny, but without understanding the message. Nowadays, television does not attract me as much. I am just interested in informative programs. After I became part of the PB process, I discovered things that in the past did not form part of my world. I learned what comprises executive and legislative authority. I learned what is culture. I learned too, that I am black. Before, for me, discrimination was almost natural, to which you do not have to pay attention. Today, there are things that I no longer accept; I exercise my rights as a citizen in all areas. I learned to listen and read. I learned, finally, that the life of the rich is good, and that they eat and dress well, while we live with cockroaches and rats, while the cold seeps through our clothes, while we die outside hospital doors because we do not have means to pay a specialist or to get medical treatment. The PB taught me all of this. (Organização Não-Governamental Solidariedade 2003, 101–2)

In a similar vein, Claudia Gomes Pinto, a thirty-one-year-old delegate of the region Cristal who earns a living as a domestic worker, notes that during her first few meetings in the PB process, "I was very scared that I would speak erroneously, that I would say only nonsense." But she later gained confidence as she continued to participate. "The [PB] process," she suggests, "enabled us to secure some improvements in our living conditions. But above all, I learned to struggle, to leave aside my fears and my apprehensions" (Organização Não-Governamental Solidariedade 2003, 109–10).

As suggested by these interviews, most PB councilors and delegates got involved in the PB process mainly to advance some common need in their communities and often felt unsure of themselves when elected to key positions. Taking part in the PB process, however, eventually led them to understand broader issues of rights, inclusion, and citizenship, and to appreciate their demands in light of these ideas. Sociologist Luciano Fedozzi's (2007) survey of PB participants further amplifies these connections between participation in the PB process and broader conceptions of citizenship and democracy. This study is particularly useful for investigating such issues because it adopts a longitudinal perspective, having incorporated earlier survey findings of PB participants.

A question in the study asks what motivated people to take part in the PB process, allowing for multiple responses. As in previous surveys, Fedozzi (2007) found that a significant share of respondents, or 46 percent in this case, participated to advance some demand relevant to their communities. Meanwhile, those who cited notions like "democracy," "citizenship," "the value of participation," and "the need to fiscalize the process" composed some 13.7 percent of respondents (Fedozzi 2007, 35). Interestingly, when correlated with the number of years that respondents had taken part in the PB process, the results suggest the significant effect of participation on their perspectives. These issues are illustrated in figure 11.1.

As seen in figure 11.1, a significant share of respondents across all categories participated in order to advance some concrete demand. However, beginning with those who had participated five years or more in the PB process, there was a marked increase in respondents who saw their participation as linked to "democracy," "citizenship," "the value of participation," and the "need to fiscalize the process," as well as with "community values linked to democracy" and the "satisfaction they found in participating" (Fedozzi 2007, 36). This suggests that even if participants initially became involved in participatory budgeting to advance a particular demand, further engagement with it tends to broaden their outlook and politicize them, generating ideas of citizenship and participatory democracy that could sustain their involvement in the process, even after their initial demands had been met, as noted by previous interviews. Corollary to this finding, the percentage of respondents who participated in order to "know," "be informed," "because they were invited," or "to complain about badly done projects" declines among those who had participated in the PB process for a much longer time.

Finally, it is significant to note too how participatory budgeting seems to have cultivated a sense of solidarity, of thinking more broadly about the city, especially among those in leadership positions in the PB process. But this too did not occur immediately. Indeed, according to Workers' Party activists who helped coordinate the PB, budget councilors initially tended to seek

FIGURE 11.1. Reasons for participating and number of years in PB

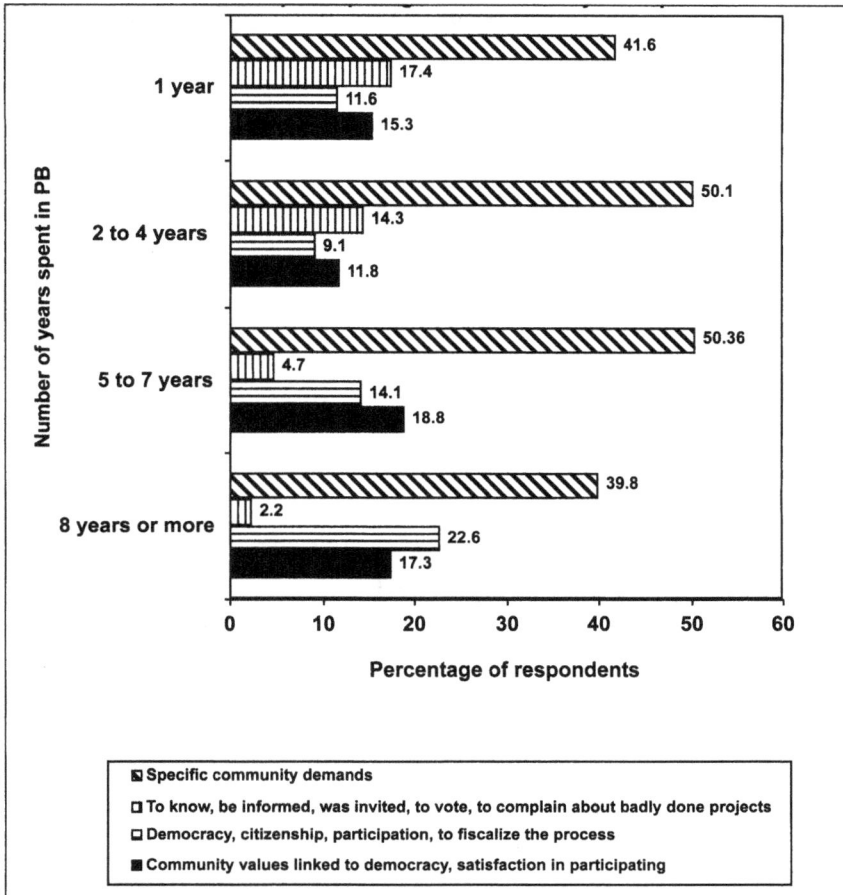

Source: Adapted and translated from Fedozzi (2007, 36)

investments only for their own regions or districts. To encourage councilors to think more broadly, party activists took them on bus trips all over city, seeking to expose them to the needs of various communities (Harnecker 1999, 18). As these councilors learned more about problems in the city, they encouraged PB participants to consider other communities' needs, seeking to negotiate competing claims for limited resources.

Roselaine Marques Neto, a councilor of the Centro-Sul region, reflects on the shift in her perspectives generated by participatory budgeting: "Even I, when I first participated in the PB process, I was only thinking of my street. But I encountered other people, other communities, and discovered problems that were worse. What I thought to be a major problem was nothing compared to the situation of other people. They did not have homes, they slept under makeshift awnings, they had open sewers where children played and walked on. I forgot my street and even now, it is still not paved" (Organização Não-Governamental Solidariedade 2003, 105). On the other hand, Altermir Duarte, a councilor of the Lomba do Pinheiro region, acknowledges that not all districts in his region appreciate the need for such broader solidarity; still, he and fellow PB activists persist with this vision. As he explains:

> Our goal was always to search for another culture, was always for communities to sit at the table to have a discussion at a higher level and look for unity. For example, everyone is going to organize and work together for a common demand, in a more systematic form, so that it will have more weight. And here is where the secret lies: negotiation. Some need a school while others need a day care? Then let us discuss what is more critical, and within this discussion, we are going to open our hand from one thing to accomplish another. This implies having a consciousness of and sensitivity to one another. To be human, one has to take note of the other with new eyes, like a brother, and not like an adversary. (Organização Não-Governamental Solidariedade 2003, 106)

But as a 2001 conference to evaluate the first decade of participatory budgeting suggests, this tension between "solidarity" and "competition" among communities remains one of its key challenges. At times, the PB process accordingly had difficulties incorporating new communities because those that were already integrated into the initiative saw them as another competitor for the city's limited resources. For conference participants, more extensive discussions of the PB regions' internal criteria for defining regional priorities could attenuate such competition, promoting broader solidarity and openness among existing participants and new entrants to the PB (Verle and Brunet 2002, 17).

PB AND SOCIAL INCLUSION

If the PB process generated claims to citizenship and encouraged further political participation, how in turn has this affected social inclusion? To what extent has it given the poorest communities more institutionalized access to public goods, in the process strengthening their social citizenship rights? Thus far, Porto Alegre–based economist Adalmir Marquetti (2008; 2003; 2002) has done the most extensive work on this issue, providing initial evidence on the socially inclusionary impacts of the PB.

For instance, in an early study, Marquetti (2002) examined the distribution of investments per capita for each PB region from 1992 to 2000[9] and correlated them with four indicators of poverty in the regions: the average nominal income of household heads, expressed as a multiple of the federally mandated minimum salary (*salario minimo*, MS);[10] the percentage of women with children and who did not complete primary school; households found in slums and other informal settlements; and inhabitants in each region who were less than fifteen years old. Poorer regions generally have lower average household incomes and a higher percentage of the last three indicators. The study found that the higher the average incomes of household heads in a region, the less investments per capita it received via the PB process. Conversely, the poorer the regions, the more they received in investments per capita (Marquetti 2002).

In another study, Marquetti (2003) classified the PB's sixteen regions from low to high according to the average nominal income levels of household heads (expressed in minimum salaries, or MS) in 1991, and correlated this with the amount of investment per capita in each region from 1992 to 2000, and the number of projects per one thousand inhabitants in each region from 1989 to 2000, via the PB. The results are seen in table 11.1.

As seen in table 11.1, the distribution of investments per capita via the PB process from 1992 to 2000 was again generally redistributive, with the four low-income regions, Extremo Sul, Nordeste, Lomba do Pinheiro, and Restinga, receiving the highest average investment per capita, of between four to sixteen times more than the high-income regions (Avritzer 2009, 105). Likewise, two of the four medium-low income regions, and all four medium-high income regions received slightly higher investments per capita than the high-income regions, most especially Centro, which includes many of the middle- and upper-class areas in the city's center. Those regions that did not follow this trend, namely Partenon and Eixo da Baltazar, had a much bigger population relative to other regions, thus significantly lowering the amount of investment per capita (Marquetti 2003) and deviating from the overall redistributive trend in investments.[11] Nonetheless, table 11.1 suggests once again that the general pattern in the PB process has been redistributive,

Table 11.1. Per capita investments for participatory budgeting regions, various years

Region	Investment per capita (in R$) *1992–2000	Number of projects per 1,000 inhabitants 1989–2000	Average income of household head in 1991
Extremo Sul	1,650	More than 3.8	Low
Nordeste	1,200	More than 3.8	Low
Lomba do Pinheiro	900	3.2 to 3.8	Low
Restinga	650	3.2 to 3.8	Low
Partenon	250	0 to 2	Medium-low
Eixo Baltazar	350	3.2 to 3.8	Medium-low
Norte	500	2 to 3	Medium-low
Glória	600	more than 3.8	Medium-low
Centro-Sul	500	0 to 2	Medium-high
Cruzeiro	500	2 to 3	Medium-high
Humaitá/Navegantes/Ilhas	450	more than 3.8	Medium-high
Cristal	750	3.2 to 3.8	Medium-high
Leste	400	2 to 3	High
Sul	350	2 to 3	High
Noroeste	200	0 to 2	High
Centro	100	0 TO 2	High

Source: Marquetti (2003) for the third and fourth columns; Avritzer (2009, 106) for the second column;

* in Brazilian reais (R$)

giving poorer regions more access to public goods and enabling them to achieve a measure of social inclusion.

EMERGING CHALLENGES

Although Porto Alegre's PB process has clearly accomplished much in advancing the citizenship rights of grassroots communities, the initiative is not without problems or vulnerabilities. Indeed, as I discussed elsewhere (Melgar 2014), since 2004 the PB has experienced significant weakening amid the defeat of the Workers' Party in consecutive mayoralty elections. While in power, the Workers' Party gave strong political, institutional, and administrative support to the PB process, enabling it to democratize local public spending decisions.

But since 2004, a series of more conservative local governments in the city have progressively reversed state attitudes toward the PB process. While maintaining participatory budgeting in form, these governments have relegated it to a less central role in budget making, depriving it of significant administrative, political, and financial support in favor of more restrictive models of citizen participation in governance (Melgar 2014). Inspired by neoliberal ideas in managing the city, these administrations have been less inclined to support the citizenship rights-based, broadly participatory processes pioneered by participatory budgeting, preferring instead to generate "partnerships" with select business and civil society groups to fund, deliver, or manage those state services that used to be decided upon and funded through the PB process.

The current lack of institutional support for participatory budgeting despite official rhetoric is best seen in the implementation of PB projects. Since 2005, local government implementation of PB projects has precipitously declined. Studies by the Porto Alegre–based NGO CIDADE, which has monitored the PB process over time, show that based on official figures, the first two post–Workers' Party administrations of Mayor José Fogaça (2005–8; 2009–10)[12] completed only an annual average of 47.5 percent of all PB projects from 2005 to 2010, in stark contrast to the 97 percent annual average of various Workers' Party administrations from 1992 to 1999.[13] In turn, the low level of government completion of projects has threatened to diminish community support for the initiative (Melgar 2014) and belief in the efficacy of popular participation in governance.

These developments in Porto Alegre have significant implications for the sustainability of participatory budgeting as a mechanism for advancing citizenship rights to political and social inclusion. Although participatory budgeting provided the locus for strengthening such rights, its sustainability still depended on the institutional support of the local state (Melgar 2014). Particularly under the Workers' Party administrations, the local state mobilized activists to coordinate community assemblies, made government data available to communities, refined the PB's institutional design with grassroots activists, and worked to ensure that PB priorities were indeed reflected in the budget and carried out by municipal departments. In this context, enabling state actions directly supportive of the citizenship-enhancing goals of participatory budgeting remain critical to its sustainability. But without programmatic support from the local state and a strong commitment to implement PB priorities, Porto Alegre's PB activists are hard-pressed to sustain the broad, energizing impact that participatory budgeting had on the grass roots' sense of themselves as citizens able to directly shape state policy.

CONCLUSION

This article has explored how citizenship, understood in terms of social inclusion and direct participation in governance, became pivotal to the efforts of Porto Alegre's poor communities to organize themselves during Brazil's authoritarian years, and eventually shaped the construction of participatory budgeting. Following Brazil's democratic transition in 1985, the same vision of citizenship as social inclusion and direct political participation infused the efforts of grassroots activists to open the state to popular input via participatory budgeting. By enabling ordinary citizens to directly participate in municipal budget making—hitherto an exclusive prerogative of local political elites—and providing poor communities more institutionalized access to public goods, participatory budgeting in Porto Alegre has contributed to the deepening of political and social citizenship rights.

The Porto Alegre experience, however, also raises broad questions about the challenges faced by citizenship-enhancing innovations like participatory budgeting. This is critical to note as participatory budgeting has spread globally; state reformers and civil society groups are experimenting with similar mechanisms to democratize policy-making processes, seeking to empower ordinary citizens to directly shape their content, character, and direction. Such initiatives to deepen and extend citizenship rights to the most politically excluded typically contest entrenched elite privileges and practices, thus likely generating opposition to their inclusionary goals. In this environment, the state's robust institutional support for these initiatives, when extended in ways that do not compromise their autonomy and dynamism, strengthens the chances of fulfilling their promise.

At the same time, the PB experience opens an important window for imagining what Rogers Smith (2013) refers to as the changing sites for political membership and inclusion beyond the national state. In the case of Porto Alegre, the growth of participatory budgeting suggests that local communities and polities can become viable arenas for membership, inclusion, and belonging, cultivating them via state-supported participatory processes that enhance ordinary citizens' control over political decisions that affect their lives. It also illustrates how democratic participation and deliberation can secure the material basis for inclusion in ways that promote equity. By giving grassroots communities a meaningful voice in public spending decisions, participatory budgeting had the effect of redistributing state resources, opening up long-denied opportunities for the hitherto excluded to live dignified lives.

NOTES

1. This article draws on and updates some of the key arguments of my PhD dissertation. For the complete dissertation, see Melgar (2010). For enabling me to present an early version of this chapter to the "Meaning of Citizenship" conference, I gratefully acknowledge financial support from the University of the Philippines and the Center for the Study of Citizenship.

2. According to Abers (2000, 44n9), the word "combative," or "*combativa*" in Portuguese, was commonly used by community activists to describe their organizations and to distinguish themselves from more clientelist groups.

3. As I noted elsewhere (Melgar 2014), although sociologist and former Dutra administration official Luciano Fedozzi's (2007, 23) estimate is likely conservative given methodological difficulties in determining the actual number of PB participants per year, his figures still demonstrate annual increases in participation rates. Accordingly, in 1990, only 628 participants attended at least one of two rounds of PB regional assemblies in 1990; by 1999, some 14,776 attended at least one of two rounds of PB regional or thematic assemblies. See Fedozzi (2007, 23) for a breakdown of PB attendance figures from 1990 to 2006.

4. In recent years, the total number of PB regions increased to seventeen due to the division of the Ilhas/Humaitá/Navegantes region into two distinct regions.

5. Beginning in 2002, the two rounds of regional and thematic assemblies were reduced to only one round to simplify the process.

6. The delegates were elected based on the formula of one "delegate" (*delegado*) for every ten people present in each regional or thematic assembly. After the first round of regional or thematic assemblies where some delegates were chosen based on such criteria, these assemblies selected the rest of the delegates in subsequent "intermediate meetings."

7. "Vila" is the term often used to refer to slums in Porto Alegre.

8. Members of the Council of Participatory Budgeting (COP) are called councilors.

9. Marquetti (2002) examined only those investments that went specifically to the PB regions, comprising a yearly average of 35 percent of total investments from 1992 to 2000; the other 65 percent went to projects covering the entire city.

10. The "minimum salary" (MS) for Brazil has varied over the years; in 1998, a monthly minimum salary was set at 120 Brazilian *reais* (R$) or about US$104.

11. On the other hand, Cristal, a medium-high-income region had a much smaller population, thus resulting in a much higher level of investment per

capita, especially compared to medium-low-income regions. See Marquetti (2003, 139).

12. José Fogaça ran for the governorship of Rio Grande do Sul in 2010, thus completing only two years of his second term as city mayor.

13. All figures computed from data in CIDADE, "Demandas do OP concluídas por ano," *De Olho na CIDADE*, April 2012, p. 1. Since this study contained some minor errors in the computation of percentages for the post-2004 period, I used only the raw data it provided and recomputed the percentages.

WORKS CITED

Abers, Rebecca Neaera. 2000. *Inventing Local Democracy: Grassroots Politics in Brazil.* Boulder, CO: Lynne Rienner.

Avritzer, Leonardo. 2009. *Participatory Institutions in Democratic Brazil.* Washington, DC: Woodrow Wilson Center Press and Johns Hopkins University Press.

Baierle, Sérgio Gregorio. 1992. "Um novo princípio ético-político: Prática social e sujeito nos movimentos populares urbanos em Porto Alegre nos anos 80." Master's thesis, Universidade Estadual de Campinas.

————. 1998. "The Explosion of Experience: The Emergence of a New Ethical-Political Principle in Popular Movements in Porto Alegre, Brazil." In *Cultures of Politics, Politics of Cultures,* edited by Evelina Dagnino and Arturo Escobar, 118–38. Boulder, CO: Westview Press.

Baiocchi, Gianpaolo. 2005. *Militants and Citizens: The Politics of Participatory Democracy in Porto Alegre.* Stanford, CA: Stanford University Press.

Bodea, Miguel. 1973. *A greve de 1917: As origens do trabalhismo gaúcho.* Porto Alegre, Brazil: L and PM Editoras.

Borges, Stella. 1993. *Italianos: Porto Alegre e trabalho.* Porto Alegre, Brazil: Suliani-Editografia.

Cassel, Guilherme, and João Verle. 1994. "A política tributária e de saneamento financeiro da Administraçao Popular." In *Porto Alegre, o desafio da mudança: As políticas financeira, administrativa e de recursos humanos no governo Olivio Dutra,* edited by Carlos Henrique Horn, 27–47. Porto Alegre, Brazil: Editora Ortiz.

Castles, Stephen, and Alastair Davidson. 2000. *Citizenship and Migration: Globalization and the Politics of Belonging.* New York: Routledge

CIDADE (Centro de Assessoria e Estudos Urbanos). 2009. "Orçamento participativo: Qual vai ser a disculpa para não investir no OP em 2009?" De Olho no Orçamento. April 2.

————. 2012. "Demandas do OP concluídas por ano." De Olho na CIDADE. April 1.

Fedozzi, Luciano. 1997. *Orçamento Participativo: Reflexões sobre a experiência de Porto Alegre*. Porto Alegre and Rio de Janeiro: Tomo Editorial and Observatório de Políticas Urbanas e Gestão Municipal (FASE/IPPUR).

————. 2000. *O poder da aldeia: Gênese e história do Orçamento Participativo de Porto Alegre*. 1st ed. Porto Alegre, Brazil: Tomo Editorial.

————. 2007. Observando o Orçamento Participativo de Porto Alegre: Análise histórica de dados: Perfil social e associativo, avaliação e expectaticas. Porto Alegre, Brazil: Tomo Editorial.

————. 2008. *O eu e os outros: Participação e transformação da consciência moral e cidadania*. Porto Alegre, Brazil: Tomo Editorial.

Filho, Arno Hugo Agustin. 1994. "A experiência do Orçamento Participativo na administração popular da Prefeitura Municipal de Porto Alegre." In *Porto Alegre, o desafio da mudança: As políticas financeira, administrativa e de recursos humanos no governo Olivio Dutra*, edited by Carlos Henrique Horn, 49–67. Porto Alegre, Brazil: Editora Ortiz.

————. 1997. "Finanças públicas." In *Porta da cidadania: A esquerda no governo de Porto Alegre*, edited by Tarso Genro and Vera Spolidoro, 91–100. Porto Alegre, Brazil: Artes e Ofícios Editora.

Guareschi, Pedrinho. 1980. "Urban Social Movements in Brazilian Squatter Settlements." PhD diss., University of Wisconsin–Madison.

Harnecker, Marta. 1999. *Delegando poder en la gente: El Presupuesto Participativo en Porto Alegre*. Havana: Centro de Investigaciones Memoria Popular Latinoamericana.

Hochstetler, Kathryn. 2000. "Democratizing Pressures from Below? Social Movements in the New Brazilian Democracy." In *Democratic Brazil: Actors, Institutions, and Processes*, edited by Peter Kingstone and Timothy Power, 162–82. Pittsburgh: University of Pittsburgh Press.

Janoski, Thomas. 1998. *Citizenship and Civil Society: A Framework of Rights and Obligations in Liberal, Traditional, and Social Democratic Regimes*. Cambridge: Cambridge University Press.

Marquetti, Adalmir. 2002. "Democracia, eqüidade e eficiência: O caso do orçamento participativo em Porto Alegre." In *Construindo um novo mundo: Avaliação da experiência do Orçamento Participativo em Porto Alegre-Brasil*, edited by João Verle and Luciano Brunet, 210–35. Porto Alegre, Brazil: Guayi.

————. 2003. "Participação e redistribuição: O Orçamento Participativo em Porto Alegre." In *A inovação democratica no Brasil: O Orçamento Participativo*, edited by Leonardo Avritzer and Zander Navarro, 129–56. São Paulo, Brazil: Cortez.

————. 2008. "Orçamento participativo, redistribuição e finanças municipais: A experiência de Porto Alegre entre 1989 e 2004." In *Democracia participativa e redistribuição: Análise de experiências de Orçamento Participativo,* edited by Adalmir Marquetti, Geraldo Adriano de Campos, and Roberto Pires, 31–54. São Paulo, Brazil: Xamã Editora.

Marshall, T. H. 1973. *Class, Citizenship, and Social Development: Essays by T. H. Marshall.* Westport, CT: Greenwood Press.

Melgar, Maria Teresa. 2010. "Constructing Local Democracy in Post-Authoritarian Settings: A Comparison between Porto Alegre, Brazil, and Naga, the Philippines." PhD diss., University of Wisconsin–Madison.

Melgar, Teresa R. 2014. "A Time of Closure? Participatory Budgeting in Porto Alegre, Brazil, after the Workers' Party Era." *Journal of Latin American Studies* 46 (1): 121–49, DOI: 10.1017/S0022216X13001582.

Menegat, Elizete M. 1995. "'Coragem de mudar': Fios condutores da participação popular na gestao urbana em Porto Alegre." Master's thesis, Universidade Federal do Rio de Janeiro.

Organização Não-Governamental Solidariedade. 2003. *Caminhando para um mundo novo: Orçamento Participativo de Porto Alegre visto pela comunidade.* Petrópolis, Rio de Janeiro: Editora Vozes.

Prefeitura Municipal de Porto Alegre (PMPA). 2005. Orçamento Participativo 2006: Porto Alegre: Regimento Interno: Critérios gerais, tecnicos e regionais. Porto Alegre, Brazil: PMPA.

Santos, Boaventura de Sousa. 1998. "Participatory Budgeting in Porto Alegre: Toward a Redistributive Democracy." *Politics and Society* 26 (2): 461–510.

————. 2005. "Participatory Budgeting in Porto Alegre: Toward a Redistributive Democracy." In *Democratizing Democracy: Beyond the Liberal Democratic Canon,* edited by Boaventura de Sousa Santos, 307–76. London: Verso.

Schmidt, Davi Luiz. 1992. "A 'desidiotização' da cidadania: A formação do cidadão para a coisa pública atraves de sua participação no processo do Orçamento Participativo de Porto Alegre entre 1989 e 1992." Master's thesis, Universidade Federal do Rio Grande do Sul.

Silva, Marcelo Kunrath. 2001. "Construção da 'participação popular': Análise comparativa de processos de participação social na discussão publica do orçamento em municípios da Região Metropolitana de Porto Alegre/RS." PhD diss., Sociology, Universidade Federal do Rio Grande do Sul.

Smith, Rogers. 2013. "The Questions Facing Citizenship in the 21st Century." Keynote lecture at "The Meaning of Citizenship" conference, Wayne State University, Detroit, Michigan, March 21.

Somers, Margaret. 2008. *Genealogies of Citizenship: Markets, Statelessness, and the Right to Have Rights*. Cambridge: Cambridge University Press.

Verle, João, and Luciano Brunet, eds. 2002. Construindo um novo mundo: Avaliação da experiência do Orçamento Participativo em Porto Alegre-Brasil. Porto Alegre, Brazil: Guayi.

12

WHAT IS AN "AVERAGE CITIZEN"?

· · · · · · · · · ·

Citizen Speech Codes as Rhetorical Resources
in Public Meetings

JAMES L. LEIGHTER

Rogers Smith (this volume) prompts us to consider, among many others, the following questions: What sorts of bonds can and should serve to hold together political communities and inspire civic engagement? And, how can and should those bonds be generated?[1] These questions reference theoretical developments first detailed in Smith's book (2003). Below, I demonstrate an empirically grounded way to evaluate some elements of Smith's theory by asking how participants in public meetings deploy the word "citizen" for the purposes of naming and characterizing persons, for calling into question actions as appropriate or not and for articulating social relationships. As an ethnography of communication,[2] this study is particularly responsive to the elements of Smith's theory that emphasize the importance of understanding how *political people making, to use his term, may get done in the practice of everyday politics.*

First, I articulate Smith's theory in terms that provide a coherent interdisciplinary frame[3] for situating the analysis. Next, I present a case study taken from public meetings convened in the city of Seattle, Washington. The case illustrates instances in which the participants are expressing notions of who they are as citizens and provides an interpretation of how such expressions of citizen personae shape the strategic, rhetorical moves made on the debate. Finally, I return to Smith's theory, offering insights for the empirical investigation of political people making.

TAKING UP ELEMENTS OF A THEORY OF POLITICAL PEOPLE MAKING

Smith's primary claim is that political science must focus on a "quite basic dimension of all political activity . . . the making, maintaining, and transforming of senses of political peoplehood" (Smith 2003, 19). Smith begins with a definition of "people making," stating it is "the generation of shared beliefs, among outsiders and insiders alike, that certain human populations comprise a political 'people'" (15). Smith suggests people or groups of people become political when they are a potential adversary of other people or groups because they have the capacity to counter the public demands of those people or groups. Smith's focus is on the divisions between actual leaders, would-be leaders of political communities, and constituents, and his intention is to make salient the ways in which stories play social and normative roles in the interactions of these groups. From the point of view of the individual, political peoplehood is one dimension of identity that may be stronger or weaker than other aspects of identity and affiliation. For Smith, "the most politically important feature of a group is the degree to which its proponents assert its priority over other associations, whether over many issues or a few" (21).

Smith's theory works to create intellectual space in two ways that are relevant for the present study. First, Smith argues for the inclusion of a wide range of types of political associations[4] for inquiry in the field of political science. He takes for granted that political peoples are neither natural nor primordial. Rather, they are "constructed." Smith goes on to stress the important influence of what he calls the "high politics" of "law-making, organized political movements, conquests, and confederations" over processes of social construction, including "culture, language, discourses, social groups, religious affiliations, economic interests, territoriality, folkways, [and] unconscious norms" (Smith 2003, 38) that contribute to political membership. This study is an investigation of processes of "social construction" that Smith would prefer not to emphasize. However, like Smith, this study takes for granted that neither micro- nor macropolitical membership can be ignored or treated as mutually exclusive of the other. More positively, this study is meant to contribute to a grounded dialogue among those who examine social constructions of peoplehood with an eye and ear toward how those social constructions are manifest in particular political circumstances.

Second, Smith argues for the inclusion of stories as a resource for investigating the nature of political memberships and the construction of political peoples. Smith writes, "narratives of peoplehood work essentially as persuasive historical stories that prompt people to embrace the valorized identities, play the stirring roles, and have the fulfilling experiences that political leaders strive to evoke for them, whether through arguments, rhetoric, symbols, or 'stories' of a more obvious and familiar sort" (Smith 2003, 45).

Much of the work Smith does to argue for the importance of stories in people making is taken for granted in communication studies and, particularly, in the study of stories as one of many types of talk found in scenes of political communication (see Black 2008; 2012). There is, however, an important distinction between notions of narrative and story that Smith uses to build his theory of people making and the ways in which my study of communication might demonstrate this notion in interaction. Smith's use of the terms *narrative* and *story* is analogous to what rhetorical scholars might call "collective memory"[5] of political peoples, on the one hand, and what cultural communication scholars might call "historically transmitted" (Philipsen 1992, 7) notions of self and persons, on the other. Whether the terminology is the same, the sentiment about how notions of political peoplehood are remembered, brought forth, constructed, and enacted is shared. The analysis below supports Smith's perspective that "stories of peoplehood do not merely serve interests, they also help to constitute them, for aspiring leaders and potential constituents alike" (Smith 2003, 45). The political interests people pursue "are constructed as much or more by their ideas of who they are and what they value as by sheer biological or material realities" (46).

What interests me most about Smith's theory is his assertion that political peoplehood, what I call in the analysis below "citizen persona," can be analyzed not merely through historical and contemporary investigations of such narratives, but also in the moment-by-moment interaction of people *doing* citizenship. The communication perspective I take assumes that "as people engage in communication practices they say something about who each person is," allowing for an analyst to ask of the practice "what does [the practice] presume, or create, as messages about identity?" (Carbaugh 2007, 175). The analysis of uses of the word "citizen" in a particular political context demonstrates how notions of political peoplehood manifest in political talk.

In sixteen hours of public meetings, the word "citizen" is spoken seventy-eight times. Below, I display and situate excerpts from the ICAP meetings that situate fifteen of these instances.[6]

I draw from ethnography of communication, speech codes theory, and cultural discourse analysis to focus attention on four assumptions about the data I present. First, when persons are referred to symbolically (Carbaugh 2007; see also Carbaugh 1988 and Philipsen 1992), observations and interpretations about models of persona in a particular cultural system may be made. Second, previous studies (Philipsen 2000; Carbaugh 2005) demonstrate that the symbol *citizen*, when it is used to refer to persons in public communicative contexts, is inextricably bound to particular modes of communicative conduct. Third, when models for persona are revealed symbolically and in juxtaposition with one another, there is the potential to interpret the types of social relations personae can and should enter into (Philipsen 1992; Carbaugh 1988; 2005; 2007). Finally, this type of analysis lends itself to a written exposition of constructs that, when crafted in combination, suggest there is a patterned or coded system of terms, meanings, premises, and rules (Philipsen 1997, 133; see also Philipsen, Coutu, and Covarrubias 2005) that provide insight into the notions of citizen personae that are deployed.

Seattle's Water Fight

Geov Parrish noted in the *Seattle Post-Intelligencer* on June 13, 2001, that the city of Seattle was involved in a water fight. Initiative 63 (hereafter I-63), a water conservation initiative, was the topic of much public discussion and debate in local print media and Seattle City Council chambers. On August 1, 2001, Mike Linblom summarized I-63 in the *Seattle Times*, writing, "I-63 would require the city to accelerate its conservation program. It would require higher water rates for homeowners and businesses that use large volumes of water, give low-income families up to $600 to install devices such as low-flow toilets, and reserve all saved water for salmon streams as opposed to 'suburban sprawl.'"

This quote captures the main ideas of the initiative but not necessarily the spirit of its proponents. Grant Cogswell wrote in *The Stranger* on June 14, 2001, "I-63 mandates water conservation by retrofitting plumbing in low-income housing units. These efforts will be paid for by making the top 10 percent of heavy 'water hogs'—mostly people watering big yards—pay a high rate for that extra water." Meanwhile, opposition to I-63 coalesced under the leadership of then Seattle City Council president Margaret Pageler. On July 23, 2001, the Seattle City Council passed a resolution allowing the city council to convene review panels for the examination of city initiatives. On July 27, 2001, the city council announced the creation of the I-63 Citizens' Analysis Panel (ICAP). Near the end of July, I-63 proponents filed a complaint with the city of Seattle Ethics and Elections Commission accusing Pageler of "stacking the panel" by selecting panelists with financial interests in opposing the initiative. On August 9, the ethics commission dismissed the complaint of "Yes for Seattle," ten days after ICAP convened for the first time.[7] In the controversy surrounding I-63,[8] one detail might be easy to overlook: the ICAP met four times between July 31 and August 21. The panel listened to expert testimony, discussed the initiative, and drafted a document for the city council to review that was submitted to the council on August 29, nearly one month before the compromise ordinance was reached.

On September 24, 2001, in the *Seattle Times*, Knoll Lowney, cochairman for Yes for Seattle, is quoted as saying, "the reason that the environmentalists objected to the panel was that the panel represented the interests of large commercial water users. Had the panel included average citizens, it would have been a different result."[9] On what grounds does the cochairman from Yes for Seattle make the claim that the panelists were not "average citizens"?

AVERAGE CITIZEN PERSONAE

The analysis begins with the examination of several spoken instances by one speaker from ICAP, Sarah.[10] Sarah's talk provides the basis for comparative analysis of meaning when she and her interlocutors use the term "average citizen."

Instance 1: Playing the Average Citizen

The first instance of the term "average citizen" occurs in the first meeting in which the panelists are posing "questions for Ted." Ted, an expert in water law, has just concluded a presentation in which he has, in his words, "raised" "issues" about the feasibility of I-63. A few panelists ask questions of Ted and, then, Sarah speaks.

> At the first meeting Bill talked about uh sometimes playing the fool?
> And sometimes I feel like I have to play the *average citizen*, and
> you know make myself uh dumbed down a little bit. But you know,

basically what he just explained there sounded very mysterious. It sounded like there were a lot of questions that we can't possibly hope to answer because you know I don't think many of us are as qualified as he is in water rights law, and and he didn't have answers for them so I don't know to me it was ih-causes a lot of consternation. but I assume that there are some precedents and that the utility has already grappled with some of these issues. I know in uh working on the Cedar River watershed HCP they've already dealt with a lot of these and I guess I would like to know in you know simple terms ih-talking about precedents that have already been established how we would answer these as opposed to just creating a lot of questions that make us nervous. I I guess I didn't feel like that was i-i-it wasn't really fair to people like me who aren't versed in in water law to raise all these questions and not be able to answer them in in some plain language.

Sarah's first move is to express a social position from which she will be speaking by saying "sometimes I feel like I have to play the *average citizen*." Sarah compares her playing the "average citizen" to the way that the moderator will be "sometimes playing the fool," but not as analogous symbols. Rather, Sarah is calling attention to her way of speaking that is similar to a way of speaking the facilitator used in earlier talk.[11]

Sarah's use of the symbols "myself" and an "average citizen" are juxtaposed and differentiated: the latter is "dumb[ed] down" "a little bit" from the former. Thus, Sarah has introduced a distinction between an "average citizen" and another type of social actor, "myself," the former having less knowledge of the topic of water law. This expressed distinction in topic knowledge is reinforced in the way she plays the "average citizen." As an "average citizen," Sarah says what Ted "explained" "sounded very mysterious" and it "sounded like there were questions that we can't possibly" "answer." To the "dumb[ed] down" "average citizen," Ted's explanation sounded unexplainable and his questions sounded unanswerable. Sarah supplies an explanation as to why "we can't" "answer" the questions Ted has raised by calling attention to differences of knowledge. The questions cannot be answered "because" "I don't think many of us are as qualified as he is in water rights law" and "he didn't have answers for them." Thus Sarah's use of "average citizen" emphasizes a distinction, knowledge of the topic, between the "average citizen" and other participants.

Sarah's second move continues to challenge what Ted has done in his presentation. The way Sarah challenges Ted, however, contrasts with her first move because in it she expresses some knowledge of the topic. After "play[ing]" the "average citizen" for a few moments, she ceases to speak as though she has "dumb[ed]" herself "down." Sarah demonstrates knowledge of the topic by making a claim backed with evidence from her experience. She says she "assume(s) that there are some precedents," and that "the utility has already grappled with some of the issues" that Ted has raised. She adds she "know(s)" from her work on "the Cedar River watershed HCP" "that they've already dealt with a lot of these." Sarah, thus, briefly abandons playing the "average citizen" in order to speak with knowledge as a person who has some understanding of the topic.

In Sarah's third move she resumes playing the "average citizen." Above, I have labeled Sarah's speech act as a challenge. More precisely, it is the opening step in a specific communicative sequence known prototypically as a social drama.[12] The conduct Sarah is challenging[13] is that Ted "raise[d] all these questions" and "didn't answer them" "in some plain language." Sarah invokes a sense of immorality and inequity, saying "it wasn't really fair" "to raise all these questions and not be able to answer them." Sarah suggests Ted's conduct may have been "fair" to some people, but not "to people like me who aren't versed in water law." Someone "versed in water law" should not do what he did to "people like me who aren't."

Sarah, speaking as the "average citizen" once more, attempts to commit Ted to a particular way of speaking. She says, "I would like to know in you know simple terms ih-talking about precedents that have already been established how we would answer these as opposed to just creating a lot of questions."

Instance 1 reveals a type of person linked with the symbol "average citizen." The semantic dimension of contrast between the "average citizen" and other symbols differentiating types of persons is the knowledge of or expertise on the topic. Additionally, Sarah uses the term "average citizen" to criticize Ted's conduct and emphasize that an "average citizen" has limited knowledge and, therefore, to place limits on Ted's communicative conduct.

Instances 2 and 3: A Conglomeration of Average Citizens

Sarah's second and third spoken instances of the term "average citizen" occur in a meeting in which the facilitator, Bill, has opened the floor for the panelists to "comment now about process and how you see the group dynamic occurring."

Sarah begins by referencing two aspects of the "resolution from the city council" that formed the ICAP. First, Sarah asserts that the panel should create a "report" and not a "recommendation," a distinction that receives considerable attention in the meetings and a topic that gets picked up by Mary in her response to Sarah. Sarah's position is clear when she says, "I feel very strongly that we should not be making recommendations. That's not what we were charged to do." The second aspect of the resolution Sarah "comments" on is the character or quality of the panel. In her utterance, Sarah makes a distinction between a "citizens panel," comprised of a "conglomeration of average citizens," and a "panel of" "interested parties." She says:

> I also feel like this resolution set up a citizens panel. And we basically decided that we didn't dec-define ourselves as a citizens panel. We're a panel of interested parties. And so therefore I think it's really important that we identify who we are and who we represent as we make our points. Um as opposed to just having a you know consensus or presenting alternative views. Some people on the panel thought this other people on the panel thought that. I think it's very important given the fact that we're not just a conglomeration of average citizens that we also reflect that in our report to the council which interests felt a certain way and which interests felt another way.

Sarah says that the panel had "decided that we didn't" "define ourselves as a citizens panel." For her, the panel is a "panel of" "interested parties" that in their "report to the council" should "reflect" "which interests felt a certain way and which interests felt another way." Following Sarah's logic, "a citizens panel" is "a conglomeration of average citizens" and distinct from "a panel of" "interested parties." Thus in Sarah's comment the term "citizen" is semantically coterminous with "average citizen." Sarah has also introduced "interests" as a distinction between panels of "average citizens" and "interested parties."

Mary responds to Sarah by de-emphasizing the significance of any label for the panel. She says, "I think every panel is a compilation or a composition of people with their own interests. Whether we're quote a citizens panel or not. You know itsa-what's your work background where you come from so while it might be interesting to note that as recommendations or

observations or conclusions are grouped by sort of our professional back-
grounds which I think is really what we're talking 'bout. I I'm not sure that
th-that is necessarily the issue."

For Mary, whether the panel is "quote a citizens panel or not" is insignificant. Mary's response centers on her assumption that the nature of the
panel is not affected by the labels used to name it because "every panel is
a compilation or a composition of people with their own interests." Mary
characterizes this concern of Sarah's in terms of "work background." Using
Mary's words, "what we're really talking 'bout" is grouping "recommendations or observations or conclusions" by "professional background" and this
is not "the issue." Mary continues, "And you know I mean whether we call
ourselves a citizen or a stakeholder or whatever we we're we are appointed as
a citizens task force. So I'm I I I'm in sort of in a favor of a of a report that
un-unless we truly have fourteen different positions but that that talks about
these are the issues that are important for these reasons and then if someone
feels very strongly or several then sort of like a minority or in an addition to
a short letter."

Mary's response is curious in that she separates the labels used for the
panel, "a citizen or a stakeholder or whatever," from the essential quality of
the panel. In her words, "we are appointed as a citizens task force." Despite
her assertions that the labels used for the panel are "not necessarily" "the
issue," Mary's own characterization of the panel includes the word "citizen."
From this instance, I am not able to interpret Mary's meaning of "citizens
task force," but her concern for the use of any label is revealed. Mary's central
concern with Sarah's suggestion that the panel is one of "interested parties"
is that the "report" will unnecessarily reflect "fourteen different positions."
Thus I interpret Mary's concern with recognizing the panel as a "panel of"
"interested parties" will undermine the appearance of unity.

Mary's full response does not dispute that the panel is not a "citizens
panel," but rather is an attempt to suggest that "whatever" label is used for
the panel is insignificant. Sarah responds by providing evidence for her claim
that the panel is not "a panel of citizens." She says, "I mean I think my point
is that i-a panel of citizens if we were just trying to get some geographic and
other sort of diversity in a panel of uh ratepayers and voters would look very
different from the panel here. You know we are people who have expertise
who have interests who are stakeholders. And you know I don't think we

should just pretend like we're just average citizens with no real interest in this. I don't think that's genuine."

Here, Sarah expresses some characteristics that a "panel of citizens" would have: "some geographic and other sort of diversity" that would reflect this "sort of diversity," as well as representation of a broad range of "ratepayers" and "voters." She adds, the "panel here" is "different" because it includes "people who have expertise" and "interests," and "who are stakeholders." Thus, Sarah has reemphasized the expertise/knowledge distinction between "average citizens" and other participants while also pointing out the distinction of "interests." Finally, Sarah picks up a term that Mary used in her utterance, "stakeholders," and suggests this is distinct from "average citizens."

That Sarah and Mary do not agree on the significance of labeling the panel as "a citizens panel" is an important aspect of the present analysis. The analyses of Instances 1, 2, and 3 provide an initial sketch of a typification of an average citizen as a distinct type of citizen persona. Mary's disagreement is important because it highlights the way in which agreement about the central character of the panel need not be achieved in order for cultural understandings to be understood. That is, Mary's disagreement with Sarah speaks to the position Sarah has taken in the social action of the meeting. It does not, however, call into question the typification of the average citizen persona that Sarah is expressing.

Instance 4: Just Average Citizens Interested in Fair Process

Sarah's fourth spoken instance of the term "average citizen" occurs in a meeting in which Bill, the moderator, invites the panelists to "talk briefly about the panel process." Sarah responds to Bill saying, "I think that over the course of these four meetings we've had some really helpful testimony from the public regarding this issue. From uh folks from the University of Washington from the League of Women Voters and uh you know just average citizens who are interested in the fair process."

Sarah suggests to the panel that they should consider "testimony from the public regarding this issue." The "issue" Sarah is referring to is "the panel process." From both the segment of talk displayed above and the audio record of this utterance, it is unclear to me whether Sarah uses the term "average citizens" as an appositive for "folks from the University of Washington from the league of Women Voters," or if this term refers to a third group of persons who

Table 12.1. Semantic dimensions for "average citizen"

	Semantic Dimension	Term of Contrast
"average citizen"	*expertise/knowledge*	"expert"
"average citizen"	*"interest(s)"*	"interested parties"
"average citizen"	*having a stake*	"stakeholder"

gave testimony. Characterizing Sarah's use of "average citizens" as a reference to "folks from the University of Washington from the League of Women Voters" as "average citizens" would seem to be in contradiction with the interpretations of Instances 1 through 3, because people from the university and the league could probably also be labeled as "experts" or "people with interests."

Nevertheless, either interpretation suggests that Sarah's use of the term emphasizes a particular quality of the people she is referring to. These speakers "from the public," including "average citizens," "are interested in the fair process." This claim, that "average citizens" "are interested in fair process," is supported by an additional instance in which the term "average citizen" co-occurs with the term "fair." Recall from Instance 1 when, "average citizen" challenges the expert for acting in a way that was not "fair."

Meanings of the Term "Average Citizen"

The descriptions and interpretations of Sarah's four uses of the term "average citizen" provide an initial sketch of the average citizen as a distinct type of citizen persona. The term "average citizen" differentiates a type of person who is less knowledgeable and has less expertise than other participants in these meetings. Moreover, this symbol also differentiates a type of person who has less interest and less of a stake in the matter.

Table 12.1 includes an additional interpretive element indicating directionality of these semantic dimensions. One way to read this table is the more expertise a person has, the less she or he is an average citizen. Directionality of these semantic dimensions is important because it explains an aspect of Sarah's talk not discussed in the analysis above. A person cannot be an "average citizen" if she or he has expertise, interest, and/or a stake. A person possessing these qualities is pushed, semantically, toward the social positions to which the symbols "expert," "interested parties," and "stakeholder" refer.

This additional interpretation explains why "experts," "interested parties," and "stakeholders" have to "play" or "pretend to be" an "average citizen."

To "play" the average citizen is (as in Instance 1) a desirable action if one is challenging an expert. In contrast, "pretend[ing] to be" an average citizen is inappropriate conduct if one is (as in Instance 3) trying to conceal, or at least be unreflective about, his or her social position as an "interested party."

As was suggested above, one other symbolic relationship exists, between the terms "average citizen" and "fair." The latter indicates an aspect of the "process" about which the former is "concerned," whether it be in the ways of speaking of the expert speakers (as in Instance 1) or in the totality of the "process" in its own right (as in Instance 4).

PREMISES AND RULES FOR THE TERM "AVERAGE CITIZEN"

What is revealed in the examination of these four instances can be formulated into statements of relationship among the key symbols and in the form of premises and rules. Although Sarah does not express explicitly the rule she uses to challenge Ted's communicative conduct, a rule may be formulated using Sarah's words and logic: *In a public meeting, on a given topic, an expert should not raise questions and not be able to answer them in some plain language.* The rule prohibits the expert from a particular way of speaking. The premise upon which the rule is grounded provides a way to interpret the expert's conduct if he (or she) enacts this way of speaking. *For an expert to raise questions on a given topic and not be able to answer them is not fair to the average citizen.* It is from this premise that Sarah makes the judgment of Ted's conduct as not "fair." Additionally, *an expert should speak in simple terms to the average citizen. An expert should not raise questions and be unable to answer them in some plain language. A person cannot be an "average citizen" if she or he has expertise, interests, or a stake in the matter at hand.*

We're a Panel of Knowledgeable People . . . and That May Be Beneficial

To cement the point that Sarah is not the only speaker who articulates these meanings, premises, and rules associated with the term "average citizen," several additional instances in which the panelists are discussing the "the panel process" are displayed and analyzed. Talk "about the panel process" occurs in the ICAP in the third meeting and at a time in which the panelists have nearly completed their discussions of the initiative and their participation on the panel. Will is the first to speak. He says,

I have several observations and I'll just tick them off and see ((unin-terpretable)). One uh a (3) a review of the initiative by a panel of uh (1) of uh knowledgeable people can help uh inform city council of the substan-of the substance of a particular initiative and is thus may be beneficial. Second is (2) it's important to distinguish between a quote citizens panel (1) vers-and a panel of knowledgeable people because there are differences that are needed (1) and that we might encourage the city council to gi-give some thought to what would best suit its needs. The third observation would be in constituting a panel be it a panel of knowledgeable people or a citizens panel uh we would encourage a highly transparent and uh objective process.

First, Will makes it clear there are "differences" between a "citizens panel" and a "panel of knowledgeable people" and that recognizing these dif-ferences is "important." Only one such difference may be found in Will's talk: that a "panel of knowledgeable people" "can help" "inform city council of" "the substance of a particular initiative." Second, although it is not clear whether Will believes a "citizens panel" could perform this same informative function, he seems to suggest that a "panel of citizens" would be useful for a different purpose. Will does not express what this purpose is but that "we might encourage the city council to" "give some thought to what" type of panel "would best suit its needs." Third, Will suggests that if the city coun-cil were to constitute either a "panel of knowledgeable people or a citizens panel," the selection of the panel should be a "highly transparent and" "objec-tive process." Finally, Will mentions "constrained" "time" as a barrier to the panel doing "a good job."

Will's third "observation," that the panel selection process should be "highly transparent" and "objective," leaves open the question of how the process can and should be judged as "transparent" and "objective." Sarah's and Jeff's responses appear to attempt to provide an answer.

This Panel Did Not Have an Appearance of Fairness

Sarah responds to Will's comments and, in so doing, the theme of "fairness" is raised once again. This theme is further connected with notions of citizen persona when Sarah expresses several justifications that the process "is not fair." She says,

I think it's important that whatever process the city council comes up with in the future for a citizen or a expert panel on initiatives that it has a very strong appearance of fairness. And I feel like I was very uncomfortable sitting on this panel because it did not have an appearance of fairness. And I'm not making accusations about people's intentions but because of the the very fast nature of putting together the resolution and passing it on the city council because of who was involved in selecting the participants because of who the participants are that it it did have a a flavor that you could definitely construe that it is not fair process. And I I just think in the future it would be great for the city council after the initiative season has passed you know in in December whenever to really have some some (1) some s-strong discussions with people who are experts in this citizen panel or whatever process to come up with a fair a fair process independent of which initiatives are on the ballot. I think this was definitely compromised by the fact that the process was set up after we already knew what the initiatives were and who the proponents and opponents of it were as well. So I don't know if I'm being clear but (1) I feel like a lot more thought needs to go into this process if it's ever going to be done again. And I think it's best to do that thought after the th-not in the heat of the moment and to make sure that the people who are involved in it are not folks who have already taken sides on the initiatives at stake.

Like Will, Sarah expresses a premise that there is a distinction between "a citizen" "panel" and an "expert panel." Sarah criticizes "the very fast nature of putting together the resolution" that created initiative review panels. For Sarah, "the very fast nature" is evidence for her criticism that the "process" is not "fair."[14] The "panel" includes "people who have expertise" and "interests," and "who are stakeholders." Building from the analysis of Sarah's talk above, for "this panel" to be "fair," its participants should be "average citizens." Sarah's criticism that "this panel" "did not have an appearance of fairness" was because "the process was set up after we already knew what the initiatives were and who the proponents and opponents of it were as well." Sarah offers that the "the process" could be "fair" if "the people who are involved in" had not "already taken sides on the initiative at stake." Such persons would presumably be "average citizens" because they do not have "interests" or a "stake" in the initiative.

Gathering a Group of Knowledgeable People Was Appropriate

Following Sarah's critique, Jeff defends "the panel process" as "appropriate." Jeff says,

> I think this is a very complex initiative. I think it was appropriate to get to gather a group of people who are knowledgeable. I think is important that in the future there be a choice between interest groups or citizens or knowledgeable people or specialt-specialists in particular areas and i-I guess under inters-interest groups I'd also call that stakeholders. but it was my understanding that the main reason for selecting this group was to move quickly uh given that it was a a complex uh initiative. An initiative that focused on perhaps just one issue uh might not require the same amount of time. The thing that really comes back to me on this is that here we are we're all knowledgeable uh this is within the areas of of our expertise and yet we've needed sixteen hours to begin to understand it and there's still a whole series of questions I have.

Like Will and Sarah, Jeff expresses differences between "people who are knowledgeable" and "citizens," both of which are different from "interest groups" and "specialists in particular areas." In his consideration of these possibilities for types of panelists, Jeff expresses that it was "appropriate" "to gather a group of people who are knowledgeable." For Jeff, "the main reason for selecting this group" "of people who are knowledgeable" "was to move quickly" "given that it was a" "complex" "initiative." Jeff does not favor a panel of "knowledgeable people" in all circumstances. Rather, Jeff expresses that it "is important that in the future there be a choice between" "interest groups or citizens or knowledgeable people" or "specialists in particular areas."

Meanings, Premises, and Rules of a "Citizen Panel"

These additional excerpts extend the interpretation of semantic dimensions among the term "average citizen" and other symbols for persons to "panels" composed of such persons.

Table 12.2. Semantic dimensions of distinction for "citizen panel"

	Semantic Dimension	Terms of Contrast
"citizen panel"	*expertise/knowledge*	"expert panel" "panel of knowledgeable people" "specialists in particular areas"
"citizen panel"	*"interest(s)"*	"interested groups"
"citizen panel"	*"anonymous"*	"interest groups" and "experts"

Table 12.2 indicates the more expertise, knowledge, and/or interest a panel has, the more it is pushed symbolically away from being a "citizen panel." Additionally, the more anonymity a panel has, the more it is pushed symbolically toward being a "citizen panel."[15]

Premises for Evaluating a Panel Process

Premises and rules are also expressed as the means with which Will, Sarah, and Jeff evaluate the "panel process." For Will, the selection of panelists needs to be a "highly transparent" and "objective process." Sarah and Jeff disagree on their judgment about the "panel process," using the terms "not fair" and "appropriate" respectively. Sarah's logic informs a series of premises that stipulate conditions under which a "panel process" could be determined to be "fair": *An initiative panel process is fair if it is put together over a long period of time, if there is a selection of the participants by a neutral party, if the participants are "average citizens," and if the participants are unaware of both the initiative content and the identities of the proponents and opponents.*

In contrast, Jeff's logic informs a premise that validates the ICAP process: If time is limited and the initiative is complex, a panel of knowledgeable people (and not a panel of citizens) is appropriate.

EMPIRICAL EVIDENCE FOR A THEORY OF POLITICAL PEOPLE MAKING

In the meetings analyzed, the word "citizen" thematizes notions of political identity in the social scenes in which it is evoked. Moreover, the ICAP participants deploy the word "citizen" as a particularly powerful *rhetorical* resource, one that can be invoked to make and back claims with great efficacy when it is used in the context of public meetings about important community matters. Finally, the term "average citizen" calls forth a range of meanings, premises, and rules for a distinctive type of citizen persona that is not randomly deployed. Rather, when examined closely, uses of the term "average citizen" reveal elements of a cultural system of symbols, meanings, premises, and rules in this context.

I use the term *citizen personae* to draw attention to the ways uses of the term *citizen* call forth patterned notions of persons, communication, and sociality. Although these notions are not perfectly aligned with what Rogers Smith calls *political personhood*, this investigation does demonstrate a useful way for noticing, describing, and interpreting the ways in which citizens conceptualize and enact citizenship. I have demonstrated a mode of inquiry, drawing from a cultural communication perspective, that is productive for illuminating the "quite basic dimension of all political activity . . . the making, maintaining, and transforming of senses of political peoplehood" (Smith 2003, 19), as people do so in their own words.

This mode of inquiry provides a way to interrogate and refine claims about what citizenship means, particularly in the United States. As a cultural system, the elements of the speech code illustrated here no doubt draw from historical notions of American citizenship. For instance, the term "average citizen" may invoke for some notions citizenship found in a "politics of community," where the idealized citizen is one participating in the face-to-face activities of a "self-governing small town." Certainly, the semantic dimension of "interest" articulated above has roots in a "politics of interest" in which groups, coalitions, lobbyists, and the like compete for scarce resources (Bellah et al. 1985, 200). Finally, "average citizens" because of their lack of expertise and interest, suggests some analogy to the "rights-regarding citizen," a person who conflates public political action with elements of everyday life (Schudson 1998, 299). While traces of these historical elements of American political culture are no doubt present in the talk of the participants of the ICAP, the focus here remains fixed on socially constructed, expressed manifestations of political culture in order to make sense of how people call forth these notions for practical, rhetorical ends in situated political talk. Participants in ICAP are no doubt constrained by both the institutional design of this particular citizen panel and the choices those who convened the ICAP made for framing the interaction between "citizens" and "experts." Such is the case with all political interaction, not just that which is displayed in this analysis. This fact substantiates the value of close inspection of political talk, as it is situated within such constraints, in order to come to terms with an empirically grounded interpretation of the meaning of citizenship.

This study demonstrates the specificity with which inquiry into different types of political people may occur and the productive value of doing so. It is an exemplar of one type of empirical inquiry, from a communication perspective, that Smith calls for in the pursuit of understanding meaning(s) of citizenship. By intentionally articulating and referencing aspects of the context of this complex public and political debate, particularly by reporting the political moves that occurred among initiative supporters, the mayor, city officials, the courts, and the ICAP, the value of understanding meanings and uses of the terms "average citizen" and "citizens' panel" become more clear.

NOTES

1. The text of the full address was provided to all authors in this volume.
2. A programmatic field of study developed first by Dell Hymes (1962; 1972). This approach has since been applied in the field of communication by Gerry Philipsen (1992; 1997) and Gerry Philipsen and Lisa Coutu (2005).
3. I address this only briefly but, in so doing, try to create a small bridge between political science theory and empirical, data-driven communication research.
4. This point is consistent with other examinations of citizenship. Michael Schudson, for example, describes "the rights-regarding citizen" by providing several examples of the ways in which this notion of citizen is enacted. Schudson writes, "citizens still exercise citizenship as they stand in line at their polling places, but now they exercise citizenship in many other locations. They have political ties not only to elected public officials in legislatures but also to attorneys in courtrooms and organized interest groups that represent them to administrative agencies. Moreover, they are citizens in their homes, schools, and places of employment. Women and minorities self-consciously do politics just by turning up, so long as they turn up in positions of authority and responsibility in institutions where women and minorities were once rarely seen.... Others do politics when they wear a "Thank You For Not Smoking" button or when they teach their children to read nutritional labeling at the supermarket or when they join in class action suits against producers of silicone breast implants, Dalkon shields, or asbestos insulation" (Schudson 1998, 229).
5. In their examination of place and public memory, Carole Blair, Greg Dickenson, and Brian Ott outline several "assumptions" about memory that seem

consistent with Smith's notions of narrative, including: (1) memory is activated by present concerns, issues, or anxieties; (2) memory narrates shared identities, constructing senses of communal belonging; (3) memory is animated by affect; (4) memory is partial, partisan, and thus often contested; (5) memory relies on material and/or symbolic supports; (6) memory has a history (Blair, Dickenson, and Ott 2010).

6. In "Codes of Commonality and Cooperation: Notions of Citizen Personae and Speech Codes in American Public Meetings" (dissertation, University of Washington, 2007), I examine the remaining sixty-three instances. The present paper articulates aspects of the "code of commonality" that emphasize types of persons. The remaining instances illumine a code of regional citizenship in such phrases as "there's really nothing the citizens of Seattle can do." That analysis highlights the way in which "citizen" is used to articulate localized rights and responsibilities.

7. Kery Murakami, "Backers of Water-Conservation Initiative File Ethics Complaint," *Seattle Post-Intelligencer*, July 31, 2001; Chris McGann, "City Is Accused of Obstructing Water Initiative," *Seattle Post-Intelligencer*, August 28, 2001, accessed July 17, 2006, from http://seattlepi.nwsource.com/local/36793_wet28.shtml.

8. On August 21, the city council filed a lawsuit against "Yes for Seattle," asking the courts to remove the initiative from the November ballot as Tracy Johnson and Kery Murakami reported in the *Seattle Post-Intelligencer* on August 21, 2001. See also Lisa Heyamoto, "Water Initiative Violates the Law, City Tells Court," *Seattle Times*, August 22, 2001, B1. The *Seattle Post-Intelligencer* reported on August 31, 2001, that Mayor Pageler proposed an alternative to I-63, called I-63B, that was quickly criticized by Yes for Seattle because of its insufficient conservation measures. See Margaret Taus, "I-63 Backers Want Alternative Scrapped," *Seattle Post-Intelligencer*, September 5, 2001, accessed July 17, 2006, from http://seattlepi.nwsource.com/local/37724_liquido5. shtml. In the end, a compromise was reached that led to the removal of both I-63 and I-63B from the November ballot. Publicly, both sides claimed victory. Margaret Taus, "Water, Salmon Plan Ready for Approval," *Seattle Post-Intelligencer*, September 19, 2001, accessed July 17, 2006, from http:// seattlepi.nwsource.com/local/39395_water19.shtml; City of Seattle, "Settlement Reached on Water Conservation Initiative," accessed July 18, 2006, from www.cityofseattle.net/council/newsdetail.asp?ID=2089&Dept=28.

9. "The Welcome Death of Seattle's Initiative 63," *Seattle Times*, B4.

10. In a separate analysis of this data that focuses on the communication practice "raising questions," the importance of Sarah's participation in these meetings as a point of departure for analysis is demonstrated by pointing out that she is the sole supporter of I-63 who repeatedly offers criticism of the ICAP process (Leighter and Black 2010).

11. In the audio record, there are at least three instances in which the facilitator says he is, or is playing, "the fool."

12. A social drama unfolds in four steps: (1) the invocation of a moral rule challenging the conduct of another, (2) a reply to the challenge, (3) the reply is honored or not, leading to (4) the offender reintegrating or not, revealing a moral schism (Turner 1980; see an example of analysis in Philipsen 1992, 134).

13. The entire sequence will not be examined here. Responses to Sarah's turn, however, indicate that Ted and the other participants take Sarah's utterance as a challenge when her turn is followed by marked silence and overlapping laughter by the group. Ted's first spoken response is a repair, beginning awkwardly with laughter, a joking comment, and stilted speech, none of which occurred so markedly in his presentation.

14. Sarah's sentiments match those expressed in a complaint with the city of Seattle Ethics and Elections Commission. Kery Murakami, "Backers of Water-Conservation Initiative File Ethics Complaint," *Seattle Post-Intelligencer*, July 31, 2001, accessed July 17, 2006, from http://seattlepi.nwsource.com/local/33483_water01.shtml.

15. This interpretation is supported in a later discussion about the panel's "report." Sarah adds an additional dimension along which "interest groups" and experts" are distinct from "citizens": anonymity. She says, "the one amendment I would make is that at the beginning of us discussing the report I -ad said that I I hoped that we would that we would go on record as individuals about what our opinions are. So when you said that it would be anonymous I wouldn't be in favor of that. Again I feel like we are not an anonymous citizens panel we're a panel of interest groups and experts and I think it's important for the council to know uh which interest groups and experts these opinions are coming from."

WORKS CITED

Bellah, Robert, Richard Madsen, William Sullivan, Ann Swidler, and Steven Tipton. 1985. *Habits of the Heart: Individualism and Commitment in American Life.* Berkeley: University of California Press.

Black, Laura. 2008. "Deliberation, Storytelling, and Dialogic Moments." *Communication Theory* 18: 93–116.

———. 2012. "How People Communicate in Deliberative Events." In *Democracy in Motion: Evaluating the Practice and Impact of Deliberative Civic Engagement*, edited by Tina Nabatchi et al., 59–82. New York: Oxford University Press.

Blair, Carole, Greg Dickenson, and Brian Ott. 2010. "Introduction: Rhetoric/ Memory/Place." In *Places of Public Memory: The Rhetoric of Museums and Memorials*, edited by Greg Dickenson, Carole Blair, and Brian Ott, 1–54. Tuscaloosa: University of Alabama Press.

Carbaugh, Donal. 1988. *Talking American: Cultural Discourses on DONAHUE.* Mahwah, NJ: Lawrence Erlbaum.

———. 2005. "'I Can't Do That' but I 'Can Actually See around Corners': American Indian Students and the Study of 'Communication.'" In *Cultures in Conversation*, 82–94. Norwood, NJ: Ablex.

———. 2007. "Cultural Discourse Analysis: Communication Practices and Intercultural Encounters." *Journal of Intercultural Communication Research* 36: 167–82.

Hymes, Dell. 1962. "The Ethnography of Speaking." In *Anthropology and Human Behavior*, edited by Thomas Gladwin and William C. Sturtevant, 13–53. Washington, DC: Anthropological Society of Washington.

———. 1972. "Models of the Interaction of Language and Social Life." In *Directions in Sociolinguistics: The Ethnography of Communication*, edited by John J. Gumperz and Dell Hymes, 35–71. New York: Holt, Rinehart and Winston.

Leighter, James L., and Laura W. Black. 2010. "'I'm Just Raising the Question': Terms for Talk and Practical Metadiscursive Argument in Public Meetings." *Western Journal of Communication* 74: 547–68.

Philipsen, Gerry. 1992. *Speaking Culturally: Explorations in Social Communication*. Albany: State University of New York Press.

———. 1997. "A Theory of Speech Codes." In *Developing Theories of Communication*, edited by Gerry Philipsen and Terrance L. Albrecht, 119–56. Albany: State University of New York Press.

———. 2000. "Permission to Speak the Discourse of Difference: A Case Study." *Research on Language and Social Interaction* 33: 213–34.

Philipsen, Gerry, and Lisa Coutu. 2005. "The Ethnography of Speaking." In *Handbook of Language and Social Interaction*, edited by Kristine L. Fitch and Robert E. Sanders, 355–80. Mahwah, NJ: Lawrence Erlbaum Associates.

Philipsen, Gerry, Lisa Coutu, and Patricia Covarrubias. 2005. "Speech Codes Theory: Restatements, Revisions, and Response to Criticisms." In *Theorizing about Intercultural Communication*, edited by William B. Gudykunst, 55–68. Thousand Oaks, CA: Sage.

Schudson, Michael. 1998. *The Good Citizen: A History of American Civic Life*. Cambridge, MA: Harvard University Press.

Smith, Rogers M. 2003. *Stories of Peoplehood: The Politics and Morals of Political Membership*. Cambridge, Cambridge University Press.

Turner, Victor. 1980. "Social Dramas and Stories about Them." *Critical Inquiry* 7: 141–68.

IV

. . . .

Defining and Resolving Conflicting Civic and Personal Obligations

13

DEMOCRATIC HOPES
AND MAJORITARIAN FEARS

· · · · · · · · · ·

Emerson as a Man on the Street in the Election of 1834

T. GREGORY GARVEY

Immediately after moving to Concord, Massachusetts, in the fall of 1834, Ralph Waldo Emerson went to New York to fill a temporary opening at a Brooklyn church. In a letter to his brother William, he describes the trip as a kind of mock-epic vacation: "Before I establish my inkstand at Concord, the country mouse shall refresh his ears with the roar of a metropolis" (Emerson 1939–95, 1: 421). His sojourn in New York put him in the city for the climax of the 1834 midterm congressional campaign. This election was a watershed in American politics because it represented the first face-off between two evenly matched, mass-democratic political parties. The Democrats had been organized for several election cycles, and the Whigs played catch-up throughout the early 1830s. But the Whigs' success in the spring municipal elections made them feel ready to stand as equals against the Democrats.

Emerson's day-by-day response to this election says much about the possible role political equality might play in the newly enfranchised citizen's sense of self. It also says much about the fears provoked as the modern party system emerged to organize the electorate. At its root, the tension that animates his commentary articulates how democratization amplified individual rights but also sublimated the voices of actual individuals to the impersonal mechanics of majoritarian politics.

Witnessing what has grown into the political culture of mass democracy, to Emerson, democratization enhanced citizenship by adding an important dimension to the identity of the newly enfranchised citizen. It recognized that to have investment in public life was important to the private dignity of each individual. Democratization, by broadening the base of consent for government, enhanced the legitimacy of elections, and thus, of political authority in general. But Emerson cared little about issues of institutional authority or legitimacy. What he cared about was the implications of political enfranchisement in the private identities of individuals. Most importantly, enfranchisement dignified the individual and gave each citizen new reasons to take himself (and eventually, herself,) seriously as a person.[1] The Democracy, as Emerson's generation called it, had been expanding throughout the 1820s. This expansion meant that hundreds of thousands of white male citizens no longer had to defer to the political authority of entitled elites (Keyssar [2000] 2009, 28–35, 54–56; Chute 1969, 295–316; Williamson 1960, 26ff.). But enhancing the dignity of individuals also came at a high cost. Even though the political system recognized new rights for individuals, as politics shifted from a republican to a democratic foundation, the voice of any particular citizen became less important in its own right and came to matter primarily in numerical terms. To control policy in a majoritarian system, numbers are what matter, and since majoritarian democracy functions by aggregating the voices of independent citizens into expressions of the will of majorities, the democratization Emerson witnessed was also subordinating the individual to the party system through which majority opinion was shaped and expressed.

On his return to rural Massachusetts after the election, Emerson puts his anxiety about the depersonalizing quality of majoritarianism out of his mind in order to affirm the way that democratic enfranchisement can change how an individual perceives him- or herself. He concludes in late November that "the root and seed of democracy is the doctrine, judge for yourself. Reverence thyself. It is the inevitable effect of that doctrine, where it has any effect (which is rare), to insulate the partisan, to make each man a state" (Emerson 1960–82, 4: 342). Then, in December he returns to this language and develops the sentiment further: "Democracy, has its roots in the sacred truth that every man hath in him the divine Reason or that though few men live according to the dictates of Reason, yet all men are created capable of so doing. That is the equality & the only equality of all men. To this truth, we look when we say 'Reverence thyself. Be true to thyself'" (4: 345). Positioning each individual as a sovereign political actor with autonomy inside its borders and equality alongside its fellows on the stage of public affairs, Emerson isolates how a change in political standing can have profound implications for the identity of the private individual.

Democratization, by reconstructing the political structure so that every enfranchised person, regardless how humble, is an autonomous agent analogous to a sovereign state in world affairs, raised the stature of each new citizen *in his own eyes*. But for the individual to maintain this new stature required a type of poised independence that was threatened by the organizations that were emerging to structure the larger electorate. At its best, whenever democracy genuinely "affects" a society, Emerson holds, it enhances the independence of each citizen by prying the partisan free from ideological collectives and compelling him or her to embrace a standard of self-respect consistent with his new standing in politics. Although this call for the individual to take him or herself seriously may always be implicit in democratic enfranchisement, it often seems drowned out by the roar of hard-fought campaigns.

DEMOCRATIZATION AND NEW YORK'S YEAR OF RIOTS

Falling in the middle of Andrew Jackson's second term as president, the election of 1834 tested the apparatus of nascent party coalitions. Everyone knew that "the Democracy" had the political initiative, but no one could predict exactly what kind of civil society democratization would produce. Electoral majorities were slim, and the Whig Party was just emerging as a cohesive institution. As early as 1828, however, the Jacksonians had developed a functioning infrastructure for appealing to the new voters who had been entering the rolls throughout the decade. They adapted the political practices of the early republic by expanding parades, picnics, and pole raisings into mass rallies that attracted crowds and generated enthusiasm. Celebration and public spectacle had always attended American politics, but with the expansion of the franchise, the scale, stakes, and importance of public events took on a variety of new meanings (Waldstreicher 1997, 27–32; Altschuler and Blumin 2000, esp. chap. 3, 87–118; Formisano 1983, 250–80, which most directly addresses party politics and elections in the 1830s; also see Holt 1999; and Brown 1985).

The achievement of universal white male suffrage undermined the viability of civic republicanism by regrounding political legitimacy in a majoritarian model that valued public opinion and raw numbers above universalized ideals of virtue. This redefinition of political legitimacy facilitated the emergence of modern parties as organizers developed techniques for winning over new voters. As long as the supporters of Daniel Webster, Henry Clay, and other conservatives were still "largely leader oriented rather than voter oriented," as Michael F. Holt puts it, they would remain at a disadvantage as political power shifted from individual leaders to party organizations (Holt 1999, 9). Emerson's Massachusetts, despite its growing textile industry and its population of industrial workers, had been a bastion of Federalism during the early republic and was becoming, almost by reflex, a site of strong Whig opposition to the Democratic Party (Laurie 2005, 17–19).

But New York City was different. In contrast to conservative Boston, New York was a Democratic stronghold. For both good and ill, the city and its politics symbolized the changes that were driving the transition to majoritarian politics. High population density, a concentration of recent immigrants, and the growth of industry all made New York a metaphor for modernity and futurity. Ronald Formisano describes the relationship between Boston and New York by noting that just "as the Commonwealth's merchant capitalists looked anxiously to the booming port of New York as a pacesetter in material growth, so, too, did the middling classes and artisans of Boston receive notions and inspiration from the Empire State and its metropolis" (Formisano 1983, 224). Richard Hofstadter remarked that "politicians throughout the country looked anxiously to the New York City elections in off years to determine which way the winds were blowing" (Hofstadter 1943, 586). Emerson understood these facts and the importance of Democratic machine politics in New York. From the perspective of a Bostonian with Emerson's pedigree, the country's repudiation of President John Quincy Adams in favor of Andrew Jackson in 1828 marked a cultural shift that had complex implications for citizenship.

In Boston, 1834 saw a peak of early union and workingmen's movements, and electoral politics signaled some unrest. But in New York, the bricolage of constructing electoral processes to accommodate the democracy was making elections not just restive, but dangerous. With the expanding franchise, the nuts and bolts of elections were changing. There was no voter registration, so voting in multiple precincts was a common practice, and the parties often facilitated fraud. There were no nonpartisan election commissions, so parties printed ballots, which created opportunities for mischief such as intentional misspelling and the obfuscation of opposition candidates. Intimidating gangs formed at polls. Since the secret ballot was often considered unmanly, voters frequently had to travel to find a polling place where they would not be mauled (Holt 1999, 33–38; see also *Democratic Party of the State of New York* 1905, 1: 130–39; Pessen 1949, 262–74; and Foner 1947, 143–67).

Worse, throughout 1834, mobbing had inflamed New York, and it was an especially tense fall. As the spring voting took place for mayor and city council, political rhetoric was subsumed in riots. The state constitution had recently been changed so that April 1834 was the first time the mayor of New York was democratically elected. Both parties campaigned intensely and promoted distrust of the opposition. A group of Whig supporters crafted a parade float in the shape of a square-rigged ship, named it "Constitution," and paraded it through the streets. During the course of a few hours thousands were cheering in its wake. The Jackson men responded by constructing their own parade wagon, also shaped as a ship, and named it "Veto." A conservative historian of antebellum riots concluded that "it was impossible for these two processions to meet without a fight occurring. . . . But the 'Hickory poles' had inaugurated a new mode of carrying on political campaigns." In the Democrats' strategy, "appeals were made to the senses, and votes obtained by outward symbols, rather than by the discussion of important political questions." Philip Hone, a prominent Whig whom Emerson would hear speak at a rally in November, recorded in his diary that "suddenly the alarm was given, and a band of Irishmen of the lowest class came out of Duane Street, from the Sixth Ward poll, armed with clubs, and commenced a savage attack upon all about the [Whig's] ship" (Hone 1927, 1: 12). The result was, as a historian of the city observed, "Civil authorities were for the first time obliged to call for military aid in maintaining the peace of the city" (Lamb 1881, 2: 724; Headley 1873, 70).

After the dust of the April election riot settled, the *North American Review* concluded, "The real objection" to the expanded franchise and the growth of the parties, "so far as there is any, is not that it brings out men of an inferior class, which, in fact, is not the case, but that it is a cumbrous, tumultuous, and perhaps, under some circumstances, unsafe mode of doing what might be . . . done by a much simpler process. The whole country is kept in a state of permanent excitement which . . . may not improbably take the form of civil war, upon the question of the presidency."[2] David Grimsted, in his history of civil unrest, situates these riots in the context of emergent majoritarian politics. He concludes: "Eighteen thirty-four was a crisis year of the second American party system as party alignment became a national reality." Jackson's refusal to renew the bank "confirmed the opposition's angriest fears," but it also "invigorated the devotion of his supporters" to create a uniquely polarized atmosphere (Grimsted 1998, 34–36, 200; also see Bernstein 1990, 5, 119–20; and Binders and Reimers 1995, 62).[3]

Rather than settling the issue, the results of the spring election encouraged partisans on both sides of the fray. The Democrats won the mayor's race, but the Whigs won a majority on the city council. Both parties claimed victory and turned with enthusiasm to their congressional campaigns in the fall. The Democrats, exhilarated at their victory in the mayoral race, announced the "Glorious Triumph" under the headline "THE BANK DEFEATED" and touted the common man's victory over the moneyed classes.[4] Philip Hone noted in his diary that the city's "Common Council is reformed" by the Whig victory and believed that his party was poised to "succeed in the great Fall election. It is a signal triumph of good principle over violence, illegal voting, party discipline, and the influence of officeholders." The Whigs celebrated their victory with "three pipes of wine and forty barrels of beer . . . the beautiful little frigate *Constitution*, which had borne so conspicuous a station in the late struggle, was placed upon the top of the building . . . from which she fired a salute" (Hone 1927, 1: 124).

The elections of 1834 solidified the Whig Party's identity as the alternative to the Democrats and instantiated the competitive two-party structure as a lasting framework for debate in the American political system. The name "Whigs," which opponents of Jackson began to adopt in 1832, evoked a British tradition of republican citizenship. It stood for government by men of character who were capable of setting aside private interests to advocate for the common good. In its emphasis on good character, the emergent Whig identity captured one of Emerson's principal objections to majoritarianism and linked individuality to a tradition of principled, civic-minded dissent that Jackson's opponents were eager to claim. With the coalescence of this opposition party after the spring elections, the Democrats and the Whigs began to assume stable public profiles that permitted each to claim the status of a national party. Struggle between these two parties would define the political landscape until the Whigs disintegrated in the mid-1850s (Holt 1999, 91–95; Brown 1985, 29).

Landing in New York City in the midst of this clash, Emerson witnessed a new phenomenon: a political culture that expanded and democratized the electorate, but that also amplified the importance of anonymous masses, numbers, and the skill of professional organizers. In a very literal sense the New York election cycle of 1834 was a trial run for this political prototype. For the first time a mass electorate was working within an organized political landscape that was constructed and managed by cadres of professional partisan politicians. It is worth pointing out here that political parties were (and remain) extraconstitutional organizations. As deeply embedded as they are in the structure of American government, they are not required by the Constitution. They emerged as ad hoc organizations during Emerson's lifetime in order to organize political coalitions that could win national elections. The parties that Emerson saw in 1834 were new institutions, and they appeared to him not as a necessary and natural part of democratization, but as one of several paths that could link political equality for individuals with procedures for legitimizing civil authority.

The United States, and within it, New York City, was arguably the most democratic place in the world, and that fact alone marked a high point for human dignity. But in what ways did the democracy promote the doctrine, "judge for yourself. Reverence thyself"? In what ways did it work to "insulate the partisan, to make each man a state" and thereby to amplify the dignifying effect of democratic citizenship by asking each citizen to take himself or herself more seriously? What good was democratization if its real effect was to sublimate the dignity of political equality for each and all to the inarticulate roar of an election parade?

INDIVIDUALITY AND MASS DEMOCRACY

Emerson arrived in Brooklyn on Saturday, October 18, and was scheduled to pastor the Second Church for the next four weeks. While he was in New York he witnessed some electioneering, attended a Whig caucus, and watched the actual voting. Immediately after arriving, he learned that his brother Edward had died of tuberculosis. Grief amplifies the pessimism of the journal entries he writes during his stay, but it does not eclipse his interest in the partisan struggle. The voting took place on the second Tuesday, Wednesday, and Thursday of November. He sarcastically notes in his journal that the political operatives were in a flurry because "they count that 1600 minutes are all the time allowed in all three days" to get supporters to the polls (Emerson 1960–82, 4: 333). He left New York shortly after the election results came in, arriving home in Concord on November 11. In Emerson's district in Massachusetts, the Whig candidate, Samuel Hoar, a personal acquaintance, won by a narrow margin.

Grief mingles with pessimism as Emerson reacts to the political environment he enters in New York. He evokes George Washington as a foil for the rise of partisan politics. On October 27, he asks:

> Who that sees the Spirit of the Beast uppermost in the politics & the movements of the time, but inly congratulates Washington that he is long already wrapped in his shroud & forever safe, that he was laid sweet in his grave the Hope of humanity not yet subjugated in him. And Edward's fervid heart is also forever still, no more to suffer from the tumults of the Natural World. And they who survive & love men have reason to apprehend that short as their own time may be they may yet outlive the honor, the religion, yea the liberty of the country.

He tries weakly to rally himself against the expected Whig loss by remembering a couplet from Wordsworth's "Sonnets Dedicated to Liberty":

> Yet is
> "Hope the paramount duty which Heaven lays
> For its own honor, on man's suffering heart."
> Otherwise one would be oppressed with melancholy & pray to die whenever he heard of the orgies of the Julien Hall or of the outrages of a mob. (Emerson 1960–82, 4: 325–26)[5]

This lament begins a series of journal entries through which Emerson evaluates the new electoral system. As he processes the street-level campaigns, his suspicion of mass politics competes with his conviction that democratization is a necessary step forward in the expansion of human rights.

On the one hand, Emerson's politics is very elitist, and not just through the snobbery of his position in Boston society. He seeks heroes, constantly alludes to the great men of history, and treats the will of the genius as the driving force of history. Watching the electioneering crowds, he tries to inoculate himself against the democracy by jotting down lists of great men: "Channing, Coleridge, Wordsworth, Owen, Degerando, Spurheim, Bentham. Even Saul," counterbalance the partisans. A couple of entries later,

"Michel Angelo Buonaroti: John Milton: Martin Luther: George Fox: Lafayette: Falkland: Hampden" all embody the power of genius and stand as antidotes to demagoguery (Emerson 1960–82, 4: 326, 328). A long tradition of commentary emphasizes Emerson's elitism and situates him along with Carlyle and Nietzsche (an odd pair, but valid in this context) as an advocate of hero worship and supermen (Van Leer 1986, 7–11; Lopez 1996).[6] But on the other hand, Emerson's egalitarianism links his politics to the Jacksonians' effort to undermine the power of arbitrary authority. In "History" he ticks off what he sees as the political evolution that anticipates American democracy: "Epoch after epoch, camp, kingdom, empire, republic, democracy" shows the slow unfolding of civil forms that offer incrementally higher standards of dignity to the individual (Emerson 1971, 2: 3).[7]

Although slightly counterintuitive, it is important to see this Whiggish sense that democratization can mark civil progress as part of the political legacy of Jeffersonian democracy because it reflects the early Whigs' effort to reconcile republican elitism with democratic egalitarianism and their assumption that public-spiritedness is a dimension of private identity. Rather than being repulsed by the democracy and retreating into an insular cultural or religious community, Emerson's reflexive response is to recognize that enhancing the public standing of the individual creates opportunities to develop character and dignity on a new stage. The challenge of political democracy was to imagine means of individuating the identities of the members from the mass opinion of the group *within* the conditions of democratic equality.

Situating this effort in Jacksonian politics requires a finer distinction than that between aristocratic Federalists-turned-Whigs and working-class Jeffersonians-turned-Democrats. Michael Holt's analysis especially asserts that American Whigs claimed descent from the Jeffersonian Republicans as legitimately as did the Democrats. Rogers Smith underscores the combinations that defined Jacksonian political identities: "If ever an era fit a 'multiple traditions' account in which racist, nativist, and patriarchal views structured American political development . . . as fully as liberal republican ones, this is it" (Smith 1997, 199). Complementing Smith's and Daniel Walker Howe's emphasis on the Jacksonian politics of racial and gender supremacy, Bruce Laurie's recent study (2005, 25–31) of the antislavery movement "beyond [William Lloyd] Garrison" underscores the complexities of class politics in the 1830s.[8] One of the issues at stake in these analyses of the changing nature of partisan identification is the problem of setting boundaries on the right of access to political discourse. What is most important for my purpose is that this debate about the right to participate in the legitimization of political authority also involves an effort to imagine public enfranchisement as a means of redefining the private self-perception of individuals.

John Holzworth develops this link between the rise of majoritarian politics and Emerson's effort to "democratize" processes of thinking through public concerns. Defending Emerson's "insistence on the capacities of ordinary people" against theories that ranked different types of people in a hierarchical order, Holzworth concludes that "Emerson's disappointment" with the low standard of individuality that democratization was promoting "is not an expression of serious doubt about human potential. Rather, it is part of his argument that significant potential is everywhere being squandered," and thus, that the majoritarian system was suppressing much of the dignity that democratization offered to newly empowered citizens (Holzworth 2011, 314–16). The identity that the emerging structure was promoting—an identity that sought partisan conformity over the ability to "Think your own thoughts and think them through"—was made vivid by the campaigns of both parties (Kateb 1995, 209).

Campaign updates in the *Niles Weekly Register* convey a sense of the ferocity and anticipation that the impending election evoked. The *Register* was published in Baltimore, but it spoke to a national audience and functioned much like the wire services do today. Alluding to the violence of the spring election and the confrontation of mass parties, on November 1 it reported that "There will be, as it were, battles of giants in New York on Monday, Tuesday, and Wednesday—the one party [the Whigs] to win the city and state, the other to retain its long held dominion; but we hope that in the generally apprehended dangers of riotous proceedings, security will be found for the preservation of the public peace." Emphasizing the partisan machinery, it records that "the Whig merchants and dealers of New York held a great meeting at the Exchange in the afternoon of Monday last—and on the same day, the Jackson party [rallied] . . . at the Castle Garden. We shall not now give particulars of the extraordinary strength and spirit displayed [even though they] shew as powerful and as perfect an arrayment of parties as we ever heard of."[9]

In an impressionistic response to the meetings and rallies that gathered the week before the election, Emerson gleans a few trends that might portend redirection of the public identity away from partisan confrontation. He decides that, "The best sign I can discover in the dark times is the increasing earnestness of the cry which swells from every quarter that a systematic Moral Education is needed." This hopeful sign leads him to think about popular entertainment and the possibilities of co-opting it for a form of education that will promote individuality: "Not Universal Education but the Penny Magazine has failed. Brougham may have failed but Pestalozzi has not. Leibnitz said; 'I have faith that man may be reformed, when I see how much Education may be reformed.' Why not a moral Education as well as a discovery of America?" (Emerson 1960–82, 4: 326–27). The "Penny Magazine," Emerson's shorthand here for working-class literary tastes, will never offer a decent popular education. But equally, to educate the newly enfranchised workingman by distributing Lord Brougham's *London Quarterly Review* at Castle Garden or the Exchange would be as absurd as hawking *The Economist* at professional wrestling matches.

Nonetheless, these missed opportunities did not imply that political rights should be withheld from poor and unskilled workingmen. Rather, he links the process of elevating the democracy to some form of civic education. By linking the expansion of political rights to education, Emerson articulates a widely shared conviction that the public empowerment of a new class of citizens must be supported by the development of common schools that prepare young men for their public responsibilities (Smith 1997, 216–19). F. A. Packard, a contemporary advocate of developing universal education to complement universal suffrage, links public education to tranquility in civil society. A national system of schooling would teach the rising generation the "immutable principles on which all rational liberty is founded." Students should "be made acquainted with their rights as citizens—that they may know them well and feel their value—whenever they shall come to that honourable and responsible station" (Packard 1836, 10). This connection between public education and political enfranchisement is crucial because, as another advocate noted:

If a man comes to the polls without the substance of this knowledge, he may be enrolled as a freeman, and he may vote as a freeman; but he has neither the intelligence nor the independence which alone constitute a freeman; and whenever the state of public feeling prepares the way, it will be found that he values much more highly and exercises much more intelligibly, the right of throwing brickbats, demolishing houses, and burning machinery, than the lawful and invaluable rights of an American citizen." (Blarter 1826, 11)

This critic's linking of intelligence and independence anticipates the connection Emerson makes between reverence and judgment. The intelligence developed by education will allow the citizen to act with independence. Equally, a standard of self-reverence will compel one to judge issues independently—and to take one's own right of judgment seriously. The challenge that the democracy posed was not that of figuring out how to re-disenfranchise the poor man and then reconcile him to a permanent state of political exclusion. By Emerson's reasoning, the challenge also could not be met by promoting a homogeneous civic education that prepared countrymen for party membership. Indoctrination might improve civil order, but it would also stunt individuality before intellectual independence had a chance to blossom. The challenge was that of cultivating identities that allow rising citizens to assert intellectual independence and thereby to individuate from parties and mobs.

He thus turns away from the popular press to consider the virtues of an unusual type of educational reform. To Emerson's circle of New England activists and intellectuals, the theories of Swiss philanthropist Johann Heinrich Pestalozzi represented an especially attractive set of techniques because they were intended to cultivate individuality even as they meliorated class difference. As such, his proposals seemed well suited to redress the sources of majoritarian alienation that threatened to squander so much human potential. While much educational theory sought conformity, Pestalozzi's method cultivated intellectual and creative expression. In February 1834, Emerson had borrowed Charles Mayo's *Memoir of Pestalozzi* from the Boston Atheneum. He had read Edward Biber's book on Pestalozzi two years earlier (Von Frank 1994, 89; Richardson 1995, 121). Biber presents Pestalozzi's educational theory in terms that are both Transcendentalist and utopian. Biber explains that Pestalozzi:

Was deeply convinced that pauperism and vice, so far from being counteracted by extreme relief funds and strict police measures, relied, on the contrary, on additional stimulus and new nourishment. . . . He felt that the improvement of the lower orders required an internal stimulus to be awakened in their own breasts; that no correction [or punishment] would make them good, and no support happy, unless there were a determination on their part to be good and happy. He saw, moreover, that even such a determination could be of no avail, unless they had it in their power to rise from the low condition to which they had sunk; and he turned, therefore, toward education. (Biber 1831, 11)

To test his assumptions, Pestalozzi established a school that became famous among American reformers. Emerson sought a "moral education" that could provoke democratic individuality in much the same way Pestalozzian education sought to provoke intellectual self-confidence. Such an education could shape the emerging democracy in much the same way that the discovery of America had fueled modernity. Indeed, as he stands amid the discord of the election hoopla, proposing the moral education of the Jacksonian mob seems an analogously bold idea to Columbus's proposition to get East by sailing West.[10] "Why not a moral education as well as a discovery of America?" Why not a society of individuals as well as a democracy?

Sacvan Bercovitch, in addressing tension between self and society in Emerson's thought, unpacks the give and take between Emerson's effort to imagine a society grounded in an organic civility and his impulse to reject *all* civil institutions as unnatural constraints on the individual's quest for unity with the Spirit. For example, Bercovitch cites Emerson's 1840 validation of communitarian social experiments: "The World is waking up to the idea of Union and already we have communities, Phalanxes and Aesthetic families, & Pestalozzian institutions." These efforts represent utopian gestures. Emerson euphorically affirms their spirit: "It is & will be magic," to see the lasting reforms that these pioneering efforts will produce. But, as Bercovitch emphasizes, by Emerson's reasoning, social experiments must mediate a paradox: authentic community can only happen in a context of radically unencumbered selfhood. Defending the free individual against the discipline of party committees, utopian associations, and even reform movements, Emerson articulates the paradox that limits his effort to reconcile individuality with community. He is all for society, but, he complains:

The Union is to be reached by a reverse of the methods they use. It is spiritual and must not be actualized. The Union is only perfect when all the uniters are absolutely isolated. Each man being the Universe, if he attempt to join himself to others, he instantly is jostled, crowded, cramped, halved, quartered, or on all sides diminished of his proportion. And the stricter the union the less & more pitiful he is. But let him go alone, & recognizing the Perfect in every moment with entire obedience, he will go up & down doing the works of a true *member*, and, to the astonishment of all, the whole work will be done with concert, though no man spoke; government will be adamantine without any governor. (Emerson 1960–82, 8: 251)[11]

For the purpose of using Emerson's response to the election of 1834 as a means of underscoring how political equality both holds out the potential of dignifying private selfhood and calls into being its own sublimation to mass party politics, two things are important here: first, Emerson's defense of individuality is explicitly public. His ideal of the individual is no apolitical hermit. On the contrary, he does the work of a "true *member*" so that the "whole work" of the society takes place. Second, Emerson imagines this utopic anarchy in direct response to the political and cultural trends that he saw as jostling and cramping people into identities that work against a public selfhood that dignifies the individual and thus permits "true" membership in civil society. The problem with majoritarian politics, as Emerson sees it, is that as parties come to dominate political relationships, they leave individuals "diminished" in proportion. Political equality enhances each individual, but actual political participation seems to cut one into halves and quarters. As he puts it, the individual has no adequate resistance to incorporation into a mass. As he watches the campaigns come to fruition in the election, this problem remains unresolved. He fails to find a clear instrument to amplify the dignifying effect of expanded citizenship and to muffle the depersonalizing demands of majoritarian politics.

THE PROBLEM OF REAL VOTES

Yet far from insulating himself by remaining outside the partisan fray, Emerson expresses strong political affiliations and mixed emotions as the election period arrives. He even adopts the Whigs' pejorative slang for Jackson loyalists. Looking at the election paraphernalia, he admits that "on all the banners equally of Tory & Whig good professions are inscribed." The Jacksonians proclaim their desire for ends that he embraces: "The Jackson flags say 'Down with Corruption!' 'We ask for nothing but our Right.' 'The Constitution, The

Laws' and so on." These hearten Emerson so that, should "the Whig Party fail, which God avert!" the "latent i.e. deceived virtue which is contained within the Tory party" might prevent a descent into intentional evil. Standing firmly with the Whigs, he petulantly condemns the Democrats: "it is notorious that the Jackson party is the *Bad* party in the cities & in general." A few paragraphs later, he amplifies this judgment by accusing the Democratic Party of fraud. "The Whigs can put in their own votes. But the Tories can do this & put them in again in another ward or bring a gang of forsworn gallows birds to boot, to elect the officers that are to hunt, try, imprison, & execute them" (Emerson 1960–82, 4: 333). Yet despite their embodiment of the "spirit of the beast," the Democrats' rhetoric indicates that "they have not yet come to the depravity that says, 'Evil be thou my good'" (4: 332).

Although he identifies as a Whig, he knows that his party shares many vices with the democracy. He attended a Whig rally that grew in attendance far beyond the organizers' expectations. A newspaper report on the event makes vivid the rapid growth of the electorate and the efforts of political organizers to deal with the changing context of elections:

> On Tuesday evening there was an immense gathering at the Masonic Hall to hear the report of the Whig nominating committee. A meeting was first organized in the great room, capable of holding about 5,000 persons—but that being instantly jammed, another meeting was organized in the long room on the first floor, and that also being found insufficient—an omnibus being drawn up, and chairs placed on its top for the accommodation of the officers, a third meeting was organized in the street. This will shew what is doing[!] And at this meeting in resolution, recommending the mechanics to leave their shops and "give up the three days to the cause" was adopted. It was also ordered that the splendid steamboat *Ohio*, which plies on the Hudson, should be chartered to proceed to Albany, (with the little frigate "Constitution" on board), saluting at each of the landing places, and firing two hundred guns at Albany.[12]

After attending this rally the week before the polling took place, Emerson concluded that: "It is rather humiliating to attend a public meeting such as this New York Caucus" and see "what a low animal hope & fear patriotism is" (Emerson 1960–82, 4: 327). The speakers had whipped up the crowd with a "party-lie" designed to gain the "votes of that numerous class of indifferent, effeminate, stupid persons who in the absence of all internal strength obey whatever seems the voice of their street, their ward, their town, or whatever domineering strength will be at the trouble of civilly dictating to them." It is worth noting that this is his own party he is condemning, and the demagogic Whig leaders who mesmerize the masses share in the general alienation. In a passage that curiously anticipates the transparent eyeball passage of *Nature*, Emerson describes a Whig orator who becomes "part and parcel" of the multitude he addresses: "Heard Mr. Maxwell at the Masonic Hall[,] a thoroughly public soul[,] the mere voice of the occasion & the hour. There are these persons into whom the general feeling enters & through whom it passes & finds never a hitch or hindrance; they express what is boiling in the bosoms of the whole multitude around them," and they thus speak not as individuals but as transparent windows into the unmediated impulses of the crowd (4: 334). Whig or Democrat, the problem with the partisans, Emerson notes acidly, is that "their votes count like real ones."

As the voting begins, he writes: "Nov. 5. The elections . . . Noisy Election; flags, boy processions, placards, badges, medals, bannered coaches[—] everything to get the hurrah on our side" (4: 328, 332–34). Steeling his party for political exile after the defeat everyone was now expecting, Emerson imagines the Whigs as a redemptive phoenix: "Let the worst come to the worst & the Whigs be crushed for a season & the Constitution be grossly violated, then you should see the weak Whig become irresistible. They would acquire the gloom & the might of fanaticism & redeem America as they once redeemed England & once aforetime planted & emancipated America." This private commentary echoes the hysterics of the Whig press, and parrots the cheap shots that Whig politicians were taking against the Democrats. He even lets himself stoop so low as to record that "Mr. [Philip] H[one] says the Tories deserve to succeed, for they turn every stone with an Irishman under & pick him up" (4: 334, 333). Succeed they did. The final tally was closer than many expected, but the Democrats got more votes and sent their slate to Congress. In the district that Emerson was watching, Ely Moore became the first workingman's union organizer to be elected to national office.

Emerson's final comment before leaving New York is a revealing bit of psychoanalysis that ironically describes the new majoritarianism as a potential source of class-based civil anarchy. He muses that "It is a great step from the thought to the expression of the thought in action. Without horror I contemplate the envy, hatred, & lust that occupy the hearts of smiling well dressed men & women. [B]ut the simplest most natural expressions of the same thought in action astonish & dishearten me. If the wishes of the lowest class that suffer in these long streets should execute themselves, who can doubt that the city would topple in ruins. Do not trust man, Great God!, with more power until he has learned to use his little power better" (Emerson 1960–82, 4: 334–35). Emerson makes a psychological as well as a class distinction. The character that enables self-control is always tenuous and subject to momentary lapses. The good manners that he implicitly associates with wealth and with the Whigs is itself a sort of costume that masks repressed desires and impulses. This masking, however, represents an internalized policing that permits civil society. He sees little to fear in the idea that every "well-dressed" exterior masks a barbaric interior realm of repressed desire. But when those repressed desires eclipse culture, even in the "simplest most natural" forms, he is reminded of how close the "orgies of the Julien Hall" and "the outrages of a mob" are to the surface of society.

In the context of the election of 1834, this personal debriefing marks an important limit on Emerson's ability to see democratization as a means of enhancing the standing or opportunities of individuals. The "lowest class," the undifferentiated mass of recently enfranchised voters "who suffer in these long streets," embody the envy, hatred, and lust that are repressed by those who could take political power for granted. The sentiments of the mob are authentic, visceral, and may well be justified. But their "power" is also undisciplined by the very standards that Emerson usually gives the back of his hand. The expanding democracy forces him to recognize the legitimacy of political equality, but his clear association of the street life of democratic politics with "envy, hatred, & lust" makes vivid his inability to resolve the problem of imagining a majoritarian democracy in which "real" citizens cast "real" votes. In the big picture, the ascendance of the Jacksonian "Tories" represents a necessary step on the road to a democratic public sphere in which participation in civil discourse serves to "insulate the partisan, to make each man a state." But when seen from the point of view of a man on the street in late fall of 1834, it also represents the liberation of uncontrolled desire and anonymous violence.

The political identities that the emergent world of partisan mass electoral politics was creating draws out tension between the way political enfranchisement can dignify the new citizen and the way mass political equality calls into being an apparatus that asks for conformity rather than individuality. As Emerson watched majoritarian politics take shape in the early 1830s, he shared Alexis de Tocqueville's "religious dread" of the democracy juggernaut, though he does not juxtapose it against a nostalgia for aristocracy. Rather, Emerson offers a running commentary in which he vacillates between expressions of democratic hope and majoritarian fear.

His key point of interest has almost nothing to with democracy as a system of government. Rather, his interest is the implication of democratization for individuality—in terms of increased self-respect and in terms of the implications of mass democracy for self-representation on the public stage. In 1834 he finds the masses and demagoguery of politics disheartening, but he also concludes that political equality is the legitimate and necessary foundation of a civil society in which each individual can claim the full measure of human dignity. Writing slightly earlier, but also about the politics of Jacksonian America, Tocqueville vividly articulates this tension between democratic hope and majoritarian fear: "I see clearly two tendencies in equality; one turns each man's attention to new thoughts, while the other would induce him freely to give up thinking at all. . . . There is matter for deep reflection here. I cannot say this too often for all those who see freedom of the mind as something sacred and who hate not only despots but despotism. For myself, if I feel the hand of power heavy on my brow, I am little concerned to know who it is that oppresses me; I am no better inclined to pass my head under the yoke because a million men hold it for me" (Tocqueville 1966, 436). In theory, democratization was not just good, it was necessary to liberate human beings from arbitrary forms of power. But as he stood among the rough-hewn timbers of the Whig and Democratic Parties, Emerson saw the same two "tendencies" that Tocqueville had seen. From the perspective of one who was more interested in the individual than in the system, the challenge was stringent. It was to amplify the dignifying effect of democratic citizenship even though citizenship would have to function in an electoral process more interested in the will of the majority than in the dignity of any particular individual.

Emerson left New York a few days after the election. On arriving back in Concord he sings the praises of home and heritage: "Concord, 15 November, 1834. Hail to the quiet fields of my fathers! . . . Bless my purposes as they are simple and natural." As a man working to carve out a career as a professional lecturer, he also takes some lessons about how he might avoid complicity in the forms of alienation he had witnessed in New York: "Henceforth I design not to utter any speech, poem, or book that is not entirely and peculiarly my work." To define the originality he was aiming at, Emerson commits to speaking on "things which I have meditated for their own sake" rather than laboring on a lecture "to make a good appearance" at the scheduled gathering (Emerson 1960–82, 4: 435). Over the next few years, setting these standards would help him to gain recognition as a public intellectual with a distinctive and compelling voice, but it did not keep majoritarian politics from infiltrating the quiet fields of Concord. As the next midterm election approached in October 1838, Emerson overheard a Democratic organizer doing his work, and he lets off a little steam: "I passed by the shop & saw my spruce neighbor the dictator of our rural Jacobins teaching his little circle of villagers their political lessons. . . . I hate persons who are nothing but persons. I hate numbers. He cares for nothing but numbers" (Emerson 1960–82, 7: 99). In 1837 the Whig Samuel Hoar had lost his bid for reelection and for the first time Concord sent a Democrat to Washington. Emerson's new congressman, William Parmenter, a naval officer, would be his representative until 1844.

NOTES

1. Rogers Smith and Daniel Walker Howe especially emphasize the sexism and racism of Jacksonian revisions of citizenship. In the view of both Smith and Howe, the movement that became the Democratic Party redefined access to political power in ways that simultaneously enhanced the power of white men and inscribed prohibitions on the rights of women, African Americans, Indians, and other minorities. Alex Keyssar interprets this period of reconstructing citizenship in terms that imply slightly less diabolical intentionality. Sean Wilentz offers an analysis that defends the Jacksonians efforts to expand democratic political rights even as it recognizes the exclusionary legacies it left in political equality. See Smith (1997, esp. chap. 8); Howe (2007, esp. chap. 11). See also Keyssar ([2000] 2009, 28–35, 54–56); and Wilentz (2005). Indispensable to thinking about political equality, also see Pole (1993); Chute (1969, 295–316); Williamson (1960).

2. *North American Review* 41 (1835): 143.

3. New York was wracked again between July 7 and 11 by an antiabolition riot that destroyed the Tappan House on Rose Street and Saint Philips African

Episcopal Church on Centre Street. Also see Bernstein, *The New York City Draft Riots*, 5, 119–120, and Binders and Reimers, *All the Nations*, 62.

4. [George Evans?], *Working Man's Advocate*, April 12, 1834.

5. Patrick Keane (2005, 439ff.) analyzes Emerson's use of Wordsworthian Hope.

6. To the context addressed here, Judith Shklar's essay "Emerson and the Inhibitions of Democracy" (1998) is especially relevant because it emphasizes the pull and tug between Emerson's competing attractions to genius and democratic equality.

7. Both Neal Dolan and Eduardo Cadava have addressed Emerson's thought about the relationship between historical change and social progress. Cadava emphasizes the inseparability of natural metaphors from Emerson's thought about history. Dolan links Emerson's progressive assumptions about historical change to broad trends in eighteenth- and early nineteenth-century political theory. See Dolan (2009, 170–74); and Cadava (1997, 99–106). Also see Kateb (1995, 173–96).

8. At the very beginning of *The Rise and Fall of the American Whig Party*, Michael Holt makes this point emphatically. Although historians have often parroted the rhetoric of the Democrats to align the Whigs with the Federalists, "Experts now know better. Massive research in the past forty years has shown that the Whig party evolved not from the Federalists but from divisions within the Jeffersonian Republican party" (Holt 1999, 2). Also see Benson (1969); Livermore (1962); McCormick (1966).

9. *Niles Weekly Register*, November 1, 1834.

10. On the importance of Columbus to Emerson's thought about both individuality and democracy, see Fresonke (2003, 90–92).

11. Bercovitch builds an entire chapter around these quotations. He sees them as the fulcrum in Emerson's effort to imagine community through the terms of radical liberalism. See Bercovitch (1993, 307–52).

12. *Niles Weekly Register*, November 1, 1834.

WORKS CITED

Altschuler, Glenn C., and Stuart M. Blumin. 2000. *Rude Republic: Americans and Their Politics in the Nineteenth Century*. Princeton, NJ: Princeton University Press.

Benson, Lee. 1961. *The Concept of Jacksonian Democracy: New York as a Test Case*. Princeton, NJ: Princeton University Press.

Bercovitch, Sacvan. 1993. *The Rites of Assent: Transformations in the Symbolic Construction of America*. New York: Routledge.

Bernstein, Iver. 1990. *The New York City Draft Riots: Their Significance for American Society and Politics in the Age of the Civil War.* New York: Oxford.

Biber, Edward. 1831. *Henry Pestalozzi and His Plan of Education.* London: John Souter.

Binders, Frederick, and David Reimers. 1995. *All the Nations under Heaven: An Ethnic and Racial History of New York City.* New York: Columbia University Press.

Blarter, James G. 1826. *Essays upon Popular Education.* Boston: Bowles and Dearborn.

Brown, Thomas. 1985. *Politics and Statesmanship: Essays on the American Whig Party.* New York: Columbia University Press.

Cadava, Eduardo. 1997. *Emerson and the Climates of History.* Stanford, CA: Stanford University Press.

Chute, Marchette. 1969. *The First Liberty: A History of the Right to Vote in America, 1619–1850.* New York: E. P. Dutton.

Democratic Party of the State of New York, 3 vols. 1905. Edited by James K. M. McGuire. New York: United States History Company.

Dolan, Neal. 2009. *Emerson's Liberalism.* Madison: University of Wisconsin Press.

Emerson, Ralph Waldo. 1939–95. *The Letters of Ralph Waldo Emerson.* Edited by Ralph Rusk and Eleanor Tilton. 10 vols. New York: Columbia University Press.

———. 1960–82. *The Journals and Miscellaneous Notebooks of Ralph Waldo Emerson.* Edited by William H. Gilman, Alfred R. Ferguson, George P. Clarck, Merrell R. Davis, Merton M. Sealts Jr., Ralph H. Orth, Harrison Heyford, et al., 16 vols. Cambridge, MA: Harvard University Press.

———. 1971–2013. *Collected Works of Ralph Waldo Emerson.* Edited by Robert E. Spiller, Alfred R. Ferguson, Joseph Slater, Jean Ferguson Carr, Wallace E. Williams, Douglass Emory Wilson et al. 10 vols. Cambridge, MA: Harvard University Press.

Foner, Philip S. 1947. *History of the Labor Movement in the United States.* 2 vols. New York: International Publishers.

Formisano, Ronald P. 1983. *The Transformation of Political Culture: Massachusetts Parties, 1790s–1840s.* New York: Oxford.

Fresonke, Kris. 2003. *West of Emerson: The Design of Manifest Destiny.* Berkeley: University of California Press.

Grimsted, David. 1998. *American Mobbing, 1828–1861: Toward Civil War.* New York: Oxford University Press.

Headley, J. T. 1873. *The Great Riots of New York.* New York: E. B. Treat.

Hofstadter, Richard. 1943. "William Leggett, Spokesman of Jacksonian Democracy." *Political Science Quarterly* 58 (4): 581–94.

Holt, Michael F. 1999. *The Rise and Fall of the American Whig Party.* New York: Oxford University Press.

Holzworth, John. 2011. "Emerson and the Democratization of Intellect." *Polity* 43: 314–16.

Hone, Philip. 1927. *The Diary of Philip Hone, 1828–1851.* 2 vols. Edited by Allan Nevins. New York: Dodd, Mead.

Howe, Daniel Walker. 2007. *What Hath God Wrought: The Transformation of America, 1815–1848.* New York: Oxford University Press.

Kateb, George. 1995. *Emerson and Self-Reliance.* Thousand Oaks, CA: Sage.

Keane, Patrick J. 2005. *Emerson Romanticism and Intuitive Reason.* Columbia: University of Missouri Press.

Keyssar, Alexander. [2000] 2009. *The Right to Vote: The Contested History of Democracy in the United States.* Rev. ed. New York: Basic Books.

Lamb, Martha J. 1881. *History of the City of New York: Its Origin, Rise, and Progress.* 2 vols. New York: A. S. Barnes.

Laurie, Bruce. 2005. *Beyond Garrison: Antislavery and Social Reform.* New York: Cambridge University Press.

Livermore, Shaw. 1962. *The Twilight of Federalism: The Disintegration of the Federalist Party, 1815–1830.* Princeton, NJ: Princeton University Press.

Lopez, Michael. 1996. *Emerson and Power: Creative Antagonism in the Nineteenth Century.* DeKalb: Northern Illinois University Press.

McCormick, Richard P. 1966. *The Second American Party System: Party Formation in the Jacksonian Era.* Chapel Hill: University of North Carolina Press.

Packard, F. A. 1836. *Thoughts on the Condition and Prospects of Popular Education in the United States.* Philadelphia: A. Waldie.

Pessen, Edward. 1949. "Did Labor Support Jackson?: The Boston Story." *Political Science Quarterly* 64 (2): 262–74.

Pole, J. R. 1993. *The Pursuit of Equality in American History.* Rev. ed. Berkeley: University of California Press.

Richardson, Robert D., Jr. 1995. *Emerson: The Mind on Fire.* Berkeley: University of California Press.

Shklar, Judith. 1998. "Emerson and the Inhibitions of Democracy." In *Redeeming American Political Thought*, edited by Stanley Hoffmann and Dennis Thompson. Chicago: University of Chicago Press.

Smith, Rogers M. 1997. *Civic Ideals: Conflicting Visions of Citizenship in U.S. History.* New Haven, CT: Yale University Press.

Tocqueville, Alexis de. 1966. *Democracy in America.* Translated by George Law-rence. Edited by J. D. Mayer. New York: Harper and Row.

Van Leer, David. 1986. *Emerson's Epistemology: The Argument of the Essays.* Cam-bridge: Cambridge University Press.

Von Frank, Albert J. 1994. *An Emerson Chronology.* New York: G .K. Hall.

Waldstreicher, David. 1997. *In the Midst of Perpetual Fetes: The Making of Ameri-can Nationalism, 1776–1820.* Chapel Hill: University of North Carolina Press.

Wilentz, Sean. 2005. *The Rise of American Democracy: Jefferson to Lincoln.* New York: Norton.

Williamson, Chilton. 1960. *American Suffrage: From Property to Democracy, 1760–1860.* Princeton, NJ: Princeton University Press.

14

FRENCH CITIZENS
AND MUSLIM LAW

· · · · · · · · · ·

The Tensions of Citizenship in Early Twentieth-Century Senegal

LARISSA KOPYTOFF

On September 29, 1916, the French National Assembly in Paris passed a law declaring the inhabitants of Senegal's Four Communes—the coastal towns of Dakar, Gorée, Saint-Louis, and Rufisque—and their descendants to be French citizens. The law, presented as a means by which to aid the wartime recruitment of troops from France's West African colonies, appeared to settle a long-running debate about the political and legal rights claimed by the communes' African inhabitants, commonly referred to as *originaires*. Yet it also revived old questions and raised new ones about the rights and obligations of citizenship in the French empire and about the relationship between French civil status and Muslim law in West Africa.

As *communes de plein exercice* (that is, full-fledged French municipalities with elected councils and designated budgets), the Four Communes held a legal and political status distinct from the rest of Senegal and French West Africa.[1] Saint-Louis and Gorée, island trading posts with French settlements dating to the seventeenth century, were home to *métis* (mixed-race) communities heavily involved in French commercial activity in the region, and their inhabitants were thought to be more fully "assimilated" to French traditions

than other Africans in the region.[2] Rufisque and Dakar, settled more recently by the French and lacking the long history of close engagement with
Europeans that existed in Saint-Louis and Gorée, were by the beginning
of the twentieth century fast-growing economic and administrative centers
of the colonial state. Although people moved into, out of, and through the
communes on a daily basis, and despite the strong ties that many in the communes maintained with family members and others living elsewhere in the
region, the *originaires* were often regarded as culturally distinct from those
living in the surrounding areas. Furthermore, they had long held some of the
rights of French citizens, including the right to vote in local elections and to
elect a deputy to the French legislature. Yet before 1916 their status as full
French citizens was ambiguous at best.

RIGHTS, OBLIGATIONS, AND TENSIONS OF CITIZENSHIP

In part, this ambiguity stemmed from the fact that the *originaires*—the vast
majority of whom were Muslim—retained their *statut personnel* (personal
or religious status), which enabled them to use Muslim courts to adjudicate
personal and family affairs even while exercising certain rights of French
citizens, a situation known as *citoyenneté dans le statut*.[3] This was an exceptional, though not entirely unique, state of affairs within the French empire;
most indigenous inhabitants of French colonies—considered French nationals and French subjects—could become French citizens through individual
naturalizations "only if they gave up their personal status ... accepted the
rules of the French civil code over marriage and inheritance, and convinced
administrators that they had fully accepted French social norms" (Cooper
2014, 6).[4] Adherence to the French civil code (and so, forswearing the use
of Muslim law seen as incompatible with that code) was often considered
a defining characteristic of the French citizen, yet in the Four Communes,
originaires held certain citizenship rights while still settling their civil affairs
under Muslim law.

The *originaires'* position had become increasingly precarious in the first
years of the twentieth century, as colonial administrators sought to restrict
the legal and political rights available in the communes. In 1914, the *originaires* responded to these restrictions by exercising their right to vote, electing Blaise Diagne as Senegal's deputy to the National Assembly. Diagne was

himself an *originaire* (of Gorée) and the first black African deputy elected to the chamber.[5] He had campaigned on promises to secure the *originaires'* citizenship status, and in 1916 he introduced the law that would declare *originaires* and their descendants to be French citizens.

The 1916 law resolved the question of the *originaires'* citizenship status, stating that "the natives of the *communes de plein exercice* of Senegal and their descendants are and remain French citizens subject to the military obligations of the law of 19 October 1915."[6] (That law had incorporated *originaires* into the ranks of the French army "subject to the same obligations and benefits" as French soldiers.[7]) Yet the law also renewed debate among colonial officials, politicians, *originaires*, and others about what they imagined to be the rights and obligations of colonial subjects and citizens and about the processes through which French citizenship could and should be acquired, granted, or recognized. It raised questions about how French citizenship in the communes—and the *originaires'* official position vis-à-vis the colonial state—related to the other markers of identification, affiliation, and difference operating in French West Africa, including race, ethnicity, language, and religion. Its uneven application and enforcement in the coming months and years cast doubt on the ability of the colonial state to effectively manage its own legal categories and the consequences of its laws. And, as Richard Roberts has noted, the law "maintained the ambiguities surrounding French civil and Muslim personal status" (1990, 451n10).

The law's single article made no mention of personal or religious status or the French civil code. Could Muslims in Senegal be full French citizens without renouncing their personal status? Had their citizenship status in fact changed with the passage of the 1916 law, or had the law merely served as formal recognition of the previously existing *citoyenneté dans le statut*? What did French citizenship mean if not the acceptance of the French civil code? And what would French citizenship mean to the *originaires* if its acquisition *did* in fact require the renunciation of Muslim law?

The extent to which the *originaires'* French citizenship and Muslim personal status could legally coexist would affect *originaires'* daily lives and the governance of the communes in myriad ways. To cite just a few examples, it could influence the payment of a pension to a veteran with multiple wives under Muslim law, whether a contested will was legally recognized, and the court before which a land dispute was brought. In short, citizenship was not just an abstraction, and questions regarding its reach and ramifications were not theoretical musings.

French citizenship came with significant benefits, among those the right to vote. If the 1914 election served as evidence of the electoral strength of the *originaires*, Diagne's legislative achievements in Paris were a reminder of the consequences that might follow from such strength. Elections mattered. But citizenship was, for many in the Four Communes, not only—and perhaps not primarily—about voting.[8] Citizenship also offered legal protections, particularly important for many *originaires*. French colonial subjects came under the jurisdiction of the *indigénat*, a repressive and often arbitrary legal code; protections from the abuses of the colonial state made citizenship desirable to many (see Mann 2009).

Yet citizenship was not just a matter of benefits or protections. It was an intricate web of opportunities and restrictions, rights and obligations. Young men in the communes were confronted with one particularly weighty obligation in 1916: conscription into the French military during the First World War.[9] Although colonial subjects were (at times forcibly) conscripted during the war, and despite the fact that those conscripts often served under worse conditions and with fewer benefits than did citizens, the colonial administration generally dedicated greater resources to keeping track of its citizens and its citizen-recruits than it did to keeping track of its subjects. Did this make acquiring French citizenship less desirable—or, at the least, did it make avoiding (even temporarily) being classified a French citizen *more* desirable—for some *originaires*? Some officials believed that while certain individuals might actively (and perhaps fraudulently) seek the opportunities that came with French citizenship, others might just as actively (and just as fraudulently) seek to avoid its obligations and demands. This is clear in the archival trails left by colonial officials' attempts to locate *originaires* who were thought to have left the communes or otherwise tried to avoid enlisting in the appropriate class of military recruits.[10] For Muslim *originaires*, the possibility that the new citizenship law might not allow for the continuation of *citoyenneté dans le statut*—that it might require the renunciation of Muslim law—also served as a reminder that the demands of citizenship, on both individuals and communities, could be significant. French citizenship had a great many benefits, but it did not necessarily come without costs.

FRENCH CITIZENSHIP IN COLONIAL SENEGAL:
AN "EVER DELICATE QUESTION"

For many *originaires*, the significance of the 1916 law was not reducible to the acquisition of rights or protections, or to a pragmatic calculus of costs and benefits. Nor, however, was its significance solely, or even primarily, symbolic. The law was also the official and unequivocal acknowledgment of a position in society that they believed they already held, one they believed they had acquired decades earlier.

By the early twentieth century, the question of whether the inhabitants of the Four Communes could, should, or did hold French citizenship already had a long history; a 1913 report on the issue refers to the status of the *originaires* as "an old but ever delicate question."[11] That delicacy resulted from evolving interpretations of official language concerning the *originaires*, from the gap between the concerns and perspectives of legislators in France and those of local colonial officials in Senegal, and from changing ideas of what it meant to be French throughout the nineteenth century, a time of dramatic changes for France and its empire. By the early 1900s, the varied (and sometimes conflicting) interpretations of the *originaires'* rights and status had become a point of contention between the *originaires* and the French colonial administration in Senegal. Briefly tracing some of the legislative and administrative turning points in this history of French citizenship in the Four Communes enables us to better understand how early twentieth-century colonial officials and *originaires* themselves used this history to frame their arguments about the tension, or balance, between French citizenship and Muslim law.

The French Revolution brought with it new ways of thinking about citizenship. It also brought the French empire into discussions about who was considered a French citizen, what political and legal rights and obligations accompanied citizenship, and what other affiliations might be in tension with citizenship.[12] These discussions would continue throughout the nineteenth century, and, indeed, they continue to the present day, most visibly with respect to immigration, cultural assimilation, and the place of religion in the French public sphere. That some in Senegal joined the debates about what it meant to be French during the revolution can be seen in the *cahier des doléances* (register of grievances) drafted by a group of notables in Saint-Louis in 1789 to be sent to the Estates-General in France. Focused largely on the trade privileges of merchants, the concerns voiced in the *cahier* were those of a community presenting itself as French—whatever that might have meant at that particular moment in French history—and entitled to make certain claims on that basis.

The following decades saw the introduction of various French political, administrative, and judicial processes and institutions to Senegal, at times somewhat haphazardly (see Diouf 1998; Idowu 1969). As Mamadou Diouf has written, through the 1830s and 1840s, "the colonial administration tried to formalize the collection of rules in a situation where the juridical norms of the magistrates conflicted with the political rationales that governed the norms of the colonial administrators." The result was often "a trial-and-error approach to the administration of justice in the colony" (Diouf 1998, 686–87).

Among the attempts to "formalize" colonial administration was the extension of the French civil code to Senegal in the 1830s, which granted all freeborn men and liberated slaves the political and civil rights of French citizens (Diouf 1998, 687). Although the extension of the civil code "fell short of granting citizenship, it was widely interpreted to mean that Senegalese were French citizens" (Shereikis 2001, 263). That interpretation was fluid, however, and the extension of the civil code was invoked frequently, to different ends, in the early twentieth-century debates about *originaires'* rights. Those who argued that the *originaires* were already full French citizens before 1916 cited the civil code as evidence of just how long they had been considered French. Those seeking to stress the historically limited reach of French citizenship in Senegal emphasized that the inhabitants of Saint-Louis and Gorée had, in the 1830s, been granted the *rights of* citizens but *not* citizenship itself.

On April 27, 1848, amid another revolution in France, the provisional government in Paris issued a decree formally ending the institution of slavery in the French empire (for the second time) and extending to all French colonies and possessions the principle that slaves who reached French soil were free.[13] The decree also declared those recently freed individuals to be citizens and granted French colonies representation in the French legislature. It stated explicitly, and more than once, that these provisions were to apply in *all* French colonies and possessions, stressing the universal applicability of French law throughout the empire.[14] Yet as French rule expanded throughout Senegal and other parts of West Africa in the second half of the nineteenth century, the principles of "free soil" and the citizenship rights granted in 1848 did not expand with it. They were, in fact, deliberately restricted.[15]

Less than a decade later, the governor of Senegal, Louis Faidherbe, made explicit the geographical limitations being placed upon the 1848 law when he wrote of recently conquered areas: "The emancipation decree of 27 April 1848 does not apply to the villages and territories annexed after the time the decree was implemented. . . . Elsewhere the natives became *French subjects, but not French citizens.*"[16] Already, the 1848 decree had become a means by which to distinguish the territories that would become the Four Communes from the rest of Senegal rather than a law to be applied in *all* French colonies and possessions.[17] By seeking to limit the reach of the decree outside of those coastal towns, however, Faidherbe implicitly acknowledged that he considered those within them to indeed be citizens.

Further complicating the status of the *originaires*, the French administration, under Faidherbe, established a Muslim tribunal in Saint-Louis in 1857 to oversee "affairs between Muslim natives regarding questions that concern Civil Status, Marriage, Inheritance . . . and Wills."[18] Muslim inhabitants of the town had petitioned the colonial administration for such a tribunal for years, and it served a useful purpose for the French administration as well. David Robinson writes that "[i]t would be hard to overestimate the importance of the tribunal for the image of Saint-Louis as a Muslim center—and the image of French toleration" at a time when French officials sought to cultivate good relationships with local Muslim leaders (Robinson 2000, 80).

By the early twentieth century, however, the existence of the Muslim tribunal was regularly cited by colonial officials as justification for why they did not consider the *originaires* to be full French citizens despite the extension of the French civil code to the colonies in the 1830s and the 1848 decree; they had given up that right when they "chose to revert" to Muslim law and to accept the rulings of the Muslim tribunal rather than bring their civil affairs to a French court.[19] As Patrick Weil writes, colonial legal doctrine of the early twentieth century deduced that the *originaires*, "who had been citizens until the decree of 20 May 1857, had become subjects again" (Weil 2008, 356n147).

As military campaigns gave way to civilian administration in much of French West Africa at the end of the nineteenth century, colonial administrators—increasingly concerned with consolidating their rule over the region—questioned even more pointedly the rights of the *originaires*. Some noted the challenges of effectively governing through "a complex patchwork of overlapping legal jurisdictions"; others warned that colonial subjects throughout the region would demand citizenship rights as well (Mann and Roberts 1991, 16).[20] Statements from French officials and politicians accepting the *originaires'* citizenship status—even if only to distinguish it from the status of those living outside the boundaries of the communes, as Faidberbe had done—became less common, replaced by declarations that the *originaires* had never been French and that, by continuing to adhere to Muslim civil law, they had embraced a status fundamentally incompatible with French citizenship. Such statements emphasized that while the *originaires* had been granted local electoral rights, those rights did not in any way imply or confer portable, comprehensive French citizenship.[21]

The first years of the twentieth century saw a series of reforms of the judicial system of French West Africa, as well as other administrative reorganizations (see Conklin 1997, esp. chap. 3).[22] In the eyes of some colonial officials, these were overdue opportunities to rein in political and legal rights run amok in the Four Communes. For many *originaires*, they were attacks on a status long assumed and legitimately held. In 1912, a particularly controversial law limited the *originaires'* rights when they traveled or lived beyond of the boundaries of the communes—potentially subjecting them to the *indigénat*—and required that all naturalizations include a renunciation of Muslim personal status.[23]

As noted above, the *originaires* responded at the ballot box, electing Blaise Diagne in 1914 as Senegal's deputy to the French legislature in Paris. Two years later, Diagne succeeded in securing formal recognition of the *originaires'* status as full French citizens. The law was passed without discussion in the National Assembly. Outside of the assembly, however, debate about the law's immediate consequences and possible implications was already underway in France, Senegal, and throughout the empire.

FRENCH CITIZENS AND MUSLIM LAW

The 1916 law was strikingly direct in its statement that "[t]he natives of the four *communes de plein exercice* of Senegal and their descendants are and remain French citizens." Yet it did not mention the civil code or the *originaires' statut personnel.* It did not address, either implicitly or explicitly, whether adherence to Muslim law would preclude *originaires* from being considered full French citizens. Some argued that the extension of the French civil code to Senegal and the decree of 1848—not to mention the exercise of voting rights in the communes—made clear that the *originaires* had already been considered French citizens without having had to renounce Muslim law. The 1916 law, on this view, had simply provided formal recognition of a citizenship status already in existence, with no mention of a new requirement that *originaires* renounce their personal status. Others argued that the vague language of the civil code's extension, which granted the rights *of* French citizens, as well as the continued acceptance and use of the Muslim tribunal meant that the *originaires* had *not* been considered French citizens before the passage of the 1916 law. The law, on this view, had created *new* French citizens in the Four Communes without noting any exception to the standard requirement that those becoming French citizens first renounce their personal status.[24] The documents described below—a report from a French colonial administrator about the possible consequences of the law and memoranda regarding the allocation of pensions for veterans or veterans' widows from the communes—illustrate ways in which these divergent views made their way into the debates over, and the application of, the law of 1916.

Even before the National Assembly passed the citizenship law, officials in Senegal, France, and elsewhere expressed concern about its potential consequences. On September 3, 1916, Gabriel Angoulvant (at the time governor of Côte d'Ivoire, and later the acting governor general of French West Africa) wrote a report detailing what he saw as the law's foreseeable and negative impact. Among the many dramatic consequences he cited, with a characteristic rhetorical flourish, was increased hardship for the many polygamous Muslim families in the Four Communes: "30,000 children at least will suddenly become bastards; 12 or 15,000 women who are second, third, or fourth wives in polygamous unions, which are permitted by Muslim law, will be thrown to the streets."[25] (It is clear from the full report that Angoulvant was less concerned with the fate of these women and children than with the fate of the French empire. Arguing that a similar policy of granting citizenship to "natives and foreigners" led to the downfall of Rome, he suggested that France, now "unable" to reject claims for citizenship from its colonial subjects in Algeria and Indochina, would soon decline in a similar manner.[26])

Angoulvant never explicitly stated the premise for his argument about these women and children, merely implying that declaring the *originaires* to be French citizens would automatically lead to the retroactive delegitimization of thousands of marriages and the children resulting from those unions, recognized under Muslim but not French law. French citizens could not choose to conduct their civil affairs according to Muslim law, and the passage of one new French law (and one that did not state any exception to that rule) could not make it so.

Even within the colonial administration, not everyone agreed with the assumptions upon which arguments such as Angoulvant's rested. Instead, memoranda regarding pension applications from the communes' veterans, as well as those from veterans' widows, present claims based upon the assumption that the *originaires*' continued adherence to Muslim law would not interfere with their treatment as full French citizens (or with their receiving the pensions due French citizen veterans). Stating matter-of-factly that they needed their pensions in order to support multiple wives "with whom [they were] married according to Muslim law," some of these veterans encountered colonial officials who—rather than declaring their children or wives to be illegitimate or not recognized by French law—began the task of determining exactly how such requests, and such marriages, should be cataloged.[27] One report notes that "we envisage multiple categories of French citizens" among West Africans, and presents a chart of the acceptable forms of proof of marriage, legitimate birth, or other civil status for each category.[28] For some officials, it would appear, the *originaires*' status was first and foremost a matter of paperwork, a bureaucratic hurdle, rather than an insurmountable obstacle for the governance of the French empire.

Much like Angoulvant, these petitioners and colonial officials did not explicitly articulate their premises or explain how a French citizen could have more than one wife. For these veterans, as well as for some of the officials charged with handling their requests—the requests of citizens who happened to adhere to Muslim law—Muslims *could* be French citizens without renouncing Muslim law, as the 1916 law made no mention of such a requirement. Whether that had been the case before 1916 or not, the passage of this particular law had, clearly, made it so.

CONCLUSION

Whether the Muslim *originaires* could maintain their *statut personnel* while holding full French citizenship remained a source of debate for years after the passage of the 1916 citizenship law, as did the law itself. The law remained in effect in the Four Communes, though the colonial administration was careful to limit its reach beyond the boundaries of Dakar, Gorée, Saint-Louis, and Rufisque. We should bear in mind, though, that the fate of the law was both unknown and unknowable to those writing and speaking on the issue at the time. They did not and could not have known that the law would not at some point be repealed, amended, or expanded—and proposals for all of these options were discussed at various points. The wide range of responses to the law and the myriad debates that accompanied its passage—of which the question of civil law and personal status was only one—reflect the *un*certainty surrounding an event that scholars have generally considered significant because of the *certainty* it supposedly brought to the fraught and "delicate" issue of French citizenship in Senegal's Four Communes.

The ambiguous coexistence of French citizenship and Muslim law continued to pose challenges for the administration of French West Africa as colonial officials, magistrates, subjects, and citizens sought to navigate that "complex patchwork of overlapping legal jurisdictions." A series of court rulings in the 1920s "paradoxically . . . granted Muslim *originaires* the power to choose the venue for their litigation on a case-by-case basis even as they progressively restricted the scope of the jurisdiction of Muslim law" (Sarr and Roberts 1991, 138). If the *originaires*' French citizenship was not to be revoked, the argument went, at least the reach of the Muslim courts could be limited. These rulings led to concern (and annoyance) within the colonial administration; in 1930, the governor general of French West Africa complained that the *originaires* were "'citizens' who can, at their discretion and following the interests of the moment, claim civil code or customary [Muslim] code. They are, truly, 'supercitizens' enjoying a privilege heretofore unknown: that of choosing their law in all circumstances."[29] On November 20, 1932, a decree was issued that explicitly recognized the special legal status of the *originaires* and restored the jurisdiction of the Muslim tribunals for the civil matters of the communes' French citizens, ending decades of legal ambiguity regarding French citizenship and Muslim law in the Four Communes.

Elsewhere in the French empire, the place of Muslim law in the lives of French citizens, and the possibility, or impossibility, of creating French citizens within Muslim communities, remained contentious issues through the following decades. They remain so today within France itself.[30] As Frederick Cooper shows in his recent study of citizenship "between empire and nation" in 1940s and 1950s French Africa, France and its colonies fundamentally reconsidered and renegotiated conceptions of citizenship, empire, and nation in the years following World War II. In 1946, Cooper writes, "it was the Senegalese system of citizenship that became the basis of French constitutional law" as Africans "obtained the 'quality'—and the rights—of the citizens of 1789, but they did not have to abandon the legal marker of their social and cultural distinctiveness, their personal status" (Cooper 2014, 8). As we note the impact that "the Senegalese system of citizenship" would have on later colonial relationships and institutions, we should bear in mind that this system was not a foregone conclusion in the Four Communes, even after 1916. The law that "settled" the issue of citizenship in colonial Senegal was not at the time thought to have resolved—or even addressed—many of the accompanying questions, including that of the tension between French civil law and Muslim personal status. The structuring and governing of difference in the French empire was not a straightforward staple of colonial rule, but a continuously contested process.

As Rogers M. Smith notes in this volume, "the social and political processes of citizenship construction, contestation, and transformation will continue"—and those processes will continue to raise more questions than they will provide answers (Smith 2015). Indeed, we find echoes of the history of French citizenship in Senegal's Four Communes in current discussions about immigration, cultural assimilation, and religion in France and elsewhere. This particular history should remind us that the relationships between the policies, practices, and institutions of states and the individuals and communities within those states are regularly shaped and reshaped—often in unpredictable ways—by cultural negotiations, historical ambiguities, unstated assumptions, and ad hoc solutions. With that in mind, perhaps we ought not to be surprised when we find ourselves wrestling with the "old but ever delicate question" of how to define and reconcile our conflicting civic and personal affiliations and obligations.

NOTES

Research support for this project was provided by the Fulbright-Hays Doctoral Dissertation Research Abroad Program. The author would like to thank Frederick Cooper, Edward Berenson, Michael Gomez, Adrian O'Connor, and the organizers of and participants in the 2013 Conference of the Wayne State Center for the Study of Citizenship, especially Marc W. Kruman and Helen Callow. The author would also like to thank the two anonymous reviewers for their insightful comments on a previous draft of this essay.

1. Saint-Louis and Gorée were declared *communes de plein exercice* in 1872; Rufisque and Dakar acquired the status in 1880 and 1887, respectively. Here I

refer to the towns as "communes" even when discussing events before these dates. Similarly, though Dakar and Gorée were, at times, blended together as a single commune, I use the term "Four Communes" throughout to refer to those territories in which the 1916 citizenship law applied.

2. Recent analyses of how "assimilation" shaped citizenship, community, and identity in the communes include Coquery-Vidrovitch (2001) and Diouf (1998). On the influential *métis* community in Saint-Louis, see Jones (2013). The complex relationships of Muslim communities and the French colonial administration in Senegal is detailed in Robinson (2000).

3. Inhabitants of French possessions in India also held *citoyenneté dans le statut*: they exercised the right to vote while retaining their personal status. On French citizenship and personal status in French India, see Deschamps (1997).

4. As Patrick Weil has noted, this requirement "did not oblige . . . Muslims to renounce their religion—they could retain it as a moral code and a collection of religious prescriptions—but it did oblige them to respect the French Civil Code, that is, to refrain henceforth from practicing the five customs that were incompatible with that code," including, and discussed most often in Senegal, polygamy (Weil 2008, 216). The renunciation of personal status in order to claim French citizenship did not apply to Jews in French Algeria after 1870, when the Crémieux Decree made Algerian Jews French citizens en masse. See Weil (2008, 209–11). Such granting of citizenship by legislation was rare; throughout the French empire, the selective and infrequent naturalization of sufficiently "assimilated" individuals was generally made on a case-by-case basis.

5. Previous deputies were white or *métis*, often from politically connected and wealthy merchant families. On the political involvement of Saint-Louis's *métis* families, see Jones (2013).

6. See the *Journal Officiel de la République Française, Lois et Décrets*, October 1, 1916, 8667–68, for the text of the 1916 law.

7. See the *Journal Officiel de la République Française, Lois et Décrets*, October 21, 1915, 7569, for the text of the 1915 law.

8. The classic work on politics in the Four Communes, and one that emphasizes voting rights before other benefits of citizenship, is Johnson (1971). Many colonial officials at the time focused on the electoral rights of citizenship, as well; allegations of electoral fraud—often regarding individuals who may have fraudulently claimed to have been born within the boundaries of the communes in order to vote in local elections—were common in the late nineteenth and early twentieth centuries.

9. There is a large literature on the recruitment of troops from West Africa, including those from the Four Communes; for a comprehensive overview, see Echenberg (1991); on the recruitment of *originaires* during the First World War and the impact of the 1915 and 1916 laws, see Lunn (1999); on the wives of West African soldiers during this period, see Zimmerman (2011). Although it blurred the line between citizens and subjects for *originaires* in the armed forces, the 1915 law was not considered to have settled the question of the *originaires'* citizenship status. It did, however, open a discussion about the exceptional place of the *originaires* in the French colonial project. It also called attention to the link between the "blood tax" of French military service and the right to be treated the same as other citizens of France. See Mann (2006).

10. See Archives Nationales du Sénégal, Dakar, Senegal (hereafter ANS) 4D26 and ANS 11D1/438 for cases of men suspected by colonial authorities of seeking to avoid being classified as *originaires* in order to avoid the military service required of a citizen. A note on women and citizenship: As documentation regarding citizenship often concerned electoral rolls and military service, the impact of citizenship laws on women—"passive" citizens even in France at this time, holding the personal and legal protections of citizenship but lacking the political rights—can be difficult to ascertain. Women in the Four Communes do enter the discussion, and the archival records, most often with respect to women giving birth (to future French citizens) within the communes or to the pensions owed the wives and widows of *originaire* soldiers. Court records provide further documentation of women navigating the citizenship regime of the communes. Archival sources show a wide range of interactions between women and the colonial bureaucrats seeking to keep track of France's newest citizens; see, for instance, ANS 23G16 on children born to the wives of *originaire* soldiers; Archives Nationales d'Outre-Mer, Aix-en-Provence, France (hereafter ANOM) AP534 on the matrilineal vs. patrilineal inheritance of *originaire* status.

11. This report appears in ANS 23G35, Document no. 64, and ANS 17G47(17), 1913 dossier.

12. Recent works on the emergence of a language of citizenship in the revolution-era French Caribbean include Dubois (2004) and Fick (2007).

13. The French Revolution of the late eighteenth century had previously abolished slavery in the French empire, although it was reinstated by Napoleon in 1802. For more on the antislavery context of the decree, see Jennings (2000).

14. Although written primarily with the plantation colonies of Guadeloupe, Martinique, Guyana, and Réunion in mind, the decree also included Senegal,

by name, as well as the other French possessions in Africa and India. The law's strongest advocate, abolitionist Victor Schoelcher, had returned from a trip to Senegal in early 1848 and later wrote of the influence of his experiences there.

15. In practice, in Senegal the decree only applied to Saint-Louis, Gorée, and a few small trading posts on the coast and the Senegal River, as these were the only areas under French control at the time.

16. ANS Kii, Document no. 6, November 14, 1857. Italics (underlining) in original. Officials in Faidherbe's administration made similar arguments regarding slavery; most were concerned with citizenship at this point primarily insofar as the emancipation decree kept French citizens from owning slaves. Instead, they focused their attention on how to support emancipation without alienating local leaders who relied upon slave labor—leaders upon whom the French themselves relied for stability in the region. Martin Klein has written of Frédéric Carrère, the chief of the judicial service under Faidherbe, who in 1855 produced a report justifying French expansion into areas in which slavery was not to be abolished: "The law, he argued, forbade slavery in Saint Louis, and made it illegal for any French citizen to own slaves. France did not, however, need to recognize those coming under French authority after 1848 as citizens. As subjects, they could continue to live under their own law." See Klein (1998, 28). On the significance of such interpretations for the establishment of a colonial legal system, see Roberts (2005, 42).

17. Similar measures were taken in other parts of the empire, ensuring that as the empire grew in the late nineteenth century, it continued to be populated primarily by French colonial subjects rather than newly French citizens. In Senegal, the decree *was* extended to Dakar and Rufisque, though not without some debate. See ANS Kii for discussions about the extension of the decree to Dakar and Rufisque; see ANOM Sénégal-IV-22 and ANOM Gorée-VIII-1 for discussions of the challenges of governing "French" areas so close to those not under French law.

18. See, among other references, ANOM Sénégal-VII-23bis, "Aux termes de l'article 2 du décret du 20 Mai 1857, 8 février1884." On the Muslim tribunal of Saint-Louis, see Sarr and Roberts (1991) and Schnapper (1961).

19. One example of this argument can be found in ANOM Sénégal-VII-8, Rapport no. 46.

20. Lauren Benton has shown that such jurisdictional "patchworks" were the rule, rather than the exception, in many colonial legal regimes; see Benton (2002).

21. Variations on one phrase—"The natives of Senegal are, according to colonial legislation, voters but not French citizens"—appear repeatedly in government memoranda and official correspondence throughout the early 1900s and 1910s. For one of many such examples, see ANOM Sénégal-VII-81, "Note sur la Formation des Listes Electorales au Sénégal, 17 juin 1914."

22. Richard Roberts details the foundations of the colonial justice system up to the early twentieth century; see Roberts (2005, chap. 2).

23. On the debates regarding the 1912 law and the law's impact on politics in the Four Communes, see Conklin (1997) and Johnson (1971); on how the law affected *originaires* living outside of the communes, see Shereikis (2001).

24. Individual naturalizations of those who were not *originaires* or the descendants of *originaires* required the renunciation of one's personal status. See Coquery-Vidrovitch (2001) and Dickens (2001).

25. ANOM AP539, "A.s. de la proposition de loi tendant à faire accorder la qualité de citoyen français aux natifs des communes de plein exercice du Sénégal, Dakar, le 3 septembre 1916."

26. Ibid.

27. ANS 4D2(81). A number of these requests are detailed, alongside discussions regarding their processing, in ANS 4D28, 4D2(81), and 4D62(89).

28. ANS 4D62(89), "Note au sujet des pensions aux familles des originaires musulmans ou polygames" (1920).

29. ANS 17G47(17), letter to the Minister of Colonies from the governor general of French West Africa regarding the *Statut des indigenes d'élite* (1930).

30. Mamadou Diouf has placed the contemporary debates over French identity, citizenship, Islam, and race within this historical narrative. See Diouf (2012).

WORKS CITED

Benton, Lauren. 2002. *Law and Colonial Cultures: Legal Regimes in World History, 1400–1900.* Cambridge: Cambridge University Press.

Conklin, Alice. 1997. *A Mission to Civilize: The Republican Idea of Empire in France and West Africa, 1895–1930.* Stanford, CA: Stanford University Press.

Cooper, Frederick. 2014. *Citizenship between Empire and Nation: Remaking France and French Africa, 1945–1960.* Princeton, NJ: Princeton University Press.

Coquery-Vidrovitch, Catherine. 2001. "Nationalité et citoyenneté en Afrique occidentale français: Originaires et citoyens dans le Sénégal colonial." *Journal of African History* 42 (2): 285–305.

Deschamps, Damien. 1997. "Une citoyenneté différée: Sens civique et assimilation des indigènes dans les Établissements français de l'Inde." *Revue Française de Science Politique* 47: 49–69.

Dickens, Ruth H. L. 2001. "Defining French Citizenship Policy in West Africa, 1895–1956." PhD diss., Emory University.

Diouf, Mamadou. 1998. "The French Colonial Policy of Assimilation and the Civility of the Originaires of the Four Communes (Senegal): A Nineteenth-Century Globalization Project." *Development and Change* 29: 671–96.

———. 2012. "The Lost Territories of the Republic: Historical Narratives and the Recomposition of French Citizenship." In *Black France / France Noire: The History and Politics of Blackness,* edited by Trica Danielle Keaton, T. Denean Sharpley-Whiting, and Tyler Stovall. Durham, NC: Duke University Press.

Dubois, Laurent. 2004. *A Colony of Citizens: Revolution and Slave Emancipation in the French Caribbean, 1787–1804.* Chapel Hill: University of North Carolina Press.

Echenberg, Myron. 1991. *Colonial Conscripts: The Tirailleurs Sénégalais in French West Africa, 1857–1960.* Portsmouth, NH: Heinemann.

Fick, Carolyn E. 2007. "The Haitian Revolution and the Limits of Freedom: Defining Citizenship in the Revolutionary Era." *Social History* 32 (4): 394–414.

Idowu, H. Oludare. 1969. "Assimilation in 19th Century Senegal." *Cahiers d'Études Africaines* 9 (34): 194–218.

Jennings, Lawrence C. 2000. *French Anti-Slavery: The Movement for the Abolition of Slavery in France, 1802–1848.* Cambridge: Cambridge University Press.

Johnson, G. Wesley, Jr. 1971. *The Emergence of Black Politics in Senegal: The Struggle for Power in the Four Communes, 1900–1920.* Stanford, CA: Stanford University Press.

Jones, Hilary. 2013. *The Métis of Senegal: Urban Life and Politics in French West Africa.* Bloomington: Indiana University Press.

Klein, Martin A. 1998. *Slavery and Colonial Rule in French West Africa.* Cambridge: Cambridge University Press.

Lunn, Joe. 1999. *Memoirs of the Maelstrom: A Senegalese Oral History of the First World War.* Portsmouth, NH: Heinemann.

Mann, Gregory. 2006. *Native Sons: West African Veterans and France in the Twentieth Century.* Durham, NC: Duke University Press.

———. 2009. "What Was the Indigénat? The 'Empire of Law' in French West Africa." *Journal of African History* 50 (3): 331–53.

Mann, Kristin, and Richard Roberts, eds. 1991. *Law in Colonial Africa*. Portsmouth, NH: Heinemann.

Roberts, Richard. 1990. "Text and Testimony in the Tribunal de Première Instance, Dakar, during the Early Twentieth Century." *Journal of African History* 31(3): 447–63.

———. 2005. *Litigants and Households: African Disputes and Colonial Courts in the French Soudan, 1895–1912*. Portsmouth, NH: Heinemann.

Robinson, David. 2000. *Paths of Accommodation: Muslim Societies and French Colonial Authorities in Senegal and Mauritania, 1880–1920*. Athens: Ohio University Press.

Sarr, Dominique, and Richard Roberts. 1991. "The Jurisdiction of Muslim Tribunals in Colonial Senegal, 1857–1932." In *Law in Colonial Africa, edited by Kristin Mann and Richard Roberts*. Portsmouth, NH: Heinemann.

Schnapper, Bernard. 1961. "Les Tribunaux musulmans et la politique coloniale au Sénégal (1830–1914)." *Revue Historique du Droit Français et Etranger* 39: 90–128.

Shereikis, Rebecca. 2001. "From Law to Custom: The Shifting Legal Status of Muslim Originaires in Kayes and Medine, 1903–13." *Journal of African History* 42 (2): 261–83.

Smith, Rogers. 2015. "The Questions Facing Citizenship in the Twenty-First Century." This volume.

Weil, Patrick. 2008. *How to Be French: Nationality in the Making since 1789*. Durham, NC: Duke University Press.

Zimmerman, Sarah. 2011. "Mesdames Tirailleurs and Indirect Clients: West African Women and the French Colonial Army, 1908–1918." *International Journal of African Historical Studies* 44 (2): 299–322.

15

WRITING TRANSNATIONALITY

$\cdots\cdots\cdots\cdots$

Locating Citizenship in Fluid Cartographies

JONAH STEINBERG

This essay finds its way into the volume by way of a rather circuitous trail. I was asked to write it in part to reflect on a book I'd written, *Isma'ili Modern: Globalization and Identity in a Muslim Community*, recognized some time later by the Center for the Study of Citizenship. Over time, however, the thoughts I'd collected for it underwent a sort of metamorphosis in which my narrative of writing it migrated from reflection to critical self-questioning. This, in turn, necessitated, I thought, a kind of personal reflection on where exactly in the course of real, lived things the ideas had found their origin.

The answer begins with a journey more than two decades in the past to a distant—and fabled—valley of northern Pakistan, Hunza, a journey that left me astonished at what I saw. The people in the Hunza Valley, along with other highland neighbors in Pakistan's Northern Chitral, Ghizar (including Yasin and Ishkoman), and Gojal (including Misghar and Shimshal), southern Tajikistan's Gorno-Badakhshan Autonomous Oblast, far western China's "Tajik" region, and far northeastern Afghanistan's Badakhshan, are part of the scattered but very well-integrated global community of Isma'ili Muslims, followers of a hereditary Imam seen as a direct descendant of the Prophet Muhammad through Ali, the current incarnation of which, Prince

Karim al-Husayni, is known as the (fourth) "Aga Khan" (and the forty-ninth imam). Isma'ilis believe that only their imam can reveal the meaning of truth and the true meaning of religion, and that an imam is charged with interpreting (through *tawil*) the truth behind revelation in every epoch. Thus to Isma'ilis doctrine is fundamentally flexible and can be adapted to changing times, based on the dicta of the imams.

Isma'ilis around the world are embedded in an exceptional institutional architecture radiating out of the imamat's governance. Prince Karim, the Aga Khan, is based near Paris, and his development institutions in Geneva. Nonetheless, villagers in remotest Baroghil, say, in Pakistan, or in Tajikistan's Khuf or Yoged or Ishkashim, feel themselves bound in a web of services, structures, and symbols provided by this institutional expanse and its devotional correlate. Hunza and its cognates have schools, roads, water distribution, bridges, and clinics and wider health care services, for example and to name only a few, provided by the Isma'ili institutional assemblage. They are bound in a lattice of political forms, including national, regional, and global constitutions, adjudication and mediation boards, and councils at every level from the village to the nation and beyond; they pay a tax-like tithe, formulated along doctrinal lines provided by the Islamic prototype of the *zakat*. They have deputy leaders, regional universities, flags and insignia, fleets of vehicles, solidarity building structures like youth camps, and narratives of participation and allegiance. Much like a state, all this; but it is, as I will discuss further, decidedly *not* a state, and yet, by virtue of its very large array of secular structures, it is also decidedly much more than "just a religion." So what is it? Is it, perhaps, an iteration of a newly possible form of transnational assemblage, with concomitant forms of citizenship? Yes, I thought, when I began to write about this. But the *yes* alone was too simple.

––––––

In 1993, at eighteen, I caught a cab from Islamabad to Rawalpindi's Pir Wadhai depot and rode a rickety Northern Areas Transport bus twenty-two hours to the highest reaches of the Pakistan Himalaya. I had been an apprentice for the summer at Save the Children Pakistan, which was tolerable to my parents; this, however would not have been, and I was thus intent on not informing my mother of my escape from the city until my return, when the fact of it would be irreversible and thus, relatively speaking, given the safe return with which I expected it would be associated, unassailable:

a fait accompli. I was endowed with a typical adolescent ignorance which, combined with a dose of knowing-it-all, convinced me that I was generally invincible and nothing could happen to me in that still-perilous transit where sectarian minorities are even now slaughtered by the busload, sprayed down with a shower of bullets as they stand lined up outside their conveyances. I paid no thought to such things, not then.

Pir Wadhai, full as it was of runaways, vagabonds, and wind-worn villagers of distant valleys, captivated me; I'd never seen anything like it, and at the time it evoked for me the sense of adventure that I believed would be associated with scaling the range at whose apex lies the likes of K2 and Nanga Parbat. Indeed it was—and remained—an adventure, though the terms of that adventure would change for me over time as I learned to be skeptical of my own orientalist longings, informed by a childhood filled with crumbling Tintins and National Geographics of the 1960s (see Lutz 1993), and critical of the inner reaches of romantic exoticism that corresponded to outer ones in the world, where weathered villagers represented something heroic and more real (as in Fabian 1983) than the (seemingly) unmarked and unexciting Harvard Square, Long Island, and Manhattan in which I'd grown up. The bus passed through the ruins of Taxila on the wide plains of what was once Gandhara (great stupa-filled seat of Greco-Buddhist sorcerers and starting point of Padmasambhava as he embarked for Tibet), and then slowly, inexorably, climbed into the pine-clad hills fringing the Indus ranges, eventually reaching prim, British Abbotabad, James Abbott's cantonment town, where Osama bin Laden would someday be killed in his unremarkable concrete bourgeois bungalow there. But nearly two decades earlier, there in 1993, the landscape of this old British hill station was scattered with Afghan refugee camps that were becoming permanent villages; these camps would become a sufficient object of fascination to form my initial doctoral topic, one that the events of 9/11/01 would replace with the study of the Isma'ilis I will discuss here.

The bus wend its way through pine-clad Shinkiari and then descended into the Indus Valley at Besham, where it entered the region once called Yaghestan, Land of the Ungoverned; the guidebooks, as the Imperial Gazetteers of a century earlier, painted a portrait all at once sinister and romantic of this "lawless" land full of insurgency. I loved the idea of cultural terrain no outsider could visit. It was what I was seeking, after all. The Indus narrowed, and the Karakoram rose, as we passed Dubair, Jijal, Dassu, Komilla, Kandia, and then we crossed near Tangir and Darel at Band-i-Sazin into the so-called Northern Areas (*Shumali Ilaqajaat*), at the time a region of Pakistani Kashmir administered from Islamabad; to make it a province, reasoned the region's low-country ministerial elite, would be to cede the division of Kashmir by accepting only part of it as Pakistan. Thus government functionaries in the area tended to be nonlocals, helping, alongside severe sectarian antipathy, to foment a sense of dissatisfaction with Pakistan. The huge mountains were black before a sea of stars as we approached Gilgit. Occasionally a hamlet glowed orange, a neat concordance of light and life in a desolate landscape. I stayed on the floor of a seedy hotel restaurant in my sleeping bag, and the next morning took a small bus across a swaying suspension bridge toward the storied Hunza Valley, upon which James Hilton (1933) had based Shangri-La in *Lost Horizon* and whose "longevity foods" fill American natural food co-op aisles. It was this enigmatic, much-misunderstood place and others near it that would impel me to ask the difficult, troubling, and intriguing questions about citizenship and belonging that came to define much of my intellectual life. These questions were about what it means to be a human being at this moment in history, what it means to be a member of something, what forms are available for membership, and what is happening to the nation-state. And, as I would learn, they pointed not to answers, but to extraordinarily complex social landscapes that led me in the end to more questions.

Rogers Smith, in his essay here, underscores neglected but important "examples of rising transnational citizenships." In this reflection I wish to ask how such questions may themselves best be asked; how, in other words, can transnationality and its manifestations in individual feelings and commitments, in the forms we identify with "citizenship," be *captured*, and authored, and mapped. What kind of atlas of allegiance would they form?

———

On that day of that season in 1993 the world was perhaps on the cusp of a major sea change of which it is now in the midst, a fundamental shift in the terms of human organization and experience, in the possible forms available for the mediation between individual and collectivity. Perhaps it was not on the cusp but already well into it, or perhaps it was already well into it but the forms in which it were to be iterated were not as well defined as they are now, or as well named. I argue that the seeds of globalization are planted with European sea-based empires, their trades in slaves and luxury commodities (see Wolf 1982), the shared experience of rule they engender (Comaroff 1985), and the flows of labor they generate. Others argue "globalization" begins much earlier (e.g., Abu-Lughod 1989; Chanda 2007), in the networks of trade along the "silk route" or in Islamic polities. But in 1993, when I stole away to the Hindu Kush, the world's understanding of the possibilities offered by the global, our explicit consciousness of it, was certainly not what it is now.

We live in an epoch where global collectivities, networks, and forms are the stuff of the daily news, habit, home, and intimate life; from global Christian organizations, including Mormonism (or Opus Dei, or global Pentecostal churches), to the proliferation of political Islamisms, including the Tablighi Jama'at (see Metcalf 1993, Masud 2000) and al-Qaeda, from embodied urbanisms like parkour and graffiti (or punk or skaterdom) to Occupy (see Graeber 2004; 2009) and Facebook, it is increasingly, exceedingly, and eminently possible to identify primarily with and participate primarily in something that is not a state (Appadurai 1996 is the classic on this). Only yesterday, it seems, as the 1948 Human Rights codices were ratified (Kelly and Kaplan 2001), or in the 1980s when the world waited with bated breath for Cold War nightmares to materialize, states were the only real game in town. They battled armies whose goal was most often statehood, when they even battled forms that were not states. No more. Now wars are fought with nonstates, treaties are signed with nonstates, and identity is derived from nonstates. Transnational forms certainly do work in and around nation-states, can be defined only in relationship to them, transecting transversing subverting transgressing, and the nation-state is far from disappearing, say some scholars. But it is not what it always has been. As Rogers Smith explains in this volume: "I agree that the era of the predominance of nation-states is not ended, but I am also conscious that this predominance is in fact a relatively recent development in world history—the age of religious and secular multinational empires is not long or even entirely past—and that nation-states have not been even in the last century the only form of political community, and that they are indeed undergoing a range of challenges and transformations. Indeed a major transformation in political organization is underway, and with it the subjective experience of allegiance and membership."

David Harvey (1990) has spoken of his own notion of an epistemic "sea change" in the way emergent modes of capitalism mediate human beings' experience of time and space; certainly this sea change is tied to that one, but it is not the same one. What, I have been compelled to ask, do these sea changes mean for individual humans? How does history feel on, in, and under the skin?

———

That first night in Hunza I was invited into a family home in a tiny hamlet next to a small village. Glacial torrents thundered thousands of feet down precipitous ravines, and thence thousands more, it appeared to my eye from the roof of an old fort, to the rapids of the Hunza below, an Indus tributary. I had been wandering around in fields that to my coddled New York Jewish eyes looked like alfalfa (maybe?), which I am now sure it was not, when some youths around my own age and younger called out to me. We struck up a conversation, and at length the boys asked me to dinner.

I returned again and again for years to this family in this place. Over and over, across many summers, I climbed the path to their tiny dwelling, caught up, ate dinner, and fell asleep alongside them in a great row of bodies (ten? twelve?), tolerating mites and bites in exchange for unending friendships and the spell of the unending torrent beneath towering peaks; I tempered that early romanticism, but I still allowed my emotional self a taste of it when I could. It is for these reasons, among others, that I cannot separate my understanding of global "sea changes" from my understanding of individual people that I know and love and trust. It is in people, after all, and stories, that history actually comes to life.

During these periods of return I worked as a kind of apprentice in the institutions of the Aga Khan Foundation, the charitable wing of the Isma'ili Muslim community, basing myself in Gilgit. It was here that, as a vaguely mad college student, I started traveling widely atop buses and cargo jeeps across the Karakoram and Hindu Kush ranges to visit or stay in isolated Isma'ili villages, from upper Yasin to Chhashi, Misghar to Arkari. It was here that I first understood the profound commitment of Isma'ilis not only to their imam but also to each other and the notion of their community in a real solidarity, but also the prescription to speak positively of it, and thus that I came to recognize in its forms not only solidarity but also ideology.

Isma'ilis exist as Isma'ilis, of course (as opposed to or alongside other things they may also be), in complicated constellations of local and regional neighbors; of other global Muslim communities; of a complex relationship between "indigenous" Himalayan Isma'ilis, on the one hand, and diasporic European and North American Khoja Isma'ilis of largely Indian Gujarati (or Kachchhi) descent by way of East Africa, on the other; and of culture and network on the planet more widely, a matter I will address further below. Thus "Isma'ili" identity is situationally and locally rendered or articulated, despite the ease with which it might be applied to all Isma'ilis around the world, and the force with which this notion of the Universal Isma'ili is promoted within and by Isma'ili institutions. This means that "Isma'ilism" becomes legible in the calculus of local configurations of collective identity; it means a particular thing, for example, in part because of its place in Tajikistan's civil war, or because of the fraught nature of sectarian politics, which charges non-Sunni identity in Pakistan's highlands under pressure from, say, revivalist groups like the Tehreek-i-Taliban or the Tablighi Jama'at or the Sipah-i-Sahaba (Rieck 1995; Sökefeld 1997), all of which level that Isma'ilism is not Islam and thus mark it as a target. These other groups of course also have complicated relationships of patronage and enmity with the state, and so triangular (or maybe polygonal) relationships enter into the local politics of transnational identity, and Isma'ilism thus comes to hold very particular citizenship-type valencies that give membership certain benefits and certain risks in the context of highly specific geographies of identity. I suspect nearly all forms of transnational citizenship are similarly fundamentally *locally* legible; they are globally articulated and locally iterated. Sometimes, in such contexts, "Isma'ili" could start out by referring to the people among a few other groups who speak a certain language (see Emadi 2000 on an isolated Pashai Isma'ili enclave in Afghan Laghman), or the people who adorn their saints' tombs in such and such a way (such as the Bibi Fatima Tomb in Ishkashim).

My engagement with the Isma'ilis was at first not scholarly but rather part of an imagined or projected career in humanitarian aid and rural development. In the end I chose scholarship, but, as I mentioned as I shared my bus-window view, I initially wanted to study the Afghan refugees in Pakistan, a group with their own predicament of citizenship. The cataclysmic events of September 11, however, saw grenades lobbed at foreigners, Daniel Pearl beheaded, and a rather unfriendly environment for research in Pakistan. Moreover, the Afghan refugees began to leave, and my mind settled on a social landscape I knew quite well from my time in Hunza. I decided to test my hypothesis that there was a nascent Isma'ili citizenship emerging by focusing a new phase of my work across the border in the Pamir Mountains of Tajikistan, where Isma'ilis had been associated with the losing resistance against the old communist guard in a vicious civil war (see Bliss 2006). As these people were so cut off from their southerly neighbors by nearly a century of affiliation with Russia and the USSR, I thought them a good test case; did they still—or now—perceive themselves part of a global community? How were they being made to feel that way?

What I found in Tajikistan, where involvement with the Isma'ili assemblage was much greater than with the state, was rather intriguing, and led me to a new assertion: that transnational sociopolitical organization is not only dependent on new modes of governance or governmentality, but also that these forms of power are fraught by virtue of their association with older colonial-era inequities, and thus that transnational polity building involves a great deal of friction and resistance, where I had always imagined it a kind of neatly packaged process. Subjecthood and citizenship came into sharp relief there. Nonetheless, I found that intensive efforts were being made to incorporate newly accessible communities into the modern Isma'ili institutional infrastructure, to teach them that they were Isma'ilis and to convey what that should mean. And what that meant, I found in time, was in part shaped by British communal categories that helped shape the idea of "Isma'ili" as a certain sort of thing. *Isma'ili* as a term for the whole community is rather new, and the variables of identities in these mountain areas have until recently been quite fluid and shaped by the particular conditions in each borderland.

The Isma'ilis are deeply invested in the notion of the modern, and of progress, and committed to capitalism, and compliance with states, pluralism, democracy, liberal multiculturalism, and cultural preservation. Many local Isma'ilis, as an Isma'ili reviewer of my book highlighted for me, saw the process of induction into transnational flows to be part of a kind of missionary drive at reforming the supposedly far-flung long-isolated subjects, objects of a kind of deep exotic desire and embodiments, perhaps, of an imagined more authentic Isma'ili past, and that this induction represented a kind of missionary *modernity*, rather than other missionary efforts where the object is primarily doctrine. As the Isma'ili reviewer suggested, in this process enacted sometimes by descendants of subjects of British empire, a new civilizing effort was born in which ghosts of empire were looming large, if only quietly and in shadows.

Nonetheless, across the parts of Afghanistan, Tajikistan, and Pakistan I mention here, with nodal connections to the other parts in India, Canada,

East Africa, the United States, and well beyond, a new Himalayan piece of a transnational polity was being slowly integrated, one of the first areas of significant Isma'ili territorial contiguity. More often than not, the arrival of global Isma'ilism in newly opened areas has been enthusiastically embraced, representing as it often has a way out of crisis and collapse, though this embracing has also been encouraged—or fostered—by the community's leadership. Territory, in general, has not been one of the fundaments of Isma'ili community building (except during the period of Aga Khan III, when the imamat, based on its autonomous princely status, asked the Crown for a piece of land to accompany recognition). It is in part this absence of territory, alongside the comprehensive architecture of something like citizenship, that suggests new transnational forms here.

Are these assertions basically mine? Fundamentally, no. As an ethnographer, I consider it my charge to transmit what people themselves feel. These dynamics are certainly not what I *expected* to find, or wanted. Are the observations contrary to what the Isma'ilis think of themselves? It depends on what one means by "the Isma'ilis." They may differ from institutional perspectives, but nonetheless they represent the tales Isma'ili villagers tell of their own experiences and their own lives.

Shortly after Tajikistan, I started the book that eventually brought me to the conference of which these are the proceedings. I struggled long with the question of how to tell the story of an enormously complex system, a polysemous, polynodal, sometimes messy, vast, transterritorial assemblage. I read various anthropological truisms about the need for multisited ethnography (e.g., in Marcus 1995), but I needed time to step back before I could start to discern a whole matrix of lives and acts in some sufficient cohesive synthesis to encourage the sense in individuals that they were primarily part of, or even "citizens" of, something that is not a state.

How, then, can transnational "citizenship" be captured methodologically?

Haltingly. Piece by piece. It was in stories that I ultimately found the answer.

I started—and infused—my nascent book *Isma'ili Modern*, the one that would eventually connect me through the Center for the Study of Citizenship with this volume—with tales of the family in Hunza, and others I met over the course of years of research. I called them with clarifications and questions. I scoured old envelopes of photos, yellowed documents, barely audible interviews, and memories. The photos: even they intimate something about history's presence (and its present) and the process of trying to capture global subjectivities (on the cover of the book, for example, is a photo of a boy on a roof beneath a massive mountain. The photo was taken in the Isma'ili village of Darkot, in the Yasin Valley: the location of an infamous "Great Game" moment, where the British political agent George Hayward was murdered, and in the first chapter is a high-pasture view of the Hunza fortress I stood atop on that day in 1993). A fine example of this is the photo across the two copyright pages of a gaggle of Wakhi-speaking Isma'ili children in Chapursan, only miles from the Afghan border. Simple enough. But the truth is, right after I took that picture, I fell backward into a ditch. I was suddenly a laughingstock, and I was rendered a foolish, hapless foreigner.

I include this little anecdote because it is an apt metaphor—falling backward into a hole. The bumbling, laughingstock ethnographer at the edge of the world—for the sake of the notion of the research experience. We stumble backward and open ourselves to ridicule. In the quest to capture some elusive object we have postulated, we fall into holes. This, I surmise, may be the only way to write transnationality. We don't know where we're going until we embrace our inner fools.

———

I claimed in the book, as I have already suggested, that the Isma'ilis exemplify or hint at the emergence of fundamentally new possibilities for human organization and membership at this moment of history, mediated by a set of historical forces like colonial empire and industrial capital, and contemporary forces of media, network organization, corporate capital, and wars on terror. When I first formally proposed the topic, I wanted to say that the Isma'ilis essentially had a nonterritorial state. Too simple, and wrong. Later, I wanted to say that where the actual nation-state was absent, deficient, or tyrannical, forming a vacuum, the Isma'ili assemblage permitted a new site for identification, and a chance to be one-up on neighbors when in conflict. Fine, but still not enough. I needed to historicize. And thus what I did not see, until reviewers (one of them, notably, the important Isma'ili intellectual Faisal Devji, identified in my book by his request) pointed it out, was the operation of power in this webwork, and its imbrication with categories and patterns created in colonial rule. Amazing that global forms of citizenship suddenly with abundant digital incarnations should have foundations in court cases of a century and a half ago (Shodhan 2001; Grondelle 2009) decreeing what an Isma'ili is, that Isma'ili should be the name for all these, and that the Aga Khan is officially the leader of all of them. Or that the transnational connections in an Isma'ili NGO office in Gilgit, Pakistan, might be shaped by trade and labor flows around the Indian Ocean rims at the turn of the twentieth century and before. These moments put Khojas in an elite seat and indirectly made others their subjects, of a sort.

But as I wrote, I grew ever more uneasy. I am uneasy even as I write this right now. I was uncomfortable. I was anxious. I found myself plagued with a fear over how what kinds of reactions what I was writing might engender, and torn between conveying how the institutional agents of Isma'ilism want to represent their structures and how Isma'ili citizen-subject-adherents represented their actual experience. I had been navigating for years a tangle of injunctions against talking about the Isma'ili infrastructure in certain ways. I had learned that the Isma'ili imamat and inner councils control their institutions' images and publicities very carefully, and that many materials go through that central directorate for approval. These fears, I came to understand, came from the same relationships, at least in part, that created the very internal tension over and within Isma'ilism I was documenting: that transnational webs are not only a site from which to reap identity and benefit and self, but also sites of disciplinary power or even surveillance. And indeed this too is a facet of polity and its realization, in individual lives, in citizenship.

———

Much of what I said in the book is captured in what I've told so far, although I have superimposed what I know now on what I saw then. When I first started gathering the stories that coalesced into the book that brought me into dialogue with the other authors in this volume, in other words, the book whose authorship I've been discussing, I didn't know I was writing it. When I first started writing this book, I didn't know what it was about. And when I knew what it was about, I wished I'd known I was writing it. What do we say about a book ten years after its idea is hatched? How do these things ferment as our own ideas change? What do we say about a community a century and a half after it is named a thousand years old? How does it become a single picture?

In sum and to recap, then, here is how the story I told goes if taken in at once: the Isma'ilis, who are led by a hereditary imam who is vested with the ability to reinterpret Islam as times change, affiliate with, participate in, and perform allegiance to a structure that has no single territorial unit, that is widely scattered, and that acts, as I say at the beginning, rather like a state, though it is not. This structure provides for its members nearly everything a polity provides, including, on the symbolic level, a site of primary allegiance, but it insists that they not look like they are violating territorial states. And, in effect, I always suggested, they are citizens of that structure, for it gives them a site for total participation and subject formation that is much more than religious and that is guided by tenets rooted in certain ideologies of modernism. But what if not everyone is not equally a citizen? This question exists at every level of the study of citizenship.

It seems necessary here to say something about why and how the Isma'ili assemblage, a term I use (following Sassen 2006) because it captures very well the nebulous yet cohesive form of the sprawl of this sort of transnational webwork, is *not* a state; this question is interesting because it points to the kind of emergent form that becomes possible perhaps only in this particular global moment. For one thing, following Weber's famous assertion, the Isma'ilis have no machinery for the legitimate use of force, or indeed any machinery for the use of force at all. They have no territory, further, and thus no sovereignty to protect or on which to infringe. No boundaries, no checkpoints, no national capital, no true government. For these reasons and others, they are in some ways not recognized as legitimate social actors. Nonetheless, the Aga Khan signs accords and treaties, secures rights for his followers, and redistributes income through his institutional structures in the form of secular services. A mixed bag, then. And on the one hand, this might seem anomalous. But that seeming anomaly is at the very heart of my argument, because perhaps it is not so anomalous after all; perhaps it is the shape of deterritorialized forms whose emergence everywhere is now possible, at the very least, if not realized.

The Isma'ili community exists at the peripheries of what is perceived by the world to be Islamdom, to borrow Hodgson's (1977) term, often persecuted, often subjected and subjugated, but it also features its own power differentials, its own internal modes of subject making. This is rooted in particular in the reframing of disparate groups loosely connected by historical threads as a single community with a single leader, and without empire this does not happen. Nonetheless, this is an uneasy assertion, for the community and its leader control their image and public relations very carefully, and their official narrative—not without iteration in historical realities—is sometimes one of organic unity deep into the past. What if one part of the community narrates or suggests one thing and the other, official part, narrates something else? Which perspective, I had to ask, was the right one to capture?

And then I realized: the multiplicity of perspectives *is* the story. It is the friction, as Tsing (2004) suggests, that captures best the nature of Isma'ili citizenship.

At the core of this, summarizing further, is that the population that constitutes the transnational community is essentially divided between people called Khoja Isma'ilis mostly drawn from East African, North American, and European diasporas tracing their genealogies to trading groups in coastal India, alongside their living kin in India itself, in the elite seat, and a group of others. The Khojas exist in extended encounter with and bound to the large populations of "indigenous" or "autochthonous" Isma'ilis that have been in the same place for a long time, mostly the Himalayan regions of Tajikistan, Afghanistan, north Pakistan, and Chinese Turkistan. These groups have a markedly different practice, and history, and until recently saw themselves as not connected or only loosely connected with the other elite now calling itself Isma'ili. But in 1866, a case in the British Bombay High Court set in motion a process by which the Himalayan subjects could quickly be incorporated into the Khojas' vision of a greater Isma'ilism, sparked the use of the Isma'ili term to cover them all, and pronounced the Aga Khan the supreme communal leader of them all.

All that is a simplification, but it suffices to capture the fervent efforts by which the Khoja institutional structure has worked to induct these Himalayan Isma'ilis into a homogenous and more standardized collectivity, beginning well over a century ago but continuing even now as political conditions in China, Tajikistan, Afghanistan, and Pakistan change. The incorporation and induction is intensive, and the Isma'ili borderlands sometimes perceive a certain imposition of culture upon them.

An essential element of the formulation of a potential contemporary global Isma'ili citizenship is the framing of the community as the realization of an antifundamentalist modernist Islam, in the wake of 9/11, people who cast off the veil a hundred years ago by official fiat, people whose official structures visibly seek states' approval, who espouse democracy and love of country and corporate capital and management ideology and environmentalism and indeed affluence. What does this mean at a moment when the notion of a transnational Islamic citizenship is charged, proscribed, tracked, circumscribed? What does it mean when several other forms of transnational Islam are so clearly critiques of the state system, capital, empire, and "The West." Does al-Qaeda have citizens? Does the Tablighi Jama'at? If so, are the Isma'ilis their transnational countercitizens? What guarantees come with nonterritorial nonstates? Can they protect? They can certainly provide, and in moments of crisis, I suggest in my book, they do. And, given this calculus of geopolitics, does this Isma'ili assemblage possess sovereignty? Not in the lexicon of legitimacy structured by the nation-state, but perhaps it does on the practical level.

Furthermore, if it does or if it does not alike, once I claim there must be a type of citizenship happening here, I am required to address another question: recognition. In what sense are individuals written in to a political, social, and cultural vision *as* citizens here? What kind of political citizenship is articulated when there is essentially no state, and when the Isma'ili polity is the only site for not only participation but also administration or even survival? What motivates the Isma'ili imam to sign treaties and pacts with the leaders of states his constituents live in? How can recognition be made of such people as citizens of something that is not a state or a corporate entity in the context of states structured by corporate entities? Is there a laissez-faire sort of tacit agreement that the Isma'ili assemblage is to govern subjects in these areas, as long as that is never uttered, as long as it never discredits the state?

Other groups, notably the Roma in Europe, have made defiant pleas for a transnational nonterritorial citizenship (see Goodwin 2004), with passports, declarations of nonterritorial nationhood, and all. Isma'ilis are called upon in general to say that they are first citizens of the states they live in and only secondarily members of Isma'ilism. I heard this first from my Hunza friends in 1994, and from others in Yasin. And yet it looks notably different when we just observe—the ethnographer's basic predicament—and the insistence on needing a formulation to be *told* to say this forces us to look at *just why.* Why is it necessary to be told to say it? The imperative of secrecy tells us a lot here, and points to processes that the community's leaders would prefer not be visible, for they are dangerous, in states' views and in Isma'ilis', and indeed empirically, and also threaten to disrupt the fragile détente that the Isma'ili leadership has labored so hard to construct.

A book, such as the one whose writing I'm mulling over here, is of course also its own naming. It is part of the process it describes. It enters into the actual reality of transnational community self-imagining, to a limited degree. It manifests, produces, and suggests itself, it is an iteration of some interpretive overlay, and thus itself imposes a certain narrative about what a community is, and how it should be seen. In this way, among others, textual choices matter.

I have long felt the atlas is my favorite book for the stories it tells and hides. I strove to express in the sum of stories in *Isma'ili Modern* a cartographic methodology, an approach that moves across a terrain of relationships, intimacies, times, and spaces, the spinning and imagining of multiple overlapping maps and domains of mood and mind. The socially "real" is always rendered real, I suggest, in those emotive domains. History is lived by individuals, by homes, in loves and in losses, and it is with that living of history, with the historical mediation of self and experience that I was concerned as I envisioned—or imposed—unity on a scattered, nonterritorial, transnational sociopolitical fabric. I believe the unity is there. But in time I became concerned with the process of its effecting.

———

We have heard a lot in the last four decades, if not perhaps too much, about the multisited ethnography. All ethnographies are, I imagine, multisited, even if they skip only from soul to soul, room to room, or home to home; it is really a question of scale. Connections across space can extend over great distances depending on the available vehicles of communication and movement. But what about the multi*timed* text, where we must overlay moments and modalities of experience upon each other, where that unsanctioned trip to Pakistan's mountains at eighteen requires to be interstitched with fieldwork a decade later, where the stuff of friendship must be teased apart or twined together with the stuff of archives of voices captured on machines, where the stuff of fervent belief must be put in the box with the rulings of Imperial High Courts? As I sat down to write, I had at last a perspective on transnational citizenship, less unwitting than ever, and yet I was more uncertain than ever how to start. This is why I conjured atlases, anatomies, maps involving nodes, filaments, and interstices—the nodes people and their collective forms, the interstices their relationships. But a cartographic mode alone is aloof and not enough; scholarly writers have to borrow something from novelists who know characters in all their complexity. That is why I insist, again, upon contrasting it with the affective, the emotive, the intimate—and ultimately the phenomenological.

The view from the fortress roof I stood on was of a landscape that has evolved and changed. At that time, Shi'i villagers still carried giant blocks of glacier ice from the upper reaches of the Bagrot Valley with which to make shaved ice in Gilgit. The children who roared with laughter at me as I fell into a hole likely do not remember the moment; to me, however, it has become a feature of the story, almost fabular. I still remember explaining e-mail to the villagers in Hunza I first encountered on this long journey: *like a letter that shows up on a television screen,* I said. The friend I called Sultan in the book stared at me blankly. Now they are on Facebook and their faces are in books. The way that global identity and citizenship feels, looks, and is rendered into culture and language are for them now much changed; the "sea change" is one that they ultimately embody as the meaning and role of territory change. Will they one day be able to be recognized as nonnational citizens by virtue of membership in a transnational polity? Could a parallel system evolve? For now that is not happening, and thus these formations, assemblages, and narratives remain in a sort of shadow zone of recognition and legitimacy, an alternate world existing alongside the world of formally allowable actors. These are, then, for now, noncitizens *except* when they move through this other domain of life that transects and transcends boundaries.

———

I sometimes define globalization in the classroom, for the sake of illustration, as a name for a historical moment, part of a Braudelian periodization in which the current moment represents a certain modality of being, a subjective experience interacting with large-scale forms and processes. Globalization, I say, is an era. Globalization is the name for the way people experience a certain historical time. Globalization, to be globalization and not just different people in different places, requires that its subjects recognize it consciously as a defining feature of their epoch.

But it is something at once much more and much less. Once I perceived globalization and transnationality were static, essential phenomena that happened to the world: chapters, like I also perceived the nation-state, in a nonteleological progression of floating historical forms. Lately, however, I've come to think that transnationality, though mediated by macrohistorical forces and configurations, is something that is *felt*, most fundamentally, above all through emergent forms of citizenship and subjecthood, and that globalization is comprised of webs and tangles of affective ties, emotive interpretations, and other modes of subjective experience well rendered by phenomenological stories. Sometimes the threads of these ties, when organized under particular rubrics, can form what to our eyes appears to be a cohesive, integrated tapestry, an architecture that constitutes a transnational polity, network, movement or society. At base, then, transnationality is in this framing an element of intimate experience, a modality through which history is lived and experienced by selves embedded in quotidian relationships, situated in enmity and friendship, home and hamlet, laughter and suffering, desire and small talk, love and aspiration.

WORKS CITED

Abu-Lughod, Janet. 1989. *Before European Hegemony: The World System A.D. 1250–1350*. Oxford: Oxford University Press.

Appadurai, Arjun. 1996. *Modernity at Large: Cultural Dimensions of Globalization*. Minneapolis: University of Minnesota Press.

Bliss, Frank. 2006. *Social and Economic Changes in the Pamirs (Gorno-Badakhshan, Tajikistan)*. London: Routledge.

Chanda, Nayan. 2007. *Bound Together: How Traders, Preachers, and Warriors Shaped Globalization*. New Haven, CT: Yale University Press.

Comaroff, Jean. 1985. *Body of Power, Spirit of Resistance: The Culture and History of a South African People*. Chicago: University of Chicago Press.

Emadi, Hafizullah. 2000. "Praxis of Taqiyya: Perseverance of Pashaye Isma'ili Enclave, Nangarhar, Afghanistan." *Central Asian Survey* 19 (2): 53–64.

Fabian, Johannes. 1983. *Time and the Other: How Anthropology Makes Its Object*. New York: Columbia University Press.

Goodwin, Morag. 2004. "The Romani Claim Non-Territorial Nation Status: Recognition from an International Legal Perspective." *Roma Rights: Quarterly Journal of the European Roma Rights Center*, no. 1: 54–56.

Graeber, David. 2004. *Fragments of an Anarchist Anthropology*. Chicago: Prickly Paradigm Press.

———. 2009. *Direct Action: An Ethnography*. Oakland, CA: AK Press.

Grondelle, Marc van. 2009. *Ismailis in the Colonial Era: Modernity, Empire and Islam, 1839–1969*. New York: Columbia University Press.

Harvey, David. 1990. *The Condition of Postmodernity*. London: Blackwell.

Hilton, James. 1937. *Lost Horizon*. New York: Macmillan.

Hodgson, Marshall G. S. 1977. *The Venture of Islam: Conscience and History in a World Civilization*. 3 vols. Chicago: University of Chicago Press.

Kelly, John D., and Martha Kaplan. 2001. *Represented Communities: Fiji and World Decolonization.* Chicago: University of Chicago Press.

Lutz, Catherine. 1993. *Reading National Geographic.* Chicago: University of Chicago Press.

Marcus, James. 1995. "Ethnography in/of the World System: The Emergence of Multi-Sited Ethnography." *Annual Review of Anthropology* 24: 95–117.

Masud, Khalid, ed. 2000. *Travelers in Faith: Studies of the Tablighi Jama'at as a Transnational Islamic Movement for Faith Renewal.* Leiden: E. J. Brill.

Metcalf, Barbara Daly. 1993. "Living Hadith in the Tablighi Jama'at." *Journal of Asian Studies* 52 (3): 584–608.

Rieck, Andreas. 1995. "Sectarianism as a Political Problem in Pakistan: The Case of the Northern Areas." *Orient* 36 (3): 429–48.

Sassen, Saskia. 2006. *Territory, Authority, Rights: From Medieval to Global Assemblages.* Princeton, NJ: Princeton University Press.

Shodhan, Amrita. 2001. *A Question of Community: Religious Groups and Colonial Law.* Calcutta: Samya.

Sökefeld, Martin. 1997. *Ein Labyrinth von Identitäten in Nordpakistan: Zwischen Landbesitz, Religion und Kaschmir-Konflikt.* Culture Area Karakorum Scientific Studies, vol. 8. Cologne: Köppe.

Steinberg, Jonah. 2011. *Isma'ili Modern: Globalization and Identity in a Muslim Community.* Chapel Hill: University of North Carolina Press.

Tsing, Anna Lowenhaupt. 2004. *Friction: An Ethnography of Global Connection.* Princeton, NJ: Princeton University Press.

Wolf, Eric. 1982. *Europe and the People without History.* Berkeley: University of California Press.

CONTRIBUTORS

KRISTY A. BELTON is a postdoctoral fellow at the Human Rights Center of the University of Dayton. Her work centers on the politics of belonging (especially citizenship, statelessness, and the racialized "Other"), migration, human rights, and global justice. She has published articles in the *Journal of Global Ethics*, *Ethnic and Racial Studies*, *International Journal of Bahamian Studies*, *Alternatives: Global, Local, Political*, and *The Latin Americanist*. Her book chapter, "Statelessness and Economic and Social Rights," was published in *The State of Economic and Social Rights: A Global Overview* (Cambridge University Press, 2013).

CANDICE BREDBENNER is an Associate Professor of History at the University of North Carolina, Wilmington. Her publications on the history of US citizenship and its obligations include *A Nationality of Her Own: Women, Citizenship, and the Politics of Marriage* (University of California Press) and "A Duty to Defend?: The Evolution of Aliens' Military Obligations to the United States, 1792–1946," *Journal of Policy History* (Spring 2012).

T. GREGORY GARVEY is Professor of English at the College at Brockport, State University of New York. He is author of *Creating the Culture of Reform in Antebellum America* and editor of *The Emerson Dilemma: Essays on Emerson and Social Reform*. He has served as Fulbright Senior Scholar and as director of the SUNY Center on Russia and the United States in Moscow. Working with Russian colleagues he edited *American Society: Essays in History and Culture* for use in Russian language universities.

NORA GOTTLIEB is a postdoctoral research fellow at the University of Illinois at Chicago. She holds a PhD from Ben-Gurion University in Beer Sheva, Israel, as well as degrees in global health from Humboldt University, Berlin, and in special education from the University of Education Heidelberg, Germany. Her fields of interest include social and political determinants of health; concepts of health rights, social justice, and citizenship; migration and health; and gender and health. Nora has been working and volunteering for the Physicians for Human Rights—Israel since 2005.

LAWRENCE B. A. HATTER is an Assistant Professor of History at Washington State University. He received his PhD in early American history from the University of Virginia in 2011. He is currently revising his book manuscript "Citizens of Convenience: Empire, Nationhood, and the Northern Border of the American Republic, 1783–1820" for publication.

LARISSA KOPYTOFF is a PhD candidate in history at New York University, currently writing a dissertation titled "The Boundaries of Citizenship: Political Imagination and Colonial Administration in Senegal's Quatre Communes."

DANI KRANZ is a social anthropologist specializing in the anthropology of migration, legal anthropology, and interethnic (couple) relationships. She has been conducting long-term ethnographic research work on Jews of German descent in Israel, focusing on the transmission of Germanness among them. At present, her main project focuses on the sociolegal situation of non-Jewish, foreign spouses of Israeli Jews in Israel, and the emigration of Israeli Jews to Germany since 1990. She has published and taught across her areas of expertise; her latest publication is "State Assisted Return Migration Programs and the Risks of Home-Coming: Israel and Germany Compared," coauthor Nir Cohen, *Journal of Ethnic and Migration Studies*, 2014, DOI: 10.1080/1369183X.2014.948392.

JAMES L. LEIGHTER, PhD (University of Washington 2007), is an Associate Professor of Communication Studies at Creighton University. He specializes in the ethnography of communication, particularly in applied contexts. His work focuses on the intersections of cultural communication, public deliberation, and sustainability. Three questions serve as the impetus for his research, teaching, and participation in community life: (1) How are moments for speaking culturally influenced? (2) How do people make decisions about the community in which they live? And (3) How can communities improve decision-making quality through attention to local, cultural understandings?

HOWARD N. LUPOVITCH is Associate Professor of History and the director of the Cohn-Haddow Center for Judaic Studies at Wayne State University. He earned a PhD in history from Columbia University and specializes in the history of Hungarian and Habsburg Jews. He is the author of *Jews at the Crossroads: Tradition and Accommodation during the Golden Age of the Hungarian Nobility* and *Jews and Judaism in World History*, and is currently completing a history of the Jews of Budapest and a writing history of the Neolog Movement in Judaism.

TERESA R. MELGAR is currently Assistant Professor of Sociology at the University of the Philippines–Diliman. She holds a PhD in sociology from the University of Wisconsin–Madison and has research interests in citizenship, democratization, participatory governance, development, and Latin America, particularly Brazil. In recent work, Dr. Melgar has been examining the sustainability of democratic innovations like participatory budgeting in countries of the global South.

ROGERS M. SMITH is the Christopher H. Browne Distinguished Professor of Political Science and Associate Dean for the Social Sciences at the University of Pennsylvania, and Chair of the Penn Program on Democracy, Citizenship, and Constitutionalism. He is the author or coauthor of many articles and seven books, including *Political Peoplehood* (forthcoming, University of Chicago Press, 2015), *Still a House Divided: Race and Politics in Obama's America* with Desmond S. King (2011), *Stories of Peoplehood: The Politics and Morals of Political Membership* (2003), and *Civic Ideals: Conflicting Visions of Citizenship in U.S. History* (1997). *Civic Ideals* received six best book prizes from four professional associations and was a finalist for the 1998 Pulitzer Prize in History.

Smith was elected a Fellow of the American Academy of Arts and Sciences in 2004 and of the American Academy of Political and Social Science in 2011.

JONAH STEINBERG is Associate Professor of Anthropology at the University of Vermont. He received his BA from Swarthmore College, and his PhD from the University of Pennsylvania. His first book, *Isma'ili Modern: Globalization and Identity in a Muslim Community*, was published by the University of North Carolina Press and awarded the inaugural biannual Citizenship Book Prize from Wayne State University's Center for the Study of Citizenship. In recent work, funded by a grant from the National Science Foundation, Dr. Steinberg has been exploring the complex lives and journeys of child runaways in urban and rural settings in postcolonial India.

KAREN THOMAS-BROWN is an Associate Professor at the University of Michigan–Dearborn in the College of Education, Health, and Human Services, Department of Education. She is a Commonwealth Scholar and holds a PhD in Geography. Her research interests and publications focus on migration and the connectivities between global and transnational citizenship, and citizenship identities. Her research also focuses on multicultural identities within the context of education and forms of citizenship identities, as well as geographic literacy and culturally responsive and competent pedagogy in social studies. Thomas-Brown is actively involved in social studies and geographic education across the United States and has served on the NAEP steering committee for geography. She was a geography writer on the National Council for Social Studies 3C Social Studies Framework, and she was involved in the revision of Michigan's social studies standards.

EUGENE VAN SICKLE is an Associate Professor of American History at University of North Georgia. He earned his doctorate from West Virginia University in 2005. His research interests focus on colonization in the Atlantic World in the early nineteenth century.

DAVID WATKINS is an Assistant Professor of Political Science and Human Rights Studies at the University of Dayton, where he teaches courses in political theory and comparative politics. His current research focuses on applied democratic theory, with particular attention to judicial review and the politics of immigration and border enforcement.

INDEX

Note: Italic locators reference figures/tables in the text.

indigenous peoples, 189, 202n16. *See also* specific groups

individual vs. mass democracy, 297–315

industrialization, US cities, 152, 153, 300

inheritance: of citizenship, 63, 75–76, 76, 179–80, 322; French citizenship and Muslim law, 321, 326, 328–29; of nationality, 132

insurance. *See* health insurance firms

integration. *See* assimilation and integration

intellectual property, 197

Inter-American Court of Human Rights, 133

intermarriage: British/Native American, 41; Kickapoo, 187; mixed religions, 221–22; WWII era, 183–84

internal migration (United States), 151–52, 153–54, 186–87

International Court of Justice, 185–86

international education. *See* global education

international law: border crossing, 172, 184, 185, 186, 189, 190; enclaves, 185–86, 190; human rights, 133, 189, 202n16, 342

interviews: Brazilian political organizers, 257–59, 260–62, *261,* 267n3; on Caribbean statelessness, 130–31, 134, 135, 137–42; Israeli citizens of German descent, 72–74, 79–88, 82n4; Jamaican educator emigrants, 99–100, 103–4, 105, 106–9, 112, 113, 115–17, 118–19; research methodology, 54–55, 99–100, 130–31

"in transit" status, 133–34, 143n15

Isma'ili Modern: Globalization and Identity in a Muslim Community (Steinberg), 18, 338, 346–49, 352

Isma'ili Muslims, 338–54

Israel: borders and security, 190; citizenship policy, 53–54, 58, 62–63, 73, 84; civic responsibilities, 84; class divisions, 80, 81; German relations, 73, 74–77, 80, 89n7; migrant labor, health care rights, 49, 53–58, 59, 62–64, 65–66n6; migrant labor, history, 53; national culture and identity, 79, 84–85, 87, 90n17; population statistics, 53, 56, 76, 90n17; religious identity, 58, 62, 75, 77, 90n11, 90n12; "Third Generation," Israeli/German citizens, 72–74, 75–76, 78–88, 88n1

Jackson, Andrew, 153, 299, 300, 301, 302, 306, 310, 311

Jacobson, David, 127

Jamaica: citizenship, 97–98, 104, 109–10, 111–12, 113, 117; economy, 97–98, 102, 106, 110, 113, 114, 121; education system, 98, 109, 110–11, 114, 115, 116, 117, 120; emigrant interviews, 99–100, 103–4, 105, 106–9, 112, 113, 115–17, 118–19; government programs and planning, 102, 106, 114; outmigration, 97–98, 99, 101, 102, 111–12, 113–21; post-independence society, 105–6

Jay, John, 31

Jay Treaty (1794): abrogation, 40, 42, 43; British subjects' American rights, 27, 29–30, 31, 34, 35, 37, 38–40, 42, 43; Native American

www.ingramcontent.com/pod-product-compliance
Lightning Source LLC
Chambersburg PA
CBHW050625280326
41932CB00015B/2525